Dorothy Garrod
and
the Progress of the Palaeolithic

*Studies in the Prehistoric Archaeology
of the Near East and Europe*

Edited by
William Davies and Ruth Charles

Oxbow Books
1999

Published by
Oxbow Books
Park End Place, Oxford

© Oxbow Books and the individual authors 1999

ISBN 1 900188 87 2

This book is available from

Oxbow Books, Park End Place, Oxford OX1 1HN
Tel: 01865–241249; Fax: 01865–794449
Email: oxbow@oxbowbooks.com

and

The David Brown Book Co
PO Box 511, Oakville, CT 06779
Tel: (860) 945–9329; Fax: (860) 945–9468
Email: david.brown.bk.co@snet.net

and via our website

www.oxbowbooks.com

Printed in Britain
at the Short Run Press, Exeter

Dorothy Garrod
and
the Progress of the Palaeolithic

Studies in the Prehistoric Archaeology
of the Near East and Europe

Dorothy Garrod with a brown bear cub in Anatolia in Summer 1938.
(Photograph courtesy of the Pitt Rivers Museum, Oxford)

Contents

Foreword – *C. Renfrew*   ix

Introduction – *W. Davies and R. Charles*   xi

1.   Dorothy Annie Elizabeth Garrod: A Short Biography – *W. Davies*   1

2.   Dorothy Garrod's Application for the Disney Professorship, 1939   15

3.   The Path not Taken: Dorothy Garrod, Devon and the British   19
     Palaeolithic – *A. J. Roberts*

4.   Some observations on the British Earlier Upper Palaeolithic   35
     R. M. Jacobi

5.   Unlocking the Inhospitable – *S. Swainston*   41

6.   Garrod and the Belgian Creswellian – *R. Charles*   57

7.   Garrod and Glozel: the end of a fiasco – *P. G. Bahn and A. C. Renfrew* 76

8.   Gibraltar Palaeolithic Revisited: New Excavations at Gorham's   84
     and Vanguard Caves – *C. B. Stringer, R. N. E. Barton, A. P. Currant,*
     J. C. Finlayson, P. Goldberg, R. Macphail and P. B. Pettitt

9.   The Evolution of the Balkan Aurignacian – *J. K. Kozłowski*   97

10. The Levantine Aurignacian: 60 years of research   118
     A. Belfer-Cohen and O. Bar-Yosef

11. The Genesis and Age of Mousterian Palaeosols in the Carmel   135
     Coastal Plain, Israel – *A. Ronen, A. Tsatskin and S. A. Laukhin*

12. The Impact of Dorothy Garrod's Excavations in the Lebanon   152
     on the Palaeolithic of the Near East – *L. Copeland*

13. The Early Upper Palaeolithic in the Zagros Mountains – *D. Olzewski*   167

14. The Zarzian Industry of the Zagros Mountains – *G. A. Wahida*   181

15. "Twisting the Kaleidoscope": Dorothy Garrod and   209
     the "Natufian Culture" – *B. Boyd*

16. The Natufian: a Coherent Thought? – *F. Valla*   224

17. Nina Frances Layard, Prehistorian (1853–1935) – *S. Plunkett*   242

18. *Nova et Vetera*: Reworking the Early Upper Palaeolithic in Europe   263
    W. Davies

19. Bibliography of Garrod's Published Works   277

List of Contributors

P. G. Bahn – 428 Anlaby Road, Hull, HU3 6QP

R. N. E. Barton – Department of Anthropology, Oxford Brookes University, Headington, Oxford, OX3 OBP

O. Bar-Yosef – Department of Anthropology, Peabody Museum, Harvard University, Cambridge, MA 02138, U.S.A.

A. Belfer-Cohen – Institute of Archaeology, The Hebrew University of Jerusalem, Mount Scopus, Jerusalem 91905, Israel

B. Boyd – Department of Archaeology, University of Wales Lampeter, Ceredigion, SA48 7ED

R. Charles – Department of Archaeology, University of Newcastle upon Tyne, Newcastle upon Tyne, NE1 7RU

L. Copeland – Château de Marouatte, Grand Brassac, 24350 Tocane-St. Apré, France

A. P. Currant – Department of Palaeontology, Natural History Museum, Cromwell Road, London, SW7 5BD

S. W. G. Davies – Dorothy Garrod Laboratory, McDonald Institute for Archaeological Research, Downing Street, Cambridge, CB2 3ER

J. C. Finlayson – The Gibraltar Museum, 18–20 Bomb House Lane, Gibraltar

P. Goldberg – Department of Archaeology, Boston University, 675 Commonwealth Ave, Boston, MA 02215, USA

R. Jacobi – Dept. of Palaeontology, Natural History Museum, London, SW7 5BD

J. K. Kozłowski – Institute of Archaeology, Jagellonian University, ul. Golebia 11, 31007 Kraków, Poland

S. A. Laukhin – Institute of Geography, Russian Academy of Sciences, Moscow 109017, Russia

R. Macphail – Institute of Archaeology, University College London, 31–34 Gordon Square, London, WC1H 0PY

D. I. Olszewski – Department of Anthropology, Bishop Museum, 1525 Bernice Street, Honolulu, HI 96817, USA

P. B. Pettitt – Research Laboratory for Archaeology and the History of Art, University of Oxford, 6 Keble Road, Oxford, OX1 3QJ; Keble College, Oxford, OX1 3QJ

S. J. Plunkett – Keeper of Archaeology, Ipswich Borough Museum, High Street, Ipswich, IP1 3QH

A. C. Renfrew – Director, The McDonald Institute for Archaeological Research, Downing Street, Cambridge, CB2 3ER

A. J. Roberts – Department of Antiquities, Ashmolean Museum, University of Oxford, Beaumont Street, Oxford, OX1 2PH

A. Ronen – Zinman Institute of Archaeology, University of Haifa, Haifa 31905, Israel

C. B. Stringer – Human Origins Group, Department of Palaeontology, Natural History Museum, Cromwell Road, London, SW7 5BD

S. Swainston – SCARAB Research Centre, University of Wales College, Newport, Caerleon Campus, P.O. Box 179, Newport, NP6 1YG

A. Tsatskin – Zinman Institute of Archaeology, University of Haifa, Haifa 31905, Israel

F. R. Valla – Ethnologie Préhistorique, EP.1730 Archéologies – CNRS, 21 allée de l'université, F-92023 NANTERRE cedex, France

G. A. Wahida – 91 Glebe Road, Cambridge, CB1 4TE

Foreword

Dorothy Garrod's work has a continuing relevance today, which outlives that of many of her contemporaries. It is remarkable, thirty years after her death (and well beyond a century after her birth), that a volume of studies should be dedicated to her memory and to the issues in prehistory which she raised. On reflection it is even more remarkable that her contributions have not been more widely recognised, and that this is the first such volume to be published.

That such a volume did not come about sooner is due in part to her reluctance to make sweepingly programmatic pronouncements, and in part due to her caution as a synthesiser. She wrote no broad surveys of the kind undertaken by her exact contemporary Gordon Childe, and so far there are no published biographies devoted to her life and work (where Childe has been the subject of at least three). She was of course primarily an excavator, and it is in the excavation reports that her best work is to be found.

That this volume comes about now is a remarkable tribute to her unerring sense of problem. She illuminated, indeed in some cases she initiated, avenues of research which seem even more clearly today than thirty years ago to address some of the central issues of prehistoric archaeology. Her first and highly successful excavation revealed fragments of Neanderthal fossils in Gibraltar. In moving to Western Asia, to Kurdistan, she worked on both the Mousterian and the Upper Palaeolithic (Zarzian). Then with the wonderful series of hominid remains from Mount Carmel she effectively initiated the study in Palestine of that remarkable transition to our own species *Homo sapiens sapiens* for which the Levant turns out to be a key area. There can be no more absorbing question for archaeology than the origins of our own species, and with her excavations there she blazed a trail which, as the papers in the volume show, is increasingly seen as of great relevance.

If the emergence and dispersal of our own species represents one of the most significant transitions in human history, the shift from hunter-gathering to food production is certainly another. Here her work on what, following Garrod, is now called the Natufian culture again forms the indispensable basis for the understanding of the first farming cultures which followed, as documented so clearly a few years later at Jericho by another redoubtable fieldworker, Dame Kathleen Kenyon.

This book begins with a sequence of papers focussing upon a theme rather closer to home. They take as their starting point her first work *The Upper Palaeolithic Age in Britain*, published in 1926 when she was only 34. This is a study which her future successor as Disney Professor, Grahame Clark, himself used as a point of departure for his own doctoral dissertation, *The Mesolithic Age in Britain*, published by Cambridge University Press just six years later. As we see here the hunter-gatherer period in Britain is once again a lively field of research.

Perhaps the most impressive feature of these papers, as they relate to Dorothy Garrod, is that they address directly the problems which interested her, and yet at the same time situate themselves in the mainstream of current research. Whether the focus is upon the Upper Palaeolithic of Britain, upon prehistoric Bulgaria or on the early Levant, it is refreshing to see that so many of the central archaeological issues of today can be traced back to the work of Dorothy Garrod half a century and more ago and to the pioneering studies which she undertook to further our understanding of the early prehistory of Europe and Western Asia.

Colin Renfrew
Disney Professor of Archaeology
University of Cambridge

Introduction

William Davies and Ruth Charles

This volume draws together archaeological studies from across Europe and the Near East, reflecting the interests and legacy of Professor Dorothy Garrod. She was a very important figure, with active interests extending over a very large geographical area, and was working at a formative time for modern archaeology. The variety of her influences has enabled us to edit a book with a very wide scope, extending not just through the Palaeolithic and Mesolithic sequences of the Near East, but also into Europe and the theoretical debates about the Palaeolithic during her working life. The final two papers in the volume attempt to consider some of the influences upon Garrod; Nina Layard, the best-known female Palaeolithic archaeologist in Britain before Garrod, is here re-appraised, and her connections with Garrod documented. While self-effacing and quietly-spoken, particularly noticeable when lecturing undergraduates, Garrod possessed great reserves of inner strength and determination, evidenced by her exhaustive work in sometimes isolated and dangerous places, *e.g.* southern Kurdistan. Her dealings with Arabs and Jews alike were liberal and non-judgmental.

Johanna Mestorf had been appointed Professor at Kiel University (Germany) in 1899, when she was 70 years old: the first woman in Europe (if not the world) to achieve this status. She was a prehistorian, making a major contribution to the dissemination of the Three Age system in Germany (Díaz-Andreu and Sørensen 1998). Forty years later, Garrod became "the first woman to be a Professor in Oxford or Cambridge" (Daniel 1969: 1), but perhaps more significantly even than that, she was the first *prehistorian* to hold the Disney Professorship of Archaeology in Cambridge University (Smith, pers. comm.). As Professor, she helped to ensure that the expanded Archaeology and Anthropology Tripos was broad-based, but must have felt severely under pressure: although she resigned in 1952 at the age of 60 to resume her excavations and research, she had already decided to give up the Chair in 1950, only two years after the introduction of the new tripos (Smith, pers. comm.).

Garrod is probably best-known as a field-worker, and this practical experience enabled her to make a significant contribution towards the development of typological sequences for the Near East and the Upper Palaeolithic of Britain. She maintained a consistent interest in many geographical areas, including Britain, France, the Near East and the Balkans. Together with Suzanne de Saint-Mathurin and Germaine Henri-Martin, she was regarded in France as one of the "Three Graces". Her most substantial memorial is perhaps her work in the Near East, and this explains the large number of papers on her work in this region in this volume. Gibraltar had been the turning-point in her career in the mid-1920s, leading to her involvement with the Glozel Commission and to work in southern Kurdistan and Palestine.

The invidious misapprehension that Garrod burnt her papers still persists (*e.g.* Champion 1998: 187), and needs to be destroyed once and for all. Persistent enquiries by Pamela Jane Smith, who refused to accept this myth, revealed that the bequest by Garrod's close friend, Suzanne de Saint-Mathurin, of her archives to the Musée des Antiquités Nationales (St. Germain-en-Laye, Paris) was an archive-within-an-archive: it also contained Garrod's papers, deposited in at least fifteen boxes in the Museum's library. When these have all been sorted and catalogued (see Smith *et al.* 1997), prehistorians will have a treasure-trove of material available for study: as well as site notebooks and photographs, there are diaries, letters, draft papers (including one on the analysis of butchery marks from La Madeleine) and the unpublished type-script of a book, entitled simply *World Prehistory* and probably completed some time during the 1940s. A hat-box, with Garrod's initials on the lid, containing film negatives, some journals and three cine-films of excavations survives in Oxford, and must also be considered part of this archive.

The response which the editors received from the contributors to this volume was overwhelmingly positive and enthusiastic: testament to the continuing relevance of Garrod's work. This book was conceived to identify Garrod's achievements in the light of current research, and the resulting consensus seems to be that these have lasting currency. Her pragmatism and caution when pronouncing judgment ensured that she never over-reached herself, and she was always prepared to revise or change her opinions if the evidence appeared to demand it. 1999 marks the 60th anniversary of Garrod's appointment to the Disney Professorship, providing a useful near-millenial date to publish this volume, while 1998 marked the 50th anniversary of the admission of women as full members to the University of Cambridge and the introduction of the Archaeology and Anthropology Tripos. With the continued study of the Garrod archive in Paris, we shall obtain a more precise picture of both her achievements and those of her female colleagues in the earlier part of this century. This volume seeks to place itself at the start of this re-appraisal: a sort of "taking stock" for the research of the next century.

Bibliography

Champion, S. 1998. Women in British Arcaheology: Visible and Invisible. In M. Díaz-Andreu and M.L.S. Sørensen (Eds.), *Excavating Women: A history of women in European Archaeology*, pp. 175–197. London: Routledge

Daniel, G. 1969. Editorial. *Antiquity* 43: 1–7

Díaz-Andreu, M., and M.L.S. Sørensen 1998. Excavating Women: Towards an engendered history of archaeology. In M. Díaz-Andreu and M.L.S. Sørensen (Eds.), *Excavating Women: A history of women in European Archaeology*, pp. 1–28. London: Routledge

Smith, P.J., J. Callander, P.G. Bahn and G. Pinçon. 1997. Dorothy Garrod in words and pictures. *Antiquity* 71: 265–270.

Acknowledgements

The following must be thanked for their help in the conception and development of this volume: Derek Roe, for suggesting that we edit this book in the first place, and for advice; Chris Chippindale, for all his help and advice; Joan Oates, Jane Davies and John Stewart for their help in the editing and translation of certain papers; Pamela Jane Smith and Jane Callander for making their knowledge and research available to the editors; Antonia Benedek, Madeleine Lovedy Smith, and other members of the Garrod family for their interest and support; the Pitt Rivers Museum, University of Oxford, and the Musée des Antiquités Nationales, Saint Germain-en-Laye, Paris, for permission to use text and photographs in their care; the Registrar of the Roll, Newnham College, for help with biographical details; Mark White, Andrew Garrard and Brian Byrd for suggesting contributors; the contributors themselves for their enthusiasm and co-operation.

1

Dorothy Annie Elizabeth Garrod
(5th May, 1892 – 18th December, 1968)

A Short Biography

William Davies

Garrod came from a family of great academic distinction, some of whose members are still active today: while her paternal great-grandfather was an estate agent in Ipswich, Suffolk, his son was Sir Alfred Garrod (1819–1907), Physician Extraordinary to Queen Victoria, who evolved the "Thread Test" for uric acid in the blood and also coined the term "Rheumatoid Arthritis" (Caton-Thompson 1969). His three sons became equally eminent: Alfred Henry (1846–1879) was an F.R.S. at the age of 30 for his work in physiology and zoology, and is best-remembered for his work in the re-classification of birds; Herbert Baring (1849–1912) won the Newdigate Prize for Poetry at Oxford, and wrote upon Dante, Goethe and Calderon; Sir Archibald (1857–1936), Garrod's father, was also an F.R.S., and was the first Professor of Medicine at St. Bartholomew's Hospital, London, and later the Regius Professor of Medicine at Oxford; he is regarded as the founder of biochemical genetics (*ibid.*). Garrod thus shared a similar upper-middle class background to Nina Layard: the families knew each other well, probably because they both derived from south Suffolk (the Garrods lived in Melton). Layard was the cousin of Sir Henry Layard, the excavator of Nineveh, and began excavations in East Anglia in the late nineteenth century (see later, and Plunkett, this volume).

Dorothy Garrod was educated mainly at home, until the year before she came up to Cambridge, when she attended Birklands School, St. Albans. Her academic career began at Newnham College, Cambridge, in 1913, where she read History. Owing to illness, she obtained an *Aegrotat* in her Part I; she obtained a Class II:2 degree in 1916 owing to a complex mixture of factors, probably including the death of one of her brothers (Thomas) earlier that year on the killing fields of France (Smith, pers. comm.; Caton-Thompson 1969). She was also deeply involved with a young man, although he too was killed in the Great War (Lovedy Smith to Callander, pers. comm.). In 1917 she joined the Ministry of Munitions as a Clerk, but soon left to take a more active rôle in the war effort, serving in France and the Rhineland as an Assistant in the Catholic Women's League huts, nursing the wounded and the dying. She had converted to Catholicism from Anglicanism during World War I (Caton-Thompson 1969), although she did not tell her parents for some years afterwards

(Callander, pers. comm.); it is not known why she converted. Her other two brothers were dead by the time she had left the Catholic Women's League: Noël was killed in 1917 in France, and Basil died in the influenza pandemic of 1919 in Cologne, shortly before he was to be demobilised (Caton-Thompson 1969). By 1919, Garrod was feeling the full force of parental expectations as the only surviving child:

> "The tragedy left a permanent imprint... for they were a devoted and integrated family. She once told me that she resolved, at that dreadful time, to try to compensate her parents, as far as lay in her power, by achieving a life they could feel worthy of the family tradition."   (*ibid.*: 341)

However, there was a problem: she was then undecided about a field in which to specialise. She was a good draughtsman, and once seriously considered specialising in architecture (*ibid.*). In 1919, after she had nothing left to keep her in the Rhineland, she joined her parents in Malta, where she was encouraged by her father to study some of the antiquities. Garrod's father died in 1936, and so never lived to see his daughter become the first female Professor in Cambridge; this was perhaps one of her greatest regrets: "I wish my father had been alive, and the others [her brothers]" (*ibid.*: 340).

In 1921, she decided to enrol for the Archaeology Diploma at Oxford, under the direction of Professor Robert Ranulph Marett; Henry Field, D. Talbot Rice and Francis Turville-Petre were among her fellow-students (*ibid.*). She had met the Abbé Breuil that summer while staying at Ussat (Ariège), and had become enthused about Palaeolithic art, visiting the caves of Niaux and Tuc d'Audoubert:

> "...we also met the Abbé Breuil, who knows more than anyone about these things, and explores caves in a Roman collar and a bathing dress."
>   (letter to cousin)

The next academic year (1922–1923), having obtained a Distinction in her Diploma, she set out for Paris to "perfect her knowledge of Prehistory" (Breuil: in Garrod, this volume) with references from Professors Sollas and Marett, and funded by a Newnham College Travelling Grant. When she showed her willingness to analyse and discuss Commont's work on the Somme gravels, Breuil was assured of her industry and intelligence, "trying to really understand the subject and possessing a justifiably critical mind" (*ibid.*). She gained valuable experience in summer (1923–1924) at excavations run by Henri Martin (La Quina, with its Neanderthals in a Mousterian context), the Saint-Périers (Isturitz), Peyrony, Pittard and Bouyssonie.

With encouragement from Breuil, Garrod started research for her book on the British Upper Palaeolithic in 1924 (see Roberts, this volume), and finished writing it in 1925. Breuil may have been one of the driving forces behind this project: as a prehistorian with global interests, he would have been particularly interested to have the British Upper Palaeolithic codified and brought into line with the rest of [Western] Europe. Garrod described her book, *The Upper Palaeolithic Age in Britain*, as her "thesis", and indeed she received a B.Sc. from Oxford in 1924 for her work on this. She experienced problems with the British record, as many sites were poorly-excavated and were typologically ambiguous (see Jacobi, Swainston, this volume); she also described and named a new late Upper Palaeolithic industry, the "Creswellian", after Creswell Crags in Derbyshire (see Roberts, Charles, this volume). During the writing and research for her book, Garrod also seems to have maintained strong links with Nina Layard, as an *addendum* to her book demonstrates:

> "Miss Layard has kindly given me permission to mention that she has recently discovered an industry which appears to be Upper Palaeolithic in a deposit of the Colne Valley in Essex. The implements bear a strong resemblance to those from the Middle zone of Mother Grundy's Parlour, and would appear to be late 'Creswellian'."
>
> (Garrod 1926a: 194)

Layard had been Vice-President of the Prehistoric Society of East Anglia (PSEA) in 1920, and President in 1921, the first woman to achieve this. Her trail-blazing path and her advanced use of excavation technique (she was one of the first Palaeolithic specialists to use three-dimensional recording techniques, from *ca.*1902: Plunkett, this volume) must have given Garrod an idea of what could be achieved by women in archaeology. Unlike Layard, Garrod did not have to serve on the Committee of the PSEA before being elected Vice-President (to Marett's President) in 1927: her success in Gibraltar had ensured that she was now one of the best-known prehistorians in the country. Her Presidential year (1928) was marked by a speech, *"Nova et vetera"*, which attempted to re-define the applications of Palaeolithic archaeology, placing the emphasis more upon the behaviours of past peoples and less upon issues of the general stratigraphic succession.

Her lack of success in excavating Kent's Cavern, Devon (see Roberts, this volume), encouraged her to think about digging outside Britain. However, she did return to work briefly in her home country in 1927, excavating at Langwith Cave between April 11th and the 28th, after her excavations at Gibraltar had finished (Callander, pers. comm.). These explorations effectively marked the end of her major work in Britain and she subsequently only excavated abroad.

Gibraltar marked a turning-point in her career (see Stringer *et al.*, this volume): henceforth she would appear to move seamlessly from one project to another, to the extent that some were truncated by new work. Frustrated by her lack of success in working at Kent's Cavern in Devon, she was encouraged by Breuil to try a site which he believed had potential. He had made preliminary soundings at Devil's Tower while posted in Gibraltar in 1917 and 1919, and had found some Mousterian artefacts. As Garrod (1961) later remarked, he "waived his rights as discoverer" of the site, and the results from her seven months of excavations between November 1925 and December 1926 had a great impact. On the 11th June, Garrod's team uncovered the skull fragments of a Neanderthal child, and the telegram sent to her family at 85, Banbury Road, Oxford, at 8.20 pm on 12th June is typically terse: "FOUND MOUSTERIAN SKULL". She called this child "Abel", perhaps to suggest the voice of our "brother" calling from the soil (see Genesis 4). An article on the excavation in the *Illustrated London News* appeared on 28th August, 1926, quoting what Garrod had told the Oxford meeting of the Anthropology section of the British Association (Garrod 1926b): "She said that the Mousterian age of the skull was beyond doubt, and this opinion was confirmed during the subsequent discussion by the Abbé Breuil and Sir Arthur Keith." She had aged the skull fragments as those of a five-year-old child, and current research now favours an age between three to four years of age (Dean *et al.* 1986).

People were impressed by the clarity of both her exposition and her excavation at Gibraltar. She was awarded the *Prix Hollandais* by the Institut Internationale d'Anthropologie in Amsterdam in 1927, and was chosen at the same meeting to be the British representative on the International Commission to inspect the site of Glozel, which had been a thorn in the side of Archaeology since 1921 (see Bahn and Renfrew, this volume):

> "The difficulty in selecting members was to get archaeologists who had not already said in public what they thought about Glozel, or were not known to hold extreme views in private about the dispute. This probably explains why I was chosen. I was young, I had just finished excavating at Gibraltar, and I certainly wasn't what you might call a very well-known prehistorian. They were looking round for people who didn't already know too much about Glozel and who might be expected to take a fairly objective view about the whole affair."
>
> (Garrod 1968: 173)

On 25th September, 1927, M. Vergne (Director of Museum at Villeneuve-sur-Lot) had been surprised by a storm at Glozel, and took refuge in a disused stable on the farm; there he discovered the tools used by the sculptor, half-baked, inscribed clay tablets and half-carved schist pebbles (Daniel 1968). The Commission set to work in November 1927, scattering coins at random and excavating where they fell, yet never found any Palaeolithic objects, suggesting that the forgers found it easier to replicate pottery, *etc.*. Although Garrod found the proceedings ridiculous, there is no evidence to suggest that she found them funny: having been the youngest member of the commission, she remained a target of vituperation long after most of the other members had died (only Prof. Bosch-Gimpera survived her): "attacks on the commission that have recently started up have been directed at me" (Garrod 1968: 173). In 1990, Fradin still referred to Garrod in extremely offensive terms (see Bahn and Renfrew, this volume).

The main protagonists of the site were Reinach, who likened the unbelievers to the Inquisition *versus* Galileo, and a local doctor called Morlet, who had unwisely offered money to the Fradins from 1925 onwards to defray their expenses and to encourage further exploration.

> "Morlet had rather strange ideas and was a very excitable and uncritical person. He did not realise that Emile Fradin was merely reproducing objects which he saw in the various archaeological books which were being lent to him."
>
> (Garrod 1968: 172)

Prior to the activities of the Commission, "approved" people were permitted to open trenches at Glozel; even the King of Romania had his own trench (Jordan 1978)! The Commission reached the predictable conclusion that Glozel was archaeologically-valueless, and the Law moved in:

> "Five policemen and a commissionaire proceeded to the Fradins' farm, took the inhabitants completely by surprise, searched the premises and found unfinished tools and Glozelian objects, including inscibed tablets of clay drying in the rafters of a barn."
>
> (Garrod 1968: 176)

The subsequent police investigation and trial cleared the Fradins of fraud, but open wounds remained. Garrod, accused of trying to "frame" the protagonists of Glozel, was probably glad that she had left France before the report was published:

> "I ...left for the Near East in 1928: I began my first tour there about a month after the appearance of our report. I became absorbed in other interests and hardly gave a thought to Glozel again."   (Garrod 1968: 177)

In March 1928, on the strength of her work in Gibraltar, Garrod was asked to become a student at the British School of Archaeology in Jerusalem, and then invited out to southern Kurdistan by the Iraq Department of Antiquities (Caton-Thompson 1969). This was a preliminary exploration: she found Mousterian flakes on ground near Kirkuk, but returned to British Mandate Palestine after only a few weeks to take up the chance to excavate Shukbah Cave between April-June 1928, where she uncovered abundant human remains, associated with a microlithic industry which she attributed to the Mesolithic, and named "Natufian" after the Wady en-Natuf (see Boyd, Valla, this volume). Underlying the Natufian, in layer D, Garrod found what

Figure 1.1: Garrod surveying a cave site in the Near East. A trowel, on disturbed earth in the talus, can clearly be seen at the foot of the rock face on the right-hand side of the photograph. (Photograph courtesy of the Pitt Rivers Museum, University of Oxford.)

Breuil called the "Aurignacio-Mousterian" (Garrod 1928: 182), together with traces of human remains. Publication of Shukbah was delayed until 1942 because she had planned to return there for another season [in 1929]; however, major events were about to occur which would change her life.

Between November and December 1928, Garrod returned to southern Kurdistan in the company of Francis Turville-Petre and others, and excavated the Mousterian site of Hazar Merd and the Late Upper Palaeolithic site of Zarzi (see Wahida, this volume). An armed guard was provided during the excavations, but they were not the victims of any violence; after the horrors of World War I it seems that Garrod was prepared for anything. Several of the Kurdish villagers were employed by Garrod's team, and her presence caused much bemusement: she was the first person to search for Palaeolithic material in this region.

In 1929, Garrod was elected a research fellow at Newnham College for three years, and began work at Mount Carmel (el-Wad) between April and June (Figure 1.2). Mount Carmel, an area of surpassing archaeological interest, came perilously close to being blasted to oblivion in order to provide enough rock for the construction of the harbour at Haifa (Callander, pers. comm.). However, Garrod's work between 1929–1934 (21½ months in total) at el-Wad and then at the Mugharet-et-Tabun, was to prove one of her most impressive achievements. The cave of Skhul was also under her general direction, but directed by her Assistant, T.D. McCown. The work of the British and American Schools in Jerusalem helped to set the "Aurignacio-Mousterian" from Shukbah into a more detailed sequence.

Garrod was lucky to have had T.D. McCown (from the American School) as her Assistant, and also in the quality of the students: Hallam Movius, T.P. O'Brien, Jaquetta Hopkins (later Hawkes), Mary Kitson Clark (later Chitty) and Joan Crowfoot (later Payne) (Caton-Thompson 1969). When she was unavoidably absent in the spring of 1932, the Mousterian human remains from Skhul were recovered under the direction of McCown. She showed nothing but praise for her Assistant's handling of the excavation, although she always regretted being absent.

Her method of excavation at these sites was noteworthy: local Arab women were preferred, as they worked well, and the money they were paid would go to supply the needs of their families; men were employed to do heavier work. Garrod herself did not excavate, but supervised the analysis of the finds (92,000 implements detailed!: *ibid.*). The removal of two of the Skhul skeletons was even recorded on cine-film, showing a notable degree of historical foresight (McCown's? – Garrod was absent).

For her final year on Mount Carmel (1933–1934), Garrod obtained a Leverhulme Fellowship. The strain since 1931 had been intense, as McCown was fully engaged in the examination of the human skeletal material from Carmel in conjunction with Sir Arthur Keith. *The Stone Age of Mount Carmel*, published in 1937, was a major achievement, gaining her a D.Sc. from Oxford; the implications of her work are considered in this volume by Belfer-Cohen and Bar-Yosef. Between the 4th and 7th April, 1935, Garrod had surveyed the Atlit quarries (see Ronen *et al.*, this volume), and was the first person to record a Mousterian open-air site on the Carmel coastal plain.

Figure 1.2: Mount Carmel, 1931 season: (left to right) Theodore D. McCown, Dorothy Garrod and Francis Turville-Petre. (Photograph courtesy of the Pitt Rivers Museum, University of Oxford.)

In 1936, Garrod was elected President of Section H (Anthropology) of the British Association for the Advancement of Science, and gave a speech which made a major re-interpretation of the Eurasian Palaeolithic. She revised and shortened this paper two years later for publication in *Proceedings of the Prehistoric Society* (1938), redesigning it with the help of Breuil to attack Peyrony's (1933) new scheme for the Aurignacian (*sensu lato*) of Breuil (1912). She invented the terms "Chatelperronian" and "Gravettian" in this paper, although the full implications of her re-working took some time to take effect (see Davies, this volume).

Accompanied by James Gaul and Bruce Howe from the American School of Prehistoric Research, Garrod set off in the summer of 1938 to reconnoitre Anatolia with a view to assess its value as a geographical bridge between Palestine and Europe. Caton-Thompson (1969: 352) had begged her to work in Sinai instead, but Garrod (1936) had already proclaimed herself more concerned with a *"mirage orientale"* than a *"mirage africain"*. Although some material was discovered in Anatolia, the bureaucratic obstacles placed in her way frustrated her greatly, and after several weeks she determined to try Bulgaria instead (suggested by O.G.S. Crawford and Christopher Hawkes in 1937). The trio spent the rest of their expedition time in Bulgaria (July-August), gaining permission to excavate at Bacho Kiro on 25th July, and working there until August 8th.

A local amateur speleologist from Drênovo, Dimiter Bachev, was the first to explore the cave interior in 1935/6 (Garrod *et al.* 1939); he made some soundings in a remote part of the cave, obtaining the flint implements and cave bear bones seen by Garrod in the Natural History Museum, Sofia: "As a result of his discoveries the cave was visited by representatives of the Royal Institute and the National Museum, but the soundings made on these occasions failed to reach a Palaeolithic level" (*ibid.*: 54). Garrod and her team were to have problems with Bachev: none of her finds from reliable deposits matched the ones he had taken to the Sofia museum, and she may have suspected that she was dealing with another Glozel, where finds miraculously appeared in disturbed deposits. Her notes are more eloquent on the subject than her final report:

Thursday, 4th August, 1938

"In the morning D[orothy] G[arrod] and B[ruce] H[owe] returned to Locus IV. This is a gallery 1.45–1.70m wide terminating in an apse with an alcove to the right as one faces the apse. There is sand adhering to the roof, and the walls are much scratched by bears and ?other animals. Some scratches obviously very ancient, others have much more recent appearance. Batcheff had dug a small hole in the apse. The deposit is very sticky grey clay capped by a crumbly, slightly hardened orange sandy deposit 0.4m thick. B.H. says Batcheff's flints came out at about 0.4–0.5m below the surface. A portion of the apse (right-hand side facing inward) had been left in place. We dug first over the part probed by Batcheff, and found one point[ed blade] at the same level and some bear bones, teeth and coprolites. No finds were made in the undisturbed portion. We then marked out an area on the left-hand side, continuous with Batcheff's dig and removed topsoil down to 0.4m. In the afternoon Bruce returned and dug this out, finding nothing. He then excavated the first area to 1.10m from surface. Deposit is still grey clay, but dry and crumbly. Bottom not reached. No finds. The whole business of Batcheff's finds is very puzzling and unsatisfactory."

(From her site notebook)

"Although none of the pieces from Locus IV are abraded, they all have a slight lustre along the ridges [unlike those from the rest of the cave].

"This group of implements is remarkable not only for the size of the pieces (the longest is 125mm) but for the outstanding excellence of most of them. The same holds good for the material previously found by Bachev, and now in the Royal Institute. It is not, however, at all easy to classify this industry. When I first examined the flints in the Royal Institute I placed them as Mousterian, but the very different aspect of the Mousterian actually found in place in the cave, and the character of some of the pieces which we ourselves obtained from Locus IV, afterwards made me hesitate."

(Garrod *et al.*1939: 66)

The pieces detailed in the second [published] quotation were attributed to a "Solutréen hongrois et polonais [*i.e.* Szeletoid]" on the advice of Breuil, who examined the pieces later in 1938 (*ibid.*).

A word can be said here about the tools used by Garrod for excavation: a note in her site notebook records that deposits within two metres of the surface were "too sticky for sieving". This suggests that she was dry sieving, as glutinous deposits would present no problems if wet-sieved. Garrod seems to have used sieves since her days in Gibraltar: photographs of the excavation there in the *Illustrated London News* show them clearly, and she continued to use them for her sites in the Near East. The use of dry-sieving would have placed Garrod's excavations among the most precise ones of the day. She never returned to the Balkans to excavate, although she was very aware of the region's importance in the origins of the Upper Palaeolithic (see Kozłowski, this volume):

> "...I would suggest that we ought to re-examine more closely not only the typology but the dating of the rather enigmatic cultures of the Eastern Alps – the Aurignacian Potočka and other Yugoslav caves, and the so-called proto-Aurignacian of the Steiermark..."
> (Garrod 1953: 35)

The system of transciption from Cyrillic to Roman characters used by Garrod's team was that prepared by Professor Minns, whom she would succeed as Disney Professor the next year. Garrod's application to the University for the Chair is reproduced in this volume; it appears that she was not especially confident of success. The faculty seem to have been determined to appoint a prehistorian (Smith, pers. comm.), which meant that Garrod was competing against the likes of Christopher Hawkes and Gertrude Caton-Thompson. Garrod was deemed the best candidate on the basis of her numerous well-conducted and well-known excavations, and duly elected. It was only after the committee had presented their recommendation to the Vice-Chancellor, H.R. Dean, that the latter pointed out the problem: as women did not exist in the University's Statutes, Garrod would effectively be an "invisible" Professor (Smith, pers. comm.). The inherent absurdity of this situation was immediately realised, but the intervention of the Second World War ensured that nothing could be done about the position of women in the University until 1948. Garrod's appointment had inadvertently contributed to the re-invention of the University; other appointments of women to Professorships followed rapidly in the subsequent years.

Garrod's appointment to the Disney Chair took effect on 1st October, 1939, but war ensured that she had the barest skeleton of an Archaeology Department to lead. Although she tried to become involved in the war from the beginning, she had to wait until 1942 before she could participate: particularly galling to her strong sense of duty (Smith, pers. comm.). She used her period of enforced civilian activity to write up her work from Shukbah Cave, and was also elected to the Council of the Society of Antiquaries of London in 1941. Her war work was for the W.A.A.F. [R.A.F.] in Medmenham, Buckinghamshire, where, as a Section-Officer, she worked on the interpretation of aerial reconnaissance photographs; her colleagues included Grahame Clark, Glyn Daniel, Charles McBurney, Charles Phillips and Stuart Piggott (Caton-Thompson 1969). She was glad to have served the war effort, asserting that she "would not have missed the... experience for anything" (letter to Sir Arthur Keith, 17 June 1945: archives of the Royal College of Surgeons of England, London).

After the war, the task of rebuilding the Archaeology and Anthropology faculty began in earnest. Increasing demand for places towards the end of the 1930s had ensured that the Tripos would have to be expanded, from a Part II preceded by a Part I in another subject (History, Classics, *etc.*), into a full three-year course. It was strongly believed that a broad-based curriculum should be promoted, so that students did not become too specialised: the new, two-part Tripos began in 1948. The heavy administrative work-load eventually lost all attraction to Garrod, who in 1952 seized the opportunity, at the age of 60, to resign her position and retire to France, where she could pursue her ambition to calibrate the Near Eastern sequence using absolute methods.

She had a house ("Chamtoine") constructed near the Charentian village of Villebois-Lavallette between 1952–3, and spent the rest of her life based there (Figure 1.3). In the late 1940s she had assisted her old friend and neighbour, Germaine Henri-Martin, in her excavations at Fontéchevade, and site notebooks in her handwriting survive in Paris (Callander, pers. comm.). Between 1948 and 1963 she participated in Suzanne de Saint-Mathurin's excavations at Angles-sur-l'Anglin (Vienne), and wrote extensively in diverse publications about the Magdalenian III paintings, sculptures and engravings found therein. Her relationship with the Abbé Breuil cooled briefly in the late 1950s, owing to his attack upon Vaufrey, and also for his unequivocal support of a Palaeolithic age for all the images from Rouffignac, Périgord (Caton-Thompson 1969). She also retained weak links with the British Upper Palaeolithic, undertaking to do flint analysis for her friend E.M. Clifford in 1954. The Early Upper Palaeolithic industry recovered from layer C of Shanidar Cave by Solecki (1958) was called "Baradostian" on the advice of Garrod, who thought it sufficiently different from the Aurignacian to warrant a different name (see Olzewski, this volume). Her Zarzian at last had a precursor in the Zagros region.

In 1953 she revised her views on the origins of the Early Upper Palaeolithic in the light of her use of the raised beach deposits from the Near East (see Davies, this volume), and was not above changing her mind where she thought appropriate. Unfortunately, her capacity to re-work a general synthesis was severely handicapped by the post-war political situation:

> "…the published [Russian] evidence is quite inadequate for forming a judgment, and the material is now inaccessible. This particular piece of the puzzle must be left for solution to the prehistorians of a happier age than ours."
>
> (Garrod 1953: 34)

This final phase of her life was marked by a concentration on the Near Eastern record (at least if one scans her publications from this period), and a determination to clarify the chronological sequences of the region. Garrod had always been interested in chronology, and was one of the first prehistorians to seize upon the possibilities offered by the absolute technique of radiocarbon. Given her oft-expressed scepticism about the efficacy of using typology for relative chronologies, she must have realised that ^{14}C, at least in theory, promised freedom from subjective sequences.

The Lebanese raised beach deposits, which had previously been studied by Zumoffen and later by Fleisch, were used by Garrod to sequence her Levantine stratigraphies, and were fully synthesised in her Huxley Memorial Lecture of 1962. Three sheltered sites in Lebanon provided the focus for her last set of excavations: in 1958 the shelter of Zumoffen was excavated, followed by Ras el-Kelb Cave in 1959; finally, when in her seventies, she excavated the Mugharet-el-Bezez (see Copeland, this volume). Garrod was in England when she received an urgent call from Beirut to go out and excavate the site of Ras el-Kelb, threatened by work on a road tunnel.

Figure 1.3: Dorothy Garrod at 'Chamtoine', her house in the Charente; probably 1960s. (Photograph courtesy of Antonia Benedek and Madeleine Lovedy Smith.)

Garrod's team withstood seven weeks of noise and disturbance, but the latter, in conjunction with the hardness of the brecciate deposits, finally forced her to adopt a novel solution: the hard deposits of the breccia were removed layer by layer, measured and numbered in squares, and removed in blocks which filled 2000 sacks; these were then dissected, and their contents cleaned and studied at the National Museum in Beirut between 1960 and 1963.

This last period of excavation and analysis was clouded by periods of illness and subsequent convalescence. She was obliged to sit while delivering her Huxley Memorial Lecture in 1962, and had had a serious attack of angina in 1955 (Caton-Thompson 1969). Garrod spent her last years working in Chamtoine, Paris and England; she was awarded the C.B.E. by H.M. Ambassador in Paris for her contribution to archaeology. Her last public appearance was in May 1968, when she was awarded the Gold Medal of the Society of Antiquaries in London, the first woman to receive this honour. She had come to London to work on her Lebanese material earlier that year; during a visit to a cousin in Sussex she suffered a major stroke, and was hospitalised in London, before being transferred to the Hope House [Catholic] Nursing Home in Cambridge, where she died on 18th December, 1968. Her ashes were buried in her parents' grave in Melton, Suffolk, close to the wooden crosses in memory of her brothers.

Garrod's Catholicism provided a sturdy support for her work; after a brief period of withdrawal instigated by her studies of prehistory in the early 1920s, she returned to the fold after contact with Teilhard de Chardin at the Institut de Paléontologie

Humaine (from 1922), whose philosophy of evolution she found congenial (Caton-Thompson 1969). One might even conjecture that her relationship with Breuil may have been partly influenced influenced by his status as a priest, but this is at present unsupported. She had a wide range of interests outside archaeology, not least among them music: she played both the flute and violin, and often carried her flute with her. After the day's excavation at Mount Carmel, for instance, she could be persuaded to play her flute (Callander, pers. comm.), and her diary from 1934 gives a good idea of the atmosphere on site:

> "A little rain during the night, and the morning; Abd el-Khadir brought a letter from the Police, addressed to the 'Superintendent of Antiquatic'."
>
> (Friday, April 6th)

> "D.G. and A[nne] F[uller] started the day in a state of profound gloom, and scarcely exchanged a word from 6.0 to 7.30. Bacon and eggs produced a warming effect, and dispelled the clouds. During breakfast the important decision was reached to work till 5.0 p.m. every day, thus securing three days work free every month. After breakfast this was announced to the assembled Tibn-ites, and was well-received. The incident closed with profuse expressions of mutual esteem and regard. The afternoon was awaited with some anxiety, as Miss Hilda Wills had announced her intention of visiting the [Tibn] Towers. E[leanor] D[yott] spent the morning in extensive 'neating' operations. At 2.0 precisely Miss W.'s car was sighted turning into the 'drive'. D.G. hastened down to receive her, putting the finishing touches to her toilet as the car approached the causeway. Miss W. and her friend Miss Lea inspected the Towers from cellar to attic, and then visited the Tabun. Though ignorant of prehistory they displayed just the right amount of interest – in short behaved just like the best type of Cultured English Hat. They then drank tea in the parlour of the Towers, and drove away, leaving a cheque for Twenty-five Pounds to gladden the hearts of the Tibn-ites. ...Sabbath sherry was drunk at 6.45, the toast being 'Miss Hilda Wells'."
>
> (Saturday, April 14th)

"Tibn [the Arabic for "straw"] Towers" was the nickname awarded to the row of cabins which formed the centre of the Mount Carmel excavations.

When she received the Society of Antiquaries' Gold Medal, her response was typically modest: "Well, at least I am not forgotten" (Daniel 1969: 2). The enthusiasm shown by the contributors to this book have shown that there was little risk of this: Garrod's range of interests were so wide and covered such a large geographic area that it was never in doubt that an interesting book could be compiled. Grahame Clark, Garrod's successor as Disney Professor, wrote the following in *The Times* of 28th December, 1968 (in Daniel 1969: 2):

> "Dorothy Garrod's distinction as a prehistorian is on the record. As a person she combined a gentle and indeed forbearing manner with a quiet authority and a scorn for the second-hand and the second-rate. Her appreciation of original work by colleagues of whatever age was genuine and unfeigned."

Acknowledgements

I should like to thank Pamela Jane Smith and Jane Callander for all their help in the writing of this biography. Their ongoing work in the Garrod archive at the Musée des Antiquités Nationales de St. Germain-en-Laye is of major importance, and is still uncovering new information. Many of the quotations and sources quoted above could only be used owing to their work. All mistakes which remain are, of course, my responsibility. Readers who would like to read another biography are recommended to read the one published in *Proceedings of the British Academy* by Garrod's friend and fellow-Catholic, Gertrude Caton-Thompson (1969).

Bibliography

Breuil, H. 1912. Les Subdivisions du Paléolithique Supérieur et leur Signification. Paper presented to the *Congrès International d'Anthropologie et d'Archéologie Préhistoriques [XIVe session]*, Geneva, 1912: 165–238.

Caton-Thompson, G. 1969. Dorothy Annie Elizabeth Garrod, 1892–1968 (obituary). *Proceedings of the British Academy* 65: 339–361.

Daniel, G. 1968. Editorial. *Antiquity* 42: 165–171.

Daniel, G. 1969. Editorial. *Antiquity* 43: 1–7.

Dean, M.C., Stringer, C.B., and T.G. Bromage 1986. Age at Death of the Neanderthal Child from Devil's Tower, Gibraltar, and the Implications for Studies of General Growth and Development in Neanderthals. *American Journal of Physical Anthropology* 70: 301–309.

Garrod, D.A.E. 1926a. *The Upper Palaeolithic Age in Britain*. Oxford: Clarendon Press.

Garrod, D.A.E. 1926b. Excavation of a Mousterian Site and Discovery of a Human Skull at Devil's Tower, Gibraltar. Abstract and title in *Report of the British Association for the Advancement of Science, Section H*, pp. 385–386.

Garrod, D.A.E. 1928. Excavation of a Palaeolithic Cave in Western Judaea. *Quarterly Statement of the Palestine Exploration Fund* 60: 182–185.

Garrod, D.A.E. 1936. The Upper Palaeolithic in the Light of Recent Discovery. Presidential Address, Section H (Anthropology), Blackpool. *Report of the British Association for the Advancement of Science, 1936*: 155–172.

Garrod, D.A.E. 1938. The Upper Palaeolithic in the Light of Recent Discovery. *Proceedings of the Prehistoric Society* 4: 1–26.

Garrod, D.A.E. 1953. The Relations between South-West Asia and Europe in the Later Palaeolithic Age, with special reference to the Origin of the Upper Palaeolithic Blade Cultures. *Journal of World History* 1: 13–37.

Garrod, D.A.E. 1961. Obituary: The Abbé Breuil (1877–1961). *Man* 61: 205–207.

Garrod, D.A.E. 1968. Recollections of Glozel. *Antiquity* 42: 172–177.

Garrod, D.A.E., Howe, B., and J.H. Gaul 1939. Excavations in the Cave of Bacho Kiro, North-East Bulgaria. Part I: Description, Excavations and Archaeology. *Bulletin of the American Society for Prehistoric Research* 15: 46–87.

Jordan, P. 1978. Glozel. In R. Sutcliffe (Ed.), *Chronicle: essays from ten years of television archaeology*, pp. 67–81. London: BBC Books.

Peyrony, D. 1933. Les Industries "aurignaciennes" dans le bassin de la Vézère. *Bulletin de la Société Préhistorique Française* 30: 543–559.

Solecki, R. 1958. *The Baradostian industry and the Upper Palaeolithic in the Near East*. Unpublished Ph.D. dissertation, Columbia University, New York.

Dorothy Annie Elizabeth Garrod

Born: 5th May, 1892

Education
Privately: Birklands School, St. Albans
Newnham College, Cambridge: 1913–16. Historical Tripos (class II:2); M.A. (Cantab.).
Society of Oxford Home-Students: 1921–24. Diploma in Anthropology, Oxford (with Distinction), 1922. B.Sc. (Oxon.), 1924. D.Sc. (Oxon.), 1939.

Awards, etc.

1927:	Prix Hollandais, Institut International d'Anthropologie.
1928:	Corresponding Member of the Société d'Anthropologie de Paris.
1936:	Socio de Honor de la Sociedad Española de Antropología, Etnografía y Prehistoria.
1937:	Hon. D.Sc., University of Pennsylvania.
1937:	Hon. D.Sc., Boston College.
1937:	Elected Fellow of the Society of Antiquaries of London.
1938:	Rivers Memorial Medal of the Royal Anthropological Institute.
1950:	Hon. D-ès Sc., Poitiers University.
1952:	Elected Fellow of the British Academy.
1962:	Huxley Memorial Medal, Royal Anthropological Institute.
1965:	Made Commander of the British Empire (C.B.E.).
1968:	Gold Medal of the Society of Antiquaries, London (first woman).
Also:	Hon. D-ès Litt., Toulouse.

Positions held

1917:	Clerk, Ministry of Munitions
1917–19:	Assistant, Catholic Women's League Huts: France, Rhineland.
1922–23:	Mary Ewart Travelling Scholar, Newnham College.
1926–27:	Vice-President, Prehistoric Society of East Anglia.
1927–28:	President, Prehistoric Society of East Anglia.
1927:	British Member, Glozel Commission.
1927–42:	Associate, Newnham College.
1929–32:	Research Fellow, Newnham College.
1933:	Leverhulme Research Fellow
1933–42:	Archaeology & Anthropology Director of Studies, Newnham College.
1934–37:	Council, Royal Anthropological Institute.
1936:	President, Section H, British Association for the Advancement of Science, Blackpool.
1936:	Faculty Board of Archaeology & Anthropology, Cambridge.
1938–41:	Council, Royal Anthropological Institute.
1939–52:	Disney Professor of Archaeology, Cambridge.
1941:	Council, Society of Antiquaries of London.
1942–45:	A/S/O Technical Branch, W.A.A.F.
1945:	Council for British Archaeology.
1945–47:	Council, Royal Anthropological Institute.
1945–52:	Associate, Newnham College.
1948:	Council, Society of Antiquaries of London.
1959–68:	Associate, Newnham College.

Served on Board of Studies in Archaeology, University of London, sometime before 1939.

Died: 18th December, 1968 (Cambridge: Hope House).

2

The Application of D. A. E. Garrod, M.A., D.Sc. (Oxon.),

Director of Studies of Newnham College,
Associate of Newnham College,

as

A Candidate for the Disney Professorship of Archaeology in the University of Cambridge

NEWNHAM COLLEGE
16 *March* 1939

Dear Mr Vice-Chancellor,

I beg to submit myself as a candidate for the vacant Disney Professorship of Archaeology, advertised in the *Cambridge University Reporter* of March 7th. A summary of my career and publications is appended.

My study of prehistoric archaeology dates from the year 1921, when I began to read for the Diploma in Archaeology at Oxford. During my tenure of the Mary Ewart Travelling Scholarship (1922–23) I became a student of the Abbé Breuil at the Institut de Paléontologie Humaine in Paris, and in the summers of 1923 and 1924 I spent many weeks assisting in the excavations of M. Peyrony, Dr Henri Martin and Dr R. de Saint-Périer. My first independent excavation was in the Mousterian rock-shelter of Devil's Tower, Gibraltar (1925–26), where I had the good fortune to find the well-preserved skull of a Neandertal child. Since that date I have devoted most of my time to field work and the publication of its results. My excavation of the cave of Shukba, in Western Judaea, on behalf of the British School of Archaeology in Jerusalem, led to the discovery of a new Mesolithic industry, which I named Natufian, after the Wady en-Natuf, in which the cave was situated. This industry has since been found in other Palestinian sites, and is now a recognised stage of the Mesolithic of the Near East. The Joint Expedition of the Sladen Memorial Fund and the American School of Prehistoric Research to the Sulaimani district of Southern Kurdistan (1928), of which I was Director, was the first to enter this region for purposes of prehistoric research, and our discovery and excavation of two Palaeolithic caves, containing a Mousterian and an Aurignacian industry respectively, is still the sole evidence for the Stone Age sequence of that area. The joint excavations of the British School of Archaeology in Jerusalem and the American School of Prehistoric Research, in the caves of the Wady el-Mughara, Mount Carmel (1929–34), of which also I was Director, resulted in the discovery of a nearly complete sequence of cultures from the last stages of the Acheulean to the end of the Natufian, and thus established the main lines of Stone Age chronology for Palestine. Associated with the flint implements was a very rich fauna, which contains many new species, and has yielded much information about variations of climate during the latter part of the Pleistocene in Palestine. The human skeletal remains, which are being studied by Sir Arthur Keith and my collaborator Mr T. D. McCown, belong to two stages, the Natufian and the Lower Levalloiso-Mousterian. The latter group contains remains of at least twenty individuals, including four nearly complete skeletons. On the evidence of the associated fauna these have been dated to the close of the Riss-Würm interglacial. They represent a hitherto unknown type of fossil man having affinities both with *Homo Neandertalensis* and *Homo sapiens*.

The study of the archaeological remains from the Wady el-Mughara, which I undertook myself, involved the classification and cataloguing of more than 87,000 stone implements. The results, with a description of the excavations, together with Miss D. M. A. Bate's study of the fauna, were published in 1937 by the Clarendon Press under the title, *The Stone Age of Mount Carmel*.

In the summer of 1938 I undertook an investigation in Bulgaria on behalf of the American School of Prehistoric Research, and in a preliminary excavation in the cave of Bacho Kiro, near Drenovo in the Northern Balkans, I discovered a number of Aurignacian layers superimposed on Mousterian. This is the first Palaeolithic sequence to be found in Bulgaria, though an Aurignacian industry was already known from one cave, and sporadic finds from three others.

Ever since I was a student at the Institut de Paléontologie Humaine I have done my best to keep in touch with recent developments in the work of my colleagues, and I have paid frequent visits to France, and have visited museums and excavations in Spain, Belgium, Germany, Switzerland, Czechoslovakia, Rumania, Turkey, Syria and Egypt.

My chief interests at the moment are the Palaeolithic of Eastern Europe and the Upper Palaeolithic as a whole. I am hoping in the future to undertake in collaboration with the Abbé Breuil a general work on the latter subject.

I append testimonials from the Abbé Breuil and Sir Arthur Keith.

I am,
Yours sincerely,
D. A. E. GARROD

THE VICE-CHANCELLOR
TRINITY HALL

From ABBÉ H. BREUIL, *Membre de l'Institut, Professeur au Collège de France et à l'Institut de Paléontologie Humaine.*

It was at Ussat in Ariège, where she was resting after the War, that I first met MISS DOROTHY GARROD in 1921. I took her to see the painted cave of Niaux. Not long after (1922) Professor Sollas sent her to me in Paris to follow my lectures at the Institute of Human Palaeontology, so that she could perfect her knowledge of Prehistory. She was an industrious and intelligent pupil, trying to really understand the subject and possessing a justifiably critical mind. This was the beginning of a series of years during which I followed her rise to the rank of a great specialist.

Her first personal researches were devoted to the co-ordination of facts concerning the English Upper Palaeolithic, scattered through the literature and museums of England. She also carried out interesting personal investigations in several English caves.

I then pressed her to undertake the excavation of a site at Devil's Tower, Gibraltar, which I had discovered, and which I assured her would be an important piece of work. Having obtained an authorisation and the necessary funds she set to work with much courage and ability and found a complete series of superposed Mousterian levels containing the skull of a Neandertaloid child, resting on the beach of the last interglacial period.

The great success of this first excavation and its publication drew attention to Miss Garrod's capacity for more distant undertakings, and was the means of her being appointed to the direction of researches in caves of the Near East, to which, from 1928 onwards, she gave all her time. It was thus that with various collaborators she explored in 1928 the cave of Shukba (27 kilometres north of Jerusalem), and those of Zarzi and Hazar Merd in Southern Kurdistan. After that she explored the group of caves and rock-shelters of the Wady el-Mughara near Haifa which occupied her from 1929 to 1934. These last excavations were particularly lucky, admirably conducted and excellently described, leaving little unstudied of the prehistory of Palestine, which, thanks to her is now one of the best known, as much from the succession of the various industrial levels as for the remarkable human types discovered there.

During these long and hard researches Miss Garrod showed great energy, high capacity in the directing of difficult work, perfect comprehension of the results obtained, and wide knowledge when comparing the finds with those of different regions. In *Nature* I stated how highly I esteemed her fine book.

Besides these personally directed excavations she has constantly followed similar work on the Continent. She has studied the paintings and engraved caves and rock-shelters of the south-west of France, the north-west of Spain and Southern Andalusia, generally in my company. She has also visited the classic sites of the Somme, the Dordogne, the Pyrenees and Cantabria and the collections they yielded, and with the same end in view has travelled in Switzerland, Germany and Central and Eastern Europe.

She is held in general esteem and sympathy as an eminent, conscientious specialist, working sometimes to the limit of her strength. The fine discoveries due to her hard work are only the just recompense of her continuous effort.

If she were nominated to succeed Professor Minns in the Disney Professorship of Archaeology, her appointment would be universally applauded because of her great gifts.

Institut de Paléontologie Humaine
Paris XII

From SIR ARTHUR KEITH, F.R.S.
In my opinion the researches carried out by MISS DOROTHY GARROD place her in the front rank of European archaeologists. I have been associated with her more recent explorations and have been impressed by her leadership, her powers of organisation, her public spirit, her industry, but above all by her power to inspire and instruct those who work with her. I am convinced she has all the qualities needed for the Disney Professorship.

Buckston Browne Farm
Downe
Farnborough
Kent

3

The Path Not Taken: Dorothy Garrod, Devon and the British Palaeolithic

Alison Roberts

Despite her influential early work on the British Upper Palaeolithic, Dorothy Garrod conducted very little related fieldwork in the subject. One of only two known examples was an evaluation of several caves in the Torbryan Valley, Devon, in 1924.[1] Indeed, this short season of work appears to have been her first independent fieldwork. Plans for further excavations in Devon at Kent's Cavern were frustrated the following summer, and by the end of 1925 she had begun the work on Gibraltar which is regarded as launching her career (see Stringer et al., this volume). Nonetheless, the insights concerning the British Upper Palaeolithic which she drew during that brief phase of her career have had a persistent influence on the field.

Introduction

In July 1926, Dorothy Garrod published her first book entitled *The Upper Palaeolithic Age in Britain*. In it she set out to review and evaluate all of the diverse and scattered evidence for this period in Britain, and to place that evidence within a European perspective. She brought to the book the thoroughness and clarity of expression which was to mark all of her subsequent work, and it was justifiably well-received. The book represents a major step in the understanding of the subject, and remains a crucial text even today.

Given her early interest in the subject and the key questions raised by her work on the British Upper Palaeolithic, it seems curious that she did not conduct any major excavations of her own in this country. Indeed, her evaluation of several caves in the Torbryan Valley, Devon, for the Torquay Natural History Society in 1924, appears to have been the first of only two examples of such fieldwork which she conducted. Although the reasons behind this peculiar situation may never be fully clear, one possible cause may lie in the failure of her attempt to conduct fieldwork at Kent's Cavern.

"The Upper Palaeolithic Age in Britain"

Dorothy Garrod's long career in Palaeolithic archaeology began in 1921 when she began the Oxford Diploma in Anthropology under the supervision of R.R. Marrett, the excavator of the Middle Palaeolithic cave site of La Cotte de St. Brelade on Jersey. Marrett not only kindled her enthusiasm for the Palaeolithic, but also introduced her to several eminent French prehistorians (Caton-Thompson 1969: 342). A year later, having obtained her degree with distinction, she went to the Institut de Paléontologie Humaine in Paris for two years of more specialised training in Palaeolithic Archaeology under the direction of Abbé Henri Breuil (*ibid.*; Garrod 1961).

Her book, *The Upper Palaeolithic Age in Britain*, was researched and written between 1924–1925. In a letter to Prof. John Myres in 1925 she refers to it as a "thesis" and mentions that Breuil had a typed copy, an observation which might indicate that the work was undertaken at his suggestion (BM: Garrod to Myres 10/06/25). Breuil's opinions concerning some sites and artefacts are certainly cited in her book. Regardless of the initial impetus for the book, her goals in writing it are clearly expressed in the author's note (Garrod 1926: 9):

> "The Upper Palaeolithic industries of this country have been much neglected in the past, and no text-book is in existence which gives even a complete list of British Upper Palaeolithic sites. The reason for this is to be found in the fact that the literature relating to them is buried for the most part in ancient numbers of scientific journals, while the collections themselves are dispersed in museums all over the country.
>
> The present work is intended to render available to prehistorians such material as we possess. Many of the implements figured in the plates are published for the first time; of others only very inadequate drawings have hitherto existed."

Throughout the book she both discusses the British assemblages and compares them with material from France and elsewhere on in the European continent. In doing so, one of her major aims seems to have been to establish a relative chronology for the known British assemblages. In this aim she was hindered by the fact that many assemblages had no associated contextual or stratigraphic information, and several obviously contained a mixture of artefacts from several different periods. However, in the final section of her book she suggests a possible correlation between the British assemblages and the classic recognised succession of Upper Palaeolithic industries from Southern France: "As we should expect, traces of human occupation are scarce, but we can make out the same general succession of industries as in other parts of western Europe, with certain gaps and variations" (Garrod 1926: 191).

The Abbé Breuil wrote an enthusiastic introduction to her book, which congratulated his former student for her *"contribution si consciencieuse et documentée"* (Breuil, in Garrod 1926: 8). His preface makes clear that he considered her book to be a major piece of work which both remedied his frustration with the difficulty of gaining a good overview of the British Upper Palaeolithic, and for the first time brought the British Upper Palaeolithic into line with work in continental Europe. In particular, Breuil highlighted two aspects of her work on the British Upper Palaeolithic which merited special interest: 1) her recognition of an 'Upper Aurignacian' characterised by blade points similar to those from Spy, Belgium, and 2) the presence of a 'Final Palaeolithic' similar in many ways to the classic Magdalenian of Aquitaine and reminiscent of a facies noted in Belgium (*ibid.*: 7). Both of these were features which she interpreted as distinct local variations of the classic European sequence. Both are also still key issues for the British Upper Palaeolithic:

i.e. the role of leaf-point industries within the British Early Upper Palaeolithic succession (see Jacobi, this volume), and the relationship of British Late Upper Palaeolithic assemblages to contemporary industries in continental Europe.

The Creswellian

So distinct did she consider the British variant of the classic Magdalenian to be that Dorothy Garrod took the major step of suggesting that it should be named as an industry in its own right (Garrod 1926: 194):

> "I would suggest that this industry is sufficiently well characterised to deserve a name of its own which will serve to differentiate it on the one hand from the classical Magdalenian of France on the other from the true Upper Aurignacian. I propose tentatively 'Creswellian', since Creswell Crags is the station in which it is found in greatest abundance and variety."

The term 'Creswellian' was accepted by the archaeological community and was used to describe the British Late Upper Palaeolithic. However, research by Roger Jacobi has shown that the type-assemblages upon which her definition was based actually contained a mixture of material from different Late Upper Palaeolithic industries (Jacobi 1991). Further research on old collections and new excavation has shown that there are at least two different industries represented in what used to be thought of as the British Creswellian: a Late Magdalenian-style industry; and a 'Final Upper Palaeolithic' with similarities to the North European *'Federmesser'* industries (Barton and Roberts 1996, 1997). The term 'Creswellian', in a British context,[2] now refers only to the Late Magdalenian-style industry which contains as a type-fossil the trapezoidal semi-geometrical form noted by Garrod (*i.e.* Cheddar Point, *cf.* Bohmers 1956) (Barton 1991, 1992; Barton and Roberts 1996, 1997; Jacobi 1991, 1997; Jacobi and Roberts 1992); the refined definition reflecting the original intent of Garrod's terminology.

That Dorothy Garrod failed to identify the *Federmesser* component in the British assemblages is unsurprising, not only because of the problems of mixing and lack of context mentioned above, but also as these North European industries had as yet to be fully defined in 1926 (*cf.* Schwabedissen 1954). Breuil's concept of a "...prolongation of the Upper Aurignacian, evolved on the northern boundary of the Magdalenian province, and existing side by side with the Magdalenian in border-lands, such as Belgium..." (Garrod 1926: 193) might foreshadow the identification of Northern European Late Upper Palaeolithic industries as distinct from the Magdalenian, but that subject is beyond the scope of this paper. Garrod recognised that the British assemblages which she examined could not be classified as either true Magdalenian or 'prolonged Upper Aurignacian' although containing elements of both. This was true even for the assemblage from the 'Black Band' at Kent's Cavern which was overlain by a stalagmite floor and underlain by a cave earth, and about which Garrod states that "we are here dealing with an industry whose stratigraphical position is certain, and we no longer have to start with a typological classification" (Garrod 1926: 40). She recognised that the Black Band assemblage had clear Magdalenian influences in its bone and antler work, but lacked some of the diagnostic flint tool-types (*ibid.*:

40–43, 193). In addition, she noted the occurrence of non-Magdalenian trapezoidal backed blades, but interpreted them as part of the wide range of point types found at other English caves (*ibid.*: 42). The assemblage is now seen as a good example of the 'Creswellian', in the new definition of the term. In the mid–1920s, the fact that even the most obviously stratified British Late Upper Palaeolithic assemblage contained a combination of Magdalenian and non-Magdalenian elements seems to have convinced Garrod that she was looking at something new.

Her interpretation of the 'Creswellian' as a separate unit was undoubtedly influenced by three factors: firstly, the assumption of contemporaneity between various different Late Upper Palaeolithic assemblages in Europe before the discovery of radiocarbon dating; secondly, the presence of non-Magdalenian artefacts in the Kent's Cavern assemblage; finally, her interest in both the migration of Palaeolithic populations and local variation. Although trained as a Palaeolithic archaeologist in France and at this point in her career best acquainted with the classic French Palaeolithic sequence, she was already looking at wider issues in interpreting the Palaeolithic world. The closing paragraph of *The Upper Palaeolithic Age in Britain* is revealing (Garrod 1926: 194):

> "It has long been recognised by prehistorians that the study of local variation, such as those described above, is a fruitful field for research. We can no more expect the classification of Gabriel de Mortillet to hold good over the Palaeolithic world than we could expect the geological strata of a whole continent to be everywhere the same as those seen in section at a given point. But it is not enough merely to map distributions; we have, as it were, to set our map in motion, to reconstruct the migrations of Palaeolithic culture, and only a careful study of the material available for each region can provide the evidence necessary for such an attempt".

It is difficult to see how this could be read as a simple conclusion of research. Her identification of the need to go beyond mapping distributions in studying Palaeolithic populations, combined with recognition of the usefulness of the study of local variation, reads more like a statement of intent. Her 'mapping' was done for Britain and several key questions had been raised, especially regarding the interpretation of local variations of continental industries. Why, then, did she not pursue these questions any further, and why was this her only major publication on the British Upper Palaeolithic?

Evaluation of the Torbryan Valley Caves, 1924

In early 1924, during the time that she was researching the *Upper Palaeolithic of Britain*, Dorothy Garrod was asked by the Torquay Natural History Society (TNHS) to evaluate the archaeological and palaeontological potential of several caves in the Torbryan Valley, Devon, with the aim of finding a place where further work by the Society would be useful. Her background was ideal for such a task, as she was well-acquainted with the principles of cave archaeology due to her participation in several Palaeolithic cave excavations during her time at the Paris Institut (*e.g.* La Quina, Isturitz, Les Eyzies, and Corrèze: Caton-Thompson 1969: 343). Given the timing, it is likely that she had become acquainted with the TNHS while examining collections in their museum for her book.

Several of the caves to be evaluated (her sites B1–6) were known from the work of James Lyon Widger between *ca.*1865 – *ca.*1890 (Widger 1892; Walker and Sutcliffe 1968). Another cave (her site A1) had been discovered in the "first years of the century" by "three enthusiastic Cave-relic hunters of Torquay" (Lowe 1918: 212). Her excavations lasted 11 days and during that time she was assisted by Mr. Dowie, a TNHS member. A two page-report on her findings was sent to the Society only a week after the excavations closed, and in it she concluded that two sites might justify further work: "the only caves which offer any opportunities for excavators are A1 and B4. The former is easy to dig, as the deposit is fairly soft, but it will be necessary to shift a considerable amount of rubbish left by earlier, unscientific excavators. B4 will be difficult, and may yield very little, but might be worth trying" (Garrod 1924: see Appendix).

The Society took her advice on cave A1 (Tor Court Cave), and held two seasons of excavation there during the summers of 1924 and 1925 directed by Mr Dowie. The Society removed *ca.*17 feet of deposit from the cave, which was revealed as a deep fissure in the Devonian limestone. Finds included flint artefacts and a rich Pleistocene fauna comparable with those from caves further up the valley (Roberts 1996b). The surviving archive shows that these excavations were recorded with an attention to detail not apparent at most other TNHS cave excavations in South Devon during the 1920s and 1930s. At Tor Court, Dowie seems to have dug stratigraphically, and kept a detailed field notebook in which he recorded details of the work done each day, what was recovered, and other observations on the work in progress. Each find was individually labelled with the date of its recovery, thus enabling reconstruction of the archaeological and palaeontological sequence at the site. As Dowie apparently had little archaeological experience prior to the evaluations, it is likely that the techniques he employed were learned from Garrod during the evaluations. The excavations were published quickly and in full (Dowie 1925, Benyon 1928).

Tor Court Cave was the first of the long series of TNHS cave excavations during the inter-war years, most of them excavated under the direction of Mr Ogilvie, the TNHS museum curator (Roberts 1996a). In terms of excavation technique, recording and publication, Tor Court was also arguably the best. The worst excavation was probably that at Tornewton Cave (1936–1939) from which not a scrap of archive survives except a couple of receipts for the payment of workmen to remove deposit, and which was not published. Why TNHS standards of cave excavation declined is uncertain, and cannot be pursued in this paper. Dorothy Garrod's recommendation to conduct further work at B4, now know as Three Holes Cave, was not taken up by the Society although subsequent work has confirmed the importance of the site (Rosenfeld 1964; Collcutt 1984; Roberts 1996b). It is also worth noting that a small Creswellian (contemporary *sensu stricto*) assemblage and *in situ* hearth deposit was found at this site, and has contributed much to the modern understanding of the period (Barton 1996).

Dorothy Garrod's report on the Torbryan Caves was not published, but survives in the archives of the Torquay Natural History Society Museum along with the objects which she recovered. The report is interesting not simply for the succinct information which it contains about the caves, but also for an apparently contradictory mix of artlessness and keen insight in both her approach to the evaluations and in her interpretations of the deposits which she examined. For example, the description of the section which she cleaned inside the "Great Chamber" at Three Holes Cave (B4) is excellent, and has been confirmed on all but one point by subsequent workers.[3]

In contrast, her statement that cave B1 (Tornewton Cave) "appears to be worked out, except for a small patch of breccia on the west wall" seems extraordinary in view of both the previous and subsequent excavation history of this well-known fissure cave (Widger 1892; Sutcliffe and Zeuner 1962; Walker and Sutcliffe 1968; Collcutt 1984; Proctor 1995; Currant 1996). Widger recorded the cave as consisting of four separate tunnels, now understood to be the main rift, two side passages, and an internal void leading downwards in the main rift which was apparently removed during excavations by the TNHS in the late 1930s (A. Currant, pers. comm.). The cave is now known to contain a long biostratigraphic succession dating back to Oxygen Isotope Stage 7 (Currant 1996). Widger seems to have explored most of the deposits now known in the cave and, by a conservative estimate, he must have excavated to a depth of at least 5 m below his contemporary ground surface in order to have encountered all of the stratigraphic horizons which he mentions in his report. Even given that Widger may have worked in part from the internal void, and that said void and side passages may have been partly refilled at the time of Garrod's work, it seems very odd that she dismisses the cave so lightly.

With the benefit of hindsight, her difficulty appears to lie in a lack of preparation for the task. In the manner in which she numbers the caves, and the descriptions she uses in relation to them, it is obvious that she failed to read the original accounts of Widger's work in the caves (Widger 1892, Lee 1880), although all were available at the TNHS Library. Instead she relied entirely on the information contained in Harford Lowe's review and synthesis of Widger's work (1918). Although surviving records are few, it is obvious that Widger was a good observer and what accounts he did leave have been of great value in recent work at the caves (Roberts 1996b). In trying to simplify Widger's reports and interpret his work for a wider audience, Lowe omits key information and introduces several misconceptions which are echoed in Garrod's report. In addition, his account suggests that Lowe was particularly confused by Tornewton Cave. With Lowe's paper as her only reference for the site, it is easy to understand why Garrod did not attempt further work there given the limited time and resources for the evaluations.

Her failure to consult the Widger accounts is curious, both as she knew Lowe, and as he quotes the published accounts in his article. It is doubtful that she did not know of the existence of the original documents, and the question must be asked why this enthusiastic and thorough student of the Palaeolithic failed to read the few basic documents relating to a series of caves in which she was excavating. She also did not include the site in her book, although Late Upper Palaeolithic and Mesolithic artefacts from Widger's excavations survived at the British Museum (Christy collection), and some contextual details are provided in Widger's report. Indeed, her apparent lack of interest in the Torbryan Caves is puzzling considering the effort she must have extended in the evaluations. Perhaps she did not realise the potential of the Torbryan caves for her own research, or just conceivably her attention may already have been focused on another site in South Devon. If the latter, could her work in the Torbryan Valley have been a favour for the TNHS rather than an end in itself?

The British Association and Kent's Cavern

In her book on the British Upper Palaeolithic, Dorothy Garrod discussed the cave sites in relation to the three main geographic regions in which they occurred: Southwestern Britain, including South Wales; Northwestern Britain, including North Wales; and Central Britain. Her stated intention was to bring some sort of order, if only geographic, to the confusion which then marked the field of Upper Palaeolithic studies in Britain (Garrod 1926: 20–21). As such, it seems unlikely to be a coincidence that she begins with a long discussion of Kent's Cavern in South Devon. No other site is treated so extensively in the book, and the Lower Palaeolithic artefacts from the site also formed the subject of her only other significant publication on the British Palaeolithic (Garrod 1925). Kent's Cavern was remarkable for two reasons: firstly, the length of its Palaeolithic sequence (Lower Palaeolithic, Middle Palaeolithic, two Early Upper Palaeolithic industries, and Late Upper Palaeolithic), and secondly, for the spatial and contextual information contained in the excavation archive. Both these factors contribute to its continued recognition today as one of the most important Palaeolithic sites in the country. The cave is also a key site in the history of science, being one of the first sites where the antiquity of humankind was proven. Although known since 1824, the fame of the site derives from the excavations conducted there by William Pengelly for the British Association for the Advancement of Science from 1865-1880. Pengelly dug the cave meticulously and methodically: setting up accurate grids throughout the cave, removing sediment in 3'x1'x1' blocks, and recording every object found to the block it was found in. His methodology was revolutionary for his time, and was responsible for providing irrefutable evidence of the contemporaneity of humans with extinct animals.[4]

Her publications show that Dorothy Garrod was well-acquainted with both the artefacts and notebooks from the Pengelly excavations. She discusses his methodology, and appears to have checked the typology of the objects and painstakingly cross-checked the find numbers with the notebooks in order to gain a good understanding of the spatial distribution of artefacts and bones within the cave. In doing so she brought a new interpretation to the collection, based on where objects were found in the cave, rather than just on details of their typology and depth at which they were found:

> "I have already said that four periods appear to be represented in the cave-earth, and this classification by typology agrees with a certain localisation of each group in a different part of the cave."   (Garrod 1926: 34)

The discussion of her findings suggests that she considered Kent's Cavern as a site of critical importance in the study of the British Palaeolithic.

Archives held by English Heritage (cited in Barton and Collcutt 1986) and the British Association for the Advancement of Science (now held at the Bodleian Library, Oxford) indicate that sporadic work had taken place at Kent's Cavern by the cave's owners during the 1910s–1920s, which both highlighted the continuing scientific importance of the deposits in the cave and caused concern in the academic community. In order to preserve the site, the British Association (BAAS) attempted unsuccessfully to have the site scheduled as an Ancient Monument in 1917, and to purchase the site in the early 1920s. The extent of their interest presumably related to their involvement with the Pengelly excavations. After the proposed purchase was finally rejected by the cave's owner in 1923, the BAAS turned their attention to the proper recording of finds in the cave. This suggestion seems to have been acceptable to the owner (Bod: Dep BAAS 351, folios 118–119), and Professor John Myres expressed the private hope that continued goodwill between two parties might lead to the possibility of new scientific excavations being held there at some point in the future (Bod: Dep BAAS 351, folio 120).

The subject of new excavations at Kent's Cavern seems to have started in earnest in early 1925, and is documented mainly in the contents of a file apparently kept by Professor Myres and now held at the British Museum. At this time Sir Arthur Keith suggests to Howarth that an "endeavour should be made to safeguard Kent's Cavern and to explore it scientifically and gradually" (BM: Keith to Howarth 11/02/25). In the same letter, Keith states that he had already advised the TNHS to start such as project by appealing to the BAAS for assistance (*ibid.*). In due course, and with guidance from Keith, the TNHS submitted details of the proposed work to the BAAS along with the information that the cave's owners had given their permission for work to begin at the end of October or beginning of November of that year (BM: Lowe to Keith 30/4/25). The proposal also suggested that four of the members of the TNHS who were then supervising the workmen at Torbryan could share the superintending of work at Kent's Cavern as well. Such local supervision does not seem to have been acceptable to the BAAS, and the subject of hiring a specialist was raised by Keith: "I think from one source or another we could get the money but can we get the right man to devote his time to proper supervision?" (BM: Keith to Myres 2/5/25).

The first suggestion for the job of supervisor at Kent's Cavern was V. Gordon Childe (BM: Keith to Myres 7/5/25). Childe was offered the job (BM: Myres to Childe 10/05/25), but wrote back that although he would like the job, a "better palaeolithicer might be needed" (BM: Childe to Myres undated). Myres thereupon wrote to Haddon in Cambridge asking if Miles Burkitt might be able to supervise the project in addition to his University work (BM: Myres to Haddon 10/05/25). Haddon did not answer the letter in the affirmative for over a month (BM: Haddon to Myres 12/06/25), by which time Myres had already offered the job to Dorothy Garrod and she had accepted. A letter from Garrod to Myres confirms her interest in the site, and indicates a previous attempt to obtain permission to conduct excavations there (BM: Garrod to Myres 10/06/25):

> "Thank you very much for your letter. Kent's Cavern is very near to my heart, as I spent a month there last winter trying to unravel the culture-sequence, and have since (backed by Professor Sollas) made fruitless attempts to be allowed to dig. In fact, I do not think anyone has 'nursed' this site quite as assiduously as I have! I was able to have access to Pengelly's m.s. journal, and so have collected a certain amount of information which I do not think is generally known. For all these reasons I shall be very glad to talk over the matter with you".

Myres seems to have been happy with her selection, and politely notified the TNHS that she would be supervising the work rather than their own proposal of four local joint superintendents (BM: Myres to Lowe 16/08/25):

"... I have had a long talk with Miss Garrod, who did some exploratory work in the cavern last winter; and have her promise that if there is excavation there this winter, she will be prepared to assist if required in a voluntary capacity. This would I think be a considerable help, as it is difficult to arrange for the continuous supervision of such work among friends who have their own business to attend to".

The same letter also stated that Myres would be proposing the establishment of a Research Committee on Kent's Cavern at the BAAS meeting on August 26th, with the purpose "... to go more carefully into the question and arrange with your Society, and with other bodies such as I have mentioned already, for excavation on the lines suggested by you" (*ibid.*).

The situation would appear to have been ideal for all concerned. The BAAS would commence new excavations at Kent's Cavern directed by Dorothy Garrod who was an acknowledged specialist in the British Palaeolithic, experienced in cave excavations, and knowledgeable about the previous excavations at the site. The TNHS would be able to participate in the new excavations, with the added benefit that the BAAS specialist was well-known to them and had helped them with the Torbryan evaluations the previous year. Dorothy Garrod had the opportunity to carry out excavations in a site which she had highlighted as being of considerable interest, and which contained deposits relevant to her research. Unfortunately, this was not to be.

There is no reply to Myres' letter from Lowe in the file, and he seems to have retired as Honorary Secretary to the TNHS before their response was sent. The official response came after the BAAS Kent's Cavern research committee had been formed, and was from Mrs. Hester Julian, the daughter of William Pengelly and a formidable force on the TNHS. Her letter to Professor Myres is marked 'Private and Confidential' (BM: Julian to Myres 29/8/25):

"I am asked to tell you, privately that the lady you mentioned would not be a *persona grata* with the Cavern proprietors. I believe they said they would 'not have her in the Cave again.' I greatly dislike having to write this, and have never met her, but heard from Mr Lowe of her being very nice indeed. I have omitted a passage bearing on this, in Mr East's letter, which was not meant to be forwarded but he had no objection to my using the copy of (his) letter as I wished to send it. I feel extremely sorry about this, which I did not know when I wrote before. I write privately to spare her any pain but of course for you and Sir A. Keith to know. It is most unlucky, and to me, unexpected"

The mentioned extracts from the letter to her from Mr. H. East, then Acting Secretary to the TNHS, were enclosed (BM: East to Julian 29/08/25):

"In the absence of the President, and in the impossibility of consulting the Committee, I should advise saying to Professor Myres that it is highly advisable to make arrangements for scientific excavating at the Cavern and in that excavating, our Society will, as it aught, lend a hand, through the agency of our

Archaeological Section. It will greatly conduce to the work if there is an archaeological expert to supervise and after all the necessity is not to accumulate specimens but to safeguard knowledge which is running to waste. Our Committee will endeavour to make more satisfactory arrangements with the owners of Kent's Cavern than those already suggested. Any agreement as to relative contributions should be referred to our Committee".

Although East's letter gives assurances that the TNHS is willing to work with the BAAS as agreed but with a different supervisor, it also shows that the TNHS perhaps wished to take a more active role in the excavations than would have been possible with an active BAAS supervisor such as Dorothy Garrod. The subject of negotiating with the cave owner in order to keep her as supervisor is not even mentioned, nor is the possibility of any form of alternative role for her. Although the letter puts the blame on the cave owner alone for the rejection of Garrod as supervisor of the BAAS excavations, no explanation for his action is given. Nor is there any elucidation of his apparent antagonism towards her in any other letter in the file. In all fairness, however, it should be pointed out that the file contains no letters from the cave owner on this subject, and no first-hand information on the matter is available.

The whole question of the renewed excavations at Kent's Cavern appeared to have faltered with the added complications that there were no suggestions as to an alternative supervisor, the permission to dig in November was in doubt, and a human skull had been found during digging by the proprietor (BM: Myres to Sykes 29/10/25). The letters in the file seem to show that most people regretted that the plan to have Dorothy Garrod supervise was rejected. However, the threat of potential damage caused by the unrecorded digging, and the possibility of losing the permission to excavate necessitated a rapid revision of plans. In November, the new Honorary Secretary of the TNHS, resurrected the proposal of TNHS supervision of the work based upon their experience in working at the Torbryan Caves, and emphasising the ability of their curator, Mr. Ogilvie, to identify Pleistocene fauna (BM: Dowie to Myres 12/11/25). The proposal was eventually accepted and a small grant was approved for the work. Miles Burkitt was asked to serve in an advisory capacity as required, but not to supervise (BM: Myres to Burkitt 20/12/25; Burkitt to Myres 23/12/25). The new excavations began in January 1926, and ran under the direction of Ogilvie until 1941, when they were halted due to World War II. Dorothy Garrod was appointed to the BAAS Kent's Cavern Research Committee in 1928, and continued to serve on it until her retirement in 1952. At the time she left the Committee, the BAAS was still trying to arrange for proper publication of the excavations (Bod: Dep BAAS 351), a task they appear to have abandoned shortly thereafter.

Conclusion

In November 1925, Dorothy Garrod began her work on Gibraltar which was to establish her international career (Garrod *et al.* 1928; see Stringer *et al.*, this volume). The decision to accept the Abbé Breuil's invitation to work there must have been taken soon after the abrupt cancellation of her plans to excavate at Kent's Cavern.

Whether or not the Kent's Cavern debacle had any effect on her decision to work outside Britain, the Gibraltar excavations were a turning point in her career. Although she did not develop her research interests in the British Palaeolithic further than those expressed in *The Upper Palaeolithic Age in Britain*, in that work she left an important legacy which has influenced all subsequent workers in that field. Indeed, there has scarcely been a major work on the British Upper Palaeolithic since 1926 which does not acknowledge the influence of her book and her insights into the development of the subject.

Acknowledgements

Most of the archive research on which this work is based was completed while employed by the British Museum and working on material from Palaeolithic caves sites in South Devon in relation to the new phase of excavations in the Torbryan Valley caves. I would like to thank the Museum, Ms. J. Cook, Head of Quaternary Section, and my former colleagues for their support of this work, and for permission to quote from the Kent's Cavern file. I would also like to thank the British Association for permission to cite the letters mentioned in the text which are now held at the Bodleian Library; and Mr. B. Chandler, Acting Curator of the TNHS Museum, for permission to reprint the text of Dorothy Garrod's report concerning the Torbryan evaluations. These three institutions retain all rights over the documents cited here. Thanks are also due to English Heritage for allowing access to their *A Survey of Palaeolithic cave sites and rockshelters in England and Wales* (Barton and Collcutt 1986). Finally, I would like to thank the editors for inviting me to contribute to the volume, and for their helpful comments on an earlier version of this paper.

End-Notes

1   The other was a brief excavation at Langwith Cave, Derbyshire, in 1927 (Garrod 1927; Barton and Collcutt 1986). The results of earlier excavations at Langwith by the Rev. E. H. Mullins, 1903–1912, were discussed in her book.
2   Garrod's terminology persists in use elsewhere in Europe (see Charles, this volume).
3   The only point on which she was in error was in the stratigraphic position of the "cave-bear" remains which are contained within the Bed 1 Diamict (her layer 5) rather than the overlaying Bed 2 Conglomerate as she claimed (her layer 4). Such a mistake can easily be attributed to the speed and poor lighting conditions under which she was working.
4   The quality of his recording system is also sufficient to attempt computer-assisted spatial analysis of the excavations (work in progress by the author, Dr R. M. Jacobi and T. Higgins).

Bibliography

Unpublished letters are listed in the text according to the repository of the archive in which they are now located: *i.e.* Bod: Dep BAAS indicates the British Association for the Advancement of Science archive at the Bodleian Library; BM indicates the British Museum.

Barton, N. 1991. The *en éperon* technique in the British Late Upper Palaeolithic. *Lithics* 11 (for 1990): 31–33.

Barton R.N.E. 1992. *Hengistbury Head, Dorset. Volume 2: The Late Upper Palaeolithic and Early Mesolithic Sites.* Oxford: Oxford Committee for Archaeology Monograph 34.

Barton, R.N.E. 1996. The Late Glacial period and Upper Palaeolithic archaeology. In D.J. Charman, R.M. Newnham and D.G. Croot (Eds.), *The Quaternary of Devon and East Cornwall: Field Guide*, pp. 198–200. London: Quaternary Research Association.

Barton, R.N.E., and S.N. Collcutt 1986. *A Survey of Palaeolithic cave sites and rockshelters in England and Wales.* Unpublished report for English Heritage and CADW.

Barton, R.N.E., and A.J. Roberts 1996. Reviewing the British Late Upper Palaeolithic: New Evidence for Chronological Patterning in the Lateglacial Record. *Oxford Journal of Archaeology* 15 (3): 245–265.

Barton, R.N.E., and A.J. Roberts 1997. Systèmes économiques et modalités techniques dans l'ouest de la Grande-Bretagne au Tardiglaciaire. In J.-P. Fagnart and A. Thévenin (Eds.), *Le Tardiglaciaire en Europe du Nord-Ouest*, pp. 507–516. Amiens: Actes du 119e Congrés National des Sociétés Historiques et Scientifiques, 1994.

Benyon, F. 1928. The deposits in the Torbryan caves. *Transactions of the Proceedings of Torquay Natural History Society* 5 (2): 153–159.

Bohmers, A. 1956. Statistics and graphs in the study of flint assemblages: II. A preliminary report on the statistical analysis of the Younger Palaeolithic in Northwestern Europe. *Palaeohistoria* 5: 7–26.

Caton-Thompson, G. 1969. Dorothy Annie Elizabeth Garrod, 1892–1968. *Proceedings of the British Academy* 55: 339–361.

Collcutt, S.N. 1984. *The Analysis of Quaternary Cave Sediments and Its Bearing Upon Palaeolithic Archaeology, with special reference to selected sites from Western Britain.* Unpublished D.Phil. thesis, University of Oxford.

Currant, A.P. 1996. Tornewton Cave and the palaeontological succession. In D.J. Charman, R.M. Newnham and D.G. Croot (Eds.), *The Quaternary of Devon and East Cornwall: Field Guide*, pp. 174–180. London: Quaternary Research Association.

Dowie, H.G. 1925. The excavation of a cave at Torbryan. *Transactions of the Proceedings of Torquay Natural History Socirty* 4 (3): 261–268.

Garrod, D.A.E. 1924. *Excavations at Tor Bryan, 1924.* Unpublished report to Torquay Natural History Society dated 12/4/24. [Printed as Appendix to this paper].

Garrod, D.A.E. 1925. Le niveau inférieur de Kent's Hole: une brèche à *Ursus spelaeus* avec outillage chelléen. *Bulletin de la Société Préhistorique Française* 23: 115–120.

Garrod, D.A.E. 1926. *The Upper Palaeolithic Age in Britain.* Oxford: Clarendon Press.

Garrod, D.A.E. 1927. Excavations at Langwith Cave, Derbyshire, April 11–27, 1927. *Report of the British Association for the Advancement of Science (Leeds, 1927)*: 303.

Garrod, D.A.E. 1961. The Abbé Breuil. *Man* 61: 243.

Garrod, D.A.E., Buxton, L.H.D., Smith, G.E., and D.M.A. Bate 1928. Excavation of a Mousterian Rock-Shelter at Devil's Tower, Gibraltar. *Journal of the Royal Anthropological Institute* 58: 33–113.

Jacobi, R.M. 1991. The Creswellian, Creswell and Cheddar. In R.N.E. Barton, A.J. Roberts and D.A. Roe (Eds.), *The Late Glacial in north-west Europe: Human adaptation and environmental change at the end of the Pleistocene*, pp. 128–140. London: Council for British Archaeology Research Report 77.

Jacobi, R. 1997. The "Creswellian" in Britain. In J.-P. Fagnart and A. Thévenin (Eds.), *Le Tardiglaciaire en Europe du Nord-Ouest*, pp. 497–505. Amiens: Actes du 119e Congrés National des Sociétés Historiques et Scientifiques, 1994.

Jacobi, R.M., and A.J. Roberts 1992. A new variant on the Creswellian angle-backed blade. *Lithics* 13: 33–39.

Lowe, H. 1918. The caves of Tor Bryan, their excavator, excavation, products and significance. *Journal of the Torquay Natural History Society* 2 (4): 199–213.

Proctor, C.J. 1995. *A British Pleistocene Chronology based on U-series and ESR dating of speleothem.* Unpublished PhD thesis, University of Bristol.

Roberts, A. 1996a. Digging and delving in the diluvium: Past and present work in the caves of South Devon. *Proceedings of Torquay Natural History Society* 22: 47–65.

Roberts, A. 1996b. Evidence for late Pleistocene and early Holocene human activity and environmental change from the Torbryan Valley, South Devon. In D.J. Charman, R.M. Newnham and D.G. Croot (Eds.), *The Quaternary of Devon and East Cornwall: Field Guide*, pp. 168–204. London: Quaternary Research Association.

Rosenfeld, A. 1964. Excavations in the Torbryan Caves, Devonshire. II. Three Holes Cave. *Transactions of the Devon Archaeological Exploration Society* 22: 3–20.

Schwabedissen, H. 1954. *Die Federmesser-Gruppen des nordwesteuropäischen Flachlandes. Zur Ausbreitung des spät-Magdalénien.* Neumünster: Karl Wachholtz.

Sutcliffe, A.J., and F.E. Zeuner 1962. Excavation in the Torbryan Caves, Devonshire. I. Tornewton Cave. *Proceedings of the Devon Archaeological Exploration Society* 5: 127–145.

Walker, H.H., and A.J. Sutcliffe 1968. James Lyon Widger, 1823–1892, and the Torbryan Caves. *Transactions of the Devon Archaeological Exploration Society* 99: 49–110.

Widger, J.L. 1892. The Torbryan caves. *Torquay Directory*, 15 June 1892.

Appendix

Text of the report on evaluations in the Torbryan Valley caves by Dorothy Garrod. Reprinted by permission of the Torquay Natural History Society.

EXCAVATIONS AT TOR BRYAN, 1924

Excavations were started on Tuesday, 25 March, & closed on Friday 4th April. I have to thank Mr. Dowie, of the Torquay Natural History Society, for kindly assisting me during this time.

For purposes of this report, the caves will be numbered as follows:-
a.) Two caves on the property of Mr. Maunder at the Tor Bryan end of the ridge, Caves A1 & A2;
b.) Six caves on the property of General Kelly, at the Tor Newton end of the ridge, Caves B1–6. These are the sites explored by Mr. Widger & described by Mr. Harford J. Lowe.

I give below the results obtained from each of these stations:-

Cave A1. A small, roughly circular hole, already partially explored by visitors from Torquay. The deposits had been removed to a depth of about 3ft. Below this they appeared to be undisturbed. The filling of the cave was a reddish loam without signs of stratification. In some places a brown clay was present. A sounding was made to a depth of 3ft. below the original excavation without encountering the rocky floor. There was no time to go deeper. Animal remains were found in relative abundance in the higher levels, but lower down they became scarce, and consisted chiefly of teeth of the hyaena. No modern bones were found. The teeth were in fair condition, and included those of *Rhinoceros tichorhinus* (one specimen), horse, red deer and hyaena. A portion of red deer antler was found. The bones were for the most part too fragmentary to be identified. They were black and had a rolled appearance. No traces of human occupation were found.

In order to complete the excavation of this cave it will be necessary to remove the material thrown out by earlier excavators which probably overlies the deposits at the entrance. It would probably repay complete exploration by the Society.

Cave A2. This is a very small cave, lying at a high level, the entrance being about 20ft. from A1. It is too small to have been used as a habitation. Mr. Maunder jr. reported that he had removed a heap of stones which closed the entrance. At a depth of a few inches, in a red sandy deposit, some bones of the human foot, belonging to two individuals at least, were found. Further excavations brought to light about half-a-dozen oyster shells, a tooth of sheep, and some bones of birds and small mammals. The only other human remains were some bones of the skeleton in a fragmentary condition and two teeth. None of these relics appear to be very ancient. All are in friable condition.

A trench was made to a depth of three feet in front of the cave, but nothing further was found.

Cave B1. (Described by Widger as the Hyaena's Den) This appears to be worked out, except for a small patch of breccia on the west wall where we found a few teeth of hyaena and some bones of small rodents.

Cave B2. ("The Old Grotto") This appears never to have contained deposits. A fissure in the back wall is choked with breccia, but we left this untouched, as it was very hard and it appeared unlikely that it would yield any traces of human occupation.

Cave B3. A tunnel without ramifications. The inner part appeared to be completely worked out except for occasional patches of cave-earth on the wall. A sounding was made at the mouth, and the rocky floor was reached at a depth of about two feet. We hoped at first that the ground was undisturbed, as two flint flakes, two teeth of reindeer, one of hyaena, a portion of reindeer antler and fragments of bone in a partially mineralised condition were found. The finding of bottle-glass at the base of the section dispelled this hope, and the exploration was abandoned.

Cave B4. ("The Great Chamber") This consists of an outer and inner chamber, with a total length of __ ft [no length given here]. The inner chamber still contains a certain thickness of deposit round the walls, especially on the west side Widger appears to have ceased work when still 6 ft. from the wall of the cave. In the middle of the chamber the deposits had been removed right down to the rocky flooor. We cleaned and partially explored the deposit on the west side, and obtained the following section (from above downwards) 1. Floor of white granular stalagmite, average thickness 1 ft. In places there were hard fragments of charcoal. 2. Cave-earth in places consolidated into a hard breccia with numerous angular fragments of limestone and blocks of a pink crystalline stalagmite floor resembling the lower stalagmite of Kent's Cavern average depth 2ft. 6ins. A few fragments of bone and one flint flake were found here. The latter is small and has a yellow-white patination. An accidental chipping of the edge showed that no portion of the original flint remains. There is no secondary working, but the edge is retouched by use all round. 3. A second stalagmite floor. Average depth 1ft. It is similar in texture to the first, but tougher, and has a pink tinge. It is quite unlike the fragments of crystalline floor found in the cave earth. 4. Bed of well-rolled limestone pebbles in a matrix of red clay. Average depth 1ft. 6ins. Remains of cave-bear in a rolled and blackened condition were fairly abundant. 5. Bed of stiff clay, brown at the top and passing down to yellow, with a darker band between the two. Very rare fragments of bone were found. This clay contained at its base a portion of crystalline floor 3ft. by 2ft.

The sequence of deposits differs in some respects from that given by Widger. He places the lower stalagmite floor between the pebble bed and the clay, and describes the latter as the "bear deposit". It is probable that he was writing from memory. No trace of the sand observed by him at the base of the deposits was found.

In the absence of definite forms of industry the deposits cannot be correlated with those of Kent's Cavern. The fauna, however, is late Pleistocene. In the S. Kensington Museum there is a small coup-de-poing of Mousterian type from Tor Bryan; if this is the "steinport" described by Widger as coming from the lowest level of the "Great Chamber" this would be roughly contemporary with the base of the cave-earth of Kent's Cavern. The flint found in the cave-earth of the "Great Chamber" is probably Upper Palaeolithic, but it is quite impossible to be certain on such slender evidence.

Further excavation will be difficult, on account of the great hardness of the brecciated cave-earth, but several feet still separate the surface of the section from the wall of the cave, and it is of course possible that it may contain interesting relics.

It appears from Widger's account that this cave was not very rich in animal remains.

Caves B5–6. really form one site. 5 is a rocky archway leading into 6, a crescent-shaped rock-shelter. Two trenches, cut at right angles one to another, showed that this site had been completely worked out.

To sum up; the only caves which offer any opportunities for excavators are A1 and B4. The former is easy to dig, as the deposit is fairly soft, but it will be necessary to shift a considerable amount of rubbish left by earlier, unscientific excavators. B4 will be difficult, and may yield very little, but might be worth trying.

Melton 12/4/24.   (Signed)   D. A. E. Garrod

4

Some Observations
on the British Earlier Upper Palaeolithic

Roger Jacobi

For half a century, *The Upper Palaeolithic Age in Britain* (Garrod 1926) remained the only monograph on its subject and, in many ways, it still remains an exemplary introductory text. In offering these brief observations on the British Early Upper Palaeolithic, I am struck by how similar much of the data-base is to when Garrod produced her overview. However, there are some important differences.

There have been excavations at Soldier's Hole (Cheddar Gorge, Somerset: Parry 1931), Badger Hole (Wookey Hole Ravine, Somerset: Ashworth 1971) and Pin Hole (Creswell Crags, Derbyshire). In addition, several excavations between 1926 and 1939 in the "Vestibule" to Kent's Cavern (Torquay, Devon) have done something to clarify the archaeology of a site in which Garrod was clearly keenly interested. It is the first locality to be considered in *The Upper Palaeolithic Age in Britain* and its entry of over twenty pages is one of the longest.

Improving curation and more intensive archival research have corrected some attributions and improved our understanding of contexts. The "re-discovery" of the leaf-point fragment from the Windmill Hill Cave (Brixham, Devon: Berridge and Roberts 1991) is a good example. The more intensive scrutiny which many lithic collections have received in recent years has also led to the identification of further Early Upper Palaeolithic artefacts from locations away from the karst (Jacobi 1990), a landscape which, perhaps understandably, received only cursory attention in 1926. Particularly important has been recognition of the material found at the beginning of the century during house-building at Beedings, near Pulborough (West Sussex: Jacobi 1986).

Recently, radiocarbon dating, mainly by Accelerator Mass Spectrometry, has helped our understanding of many aspects of the European Upper Palaeolithic (for example, Mellars *et al.* 1987). However, for Britain its greater impact has been upon the archaeology of the Late Glacial rather than the earlier stages of the Upper Palaeolithic. This is largely because of the extreme rarity of cut-marked bone and human fossils which can confidently be linked to the latter. Thus, while there seems good reason to believe the Early Upper Palaeolithic to have been the contemporary of a rich grassland fauna which included mammoth, woolly rhinoceros, horse, bovines and several species of deer, the majority of bones at cave sites were introduced by hyaenas.

However, we do possess a much better understanding than Garrod of the relative chronology of the Upper Palaeolithic and of natural events, most notably the maximum extension of the late Devensian ice-sheet. Whilst the timing of this maximum remains contentious (Peacock 1997), there is little controversy about which parts of the British archaeological record belong before and after. Before, belong technologies with surface-retouched blades (so-called "leaf-points"), the Aurignacian and stray finds of Gravettian artefacts – the Early Upper Palaeolithic (Campbell 1977).

Leaf-points, usually interpreted as weapon heads, occur in many different contexts within the European Upper Palaeolithic and individual radiocarbon dates for some of these find-spots are greater than forty thousand years (Allsworth-Jones 1990a: table 2). While the British finds were interpreted by Garrod as extensions of the Solutrean, and indeed Solutrean material is known from as close as the Paris Basin (Sacchi *et al.* 1996), there appears now to be a consensus that instead they date from the earliest part of the Upper Palaeolithic (Allsworth-Jones 1986). This belief gains indirect support from a number of radiocarbon dates (Table 4.1), although in each case we are looking at contexts where natural sediment transport has probably occurred.

Leaf-points have been identified from 31 find-spots in England and Wales, the greater number in central and eastern Britain (Jacobi 1990: figs. 2 and 3; also unmapped) hinting at links eastwards across an emerged southern North Sea bed. These leaf-points may be wholly or partially bifacial and the greater number are clearly made from blades (*ibid.*: 271–2). While the extent and distribution of surface chipping are often likely to have been influenced by raw material and the degree of difficulty encountered in thinning and straightening individual blanks, it is worth noting that the three points from Soldier's Hole, Cheddar Gorge, are fully bifacial, while those from Badger Hole and the Hyaena Den in the nearby Wookey Hole

Table 4.1: Recent AMS ^{14}C dates from Britain

Soldier's Hole (Unit 4), Cheddar Gorge, Somerset

OxA-691	calcaneum of reindeer	>34,500 BP (1)
OxA-692	phalange of reindeer*	29,300±1100 BP (1)
OxA-693	astragalus of reindeer	>35,000 BP (1)
OxA-1957	humerus of reindeer	41,700±3500 BP (2)
OxA-2471	phalange of reindeer*	29,900±450 BP (2)
OxA-1777	tibia of bovine	>42,900 BP (2)

Bench Tunnel Cavern, Brixham, Devon

OxA-1620	mandible of hyaena**	34,500±1400 BP (3)
OxA-4984	unidentified bone fragment	32,400±1100 BP (4)
OxA-4985	unidentified hyoid bone	27,150±600 BP (4)
OxA-5961	mandible of hyaena**	32,500±1200 BP (4)

Pin Hole Cave, Creswell Crags, Derbyshire

| OxA-4754 | pre-maxillary of hyaena | 37,800±1600 BP (4) |

Gowlett *et al.* 1986: 210. (1)   Hedges *et al.* 1991: 123-4. (3)
Hedges *et al.* 1989: 214. (2)   Hedges *et al.* 1996: 395. (4)
* and ** indicate repeat dates on the same specimen.

Ravine are all only partly bifacial. Whether any additional parameter beyond technological, for example chronological (*cf.* Otte 1981), is necessary to explain this difference remains speculative.

While leaf-points and Mousterian artefacts are sometimes recorded from the same find-spots, there is no certain evidence for linking them. Where there appears reason to associate leaf-points with other artefacts, the latter are of Upper Palaeolithic types – as at Beedings.

Unappreciated in 1926 were the probably complex relationships between the earliest parts of the European Upper Palaeolithic and the fossil record documenting the transition from archaic (Neanderthal) to fully anatomically-modern humans. Thus, while all the hominids associated with the Aurignacian seem to be of modern type (Gambier 1989, Hublin 1990, Mellars 1992), the same cannot be demonstrated for the Szeletian. Therefore, it remains a viable speculation, based on limited fossil evidence, that this technology was produced by indigenous archaic hominids (*cf.* Allsworth-Jones 1990b). In turn, if the British leaf-points are envisaged as equivalents of the Szeletian, it becomes a further speculation that this part of our Upper Palaeolithic was produced by populations of Neanderthal type.

Aurignacian artefacts are certainly recorded from only seven British find-spots. The clearest typological markers are off-set or shouldered nosed scrapers (*grattoirs à épaulement*: Sonneville-Bordes and Perrot 1954: 332) and *burins busqués*. What is particularly striking is that all these find-spots are in western Britain. This pattern could be interpreted as evidence for settlement northwards along a coastal plain linking the Atlantic seaboard with the eastern margin of the Irish Sea.

What is also striking is that there are no typological arguments for sub-dividing the British Aurignacian. In other words, it could represent a single settlement event. The largest sample of Aurignacian artefacts comes from the Paviland Cave (Rhosili, West Glamorgan), a locality for which crude statistics have been published (Campbell 1980: 50). These strongly suggest a correlation with the *Aurignacien II ancien* of south-western France, associated with the Arcy Interstadial (Djindjian 1992), which is dated 32–29,000 years ago (Leroi-Gourhan 1997: 157). Of particular interest, therefore, is the central value of the radiocarbon date for a human maxilla (KC4: Oakley *et al.* 1971: 28) recovered from the Vestibule to Kent's Cavern in 1927 (Keith 1927). This date is:

30,900±900 BP (OxA–1621: Hedges *et al.* 1989: 209).

Although the maxilla is reported as having been found deeper than the majority of the Aurignacian artefacts in the Vestibule (Jacobi 1990: 284), many of the latter show natural damage (*concassage*) consistent with the results of sediment transport. Radiocarbon dates on humanly un-modified faunal specimens can be interpreted as providing a *terminus post quem* for the emplacement of these sediments. The dates are:

OxA–4435 molar of red deer   28,060±440 BP
OxA–4436 mandible of reindeer   27,780±400 BP (Hedges *et al.* 1996: 394).

Having said this, analysis of the material from the more recent work at La Ferrassie has demonstrated a facies of the recent Aurignacian difficult to distinguish from Aurignacian II (Delporte 1984: 204–206). This is included within Djindjian's

"Aurignacien IV", and dated to the Maisières Interstadial – 29–28,000 years ago. Clearly, fresh assessments of the British Aurignacian will need to bear this complexity in mind.

While Aurignacian artefacts and leaf-points are known from some of the same find-spots, there is no clear support for the suggestion that, therefore, they are parts of the same technology (McBurney 1965: 26–29; Campbell 1980: 43–49). At Kent's Cavern their spatial distributions are very different, an observation already made by Garrod (1926: 44–45). Thus, while the Aurignacian probably has the widest distribution of any technology within the cave, leaf-points were recovered only from its southern axis. At Ffynnon Beuno, artefacts were recorded from several locations, and it seems as if the leaf-point was a solitary find (Hicks 1886: 5–9). Elsewhere, for example Creswell Crags, obligate Aurignacian artefacts are absent from localities where leaf-points have been found.

Stemmed (Font-Robert) points are known from nine British find-spots (Jacobi 1990: fig. 5). Recent reconsideration by Bosselin and Djindjian (1994) suggests that the "Fontirobertian" belongs to the earliest part of the western European Gravettian. Later evolutionary stages, some of which appear to be represented in Belgium (Otte 1979), are absent from Britain. While there are no radiocarbon results of demonstrable stratigraphic relevance to any of these points, it is worth noting that the date of 26,350±550 BP (OxA–1815: Hedges *et al.* 1989: 209) for a male inhumation from Paviland (Paviland I: Oakley *et al.* 1971: 33–34) is not wholly irreconcilable with those from the Fontirobertian (Bosselin and Djindjian 1994: 112). This burial is reported as having had associated with it an ochre stain, periwinkle shells, forty or fifty fragments of ivory *baguettes*, and parts of two ivory bracelets (Buckland 1823: 88–89). These "…had evidently been buried at the same time with the woman [*sic*]…" (*ibid.*: 89).

While Garrod believed that "…semi-geometrical forms, derivatives of the Gravette point, of which the most characteristic is an elongated trapeze…" (1926: 181) formed a genetic link between earlier and later Upper Palaeolithic technologies, we now know all these "Cheddar points" to belong to the "Creswellian", with radiocarbon dates younger than 13,000 years ago (Jacobi 1991). Instead, unless some of the British leaf-points are indeed Solutrean, as suggested by Garrod (1926: 192), there is no lithic evidence for a human presence between the Early Gravettian and the Creswellian.

However, there are three published radiocarbon dates for bone artefacts which, taken at face value, would indicate a human presence during the period of lowered temperatures, increased precipitation and maximum ice-growth termed the Dimlington Stadial (Rose 1985). These are:

Hyaena Den, Wookey Hole Ravine, Somerset:
OxA–3451 bone/antler point   24,600±300 BP
(Tratman *et al.* 1971: Pl. 22c; Hedges *et al.* 1996: 393–394).

Paviland, Rhosili, West Glamorgan:
OxA–1790 bone knife made from horse metapodial   23,670±400 BP
(Sollas 1913: fig. 22; Hedges *et al.* 1994: 342).

Kent's Cavern, Torquay, Devon:
OxA–2845 bone pin   14,140±110 BP
(Garrod 1926: fig. 2: 10; Hedges *et al.* 1994: 342).

All are old finds with unrecorded conservation histories. The knife from Paviland has very clearly been conserved. The dates from the Hyaena Den and Kent's Cavern are much younger than would be predicted from radiocarbon dates for unmodified faunal items, those from the Hyaena Den being recently collected. While not denying the possibility that groups visited what Garrod so graphically described as "...the Ultima Thule of Upper Palaeolithic Europe..." (1926: 191) between about 26,000 and 13,000 years ago, these dates are probably not the safest upon which to base such a conclusion.

As noted above, much of the present data-base for the British Early Upper Palaeolithic was known to Dorothy Garrod. Where present interpretations differ most from those of 1926 is in the ordering of the parts. However, as in 1926, the clues to this ordering still come from work outside Britain. In seventy years' time it will be interesting to see what degree of independence has been achieved.

Bibliography

Allsworth-Jones, P. 1986. *The Szeletian and the Transition from Middle to Upper Palaeolithic in Central Europe.* Oxford: Oxford University Press.

Allsworth-Jones, P. 1990a. Les industries à pointes foliacées d'Europe centrale. Questions de définitions et relations avec les autres techno-complexes. In C. Farizy (Ed.), *Paléolithique moyen récent et Paléolithique supérieur ancien en Europe: Actes du colloque international de Nemours, 1988,* pp. 79–95. Nemours: Mémoires du Musée de Préhistoire d'Île de France, 3.

Allsworth-Jones, P. 1990b. The Szeletian and the stratigraphic succession in Central Europe and adjacent areas: main trends, recent results, and problems for resolution. In P.A. Mellars (Ed.), *The Emergence of Modern Humans: an Archaeological Perspective,* pp. 160–242. Edinburgh UP.

Ashworth, H.W.W. 1971. *Fourteen Years at the Badger Hole. From the Diaries of H.E. Balch, M.A., F.S.A. (1938–1952).* Wells Natural History and Archaeology Society.

Berridge, P., and A. Roberts 1991. Windmill Hill Cave, Brixham: setting the record straight. *Lithics* 11 (for 1990): 24–30.

Bosselin, B., and F. Djindjian 1994. La chronologie du Gravettien français. *Préhistoire Européenne* 6: 77–115.

Buckland, W. 1823. *Reliquiæ Diluvianæ.* London: John Murray.

Campbell, J.B. 1977. *The Upper Palaeolithic of Britain: a Study of Man and Nature in the Late Ice Age.* Oxford: Clarendon Press.

Campbell, J.B. 1980. Le problème des subdivisions du Paléolithique supérieur britannique dans son cadre européen. *Bulletin de la Société royale belge d'Anthropologie et de Préhistoire* 91: 39–77.

Delporte, H. 1984. *Le Grand Abri de La Ferrassie: Fouilles 1968–73.* Paris: CNRS, Études Quaternaires, Mémoire N° 7.

Djindjian, F. 1992. L'Aurignacien du Périgord: une revision. *Préhistoire Européenne* 3: 29–54.

Gambier, D. 1989. Fossil hominids from the early Upper Palaeolithic (Aurignacian) of France. In P.A. Mellars & C.B. Stringer (Eds.), *The Human Revolution: Behavioural and Biological Perspectives on the Origins of Modern Humans,* pp. 194–211. Edinburgh: Edinburgh University Press.

Garrod, D.A.E. 1926. *The Upper Palaeolithic Age in Britain.* Oxford: Clarendon Press.

Gowlett, J.A.J., Hedges, R.E.M., Law, I.A., and C. Perry 1986. Radiocarbon dates from the Oxford AMS system: *Archaeometry* datelist 4. *Archaeometry* 28 (2): 206–221.

Hedges, R.E.M., Housley, R.A., Law, I.A., and C.R. Bronk 1989. Radiocarbon dates from the Oxford AMS system: *Archaeometry* datelist 9. *Archaeometry* 31 (2): 207–234.

Hedges, R.E.M., Housley, R.A., Bronk, C.R., and G.J. Van Klinken 1991. Radiocarbon dates from the Oxford AMS system: *Archaeometry* datelist 12. *Archaeometry* 33 (1): 121–134.

Hedges, R.E.M., Housley, R.A., Bronk Ramsey, C., and G.J. Van Klinken 1994. Radiocarbon dates from the Oxford AMS system: *Archaeometry* datelist 18. *Archaeometry* 36 (2): 337–374.

Hedges, R.E.M., Pettitt, P.B., Bronk Ramsey, C., and G.J. Van Klinken 1996. Radiocarbon dates from the Oxford AMS system: *Archaeometry* datelist 22. *Archaeometry* 38 (2): 391–415.

Hicks, H. 1886. Results of recent researches in some bone-caves in North Wales (Ffynnon Beuno and Cae Gwyn). *Quarterly Journal of the Geological Society* 42 (1): 3–19.

Hublin, J.-J. 1990. Les peuplements paléolithiques de l'Europe: un point de vue géographique. In C. Farizy (Ed.), *Paléolithique moyen récent et Paléolithique supérieur ancien en Europe: Actes du colloque international de Nemours, 1988*, pp. 29–37. Nemours: Mémoires du Musée de Préhistoire d'Île de France, 3.

Jacobi, R.M. 1986. The contents of Dr. Harley's show case. In S.N. Collcutt (Ed.), *The Palaeolithic of Britain and its Nearest Neighbours: Recent Trends*, pp. 62–68. Sheffield: John R. Collis.

Jacobi, R.M. 1990. Leaf-points and the British Early Upper Palaeolithic. In J.K. Kozlowski (Ed.), *Feuilles de Pierre. Les Industries à Pointes foliacées du Paléolithique supérieur européen. Actes du colloque de Cracovie 1989*, pp. 271–289. Liège: Études et Recherches Archéologiques de l'Université de Liège, 42.

Jacobi, R.M. 1991. The Creswellian, Creswell and Cheddar. In R.N.E. Barton, A.J. Roberts and D.A. Roe (Eds.), *The Late Glacial in north-west Europe: human adaptation and environmental change at the end of the Pleistocene*, pp. 128–140. London: Council for British Archaeology, Res. Rep. 77.

Keith, A. 1927. Report on a fragment of a human jaw. *Transactions and Proceedings of the Torquay Natural History Society* 59 (1), for 1926–7: 1–2.

Leroi-Gourhan, Arl. 1997. Chauds et froids de 60 000 à 15 000 BP. *Bulletin de la Société Préhistorique Française* 94 (2): 151–160.

McBurney, C.B.M. 1965. The Old Stone Age in Wales. In I.L. Foster and G. Daniel (Eds.), *Prehistoric and Early Wales*, pp. 17–34. London: Routledge and Kegan Paul.

Mellars, P.A. 1992. Archaeology and the population-dispersal hypothesis of modern human origins in Europe. In M.J. Aitken, C.B. Stringer and P.A. Mellars (Eds.), *The Origin of Modern Humans and the Impact of Chronometric Dating*, pp. 196–216. Princeton University Press.

Mellars, P.A., Bricker, H.M., Gowlett, J.A.J., and R.E.M. Hedges 1987. Radiocarbon accelerator dating of French Upper Palaeolithic sites. *Current Anthropology* 28: 128–133.

Oakley, K.P., Campbell, B.G., and T.I. Molleson 1971. *Catalogue of Fossil Hominids, Part II: Europe*. London: British Museum (Natural History).

Otte, M. 1979. *Le Paléolithique supérieur ancien en Belgique*. Brussels: Musées royaux d'Art et d'Histoire, Monographies d'Archéologie nationale 5.

Otte, M. 1981. Les industries à pointes foliacées et à pointes pedonculées dans le nord-ouest européen. *Archaeologia Interregionalis* 1: 95–116.

Parry, R.F. 1931. Excavations at Cheddar. *Proceedings of the Somerset Archaeological and Natural History Society* 76 (2), for 1930: 46–62.

Peacock, J.D. 1997. Was there a re-advance of the British ice sheet into the North Sea between 15 ka and 14 ka BP? *Quaternary Newsletter* 81: 1–8.

Rose, J. 1985. The Dimlington Stadial/Dimlington Chronozone: a proposal for naming the main glacial episode of the Late Devensian in Britain. *Boreas* 14: 225–230.

Sacchi, C., Schmider, B., Chantret, F., Roblin-Jouve, A., Bouyssonie, M., and S. Drapier 1996. Le gisement solutréen de Saint-Sulpice-de-Favières (Essonne). *Bulletin de la Société Préhistorique Française* 93 (4): 502–527.

Sollas, W.J. 1913. Paviland Cave: an Aurignacian station in Wales. *Journal of the Royal Anthropological Institute* 43: 325–374.

Sonneville-Bordes, D. de, and J. Perrot 1954. Lexique typologique du Paléolithique supérieur. Outillage lithique: I grattoirs – II outils solutréens. *Bulletin de la Société Préhistorique Française* 51 (7): 327–335.

Tratman, E.K., Donovan, D.T., and J.B. Campbell 1971. The Hyaena Den (Wookey Hole), Mendip Hills, Somerset. *Proceedings of the University of Bristol Spelaeological Society* 12 (3): 245–279.

5

Unlocking the Inhospitable

Stephanie Swainston

Introduction

Dorothy Garrod provided an evocative characterisation of Britain in Early Upper
Palaeolithic Europe, as a "north-west cape, remote and inhospitable" (1926: 191) with
scarce traces of human occupation resulting in scanty archaeological material. Her
classic book *The Upper Palaeolithic Age in Britain* (1926) has certainly served as a sound
basis for work in this field.

As a student of the Abbé Henri Breuil, Garrod was familiar with the more
thoroughly-developed French sequence, with which she sought to associate British
finds. Only within the last 20 years (Campbell 1977, 1980; Jacobi 1980) has a British
sequence been constructed, and this mainly in order to facilitate comparisons with
more well-dated sites in the Low Countries.

In the Early Upper Palaeolithic, Garrod's Middle or "Typical" Aurignacian has
been retained as an equivalent to the Aurignacian II of France and Belgium. Garrod
followed this with the "Upper Aurignacian", in which elements of a late glacial
industry are now recognised, and which is now named "Creswellian", a term
proposed by Garrod herself (1926: 194). She described the Upper Aurignacian as
contemporary with the "Proto-Solutrean", an industry which includes leaf points on
blades usually retouched on the ends of the ventral surface only, and suggested that
the "Proto-Solutrean" substituted the true Solutrean industry in England and Wales,
but it is now known to come first in the sequence. Far from being a "special
development" (*ibid.*: 192) it is now recognised that leaf points show great similarities
with finds from Belgium (Otte 1979), Poland and Germany (*e.g.* Kozłowski 1983), and
in Britain this first Early Upper Palaeolithic industry is referred to as the leaf point
phase (Campbell's "Lincombian"), and is generally regarded as the earliest intrusive
modern human industry, contemporary with the Aurignacian (Jacobi 1980: 17).

The third and final phase of the British Early Upper Palaeolithic is somewhat
more elusive. It was described by Garrod (1926: 38) as the "Final Aurignacian of Font
Robert" and is typified by large tanged points made on blades, similar to those from
the open air sites of Maisières-Canal, and Spy Cave, Belgium (Otte 1984). On the
continent this Font Robert point phase (Campbell's "Maisièrian") is associated with
leaf points retouched on the dorsal surface, where it has been dated to 26,000 BP
(Jacobi 1980: 30). Therefore it should not be assumed that all leaf points are necessarily
associated with the earliest phase. Additionally, all three phases of settlement may

incorporate other chronologically or stylistically discrete entities which further research may distinguish.

This paper aims to review five issues which are the focus for current research into the British Early Upper Palaeolithic:

1. The process of colonisation
2. The pattern of occupation
3. The hiatus in occupation
4. Idiosyncrasies in the British Early Upper Palaeolithic
5. The typology of the British Early Upper Palaeolithic

Each issue will be illustrated by a "case study" of an individual site, regarded as particularly applicable to the question posed. It must be emphasised, however that the issues are applicable to all British sites. With a receptive approach, new research may reveal surprising and unique variations in the long-held assumptions of Palaeolithic hunter behaviour, in this area which was at the edge of their known geographical range and possibly the limit of their climatic adaptation.

The process of colonisation

The traditional interpretation of the nature of occupation in the British Early Upper Palaeolithic is one of the northward dispersal of groups, with different lithic and bone technologies which originate elsewhere, presumably on the European mainland. The finds, however, are scanty and would allow alternative interpretations. The current model supposes 15,000 years of arrivals, no continual settlement and no cultural evolution *in situ*. The model fits our characterisation of Upper Palaeolithic social organisation – small, highly mobile and migratory groups of hunters, perhaps twenty-five in a group, in a steppe or tundra environment. Brief use was made of caves and open-air sites in a pattern of movement possibly following or predicting reindeer herds in a north-west, south-east direction (Gamble 1986: 223).

An intriguing question is whether Britain served as a refuge for Neanderthal populations. There are several sites which have both Mousterian and leaf point components in their assemblages, although owing to insufficiently recorded stratigraphy, it is not possible to determine whether artefacts occur in the same or closely related layers, or whether there is a hiatus between them. The situation is in fact far from clear, as there is no skeletal evidence for classic Neanderthals from mainland British sites, and apart from a variant of Mousterian of Acheulian Tradition, none of the French typological groupings can be recognised in British Middle Palaeolithic material. However, Coygan Cave in Carmarthenshire yielded a sequence with a Mousterian occupation within the time span 64,000–38,000 BP according to uranium-series and radiocarbon dates recently published (Aldhouse-Green *et al.* 1995). The possibility of contemporary Neanderthal and modern human occupation in Britain is small, but cannot be excluded.

Creswell Crags, on the borders of Derbyshire and Nottinghamshire, is an ideal site to investigate the questions raised by a consideration of the process of colonisation. A total of twenty-four small caves and shelters are concentrated within this limestone valley, approximately one kilometre long, which is evidence for the furthest northward expansion of the Mousterian, leaf point and Font Robert phases, and possibly the Aurignacian. An argument for the Aurignacian at Creswell can be made only on the presence of a form of long end-scraper from Robin Hood's Cave, almost identical to one from Paviland Cave. That the Aurignacian did occur this far north is confirmed by a busqué burin from Ffynnon Beuno, a cave site in the vale of Clwyd, north Wales (Green and Livingston 1991). There are radiocarbon dates from Pin Hole, Creswell which would fall into the accepted Aurignacian time-span, for example 31,300±550 BP (OxA–3405) on worked reindeer antler (Hedges *et al.* 1994: 338).

Creswell Crags would have provided a natural route and a series of shelters for hunters and game (Hart 1981: 19). Three of the caves in the complex have, according to Campbell (1977), yielded Early Upper Palaeolithic material. These are Robin Hood's Cave, Pin Hole and possibly Church Hole Cave. Robin Hood's Cave retained some stratified, if disturbed, sediment at the time of Campbell's excavation (Campbell 1969). No definite Early Upper Palaeolithic evidence was found by him, but such material is known from the 1874–76 excavations by Mello and Dawkins (1876: 252). Dawkins unearthed 267 worked flints (Jenkinson 1984: 39), including two leaf points. Robin Hood's Cave also has a Middle Palaeolithic series, which was found in the "cave earth" layer (Dawkins 1876: 255). These are primarily unretouched flakes from rough-grained quartzite cobbles of a brown to pink colour, as well as two small cordiform handaxes. Quartzite "bunter" pebbles occur abundantly very near the caves, and there are several sources within a 16km radius of Pin Hole Cave (Dawkins 1876: 28). Flint, on the other hand, is about 60km distant; samples which show gravel staining and weathering may have been obtained from the Trent valley, but the finer material may have been imported from southern chalk areas.

The contrast between Mousterian and Early Upper Palaeolithic is striking. There is a clear distinction between these industries in many sites, both in terms of the distances which raw materials have been transported, and of the raw materials themselves (Gamble 1995: 23). Mousterian implements are lithic only, and are made on raw materials which are locally available. Clarification and quantification of this observation would be a useful aim for further research. It may be evidence for shorter planning depth on the part of the handaxe makers, arising from a cognitive difference or an extremely opportunistic means of procuring lithic raw material. Another hypothesis is that this contrast reflects the longer distances regularly travelled by leaf point groups, which pass through areas where high quality flint is plentiful, whereas the groups manufacturing handaxes were moving within more circumscribed areas (Jenkinson 1984: 151). Where flint handaxes do occur, they are of a very small size, perhaps indicating that the rapidity of wear results in the need for a local raw material supply. It must not be overlooked that rough-grained raw materials may have been desirable and specifically selected. The serrated edges of flaked rhyolite and quartzite provide a very efficient saw, useful to hunter-gatherers for butchery and for processing vegetable matter (Gamble 1993: 128).

Pin Hole Cave is on the same, south-facing, side of the crags as Robin Hood's Cave. Water action has disturbed the deposits and evidence of human occupation is not as abundant as at Robin Hood's Cave (Hart 1981: 19). Three retouched flint blades were found, one of which (Campbell 1977: fig. 100, 1) is very similar in working to the leaf points, and indeed was listed by Jackson (1967: 16) as a flint blade of Proto-Solutrean type. Semi-invasive scalar retouch covers both surfaces of the blade at the proximal end, and chipping and cryoturbation notching continues along both sides of the piece. This blade serves to remind us that in investigating the leaf point phase we should be searching for a technological variation or a new style of retouch which can be applied to many tool forms, rather than simply the presence of leaf points as a single diagnostic form. Pin Hole Cave produced two tanged "Font Robert" points which compare favourably with those from Belgium.

In accordance with the pattern of dispersal and colonisation (Mellars 1992), the Aurignacian II in Britain seems to appear later than on the continent, where radiocarbon dates from Arcy-sur-Cure, the Abri Pataud (Movius 1975: 15) and Vogelherd suggest a date range of around 33,000–28,000 BP (Green 1984: 27). In the Istálloskö Cave, in the Bükk mountains of Hungary, two stratified Aurignacian levels have radiocarbon dates of around 31,500 BP for the lower and 30,600 BP for the upper level (Gamble 1986: 180). These are also broadly contemporaneous with leaf point industries.

A prime question for further research should be to what extent we can rely on busqué burins as a type fossil for the Aurignacian in Britain, or whether, in this marginal area their use continued for a longer time. At the Abri Pataud itself they are present only in layers 8–6, the Later Aurignacian. If busqué burins are a tool specifically made for a functional task, for example bone working, they may not be an accurate type fossil and could be included with the Perigordian material. However, busqué burins from British sites, although including atypical examples, are by no means significantly different in morphology from those in south-west French sites.

A finer chronological definition would allow the patterns of interactions between sites to be conjectured, and would allow close links to be made between Britain and data from Continental sites. However, rather than relying on the model of "climate-controlled" colonisation in which groups of Palaeolithic hunters, permitted a northward expansion in each interstadial, reach the limits of their ranges; we should consider the possibilities raised by a variety of activities which occurred over the time-span 40,000–20,000 BP.

Pattern of occupation

Badger Hole and the Hyaena Den are two Early Upper Palaeolithic cave sites situated approximately 50m apart in the eastern face of the Wookey Hole ravine, Mendip Hills, Somerset. A third possibly Early Upper Palaeolithic site in the same area is Soldier's Hole, Cheddar (Balch 1928: 207; Campbell 1977: figs. 91 & 92). The relative density of sites in the South Wales, Somerset and Devonshire area have tempted some authors to comment on the possible patterns of occupation. However it is potentially misleading to attempt to model the nature of occupation during the Early Upper Palaeolithic in Britain, from the little evidence available.

Wookey Hole is roughly equidistant (110km) from Paviland Cave, South Wales, on the other side of what would have been the Bristol Channel Plain, and Kent's Cavern, Torquay. It is closer still (13km) to the caves at Uphill where leaf point phase material has been found (Harrison 1977: 242; Garrod 1926: fig. 22).

At Badger Hole, unifacial leaf points occur associated with an Early Upper Palaeolithic assemblage which includes retouched flakes and scrapers. Two of the four leaf points are from "definitely undisturbed" contexts in the south portion of the entrance, more or less on bedrock. Campbell (1977: figs. 88 & 89) provides an illustration of these long blades – one with intermittent bifacial working, one with complete unifacial retouch. There are no reliable dates from this site (>18,000 BP: BM–497). In addition to the leaf points, one of the blades from Balch's 1938–1952 unpublished excavations has characteristic "Aurignacian retouch" (Swainston 1997: 119).

There is one definite Early Upper Palaeolithic find from the Hyaena Den: a fragment of a leaf point. Both ends of the original blade have been lost or removed in antiquity and the ends subsequently reflaked, perhaps to trim rough edges left by the breaks and rework the implement as an end-scraper. Both edges show signs of use and, according to Tratman *et al.* (1971: 262), a notch has been created by steep retouch on the left side of the piece.

A "base site" would be a main focus of exploitation activity and would have relatively dense occupation debris, which Campbell (1977: 31) arbitrarily sets at 50 artefacts. "Transit" or "subsidiary" sites would be more numerous, placed strategically within a 10km range of the base sites. Transit sites related to migration would occur between base sites. Campbell states that a transit site would have relatively little occupation debris, and allows that it could simply be the find spot of a single implement; a dangerous assumption when the post-depositional factors influencing open-air finds are considered. Finally, an "annual territory" would be the total area exploited by a human group ("group" remains an undefined term) throughout a given year, and would have one or more "site exploitation territories" which have 10km radii centred upon base sites.

The theoretical aspect of Campbell's (1977) work is an attempt to make archaeological evidence fit an ethnographic pattern. Ethnographic accounts cannot be used to match and highlight a specific archaeological patterning, since many patterns of behaviour are possible with the present evidence. In the case of the British Early Upper Palaeolithic, taphonomic factors and preservation conditions must be emphasised. The effects of the glacial maximum and subsequent variations in sea level, as well as alterations and disturbances in the cave sediments, are so pervasive that the question remains whether it is possible to reach an understanding of the underlying pattern of human occupation. Any distribution map for the Early Upper Palaeolithic in Britain will tend to chart areas of limestone outcrops with caves allowing artefacts to be trapped, and therefore preserved. If caves were only occupied as very temporary camps there may well be only one or two days' worth of evidence for the activities of each group. Attempts to find open-air sites are frustrated by the great depth of overlying deposit (Moir 1938: 258) or scouring by glacial action which removed previous land surfaces.

In addition to the problems of preservation, the nature of human occupation itself is scarce enough to show few signs of patterning. Gamble (1983: 211) suggests that an area such as south Wales could represent the outer limits of an exploitation zone of groups, whose residential camps lay well outside the area. The settlement traces for the Early Upper Palaeolithic could therefore represent only a partial record. The lifetime territory size of a modern group of hunters is 120,000km² (Binford 1983), whereas the area of England and Wales combined (and unglaciated) is not much greater at 151,207km². Residential camps, if indeed they existed, could easily be missing from the archaeological record in Britain – an area which the nomadic hunter could regard as small. During warm periods particularly, work camps could have been created for special tasks, a possible example being Paviland Cave as an ivory working site (Sollas 1913).

European Early Upper Palaeolithic environments, like those of modern-day Eskimo hunters, are expected to impose high-level constraints on behaviour and offer little guiding information. Penalties for incorrect decisions would be prompt and drastic – the key to minimising such risks is an ability to retain accurate information about the environment and its resources (Gamble 1983: 205), together with a social strategy allowing such information to be rapidly disseminated among individual hunters. The mobility of groups could arise from a need to reaffirm social ties, rather than as a result of ecological imperatives. Even if the latter were the case, it must be recognised that social alliances provide a framework for the dissemination of information about the environment and available resources. Otte (1990) negates climatically deterministic explanations for the Late Upper Palaeolithic reoccupation of the north-west European Plain in favour of purely cultural ones.

It is worth noting that characterisation of hunting strategies in the Early Upper Palaeolithic does not change for the Late Upper Palaeolithic. The theoretical treatment of sites, and the nomenclature used, remains the same (Campbell 1977: 166). It is a restrictive model, leading Campbell to explain the presence of fossil shells from Britain (Otte, in Campbell 1977) found in Spy Cave, Belgium, as "trade", although they could have been transported by a single individual in a group with a wide annual territory. The shells *Nassarius reticulatus* and *Trivia coccinelloides* have no humanly-made markings but could have been suspended by natural perforations, a possible reason for their selection. It is not clear from which Early Upper Palaeolithic layer (Aurignacian or Perigordian) they originate, but they are roughly associated with a radiocarbon date of 22,105±500 BP (Otte 1977). The nearest known source of these shells is the Red Crag deposits in southern East Anglia, and it is assumed they had been transported by hand from there. Exchange networks are possible, but the evidence is indisputable that contact between groups, if not the range of a single group, often spanned a distance greater than 100km.

Badger Hole and the Hyaena Den provide *in situ* accumulations of material. The similarities between the finds from these sites, as well as their proximity, suggest that they are at least roughly contemporaneous. Neither seems to be a "specialist" site, if the leaf points found at the majority of cave sites are assumed to be "unspecialised".

The pattern of occupation may change while the lithic industry remains the same; associating different industries with different behavioural patterns is potentially misleading. If a pattern is to emerge, it will be through the investigation of fauna as well as lithic data and a thorough interpretation of radiocarbon dates already produced, as well as further assays.

Following theoretical model building may not be a fruitful method of research in the British Early Upper Palaeolithic. A more fluid approach is required, which considers caves as "sediment traps" incorporating artefacts from very brief occupations over a very long time-span, and associations between sites should be considered tentative to say the least. Confronted with such uncertainty, the researcher may be tempted to concentrate on specific sites and the analysis of individual artefacts – but artefacts must be placed within the social and cultural system of which they once formed a part (Gamble 1983: 203). Characterisations of the pattern of occupation of Britain during the Early Upper Palaeolithic should evolve from a knowledge of the data, rather than being led by theoretical models.

The hiatus in occupation

Britain, and indeed the whole north-west European Plain, is said to be unoccupied during the height of the last glaciation (Jacobi 1980: 15) when, as Garrod suggested, "the increased cold... brought about a return of arctic conditions and industrial remains are rare" (1926: 192). The duration of the hiatus is still a matter of debate, as is the question of whether the break in occupation was absolute. This question hinges on our interpretation of the harshness of the climate, and on our expectations of the capacities of hunter-gatherers.

For England and Wales, Campbell (1977) proposed a hiatus of at least 5000 years, following McBurney's (1965: 30) image of a "complete or virtual depopulation of northern Europe." Jacobi (1980) more than doubled the time span of this hiatus, based on continental parallels of artefact types and a lack of radiocarbon dates on humanly-worked bone throughout the period 23,000–13,000 BP. It is now customary to split the Upper Palaeolithic into Early and Late periods, which lie before and after the extreme glacial extent.

The approach to the late Glacial Maximum, from 60,000 to 25,000 BP (Mellars 1996: 25) was a period of oscillatory but relatively mild climate in which the extent of global glaciation was substantially reduced. Through detailed studies of the oxygen isotope ratios in long ice cores it has been possible to identify at least twelve significant oscillations within this stage, in which temperatures over the area of the ice sheet seem to have risen by 5–8 °C, often within 50 years (Dansgaard *et al.* 1993).

Jacobi (1980: 21) matches the industries present in Britain to reoccupation during climatic ameliorations: the leaf point phase within the Hengelo, and the Aurignacian within the Arcy interstadial, whereas the Font Robert point phase could be said to fall within the Kesselt climatic amelioration. What this actually means in terms of availability of food, raw material resources and shelter, is still a matter for further research. Oxygen isotope stages and substages (OIS) should be used for clarity. The effect of interstadials was probably not the same throughout Europe, and we will probably never be able to gain sufficient definition in British sites to be certain of a chronology for, and duration of, each phase in the lithic typological scheme.

By 26,000 BP Britain was a full tundra environment, occupied only by herds of reindeer and woolly mammoth. Even these are thought to have disappeared at least between 20,000 and 18,000 BP, the dates for maximum extent of continental ice sheets, identified at OIS 2 and corresponding to the lowest isotopic values for ocean volume in the last full interglacial-glacial cycle.

Dates can be collated which suggest the presence of a megafauna close in time to the maximum ice advance within Britain (Jacobi 1980: 28). From Wales there is a date on a woolly rhinoceros (*Coelodonta antiquitatis*) scapula from Ogof-yr-Ychen, Caldey Island, giving 24,000±620 BP (Birm–340) (Shotton and Williams 1973: 458). A mammoth carpal from Ffynnon Beuno is dated to 18,000 +1400/–1200 BP (Birm–146) (Shotton and Williams 1973). The specimens are neither burnt nor cut-marked, so it is not known whether hunters were exploiting this fauna. It must also be emphasised that these are minimum dates, owing to the uncertainties of the radiocarbon technique. The Ogof-yr-Ychen bones, whilst claimed to have been associated with a lithic assemblage of Creswellian type (van Nedervelde *et al.* 1973) and some undiagnostic flakes, were, however, found in mixed, redeposited sediments.

The earliest date for a possible recolonisation of Britain comes from Little Hoyle Cave, Pembrokeshire. Outside the southern entrance fragmentary artefacts were found associated with an unmodified fragment of bone (possibly horse or bison) dated to 17,600±200 BP (OxA–1026). Substantive recolonisation is usually taken to occur much later, during warm periods of the late glacial in the thirteenth millennium BP (David 1990). The North Sea Plain was still dry at that time and formed an important corridor for the movement of animals. It is also the most likely route of recolonisation for human populations, and therefore it is in countries near the eastern margins of the North Sea that analogues for the British Late Upper Palaeolithic sequence should logically be sought (Barton and Roberts 1996: 249).

Campbell (1986: 8) has argued against the hiatus hypothesis, claiming that it is "basically ethnocentric and probably wrong". The accusation of ethnocentricity arises from modern European conceptions of comfort and an underestimation of the abilities of hunter-gatherers to exploit difficult environments. Campbell refers to research in Tasmania and Australia which has proven occupation throughout the Devensian, with some sites closer than 10km to the ice margin. He suggests that hunter-gatherers will only normally leave land totally unoccupied if there are social or religious reasons for doing so, or if the land itself is unavailable (for example covered by glaciers). During OIS 2 ice sheets stretched over northern Britain and the uplands of Wales, but southern England and the south coast of Wales were free of ice. Ethnographic analogies must however be treated with caution – and used to give an impression of the possibilities, never the actualities. Archaeology alone provides a glimpse of the complex hunting-gathering adaptations typical of past human societies (Price and Brown 1985).

A site which most clearly demonstrates the British Palaeolithic sequence and occupation hiatus is Kent's Cavern, Devonshire. It has provided an Early Upper Palaeolithic series of 479 artefacts (Campbell 1977: 97). Excavations at this site began as early as 1825–1829 by the Rev John MacEnery, but more systematic and extensive excavations were those conducted by William Pengelly, from 1865–1880 (Warren and Rose 1994). Pengelly's diary runs to six volumes and was thoroughly analysed by Campbell (1977: 38; Campbell and Sampson 1971), who produced stratigraphic sequences from the information. Proctor (1996: 163) has recently obtained a group of uranium-series and electron spin resonance dates on speleothem samples, which provide a basic chronology for the sequence of sediments and hence for the events responsible for their emplacement.

The "Cave Earth" is Pengelly's third stratigraphic unit and includes Middle and Upper Palaeolithic artefacts, a very diverse mammal fauna (Garrod 1926; Campbell and Sampson 1971), and blocks of crystalline stalagmite from the preceding stratigraphic unit, possibly broken up by an earthquake during the early Devensian (Straw 1996: 23). Cave Earth deposition began at about 74,000 BP, according to speleothem dates and faunal comparisons (Proctor 1996: 167).

A bifacial leaf point from the Gallery (illustrated by Campbell 1977: fig. 8) has an associated radiocarbon determination of 28,720±450 BP (GrN–6202) from an unmodified humerus of *Ursus arctos* from the same grid and spit position. A unifacial leaf point, two nosed scrapers and a "saw" from the middle of the Great Chamber have an associated age estimate of 27,730±350 BP (GrN–6323) from an unmodified radius of *Bison* sp.. Lastly, two unifacial leaf points and a "saw" from the south western centre of the Great Chamber have a wider estimate of 38,270 +1470/−1420 BP (GrN–6324), from an unmodified radius of *Equus* sp. from the same spit and almost the same grid position. As Campbell states (1986: 14) we should not assume a 9000-year-long hiatus within the leaf point phase without supporting dates.

That the Cave Earth is a debris flow, and not an *in situ* deposit, places uncertainty on the dates obtained for artefacts associated with bone. Secondly, suspicions are aroused by the possible reworking or "major disruption" (Proctor 1996: 165) of earlier sediments by water action, producing erosion and reopening sealed entrances, allowing the subsequent emplacement of debris flow material. Thirdly, there is a great deal of evidence that Kent's Cavern was a hyaena den during at least part of the Middle and Upper Devensian; that bones may be introduced or moved by hyaenas render associations even more tentative. Campbell (1977: 40) comments that the Early Upper Palaeolithic "occupation" is focused on the southern half of Kent's Cavern, the Great Chamber, Gallery and South Sally Port. Scrapers and "awls" are also scattered throughout this area. In the light of the fact that the Cave Earth occupied only the outer half of the cave (Straw 1996: 20), having passed through the present entrances, presumably carrying artefacts with it, any spatial analyses of the human use of the cave during the Early Upper Palaeolithic are suspect. That leaf points and nosed scrapers appear in the same "spits" (Campbell 1977) is a significant reminder of the impossibility of stratigraphically-separating leaf point phase and Aurignacian material in this case.

The evidence from Kent's Cavern supports the 23,000–13,000 BP hiatus hypothesis as outlined by Jacobi (1980: 53). A complete break in occupation cannot be proved or disproved. The Late Upper Palaeolithic layer is the "Black Band", a dark deposit at the top of the Cave Earth, including charcoal, bone fragments and artefacts. A radiocarbon date of 12,325±120 BP (GrN–6203) from the "Vestibule" on an unmodified tibia of *Ursus arctos* is associated – although unreliably – with angle-backed and trapezoidal backed pieces.

Kent's Cavern is the only British site with a stratigraphically correlated lithic sequence from the Lower Palaeolithic to Final Palaeolithic (*sensu* Barton and Roberts 1996), but unfortunately, owing to the artefacts and bone being included in a debris flow deposit, no finer chronology can be described.

Idiosyncrasies in the British Early Upper Palaeolithic

Differences between assemblages could be expected in Britain owing to the often very small "windows" which sites provide onto the depth of time. The division of artefacts into industries is itself artificial, dependant on the recognition of specific forms of implements in more well-dated sites which may lie some distance away. In some cases, such as that of the Font Robert point phase, the variations within a grouping may be striking. "Cultures" have often been given improbably wide ranges (*e.g.* Breuil 1922: 262). On the other hand, in order to explain unexpected associations new cultures may be invented, leading to a proliferation which may be better explained in terms of functional differences (Binford and Binford 1969), or inadequate stratigraphy. Comparisons on the basis of differing numbers of the same tool type, or "proportional" comparisons (*e.g.* Hahn 1977: 307: carinated burins in Aurignacian assemblages) should be more tentative than those which rely on the presence/absence of *fossiles directeurs*, or non-lithic criteria, especially if the sample size is small. Depending on raw material, technological differences (for example uni- or bi-directional use of cores) could also be good criteria; these may be passed on through teaching, and can persist and become widely-spread.

This section will highlight a particular lithic artefact type – or rather a style of retouch which is idiosyncratic to the site of Paviland Cave, on the Gower Peninsula of South Wales – and on this basis will suggest that a percentage of the Paviland collection forms a group which differs slightly from other Early Upper Palaeolithic industries. Unfortunately it is impossible to determine the age of these types, or to know within what time span they belong, or whether they were in association with any other implements. Further research may lead to a formalised description of the Early Upper Palaeolithic industry at Paviland, in terms of the composition of standard tool types (burins, truncations, *etc.*) and assess how these compare with other assemblages.

Paviland Cave is a major Early Upper Palaeolithic site, on account of the number and quality of lithic, ivory and bone finds, and the presence of the "Red Lady" ceremonial burial (Buckland 1823, Sollas 1913, Garrod 1927: 50; Campbell 1977: 144). The first major excavation was in 1823, by William Buckland, and the second by William Sollas in 1913. Sollas' excavations produced the majority of the lithics sample: 4000 pieces of debitage and 600 retouched tools. Owing to the lack of meaningful stratigraphy (Sollas 1913: 331) it was impossible to associate pieces with each other, or with datable material. Consequently, the Abbé Breuil classified the implements solely on their morphological characteristics, and grouped them into the then-accepted cultural sequence. The Paviland lithic collection was updated by Jacobi (1980: 30) as part of the formulation of a British sequence.

The newly-recognised form of shouldered scraper was termed by Breuil a "rostrate grattoir with inverse terminal retouches" (Sollas 1913: 344). Breuil did not note that he thought it a new type so the possibility remains that he had seen something similar elsewhere in his wide experience. However an investigation of the literature has produced no comparable examples. The implements are made on flake blanks of flint and fine-grained Carboniferous chert to a form which seems standardised, with four to six diagonal retouch facets on the ventral surface. The implement should be described by the style and position of retouch, which serves to round as well as strengthen what is presumably the working edge.

Although most obvious on the shouldered scrapers, it should be noted that this distinctive retouch is also present on the end of a blade, forming an atypical end-scraper, and as a platform for a burin removal in at least two cases. Indeed, as the retouch usually slopes down from right to left, it may signify "handedness" on the part of the person who made the artefacts, as it would be easy to produce this pattern by retouching with the right hand, the blank being held in the left. Tools with this retouch make up 4% of the Paviland assemblage and may have originated from a single phase of occupation (Swainston 1997: 101). 4% may not seem a particularly high occurrence but offers evidence of contemporaneity in an Early Upper Palaeolithic assemblage for which the radiocarbon determinations span at least 23,500 years. I suggest that regional idiosyncrasies are more likely to have occurred over a short time span, than are widespread industries such as Aurignacian II.

It would be interesting to know the function of these implements. On the basis of their similarity to burins, and the large amounts of worked and un-worked ivory found in the cave (Sollas 1913: 359) it is tentatively suggested that they may be engraving tools for working bone, antler and ivory – an "isochrestic" choice (Sackett 1982: 73), to produce scrapers with an edge approaching burin-like strength.

Stylistic variations serve as an encouragement to look beyond typology in an attempt to see the hand of the individual. Variation in the British Creswellian, and in the Belgian and French Magdalenian, has been explained by an evolutionary model, involving a group becoming separated from the main population, with technological differences gradually becoming standardised in that group (Barton and Roberts 1996: 258). Differences may in fact be favoured to accentuate the cultural distance between two groups, and adhered to as an expression of group affinity. As Paviland is a marginal site in terms of its situation within Europe, lowland sites having been lost due to rising sea level, we should not be surprised that unique stylistic traits are expressed in the lithic collection.

The typology of the British Early Upper Palaeolithic

The standard statistical method for the description of Early Upper Palaeolithic assemblages (de Sonneville-Bordes and Perrot 1954; de Sonneville-Bordes 1960) includes a list of 104 (originally 92) tool types and a method of comparison involving cumulative graphs. Some of these *fossiles directeurs* have been used to construct the British sequence widely accepted at present. However, the standard typology is of use only in comparative dating and morphological description; it is limiting in the description of technological aspects. Many of the classic tool types present in the French Early Upper Palaeolithic do not occur in British sites, whereas British sites such as Paviland Cave have yielded idiosyncratic types.

The debitage from British sites has largely been ignored, although studies of debitage and raw material use would extract further information regarding both Early Upper Palaeolithic technology and reduction-sequences (*chaînes opératoires*). Ethnographic studies (Binford 1979) mention the use of otherwise unmodified flint flakes, and so the distinction between implements (retouched flakes) and waste or "blanks" (unretouched flakes) is unreliable. It is understandable that debitage has not been greatly studied since, being non-diagnostic, it may have originated in any phase of the Early Upper Palaeolithic. Any attempt to isolate material from one phase, from a palimpsest site would result in an inaccurate sample. Refitting and the description of groups, both of similar raw materials and of similar technological attributes (such as style of retouch and shape of blank), may help to overcome this problem.

There is only one example of an Early Upper Palaeolithic assemblage in Britain which is likely to have resulted from the activities of a single group at a single point in time. The assemblage is from the leaf point phase, but has striking differences which urge reassessment of the degree to which assemblages are the result of a gradual accumulation of "worn-out" items. This is the fortuitously-preserved open-air site at Pulborough, West Sussex; here 198 items survive, described by Curwen (1949: 192) and Jacobi (1980, 1986). In addition to 40 leaf points, a single burin spall, *lames machurées* and long, sometimes crested, prismatic blades were found. The platforms of the thicker blades are often faceted, bulbs are diffuse and there are usually clear lips suggestive of a "soft hammer" mode of striking (Jacobi 1986: 63). Also from Pulborough are five end-scrapers on otherwise unmodified blanks. Of these, one is combined with an inverse truncation at the opposite end of a long blade, and one or two with burins. There are nine dihedral burins and a single piercer – all in all a typical Early Upper Palaeolithic technology. Recycling of tools and knapping probably took place, as pieces can be conjoined and opposed platform blade cores are present. There are no bone, antler or ivory tools. Jacobi (1986: 64) compares inverse truncations in association with dorsal surface removals with "Kostenki knives" from Avdeevo and Kostenki, sites on the Russian Plain. The age of Pulborough is not known, but level two of Kostenki 8 is dated to 27,700±7500 BP (GrN–10509). Kostenki knives have no equivalent from any other British find spot, and serve to demonstrate how much cultural evidence is missing from the archaeological record of the British Early Upper Palaeolithic.

Originalities arising in British assemblages are usually interpreted in terms of two lines of cultural influence from France and Central Europe, leading to an anomalous mixture in the north-west which is difficult to interpret. Jacobi (1986: 66) reflects this viewpoint by writing: "technologies of Atlantic sea-board type may make up a part of any British Early Upper Palaeolithic assemblage." This is an echo of Garrod's (1926: 194) observation: "...we [cannot] expect the classification of Gabriel de Mortillet to hold good all over the Palaeolithic world."

The assemblage from Pulborough challenges the traditional usage of typology. It is a snapshot of a dynamic and adaptable way of working flint, in which any tool type can be recycled into any other form, as and when needed. The implements themselves are not necessarily final products, instead they have been discarded at one particular stage of their use. The implements serve as cores from which new implements can be knapped; they are a way of dividing and transporting raw material.

Differences exist in the morphology of tools from cave and open-air sites, which could arise from a number of causes. Jacobi (1986: 63) notes a difference in size between the "massive" Pulborough leaf points (length around 140mm) and their smaller counterparts found in caves (80mm for the complete Paviland example). The reduced size of the cave leaf points may be another example of isochrestic choice, reflecting long curation histories with frequent resharpening of implements to maintain the desired outline and symmetry.

The morphology of leaf points has traditionally been explained functionally. Bosinski (1990: 53) remarks that their retouched tips would be useful if they were used as spear points, because the thin and irregular tips might break and remain in the wound, further disabling the animal. That they are projectile points is supported by study of the Pulborough leaf points which have fluted or burin-like impact fractures (Jacobi 1986: 63). A piece from Robin Hood's Cave has a "wear facet" about three-quarters of the way along the length of the piece, which may have resulted from hafting. If these pieces were hafted as spear points, one would expect at least a third of their length to be included in the haft, and it could be predicted that this would be the part of the implement to be found most often in archaeological "hunting camp" contexts. Dawkins (1876: 252) notes that the retouch produces "a twist in the edges analogous to that which has been observed in Neolithic arrow heads, intended to make the arrow revolve in its flight." Dawkins' explanation is interesting, and could well form the focus for some experimental archaeology.

Other open-air sites, particularly those of single finds such as Cameron Road, Dorset (Campbell 1977: fig. 109; Palmer 1970: 100), Fir Hill, Wiltshire (Campbell 1977: fig. 109; Engleheart 1923: 144) and Reynoldston, South Wales (Green 1984: 26), require critical review. The pieces are described by Campbell (1977: 150) as thin, bifacial leaf points or "Blattspitzen"; those from Mauern II are dated at around 38,000 BP. However they should rather be regarded as of uncertain cultural classification, being without cryoturbation damage or water rounding, and similar in morphology to Neolithic or early Bronze Age knives. Open-air sites which are more widely accepted are Bramford Road (Campbell 1977: fig. 107) and Constantine Road, Ipswich (Garrod 1926: 170; Moir 1938: 258), which yielded leaf points deeply buried in gravels. No Aurignacian phase open-air sites are known.

Conclusion

The extent of occupation during the Early Upper Palaeolithic has been demonstrated by the collections from Creswell Crags, our characterisation of the patterns of occupation by the Wookey caves complex and the hiatus in occupation by Kent's Cavern, the only stratified site with an Early Upper Palaeolithic lithic assemblage. Idiosyncrasies in the British Early Upper Palaeolithic have been highlighted by an example from Paviland Cave, and the restrictions placed on research by an adherence to typology have been illustrated by the Pulborough assemblage. This latter is the only site which Garrod did not include in her 1926 volume.

At present, studies could understandably be decried for lack of background and solid evidence, but work is progressing in this field, most notably at Kent's Cavern (A. Roberts pers. comm.), at Paviland Cave and the Vale of Clwyd caves (S. Aldhouse-Green pers. comm.), and at King Arthur's Cave and the Wye Valley (N. Barton pers. comm.), which will add greatly to the body of evidence. Two recommendations remain for further research, the first being "to construct as completely as we can the physical environment of the stone implement makers" (Garrod 1946: 1). More precise ecological and topological models can be created for the middle to late Devensian. These would be of particular relevance in dealing with sites which are currently surrounded by the sea, like Paviland and Uphill; which require a stretch of the imagination to envisage as sites on the Bristol Channel Plain. Secondly, dating is of the utmost importance if sites are to be compared more thoroughly than in the above synopsis. The main factor holding archaeologists back from a more adventurous explanation of the British Early Upper Palaeolithic is a lack of resolution and clarity in stratigraphy. Further absolute dating and environmental modelling, along with lithic and faunal analyses are needed to "set the map in motion" (Garrod 1926: 194), and to understand the activities of hunter-gatherers in Britain and north-west Europe.

Bibliography

Aldhouse-Green, H. S., Scott, K., Schwartz, H., Grün, R., Housley, R., Rae, A., Bevins, R. and M. Redknap 1995. Coygan Cave, Laugharne, South Wales, a Mousterian Site and Hyaena Den: A Report on the University of Cambridge Excavations. *Proceedings of the Prehistoric Society* 61: 37–79.

Balch, H. E. 1928. Excavations at Wookey Hole and Other Mendip Caves 1926–1927. *The Antiquaries Journal* 8: 193–211.

Barton, R.N.E., and A.J. Roberts 1996. Reviewing the British Late Upper Paleolithic: New Evidence for Chronological Patterning in the Lateglacial Record. *Oxford Journal of Archaeology* 15 (3): 245–267.

Binford, L.R. 1983. *In Pursuit of the Past: Decoding the Archaeological Past.* London: Thames and Hudson.

Binford, L.R., and S.R. Binford 1969. Stone tools and Human Behaviour. *Scientific American* 220 (4): 70–84.

Binford, L.R. 1979. Organization and Formation Processes: Looking at Curated Technologies. *Journal of Anthropological Research* 35: 255–273.

Bosinski, G. 1990. *Homo Sapiens.* Editions Errance.

Buckland., W. 1823. *Reliquiæ Diluvianæ.* London: John Murray.

Breuil, H. 1922. Observations on the Pre-Neolithic Industries of Scotland. *Proceedings of the Society of Antiquaries of Scotland* 56: 261–281.

Campbell, J.B. 1969. Excavations at Creswell Crags: Preliminary Report. *Derbyshire Archaeological Journal* 89: 47–58.

Campbell, J.B., and C.G. Sampson 1971. *A New Analysis of Kent's Cavern, Devonshire, England.* University of Oregon Anthropological Papers No. 3.

Campbell, J.B. 1977. *The Upper Palaeolithic in Britain- A study of Man and Nature in the Later Ice Age.* Oxford: Clarendon Press. 2 Volumes.

Campbell, J. B. 1980. Le Problème des Subdivisions du Paléolithique Supérieur Britannique dans son Cadre Européen. *Bulletin de la Société royale belge Anthropologique et Préhistorique* 91: 39–77.

Campbell, J.B. 1986. Hiatus and Continuity on the British Upper Palaeolithic: A View from the Antipodes. In D. Roe (Ed.), *Studies in the Upper Palaeolithic of Britain and Northwest Europe.* Oxford: British Archaeological Reports British Series 296.

Curwen, E. 1949. A Flint Dagger Factory near Pulborough, Sussex. *Antiquaries' Journal* 29: 192–195.

Dansgaard, W. Johnsen, S.J., Clausen, H.B. , Dahl-Jensen, D., Gundesrup, N.S., Hammer, C.U., Hvidberg, C.S., Steffensen, J.P., Sveinbjörndottir, A.E., Jouzel, J, and G. Bond 1993.

Evidence for general instability of past climate from a 250-kyr ice core record. *Nature* 364: 218–220.

David, A. 1990. *Palaeolithic and Mesolithic Settlement in Wales.* Unpublished Ph.D. thesis, University of Lancaster.

Dawkins, W.B. 1876. The Bone Caves of Creswell Crags. *The Quarterly Journal of the Geological Society*: 248–258.

Engleheart, G.H. 1923. Surface Implements from Wiltshire. *Antiquaries Journal* 3: 144–145.

Gamble, C. 1983. Culture and Society in the Upper Palaeolithic of Europe. In G. Bailey (Ed.), *Hunter-Gatherer Economy in Prehistory*, pp. 201–211. Cambridge: Cambridge University Press.

Gamble, C. 1986. *The Palaeolithic Settlement of Europe.* Cambridge: Cambridge University Press.

Gamble, C. 1993. *Timewalkers.* Stroud: Alan Sutton.

Gamble, C. 1995. Lithics and Social Evolution. In A.J. Schofield (Ed.), *Lithics in Context*, pp. 19–26. Lithics Studies Society Occasional Paper No. 5.

Garrod, D.A.E. 1926. *The Upper Palaeolithic Age in Britain.* Oxford: Clarendon Press.

Garrod, D.A.E. 1946. *Environment, Tools and Man.* Cambridge: Cambridge University Press.

Green, H.S. 1984. The Old and Middle Stone Ages, 1: The Palaeolithic Period. In H.N. Savory (Ed.), *Glamorgan County History Vol. II*, pp. 11–33. Cardiff: Glamorgan County History Trust Limited.

Green, .S. and H. Livingston 1991. The Palaeolithic and its Quaternary Context. In J. Manley, G. Grenter and F. Gale (Eds.), *The Archaeology of Clwyd.* Clwyd County Council.

Hahn, J. 1977. *Aurignacien: Das Ältere Jungpaläolithikum in Mittel- und Osteuropa.* Köln: Fundamenta Series A9.

Harrison, R.A. 1977. The Uphill Quarry Caves, Weston-Super-Mare, a Reappraisal. *Proceedings of the University of Bristol Spelaeological Society* 14 (3): 233–254.

Hart, C.R. 1981. *The North Derbyshire Archaeological Survey to A.D. 1200.* The North Derbyshire Archaeological Trust, Chesterfield. pp. 17–21.

Jacobi, R.M. 1980. The Upper Palaeolithic of Britain with Special Reference to Wales. In J.A. Taylor (Ed.), *Culture and Environment in Prehistoric Wales*, pp. 15–99. Oxford: British Archaeological Reports British Series 76.

Jacobi, R.M. 1986. The Contents of Dr. Harley's Showcase. In S. N. Collcutt (Ed.), *The Palaeolithic of Britain and its Nearest Neighbours: Recent Trends*, pp. 62–68. Sheffield: John R. Collis.

Jackson, J.W. 1967. The Creswell Caves. *Cave Science: Journal of the British Spelaeological Association* 6: 8–23.

Jenkinson, R.D.S. 1984. *Creswell Crags.* Oxford: British Archaeological Reports British Series 122.

Kozłowski, J.K. 1983. Le Paléolithique supérieur en Pologne. *L'Anthropologie* 87: 49–82.

Mellars, P. 1992. Archaeology and the Population-dispersal Hypothesis of Modern Human Origins in Europe. *Philosophical Transactions of the Royal Society of London* 337: 225–234.

Mellars, P. 1996. *The Neanderthal Legacy: An Archaeological Perspective from Western Europe.* Princeton: Princeton University Press.

McBurney, C.B.M. 1965. The Old Stone Age in Wales. In G. Daniel and I.L. Foster (Eds.), *Prehistoric and Early Wales*, pp. 17–34. London.

Mello, J.M. 1876. The Bone-Caves of Creswell Crags. *Quarterly Journal of the Geological Society.*

Moir, J.R. 1938. Four Flint Implements. *Antiquaries' Journal* 18: 258–261.

Movius, H.L. 1975. *Excavation of the Abri Pataud, Les Eyzies.* Harvard University.

Otte, M. 1984. Paléolithique Supérieur en Belgique. In D. Cahen and P. Haesaerts (Eds.), *Peuples Chasseurs de la Belgique Préhistorique dans Leurs Cadres Naturel. Bruxelles*, pp. 157–97.

Otte, M. 1990. The Northwestern European Plain Around 18 000 BP. In O. Soffer and C. Gamble (Eds.), *The World at 18 000 BP, Vol. I*, pp. 54–68. London: Unwin Hyman.

Palmer, S. 1970. The Stone Age Industries of the Isle of Portland, Dorset, and their Utilisation of Portland Chert as Artifact Material in Southern England. *Proceedings of the Prehistoric Society* 36: 85–115.

Price, T.D., and J.A. Brown 1985. *Prehistoric Hunter-Gatherers: The Emergence of Cultural Complexity.* Academic Press.

Proctor, C.J. 1996. Kent's Cavern. In D.J.Charman, R.M. Newnham and D.G. Croot (Eds.), *Devon and Cornwall Field Guide, Quaternary Research Association*, pp. 163–167.

Sackett, J.R. 1982. Approaches to Style in Lithic Archaeology. *Journal of Anthropological Archaeology* 1: 59–112.

Sollas, W.J. 1913. Paviland Cave: An Aurignacian Station in Wales. *Journal of the Royal Anthropological Institute*: 325–374.

Sonneville-Bordes, D. de, and J. Perrot 1954. Lexique Typologique du Paléolithique Supérieur, Outillage Lithique. *Bulletin de la Société Préhistorique Française* 51: 327–335.

Sonneville-Bordes, D. de. 1960. *Le Paléolithique Supérieur en Périgord.* Bordeaux: Imprimeries Delmas.

Straw, A. 1996. The Quaternary Record of Kent's Cavern - A Brief Reminder and Update. *Quaternary Newsletter* 80: 17–25.

Swainston, S. 1997. *A Study of the Lithic Collections from Paviland Cave, and the Site in its Wider Context.* Unpublished M.A. thesis, University of Wales College, Newport.

Tratman, E.K., Donovan, D.T., and J.B. Campbell 1971. The Hyaena Den (Wookey Hole), Mendip Hills, Somerset. *Proceedings of the University of Bristol Spelaeological Society* 12 (3): 245–279.

Van Nedervelde, B.R.J., Davies, M., and B.S. John 1973. Radiocarbon dating from Ogof-yr-Ychen, a New Pleistocene Site in West Wales. *Nature* 245: 453–454.

Warren, C.N., and S. Rose 1994. *William Pengelly's Techniques of Archaeological Excavation.* Torquay Natural History Society Publication No. 5.

6

Garrod and the Belgian Creswellian

Ruth Charles

Dorothy Garrod's defintion of the British Creswellian in 1926 drew on continental parallels, particularly from the site of Martinrive in Belgium. Since then the existence of the Creswellian has been unquestioningly recognised on the European mainland. This paper reviews the evidence from Martinrive and other claimed Creswellian assemblages from Belgium, and concludes that there is no firm basis on which to recognise the Creswellian in this region.

Introduction

The Creswellian is a Lateglacial backed point complex most frequently recognised in Britain, although Creswellian sites have been claimed from other areas of north-western Europe. The Belgian Late Upper Palaeolithic has been under review by the author since 1990. One aspect of this has been the re-assessment of the claimed Belgian Creswellian sites. This has resulted in the question "does the Belgian Creswellian exist?" Before attempting to answer this question in detail, it seems best to first define what is meant here by the term Creswellian *sensu stricto*.

Dorothy Garrod first coined the term Creswellian (1926a, 1926b), defining it as a regional variant of the Magdalenian. Created over half a century ago, as Jacobi (1991) has noted, it was inextricably linked to other contemporary definitions of culture history and written with reference to a very different European Lateglacial database from the one with which we are now familiar. Garrod chose Creswell Crags, on the Nottinghamshire/Derbyshire border, as the type site for her definition as:

> "It is clear that the Magdalenian of this country [Britain] is of a provincial type, with very important survivals from the Upper Aurignacian, such as the ordinary La Gravette point, the shouldered point and the Noailles graver (found at Creswell). Special forms are the trapezoidal point, almost unknown in Continental deposits, and a number of small semi-geometrical points and blades similar to those found at Martinrive, a late Upper Palaeolithic station of doubtful affinities, near Liège. Finally the scarcity of typical gravers is in striking contrast with their abundance in classical Magdalenian sites...
>
> ...I would claim that it does seem to represent a local and semi-independent facies of the Magdalenian sufficiently well-characterised to deserve a name of its own, and I would suggest tentatively, "Creswellian," since Creswell Crags is the station where it is found in greatest abundance and variety."
>
> (Garrod 1926a: 301)

Since Garrod's pioneering research, much work has focused on the Creswellian, in attempts to enhance our understanding of this term and the archaeological material it signifies. Most notable are the writings of Campbell (1977, 1980) and Jacobi (1986, 1991). These present the range of different definitions and opinions which have surrounded the Creswellian in recent years.

On the one hand, Campbell advocated that the Creswellian be sub-divided into first three (1977) and then four stages (1980), linked to an extended chronology spanning the range 23,000 to 9,000 BP. This suggestion emerged from the radiocarbon evidence obtained as part of his research into the British Upper Palaeolithic. On the other hand, more recent research (Jacobi 1991) has argued for a much 'tighter' definition, in which Campbell's four stages can be discarded on the basis of inadequate sample size (*cf.* Burdukiewicz 1986: 79; Charles and Jacobi 1994: 5–6) and his radiocarbon chronology abandoned on the basis of unsuitable sample selection. Despite the wide range of opinions surrounding the nature of the Creswellian, it does appear that at least a part of Garrod's original definition still holds validity (Jacobi 1991: 131), specifically relating to the presence of trapezoidal backed points (*Cheddar points* as they are more commonly known) within true Creswellian assemblages. Creswellian toolkits also include another form of 'semi-geometrical' point (Creswell points), which are frequently, although not exclusively, broken Cheddar points. However, Jacobi argued that the Creswellian cannot simply be recognised on the presence of these trapezoidal backed points alone, as similar backed points occur in other European Lateglacial contexts, specifically within both Magdalenian and Hamburgian assemblages.

This has led to a radical solution to the problem of definition (Jacobi 1991): as the term *Creswellian* (used by Garrod to include any British Lateglacial material) is now redundant, and as other recent definitions of the Creswellian are irretrievably flawed, that the term *Creswellian* itself be abandoned, and be replaced at least in part by the term *Cheddarian* as this describes adequately the material which he considers to be the 'core elements' of the Creswellian, and offers a far 'tighter' definition which incorporates Garrod's trapezoidal points. This emphasises the differences between the British Lateglacial material and that found in mainland Europe, as the Cheddarian lacks microlithic backed bladelets (unlike the Magdalenian) and differs from the Hamburgian in the morphology of its backed points. It is really the Cheddarian in this sense which continental researchers have attempted to identify as Creswellian, as the presence of Cheddar points has generally been taken as the critical feature when identifying supposedly Creswellian industries in Europe.

One could add that in addition to the presence of trapezoidal points, Creswellian/Cheddarian blade production is characterised by butt preparation *en éperon* (Barton 1990); but that these lithic assemblages lack *burins de Lacam* (or Lacan) (Barton, pers. comm., "Burin présentant une troncature retouchée concave très oblique postérieure à l'enlèvement de coup de burin et formant un bec, dont le biseau est parfois réduit par une retouche tertiaire" (Demars and Laurent 1989: 76)). Bone work, although present, does not include as yet any harpoons, an artefact type frequently found on contemporaneous Magdalenian sites, although other forms of worked bone antler and ivory commonly found in the Magdalenian, including *bâtons de commandement* and *sagaies*, have been recognised in British Creswellian contexts (Jacobi 1991).

In 1991 Jacobi could only recognise 20 British findspots which fulfilled his definition of the Cheddarian, compared with 150 findspots claimed to be of Lateglacial age. The vast majority of these Cheddarian sites were caves, and available radiocarbon dates directly associated with the lithic assemblages (via cut marked bone or worked bone artefacts) indicated human presence between 13,000 and 12,000 BP.

The very issues which Jacobi addressed in his 1991 paper are clearly encapsulated within the Belgian Lateglacial archaeological record. The Belgian Lateglacial archaeological database indicates the presence of a number of archaeological groups during at least part of this period: the Magdalenian, Federmesser (Tjongerian) and Ahrensburgian, as well as claims for the Creswellian/Cheddarian. It is these claimed Creswellian/Cheddarian sites which are re-evaluated here in the light of recent work.

The terms *Creswellian*, *Creswello-Tjongerian* and *Creswello-Hamburgian* have been used to describe the assemblages from a number of Belgian sites believed to be of Lateglacial age. The definition of these many Creswellians has rarely been made explicit.

Numerous sites have become fixed points on distribution maps of the Belgian Creswellian, usually without any critical re-appraisal of their actual status. The main sites identified at one time or another as Creswellian (Bois de la Saute, Grotte de Martinrive, 4ᵉ Grotte de Engis, Maldegem, l'Abri de Megarnie, Grottes de Presle, Obourg «St. Macaire» and Orroir) are discussed briefly below. They have been selected due to their frequent inclusion in such distribution maps (*cf.* Otte 1984).

In discussing and identifying Creswellian/Cheddarian material Jacobi's redefinition will be followed here, as it permits a very precise recognition of one particular and distinctive component of the British Lateglacial record. Jacobi's *Cheddarian* is clearly defined on the presence of Cheddar points amongst other typological and technological features, and it is the recognition of such points which have led many continental commentators to identify the Creswellian in Europe; accordingly it is this material which is taken as the critical aspect of the Lateglacial assemblages under discussion.

What follows is a review of the Belgian sites which have been claimed to be Creswellian, highlighting current problems of identification and interpretation.

Caverne de Bois de la Saute

The *Caverne de Bois de la Saute* was discovered in 1952; major excavations were undertaken in 1977 and 1978 by an amateur archaeological group (Toussaint and Toussaint 1983: 88; Toussaint *et al.* 1979) and yielded a small lithic assemblage. Amongst the lithics from these excavations are a number of curved backed pieces (Fig. 6.1a: nos. 1–4), which were described by the authors as *Tjonger points*. Three of the four pieces are broken. Also present in the assemblage are three burins (Fig. 6.1a: nos. 6–8), some broken backed pieces (Fig. 6.1a: nos. 9–11), mid-sections of backed bladelets (Fig. 6.1a: nos. 12–13) and a fragment of an engraved plaquette. No Creswell or Cheddar points are illustrated or mentioned in the published accounts.

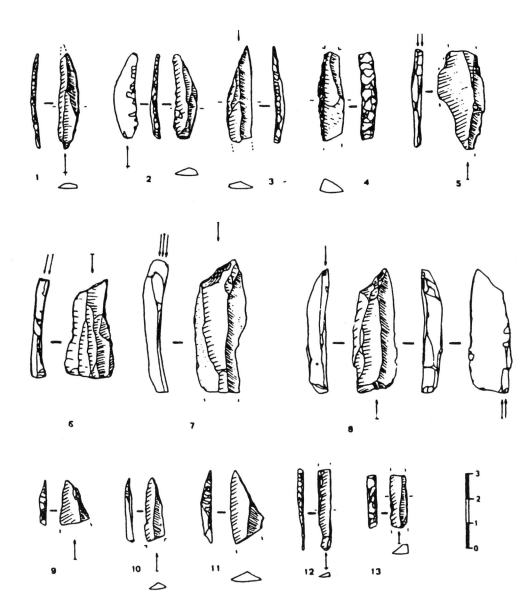

Fig. 6.1a: Archaeological material from Bois de la Saute (after Toussaint et al. 1979).

The lack of Creswellian/Cheddarian *fossiles directeurs* leaves little to suggest that this assemblage can properly be linked to the Creswellian/Cheddarian. A tentative case could be made linking it with the local Magdalenian – hinted at by the presence of segments of backed bladelets rather than blades and the presence of part of a plaquette. However, Federmesser affinities could also be suggested. The assemblage appears to be so small (13 secondarily worked pieces and 1 plaquette) that designating

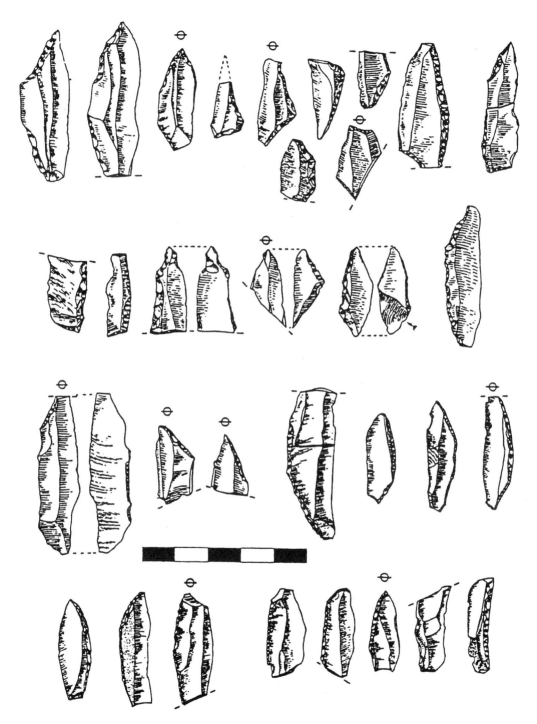

Fig. 6.1b: Archaeological material from Martinrive (after Dewez 1977).

any cultural ascription appears to be unrealistic at the moment. The one clear statement which can be made about the material from Bois de la Saute is that there is no reason why any of the material should be considered Creswellian/Cheddarian.

Grotte de Martinrive

The cave of Martinrive, actually mentioned by Garrod in her original definition, lies to the south of Liège, near the village of Comblain-au-Pont. Unfortunately, the assemblage from the site does not in fact appear to be part of what is currently accepted as the Creswellian/Cheddarian. The lithics from the site instead appear to fit within the general category of Federmesser: dihedral burins and burins on truncations are present. Piercers, *becs*, tools on blades and narrow backed blades are all absent (Lohest *et al.* 1922: fig. 3; Dewez 1977: abb. 2; and Dewez 1987 figs. 218–222). Three possible Cheddar points have been figured from the site (Fig. 6.1b) although neither of these specimens has a distinct trapezoidal outline and both lack the characteristic gibbosities (Jacobi 1986: 76) frequently found on *Cheddar points* from the UK. Sadly, three possible Cheddar points are not in themselves clear evidence for the Creswellian/Cheddarian. This assemblage has also been referred to as Creswello-Tjongerian (Dewez 1977); problems surrounding this entity will be discussed in more detail below. As far as this review is concerned, the material recovered from Martinrive may indeed be of Lateglacial age, but remains culturally undiagnostic beyond the general term *Federmesser*.

It is unfortunate that Garrod took Martinrive as the prime analogy within her definition, although understandable, since at the time of publication it was among the few sites known in the archaeological literature which did not fully correspond with the 'classic' Magdalenian of southern France, instead being something more characteristically northern European. Schwabedissen's recognition (1954) of the *Federmessergruppen* still lay some decades ahead. Radiocarbon dates are not currently available from Martinrive, and whilst the probablity is that this material is indeed of Lateglacial age, this has yet to be unequivocally demonstrated.

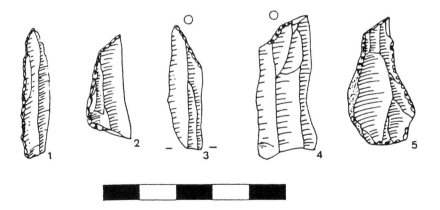

Fig. 6.2a: Archaeological material from the 4e Grotte d' Engis (after Dewez 1987).

4ᵉ Grotte d'Engis

The 4ᵉ Grotte d'Engis (also known as the 'Caverne Funéraire') is situated on the left bank of the river Meuse, to the south-west of Liège. As its name suggests, there are other caves situated nearby in the same limestone outcrop. The site of the 4ᵉ Grotte was first explored either during or just before 1899 by E. Doudou, who presented the results of his work to the Société d'Anthropologie de Bruxelles; unfortunately the paper describing his work was not published in their *Bulletin* (Jacques 1899: LII). Doudou's research was finally published privately in 1903 under the title *Explorations scientifiques dans les cavernes, les abîmes et les trous qui fument de la Province de Liège*.

Further excavations were carried out during 1896 by Fraipont and Destinez (Fraipont 1900, cited in Dewez 1987). These investigations revealed Neolithic burials, which occurred in the same archaeological/geological unit as Palaeolithic material (Dewez 1977–79: 133).

The last recorded excavations were undertaken between 1908 and 1910 by the association *les Chercheurs de la Wallonie* (de Rasquin 1910). Found alongside both historic and prehistoric pottery were a number of flint artefacts. Included amongst these were:

> "En tout environ 150 pièces, fortement patinées, que nous croyons pouvoir ranger, malgré le peu d'instruments achevés et caractéristiques, dans le magdalénien.
> (*ibid.*: 190)

Unfortunately none of these were illustrated in the 1910 report. The only illustrations of lithics from the site are given by Dewez (1977–79: fig. 1; Fig. 6.2a). Sadly, his suggestion that this assemblage might be Creswellian (Dewez 1987: 299) does not appear to be viable. Whilst the material illustrated is clearly Upper Palaeolithic in form – curved and angle-backed pieces, and a lone burin – the assemblage once again lacks the distinctive Cheddar and Creswell points. Indeed, one curved backed piece (Fig. 6.2a: no. 1) could perhaps be identified as a penknife point. It seems probable that this small assemblage (which also reputedly includes a core, 4 *lames à crête*, 25 blades, 5 bladelets and an *éclat à crête*) is of Lateglacial age. However, it cannot be clearly identified as part of any particular Lateglacial techno-complex on the basis of the present lithic collection.

L'Abri de Megarnie

Located on the right bank of the river Meuse near the hamlet of Engihoul, this small rock shelter has now been partially destroyed by quarrying. Initial excavations were undertaken by E. Doudou during the final years of the 19th Century (Dewez 1987: 301). Doudou's collection was subsequently donated to the University of Liège. Further excavations were initiated by the *Chercheurs de la Wallonie* between 1908 and 1909. These recovered lithics which were characterised as Magdalenian. Further excavations under the auspices of the *Chercheurs* took place in 1916 during the course of which they discovered a hearth. Final excavations by the *Chercheurs* in 1958 located material discarded during earlier excavations. It appears that the site has now been completely excavated. There are no absolute dates for human presence at this site currently available.

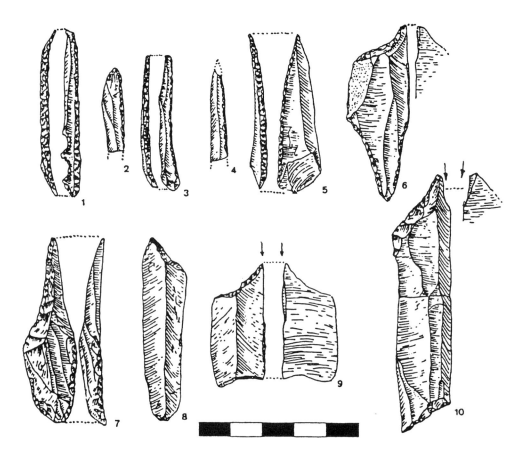

Fig. 6.2b: Archaeological material from the Abri d'Megarnie (after Dewez 1987).

    Dewez (1987: 305) briefly discussed the cultural ascription of the site, and
concludes that it is more likely to be Creswellian than Magdalenian. He reported a
total of 434 flints in the assemblage. Of these, 24 are tools, 10 of which are illustrated
(*ibid.*: fig. 201; Fig. 6.2b). None of the descriptions or illustrations seem to relate to
Creswellian/Cheddarian *fossiles directeurs* and the presence of backed blades and
bladelets (Fig. 6.2b: nos. 1–4) and *burins de Lacam* (Fig. 6.2b: nos. 6 and 7) is more
reminiscent of the Magdalenian. The assemblage is far too small to make any credible
claims about its affinities and there is no real case for supposing that any of it is
recognisable as Creswellian.

Grottes de Presle
The caves at Presle lie in cliffs by the right bank of the river Biesme, within the estate
of the Count d'Oultremont. The initial excavations in 1904 were carried out under the
auspices of the Société Paléontologique et Archéologique de Charleroi, directed by Dr
Druart, and involved the investigation of four caves (*Rapport sur les fouilles effectuées*

en 1904 dans les Grottes de Presle, in Documents et Rapports de la Société Royale Paléontologique et Archéologique de l'Arrondissement Judiciaire de Charleroi; referenced in Danthine 1955–60). Of these, the Trou de l'Ossuaire appears to have contained both later prehistoric inhumations and some curved and angle-backed blades (Debaille and Foulon 1926; Debaille 1945). This material alerted Prof. Hélène Danthine to the possibility of an Upper Palaeolithic assemblage with few existing parallels from Belgium (Danthine 1955–60: 3). Her subsequent excavations at the Presle sites (Trou du Renard, Trou des Nutons, Trou du Docteur and the Trou de l'Ossuaire) revealed numerous traces of human use and habitation. Most notable amongst these was an archaeological layer of Lateglacial age found within the Trou de l'Ossuaire. It was from this that Danthine recovered 1753 worked flints (Leotard 1985a: 53).

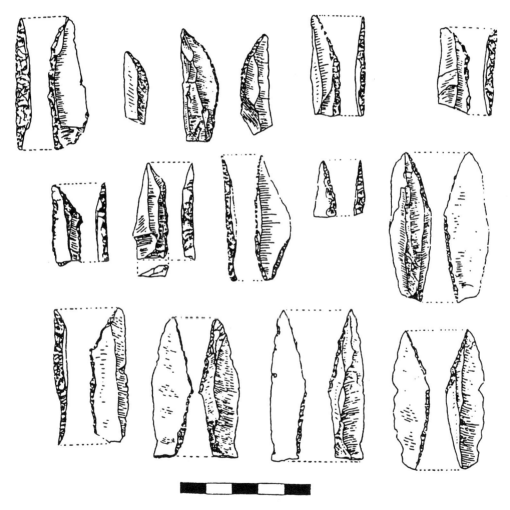

Fig. 6.3: Archaeological material from Presle (after Danthine 1955–60).

More recent excavations, instigated by Otte and Leotard in 1984, recovered further Lateglacial material. To date details of this research have only been published as interim reports (Leotard 1985b; Leotard and Otte 1985, 1988) and the final publication is in preparation. The archaeological collections from Presle are amongst the more substantial collections relating to the Belgian Upper Palaeolithic, and as such represent an important part of that country's Lateglacial heritage.

Only two radiocarbon age estimations have been linked with the Belgian *Creswellian*, both originating from the sites at Presle: Lv–1472 – 12,140±160 BP (Trou de l'Oussaire; Leotard 1985b: 132) and OxA–1344 – 10,950±200 BP (unattributed to site; Hedges *et al.* 1988: 294).

At face value, the lithics from Presle seem to give the one clear piece of evidence for a Creswellian/Cheddarian presence in Belgium. The assemblages are unquestionably Lateglacial and those from at least two of the sites, the Trou de L'Ossuaire and the Trou du Docteur, contain both curved backed and angle-backed elements (Fig. 6.3). Pieces which can clearly be recognised as *Cheddar* and *Creswell points* are present and butts *én éperon* were noted by Leotard amongst the blades he refitted (Leotard 1985a: 61).

However, there are numerous problems which form a bar to the interpretation of material recovered from these sites. From a technological viewpoint, there are strong hints that the material from Presle has at least some affinities with the local Magdalenian: a microlithic element is present and *burins de Lacam* are recorded by Leotard (1985a: 75). Both J-M. Leotard and R.M. Jacobi (pers. comm.) have indicated that they suspect the collections from the Trou de l'Ossuaire may not be the result of a single human occupation (see Leotard 1985a: 52, 108, 159–184), and both have suggested independently that there may be a mixing of both Magdalenian and Creswellian/Cheddarian material at this site.

As defined above, the Creswellian/Cheddarian is similar to the Magdalenian in many ways, but lacks certain *fossiles directeurs*, such as the *burin de Lacam*, as well as a microlithic component. Both of these can be found within the assemblage from the Trou de l'Ossuaire which is thought to have come from within a single discrete layer. Similarly Creswell and Cheddar points may occur in assemblages which are not Creswellian/Cheddarian (including the Magdalenian) – it is the predominance of them which is important. Added to this is the question of whether the collection should be treated as a single assemblage, or as a palimpsest.

There is also confusion about the exact provenance of at least some of the lithics which have been ascribed to both the Trou du Docteur and the Trou de l'Ossuaire (Charles 1994: 74). It cannot be assumed that the Lateglacial use of these sites was contemporaneous, let alone contemporary, and at present there is little to indicate how many different human groups, on how many occassions might used this complex of sites. Accordingly, it seems appropriate to ask whether one is justified in recognising the Creswellian/Cheddarian (or any other Lateglacial group) at Presle on the basis of what may well be a palimpsest incorporating material from more than one locality?

Turning to the radiocarbon evidence, it is difficult to argue that either of the existing radiocarbon dates gives much (if any) information directly relating to any Lateglacial techno-complex. If the lithic assemblage from Presle is a mixture of both

Magdalenian and Creswellian/Cheddarian, then neither of the dates mentioned above can tell us much about either group.

Lv–1472 (12,140±160 BP) does fall within the range of British dates for the Creswellian/Cheddarian, but there is little to directly link it with human activity at the site; OxA–1344 (10,950±200 BP) is at least a millennium after the time band usually associated with the Creswellian/Cheddarian. This discrepancy might be explained at least in part by the fact that the date was on an unmodified mandible of red deer and, as Professor Otte commented (Hedges *et al.* 1988: 294), its association with any archaeological assemblage may be suspect. In fact, it is likely that this date simply gives biostratigraphic information about the local occurrence of red deer during the Lateglacial.

Even if there were no questions as to a mixing of archaeological assemblages of potentially different ages, a bulked conventional date on bones and bone fragments can have little reliability even when in broad agreement with prior expectations (*cf.* Charles 1996). This very point is underlined by the two and a quarter page listing in Leotard's thesis (1985a: 110–112) of the individual bones and bone fragments, with find numbers and depth, submitted to make up Lv–1472. The material has a vertical range between 87 and 146 cm, across an area of 5 m². Sadly, no identifications to either element or species are available, and we must assume that the 75 specimens listed by Leotard were all unidentified bone fragments (*ibid.*: 112).

Overall, the significance of the Lateglacial archaeology from Presle remains unclear. The use of at least two of the caves during the Lateglacial, and the subsequent confusion over the precise provenance of many of the finds complicates matters. Leotard suggested that the lithics recovered in 1904 from the Trou du Docteur could be treated as a single coherent assemblage and saw affinities between this and material collected from Maldegem (Leotard 1985a: 178; originally described as *Creswellian* or *Creswello-Hamburgian*, but viewed here as *Federmesser*, see below), as well as recognising parallels between the 1950–60: 1983 and 1984 collections and the Magdalenian (*ibid.*: 180–181). Differences were also noted. The material from Presle was also compared by Leotard with the British Creswellian/Cheddarian and close analogues were found with Campbell's *Lower Creswellian* (Campbell 1980), alongside differences (*ibid.*: 185–186) between the points from Presle and those from Britain. Finally he suggested that at least three separate human groups used the caves at Presle during the Lateglacial – one during a cold period (suggested as Dryas I) based on the presence of a cache of female reindeer antlers (for an alternative interpretation of such accumulations of antler see Murray *et al.* 1993), another represented by the material from the Trou du Docteur found in 1904, and a third discrete group from the Trou de l'Ossuaire (*ibid.*: 188–189).

Whilst it is certainly possible that at least part of the archaeological collection from Presle is Creswellian/Cheddarian, I concur with Jacobi and Leotard that there is also material which clearly suggests a Magdalenian presence at a number of the sites, although I can see no clear basis for identifying a third group. As matters stand, the confusion over provenance and the possibility of palimpsests stand as bars to any detailed interpretation of the lithic assemblages recovered from Presles. It is hoped that the final report on this research will address the problems outlined here and clarify matters.

Obourg «Bois de St. Macaire»
This is an open air site located on the crest of a hill overlooking the confluence of the
rivers Haine and Obreceuil (Letocart 1970). Shouldered points are present (*ibid.*: Tafel
111, nos. 1–4), as are curved backed (*ibid.*: Tafel 111, nos. 7–16) and angle-backed
pieces (*ibid.*: Tafel 113, nos. 1–14). Alongside these are figured tranchet arrowheads
(*ibid.*: Tafel 113, nos. 23, 26 and 27) and a number of pieces which do not appear to
be characteristically Upper Palaeolithic in form.

Letocart suggested that the material was Late Upper Palaeolithic, and that the
Magdalenian would seem to be the most likely ascription (1970: 359). Subsequently,
however, it has appeared as a *Creswellian* dot on Lateglacial distribution maps (*e.g.*
Otte 1984). Whilst there are clearly Upper Palaeolithic elements in the collection, there
is nothing that certainly links it to the Lateglacial, let alone identifies it as either
Creswellian/Cheddarian or Magdalenian.

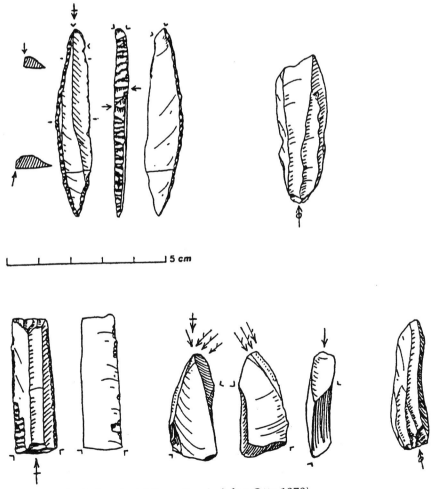

Fig. 6.4: Archaeological material from Orroir (after Otte 1979).

Orroir «Mont de l'Enclus»

One relatively obscure publication describes the lithics recovered by two amateur archaeologists (R. Putman and G. Coulon) from an unstratified context somewhere on the Mont de l'Enclus (Otte 1979). Since the 1979 publication, the locality has become a fixed point on distribution maps of the Belgian Creswellian. There are no radiocarbon dates associated with any of the finds from Orroir. The published illustrations (Otte 1979; Fig. 6.4) do not show any distinctive *fossiles directeurs* of the Creswellian/Cheddarian. Indeed, the curved backed point bears a striking resemblance to a *Tjonger point*. Otte commented (1979: 197) that there are some similarities between this specimen and a Châtelperronian point. However, this possible affiliation is ruled out, and instead a Lateglacial affinity seems to have been thought the most likely ascription (*ibid.*). The argument was that the piece is not really a Magdalenian type fossil, instead being more reminiscent of the Azilian. However, Otte notes (*ibid.*) that there are no other traces of the Azilian from Belgium, and so excludes this possibility. The question of whether the find might relate to the Creswellian/Cheddarian is also discussed, and similarities are drawn between the Orroir point and specimens from Presle. The Federmesser (Tjongerian) is considered briefly, but it is suggested that the "technique" used in point manufacture differs between the Orroir point and other Tjonger points (although the nature of these differences is not made clear). Otte's conclusion is that the Orroir point has affinities with both the British Creswellian/Cheddarian and the Belgian Tjongerian; the links are seen as being strongest with the Creswellian, more specifically a subset of material he refers to as Cheddarian! The reason for this line of argument only becomes clear, once it is realised that Otte, writing in 1979, was naturally following the finegrained evolutionary progression suggested for the British Lateglacial by Campbell (1977: 189).

Otte compared the Orroir piece with penknife points from sites such as Mother Grundy's Parlour at Creswell Crags; whilst this comparision seems perfectly valid, this does not make the material Creswellian/Cheddarian. Indeed, Jacobi (pers. comm.) specifically excludes the penknife points from Mother Grundy's Parlour as being a part of the Creswellian/Cheddarian *sensu stricto*.

At this point in the discussion it seems worthwhile to outline the basic premises of Campbell's (1977 and 1980) seriation of the Creswellian. This suggested a tripartite division of the chronology of the British Lateglacial based partly on typology. This proposed an earlier *Creswell point phase*, followed by a *penknife point phase* which was succeeded by a *transitional to mesolithic phase*; it is the *penknife point* phase with which Otte drew a parallel. This material is now thought to fall outside the Creswellian/Cheddarian *sensu stricto*, and since Campbell's pioneering research it has become apparent that where material associated with penknife points has been radiocarbon dated it has been shown to post-date the Bölling Interstadial phase. Recent AMS work by both R.M. Jacobi and R.N.E. Barton indicates that the Cheddar and penknife point phases do indeed appear to be chronologically distinct from each other, and accordingly that the typological progression proposed by Campbell is valid in this instance. However, this *penknife point phase* cannot now be regarded as an integral part of the Creswellian/Cheddarian, but rather as a separate and independent entity.

Consequently, the suggestion that the material from Orroir could be linked to the *Creswellian* cannot now be supported. It would in any case be extremely difficult to make suggestions about the cultural designation of such a small assemblage, but it is also clear that this material lacks both the distinctive Creswell and Cheddar points. The Orroir backed point does bear a strong resemblance to a penknife point and as such is viewed here as part of the *Federmesser*.

The Belgian Creswellian 'variants': the "Creswello-Tjongerian" and the "Creswello-Hamburgian"

These are an apparently recent addition to the archaeological pantheon, and at first sight their occurrences appear to be contained within the borders of Belgium. The terms have been used by researchers to describe certain Belgian Upper Palaeolithic assemblages (see, for example, Otte 1984 and Dewez 1987). The term *Creswello-Tjongerian* is usually applied to assemblages which appear to be "like" the Tjongerian (Federmesser), but which lack the Tjonger *fossiles directeurs*. Similarly, those assemblages which are seen as "like" the Hamburgian, but are again lacking the appropriate *fossiles directeurs*, are classified as *Creswello-Hamburgian*. The general composition of the industries so described appears to involve an element of angle-backed pieces, and various forms atypical of the other Lateglacial technocomplexes such as the Creswellian, Hamburgian, and Magdalenian. It is surprising to find an archaeological culture which respects modern day political boundaries; however, if one accepts the *Creswello-Tjongerian* and *Creswello-Hamburgian* at face value, this is precisely what happens. If one begins to look in detail at the precise make up of assemblages classified in this way, one begins to run into even greater problems than with those Belgian assemblages simply referred to as Creswellian.

Maldegem

A good example of the problems of typological definition outlined above is the open air site of Maldegem, to the south-east of Brugge. The site is located on the border of the Flemish valley and the Oedelem hills. Published in 1984 (Otte *et al.* 1984), the lithic assemblage was suggested to have affinities with both the *Creswellian* and the Hamburgian, and so was designated *Creswello-Hamburgian*.

Amongst the lithics from the site are 2 possible Creswell points, 2 possible *Hamburg* points, 14 fragmented backed pieces, 6 burins, 24 scrapers, 6 blade cores and 128 pieces of debitage (Otte *et al.* 1984: 114–5). Two shouldered pieces are illustrated in this publication. One of these may be a Creswell point; the other, which is suggested to be a Hamburg point, is certainly shouldered but defies any further classification. Of the other three backed pieces, two are broken. The only complete backed piece is undiagnostic. Butt preparation *en éperon* is not reported. There seems to be little reason to give any more detailed ascription to this material than that of *Federmesser*. The assemblage is small and, as with many other sites already discussed, lacks any clear *fossiles directeurs*. The suggestion that the material has affinities with the Creswellian and/or Hamburgian seems to reflect the actual situation, namely that the material can only be grouped within the broad class *Federmesser* rather than being given any more detailed designation.

Grotte Walou

A claimed *Creswello-Tjongerian* site, only preliminary reports are currently available for the Grotte Walou (Dewez 1986 and 1992) and excavation is still in progress by a multidisciplinary team. It is a collapsed cave near the small village of Trooz in the valley of the river Magne.

The main evidence for human occupation of the site is a series of Upper Perigordian layers, underlain by what appears to be a Mousterian sequence (in the initial stages of excavation); there are small pockets of Lateglacial deposits at the top of the cave sequence, which have yielded lithic material (Dewez pers. comm.). The lithic material from the Creswello-Tjongerian units at this site are said to include flakes, blades and backed pieces, most probably of Lateglacial age. To date, no illustrations of the material are available and so no comment on typology or technology can be made here.

More recently, three radiocarbon dates have been published from the site (Dewez 1992) and are presented in Table 6.1. It is difficult to discuss dates in detail when so little is known about the nature and exact occurrence of the dated sample, or indeed the archaeology of the site as a whole.

The one date assigned to the Creswellian is early Postglacial, whereas in the traditional "heartland" of the Creswellian (Britain) the latter is usually dated to the Bölling Interstadial phase of the Lateglacial Interstadial. The dated material is descibed as being "débris osseux" and must be subject to all the usual problems of bulk sampling. It remains unclear what, if any, its relationship to any archaeological residues might have been.

Table 6.1: Lateglacial radiocarbon dates from the Trou Walou.

Lab code	Date	Cultural ascription	Material dated
Lv–1556	9990±160 BP	Creswellian	"débris osseux'
Lv–1582	13,030±140 BP	Magdalenian	"débris osseux"
Lv–1593	13,120±190 BP	Magdalenian	"débris osseux"

The two Magdalenian dates cited carry with them the same problems of association. It is interesting to note that both Lv–1582 and Lv–1593 fall into Dryas I rather than the Bölling, and appear to predate accelerator dates from Belgian Magdalenian contexts (*cf.* Charles 1996) making them the earlist evidence for human settlement of this region after the Last Glacial Maximum; however, until further sample details are available they cannot be treated as reliable dates for the earliest human re-colonisation of this area of western Europe.

After extensive discussions with colleagues working on the Belgian Upper Palaeolithic, it became apparent that, rather than representing an archaeological culture, in any sense of the word, the terms *Creswello-Tjongerian* or *Creswello-Hamburgian* were generally used as a shorthand for any undiagnostic, but apparently Lateglacial flint assemblages. The terms have only been used to describe relatively small assemblages. This being the case, the immediate abandonment of these terms is advocated here, as they will simply lead to confusion. Meanwhile, any discussion of spatial and temporal distribution of the *Creswello-Tjongerian/Creswello-Hamburgian* is meaningless.

Does the Belgian Creswellian exist?

There appear to be numerous problems surrounding the Belgian Creswellian, not least of which are basic problems of classification. At present the only sites which seem at all likely to have had a clear Creswellian component *sensu stricto* are the caves at Presle. Even here, the situation is far from clear cut. If the true Creswellian is present in Belgium, then it is far more restricted than has been suggested in the literature. During my recent work on the Belgian Lateglacial, I have found it increasingly difficult to identify any distinctive Creswellian collections. The vast majority of assemblages suggested as either Creswellian, Creswello-Tjongerian or Creswello-Hamburgian are composed of a small number of backed pieces, only a few of which appear to be diagnostic in any way. Where larger broadly contemporary assemblages have been found, these are almost always readily classifiable as Magdalenian, Federmesser (Tjongerian) or Ahrensburgian.

Perhaps at this point one should ask not simply whether material which is clearly Creswellian/Cheddarian exits in Belgium, but whether such culture-historical terms continue to be useful within the current framework of Upper Palaeolithic research. The material which Jacobi termed *Cheddarian* certainly seems to form a coherent unit within the framework of the British Upper Palaeolithic sequence, but what, if any, is its relationship with contemporaneous material from mainland Europe?

During the Bölling Interstadial phase Britain was not an island (Preece 1995) but rather an extension of mainland Europe. The human groups who left behind residues of their material culture (which archaeologists now term Creswellian and Magdalenian) in Benelux, western France and Britain during the Bölling had extensive exchange networks (*cf.* Bahn 1982 and Charles 1994) implying various forms of interaction and alliance (*cf.* Gamble 1982, 1986, 1993). There is little doubt that individuals and the social groups of which they were a part were in touch with each other, and that ideas and innovations were shared and transmitted to varying extents between these groups.

Consequently what we see in the archaeological record for this period is a reflection of the common pool of ideas (Gamble 1982) intermixed with the external trappings of both group and individual identity (Wobst 1977; Weissner 1983, 1984). The archaeological database currently available for the Lateglacial in north-western Europe is intrinsically biased by both taphonomy and the excavation and survey strategies of previous researchers. We are, in effect, looking at only a part of the overall picture, which may be distorted by a whole range of factors, the majority of which are beyond our current control. In other words, we are looking at 'islands' of material culture which appear within a 'sea' of unknowns. Perhaps, rather than examining discrete archaeological entities within this region, we are instead dealing with a spectrum of variability, part functional and part chronological, together with the intrinsic variability produced as part of the negotiation of both individual and group identity on the part of Lateglacial hunter-gatherers.

The supposedly Creswellian material discussed here is typical of much of the archaeological data of this time and region. It is characterised by the presence of certain types of backed points. Regional subdivisons of material based on perceived different 'styles' of these backed points, using terms such as *Creswellian* and *Magdalenian* may well serve as much to disguise the continuous nature of regional variability as to explain it. It may well be that the problems of definition and classification encountered within this paper are a function of looking at archaeological material from the periphery/boundary of perceived archaeological entities, rather than looking at material from its 'core' region. Perhaps the time has come to re-examine our perceived boundaries between these Lateglacial groups beyond the framework of technology and typology. Approaches looking at the transport and scale of raw material procurement, the diversity and/or standardisation of butchery practice and the different kinds of spatial (and also social) organisation of the campsites of these Late Pleistocene hunter-gatherers might provide just such opportunities, whilst freeing researchers from an over-restrictive view of culture-history.

Acknowledgements

I would like to thank Marc de Bie, Roger Jacobi, Nick Barton, John Mitchell and Derek Roe, who all made valuable comments on issues discussed in this paper. Much of the research reported here was undertaken whilst the author held a British Academy Major State Studentship, additional support being given by Christ Church and The Queen's College, Oxford.

Bibliography

Bahn, P.G. 1982. Inter-site and inter-regional links during the Upper Palaeolithic: The Pyrenean evidence. *Oxford Journal of Archaeology* 1 (3): 247–268.

Barton, R.N.E. 1990. The *en éperon* technique in the British Late Upper Palaeolithic. *Lithics* 11: 3–33.

Bohmers, A. 1947. Jong-Palaeolithicum en Vroeg-Mesolithicum. In A.E. van Giffen Gedenkboek (Ed.) *Oudheidkundig Bodemonderzoek in Nederland*, pp. 108–201. Meppel.

Bohmers, A. 1956. Statistics and graphs in the study of flint assemblages. *Palaeohistoria* 5: 1–25.

Burdukiewicz, J.M. 1986. *The late Pleistocene shouldered point assemblages in western Europe*. Leiden: E.J. Brill.

Campbell, J.B. 1977. *The Upper Palaeolithic of Britain: a study of man and nature in the late Ice Age.* 2 vols. Oxford: Clarendon Press.

Campbell, J.B. 1980. Le Problème des subdivisions du Paléolithique Supérieur Britannique dans son cadre Européen. *Bulletin de la Société Royale Belge d'Anthropologue et Préhistoire* 91: 39–77.

Charles, R. 1994. *Food for Thought: Late Magdalenian chronology and faunal exploitation in the north-western Ardennes*. Unpublished D.Phil dissertation, University of Oxford.

Charles, R. 1996. Back into the North: The radiocarbon chronology for the human re-colonisation of the north-western Ardennes after the Last Glacial Maximum. *Proceedings of the Prehistoric Society* 61: 1–17.

Charles, R. and R.M. Jacobi 1994. Lateglacial faunal exploitation at the Robin Hood Cave, Creswell Crags. *Oxford Journal of Archaeology* 13 (1): 1–32.

Danthine, H. 1955–60. Fouilles dans un gisement préhistorique du Domaine de Presle: rapport preliminaire. *Documents et Rapports de la Société Royale d'Archéologie et de Paléontologie de Charleroi* 50: 1–39.

Debaille, E. 1945. Grottes de Presles: Industries Aurignaciennes. *Documents et Rapports de la Société Royale d'Archéologie et de Paléontologie de l'arrondissement judiciare de Charleroi* 45: 9–14.

Debaille, E., and L. Foulon 1926. Rapport sur les fouilles effectuées en 1904 dans les Grottes de Presles. *Documents et Rapports de la Société Royale d'Archéologie et de Paléontologie de l'arrondissement judiciare de Charleroi* 37: 3–24.

Demars, P-Y., and P. Laurent 1989. *Types d'outils lithiques du Paléolithique Supérieur en Europe.* Bordeaux: CNRS Cahiers du Quaternaire 14.

Dewez, M. 1977. Neue Grabungen in der Höhle von Martinrive (Prov. Lüttich, Belgien). *Archäologisches Korrespondenzblatt* 7 (2): 89–93.

Dewez, M. 1977–79. Le probleme du paléolithique supérieur à la quatrième Grotte d'Engis. *Bulletin de la Société Royale Belge d'études Géologiques et Archéologiques «Les Chercheurs de la Wallonie»* 24: 131–145.

Dewez, M. 1986. Campagnes de Fouilles 1985–1986 à la Grotte Walou (Trooz, Province de Liège). *Notae Praehistoricae* 6: 115.

Dewez, M. 1987. *Le Paléolithique Supérieur Récent dans les Grottes de Belgique.* Louvain-la-Neuve, Publications d'Histoire de l'Art et d'Archéologie de l'Université Catholique de Louvain LVII.

Dewez, M. 1992. La Grotte Walou à Trooz (Province de Liège, Belgique), presentation du site. In Toussaint, M. (Ed.), *Cinq Millions d'années, l'Aventure Humaine,* pp. 311–318. Liège, Etudes et Recherches Archéologiques de l'Université de Liège.

Doudou, E. 1903. *Explorations scientifiques dans les cavernes, les abîmes et les trous qui fument de la Province de Liège.* Liège, Thone.

Garrod, D.A.E. 1926a. The Upper Palaeolithic Age in Britain. *Proceedings of the University of Bristol Spelaeological Society (for 1925)* 2 (3): 299–301.

Garrod, D.A.E. 1926b. *The Upper Palaeolithic Age in Britain.* Oxford: Clarendon Press.

Gamble, C.S. 1982. Interaction and alliance in Palaeolithic society. *Man (N.S.)* 17: 92–107.

Gamble, C.S. 1986. *The Palaeolithic settlement of Europe.* (Cambridge, Cambridge University Press).

Gamble, C.S. 1993. *Timewalkers: The Prehistory of Global Colonisation.* London: Alan Sutton.

Hedges, R.E.M., Housley, R.A., Law, I.A., Perry, C., and E. Hendy 1988. Radiocarbon dates from the Oxford AMS system: *Archaeometry* datelist 8. *Archaeometry* 30 (2): 291–305.

Jacobi R.M. 1986. The Lateglacial Archaeology of Gough's Cave at Cheddar. In S.N. Collcutt (Ed.) *The Palaeolithic of Britain and its nearest neighbours: recent trends,* pp. 75–79. Sheffield: Dept. of Archaeology and Prehistory, University of Sheffield.

Jacobi, R.M. 1991. The Creswellian, Creswell and Cheddar. In Barton, N., Roberts, and Roe, D.A. (Eds.) *The Late Glacial in north-west Europe: human adaptation and environmental change at the end of the Pleistocene,* pp. 128–140. London: CBA Research report 77.

Jaques, V. 1899. Rapport sur le travail de M. Doudou sur de nouvelles fouilles dans les cavernes d'Engis. *Bulletin de la Société d'Anthropologie de Bruxelles* 18: LII.

Leotard, J.-M. 1985a. *Le Paléolithique superieur final des grottes de Presle.* Memoir de Licence presented to the Faculty of Philosophy and Letters, Art History, Archaeology and Musicology section, University of Liège. 216pp.

Leotard, J.-M. 1985b. Le Paléolithique superieur final des grottes de Presle (Aiseau). *Notae Praehistoricae* 5: 131–132.

Leotard, J.-M., and M. Otte 1985. Fouilles au site "Creswellien" de Presle (Hainaut). *Notae Praehistoricae* 5: 33–35.

Leotard J.-M., and M. Otte 1988. Occupation Paléolithique Final aux Grottes de Presle: fouilles de 1983–4 (Aiseau – Belgique. Pl. 1). In M. Otte (Ed.) *De la Loire à l'Oder: les civilisations du Paléolithique final dans le nord-ouest européen*, pp. 189–215. Oxford: British Archaeological Reports International Series S444 (1).

Letocart, L. 1970. Un Gisement du Paléolithique Final à Oburg "St. Macaire" (Hainault). Gripp, K., Schütrumpf, R. and H. Schwabedissen (Eds.) *Frühe Menschheit und Umwelt: Archäologische Beiträge* 1: 352–361.

Lohest, M, Hamal-Nandrin, J., Servais, J., and Ch. Fraipont 1922. La Grotte de Martinrive. *Revue Anthropologique* 32: 349–355.

Murray, N.A., Bonsall, C., Sutherland, D.G., Lawson, T.J., and A.C. Kitchener 1993. Further radiocarbon determinations on reindeer remains of Middle and Late Devensian age from the Creag Nan Uamh caves, Assynt, NW Scotland. *Quaternary Newsletter* 70: 1–10.

Otte, M. 1979. Documents du Paléolithique superieur au Mont de L'Enclus (Orroir, Hainault). *Paléontologie et Préhistoire. Bulletin de la Société Tournaisienne de Géologie, Préhistoire et Archéologie* 38: 195–199.

Otte, M. 1984. Paléolithique Supérieur en Belgique. In Cahen, D. and Haesaerts, P. (Eds.), *Peuples Chasseurs de la Belgique Préhistorique dans leur Cadre Naturel*, pp. 157–197. Bruxelles: Institut Royale des Sciences Naturelles de Belgique.

Otte, M., Vandermoere, N., Heyse, I., and J.-M. Léotard 1984. Maldegem et le Paléolithique récent du nord-ouest Européen. *Helinium* 24: 104–126.

Preece, R.C. (Ed.) 1995. *Island Britain: a Quaternary perspective*. London: The Geological Society Special Publication 96.

Rasquin, L. de 1910. La Caverne Funéraire d'Engis: nouvelles fouilles. *Société Belge de Spéléologie et de Préhistoire avec section de vulgarisation scientifique «Les Chercheurs de la Wallonie»* 4: 186-195.

Schwabedissen, H. 1954. *Die Federmesser-Gruppen des nord-westeuropäischen Flachlandes zur Ausbreitung des Spät-Magdalénien*. Neumünster: Wachholtz.

Toussaint, M., Cordy, J-M., Dewez, M., and G. Toussaint 1979. Le gisement Paléolithique final de la Caverne du Bois de la Saute (Prov. de Namur). *Société Wallone de Palethnologie Memoire* 1.

Toussaint, M., and G. Toussaint 1983. Le Paléolithique supérieur final de la caverne du Bois de la Saute (Province de Namur, Belgique). *Bulletin de la Société Préhistorique Française* 80 (3): 88–93.

Wiessner, P. 1983. Style and social information in Kalahari !San projectile points. *American Antiquity* 48: 253–276.

Wiessner, P. 1984. Reconsidering the behavioural basis for style. *Journal of Anthropological Archaeology* 3: 190–234.

Wobst, M. 1977. Stylistic behaviour and information exchange. *University of Michigan Museum of Archaeology Papers* 61: 217–242.

LE DOCTEUR MORLET PASSE A L'OFFENSIVE

Il nous révèle des faits graves et met en cause la procédure de la Commission d'enquête

Comme nous le disions hier, le docteur Morlet ne s'est pas incliné devant les conclusions du rapport de la commission d'enquête — qui infirme l'authenticité du gisement de Glozel, tout en reconnaissant que certaines pièces qui y figurent peuvent être authentiques.

Le docteur Morlet se prépare à protester publiquement, par une ré-

Miss Garod

~~~se qui sera publiée dans quel-
~~~ jours. En attendant des préci-

une garantie, et qui avait été l'un des promoteurs de la commission d'enquête.

Deux faits graves
sur lesquels il faut la lumière

En outre, le docteur Morlet accuse personnellement l'un des membres de la commission, Miss Garod, d'avoir, par des manœuvres frauduleuses, essayé de jeter la suspicion sur le gisement de Glozel. Cependant qu'elle opérait les fouilles, elle aurait, en effet, pratiqué sur le terrain des sortes de trous profonds, de manière à laisser croire qu'on s'en était servi pour introduire dans le « Champ des morts » les objets qu'on y découvrait par la suite.

Prise en flagrant délit, et amenée devant témoins, Miss Garod du faire le pénible aveu de sa fraude. Et, depuis ce moment, elle ne put continuer à travailler que sous la surveillance de trois assistants bénévoles dont on cite les noms.

En outre, affirme le docteur Morlet, un autre membre de la commission internationale, M. Peyrony, aurait, à l'aide de la lame d'acier d'un canif, maquillé le dessin d'un renne gravé sur une pierre. Ceci pour prouver que ces dessins n'avaient pas l'ancienneté que les glozéliens leur attribuaient... Un témoin — le docteur Morlet le nomme, le professeur Tofroli — aurait surpris cette manœuvre...

Autre fait invoqué par l-

Figure 7.1: Article [La Querelle de Glozel] from L'Écho de Paris, 27 February 1927, quoting Morlet's outburst.

7

Garrod and Glozel: The End of a Fiasco

Paul Bahn and Colin Renfrew

"...a more improbable collection of objects one could not imagine." (Dorothy Garrod)

Introduction

One of the most notorious episodes in Dorothy Garrod's illustrious career was her involvement in the International Commission that investigated the claims about the French site of Glozel. This is not the place to present a full account of the story of that site – readers are referred to the fundamental articles by Crawford (1927) and Vayson de Pradenne (1930). Suffice it to say that the finds at Glozel constitute one of the most famous and most curious cases of fakery in the history of archaeology.

In the late 1920s an amazing assemblage of objects – badly-made pseudo-Ice Age carvings and tools, pseudo-Bronze Age pots, and fired-clay tablets bearing a non-existent script – emerged from a single field on a farm near Vichy. 'Glozelians' claimed them to represent a hitherto-unknown civilisation, while 'anti-Glozelians' dismissed the whole thing as a fraud. The International Commission, which included such luminaries of the time as Peyrony, Pittard, Hamal-Nandrin and Bosch Gimpera, as well as Garrod, investigated and produced a negative verdict amid claims that they themselves had salted the site with fakes to discredit the owners. Half-made objects were discovered in the local farm, and a court case ensued, in which the young farmer, Emile Fradin, was eventually acquitted through benefit of doubt. However, Garrod and the other members of the commission had no doubts as to who had made the forgeries (see Garrod 1968).

The story then died down until the 1970s when the new dating technique of Thermoluminescence was applied to some fired-clay tablets from the site and produced a bewildering array of results, some between 700 BC and AD 100, which resurrected the controversy (see Daniel 1992, *passim*). These TL results have never been fully explained or published, and the whole affair has been left unresolved: to almost all archaeologists, Glozel is an impossibility, a fiasco, but the lunatic fringe see themselves as champions of the site against the blinkered dogma of orthodoxy.

Continuing calumnies

Most French prehistorians maintain an embarrassed silence about the whole affair – it is noticeably absent from the vast majority of books on French prehistory, even though the site's museum is under the aegis of the regional archaeological service and official signposts direct tourists to the museum, which is frequently visited by school parties. Yet a couple of scholars have been courageous enough to speak out: the entry on the site in Leroi-Gourhan's *Dictionnaire de la Préhistoire* has cast doubt on the site, calling it a "faux archéologique probable" (Demoule 1994: 449), without actually branding it a fake; whereas Jean-Pierre Adam, in two books (1975, 1988), has openly derided the site and its finds – for example placing drawings of its crude 'harpoons' next to the real thing from the Magdalenian, and pointing out that the Glozel harpoons could not have harmed an elderly arthritic carp. Most recently, a well researched article in a popular science magazine has declared the site a fake, though still falls short of daring to name the hoaxer (Chauveau 1997).

The scandal is that, apart from these lone protesters, it is the 'Glozelians' whose voices have been heard most loudly in recent times. For example, in the *Dictionnaire Archéologique de la France* (Editions Atlas, 1990, vol. 1, A to H), an anonymous article (pp. 283–9) presents an entirely favourable account of the site, especially in its captions. Books continue to appear including a recent glossy hardback, with beautiful colour photographs of the finds (Liris *et al.* 1994), dedicated to Fradin – but it takes more than colour plates to validate this dubious material, and the Glozel 'finds' look, if anything, even more clumsy and ugly in glorious colour close-ups.

Even worse, France's leading popular magazine of archaeology, *Archéologia*, not only devoted a positive edition to the site in 1983 with the disgraceful title of "Glozel: L'Affaire Dreyfus de l'Archéologie" (Les Dossiers Histoire et Archéologie, No. 74, June/July), but has even published Fradin's own memoirs (Fradin 1990), in which, naturally, all is painted as if the site were authentic, and all doubters are assigned a variety of nefarious reasons for their antagonism (*e.g.* Peyrony feared the field would become a bigger tourist attraction than Les Eyzies [sic], Capitan wanted to buy the field but was thwarted, Vayson de Pradenne failed to buy the finds, and so on).

One of the worst calumnies ever perpetrated by the Glozelians was the claim that, during the investigation by the International Commission, Garrod was caught red-handed, doctoring the site so as to introduce fakes and hence produce a negative verdict. What actually happened was set out in detail by Garrod herself in a handwritten statement (subsequently published in Ponsonnard 1984: 41–2), and later in a published article (1968). Her version was fully confirmed by other members of the commission such as Bosch-Gimpera. She was sent on ahead, on the morning of 7 November 1927, to check the complicated system of markers which had been left on the section the previous evening to ensure that nothing was disturbed. It was while she was checking this pattern left in the commission's powdering of plaster that Dr Morlet, the site's main excavator and protagonist, came upon her and furiously accused her of having tampered with the section and made a hole in it – in fact, a small piece of plaster had fallen, but there was no hole.

All those present confirmed that Morlet admitted before the whole commission that a misunderstanding had taken place, and the incident ended with a handshake – Morlet himself saying, "Voulez-vous, Mademoiselle, que tout soit oublié et que nous nous serrions la main?" (letter from Hamal-Nandrin, and testimony of Bosch-Gimpera, in Ponsonnard 1984: 37; 44). Yet the publication of the Commission's negative report led a furious Morlet to go on the offensive (in every sense) and to break his word: in the *Echo de Paris* of 27 December 1927 (see Ponsonnard 1984: 72) he accused Garrod of having used "fraudulent manoeuvres" to cast suspicion on the site, by making deep holes which would make people think they had been used to insert objects intended for discovery. He even claimed that she had been "prise en flagrant délit" and that, brought before witnesses, Garrod had admitted her fraud....

Needless to say, these were outright and disgraceful lies, which led a whole series of eminent archaeologists including Breuil to write letters of protest against Morlet's lack of honour (some are reproduced in Ponsonnard 1984: 33–52). Yet Fradin's disciples continue to advance this false and malicious version of events (*e.g.* Torchet *et al.* 1978: 27); and, far worse, Fradin himself, in his memoirs, introduces this bogus story with the disgraceful words "l'invraisemblable histoire de ce petit chameau de Miss Garrod" (Fradin 1990: 110) – as mentioned above, this book was published by France's leading archaeological magazine which should be deeply ashamed of itself for the book as a whole and for this sentence in particular. Such libels have their effect – indeed, one of us (PB) heard a French prehistorian declare in public, only a few years ago, that Garrod was caught cheating at the site. Obviously, the mud of Glozel sticks, and Garrod's name must be cleared once and for all of this unworthy charge.

Sorting out the dates

The same applies to the TL dates – more than 20 years have now passed since it was claimed that they proved the site's authenticity, and it is high time that these results should be clarified and explained by the specialists involved. They fell into three groups – Gallo-Roman (11 dates), mediaeval (2) and 18th century (1). It should also be remembered that radiocarbon analysis of bones from the site in 1958 produced a date of around 17,000 years ago (taken from the carbon in 15 different bones!); another of about 2000 years ago, and some modern results. This means that the Glozelians now have to explain how a supposedly 'Neolithic' site should contain Palaeolithic bones and Gallo-Roman tablets, all bearing the same 'script'; how a culture that is totally unknown elsewhere somehow existed unchanged in a single field, the notorious 'Champ des Morts', for many millennia, but without leaving any trace of a dwelling or a hearth. For one of the most prominent features of the material from Glozel is its strange homogeneity, despite the incredible range of dates from the site...

Between 1983 and 1990, the French Ministry of Culture carried out a campaign of fieldwork and laboratory analysis to reach a conclusion about the site – in part because, disturbingly, far-right French nationalists had begun to use Glozel as evidence that Europeans, rather than the Semites of the Near East, invented writing and civilisation (Chauveau 1997: 104)! A summary report has appeared (Daugas *et al.* 1995), and results were also divulged in a television documentary on the channel Canal Plus in 1993. Among the more important points are the following:

(i) – the handful of sites peripheral to Glozel which were supposed to have yielded 'Glozelian' finds in the past were all found to contain absolutely nothing earlier than mediaeval and modern material.

(ii) – the only examples of 'Glozelian' objects found in the Champ des Morts itself in 1983 were in sediments that had been disturbed by early excavations or subsequently. Indeed, one half of a lamp was found, clearly inserted recently into the remains of a trench of 1974, while the other half was awaiting the investigators on the grass in front of their tent when they returned to camp for lunch (Chauveau 1997: 103).

(iii) – the investigation was unable to find an intact archaeological layer containing Glozelian objects *in situ*.

(iv) – pollen analysis reveals that the site's sediments date to the subatlantic period (*i.e.* the mediaeval period and the present), and excludes the presence of an environment corresponding to the Neolithic period, let alone to a Palaeolithic period featuring reindeer (which are supposedly depicted on some of the site's crude pseudo-Palaeolithic carvings).

(v) – physical and chemical analysis of the site's deposits shows that the absence of carbonates, the scarcity of calcium and the acid pH of all levels preclude the conservation of bones for any length of time. Hence, if any bones in the field are prehistoric in date, they must have been placed there far more recently.

New dates have been obtained by the Ministry of Culture whose report (Daugas *et al.* 1995) points out that the thermoluminescence technique is subject to great uncertainties at Glozel, where the level of background radioactivity is high and varies from place to place. Another possible source of error is the circumstance that most of the Glozel objects are very badly fired, while others seem to have been made from something bigger and already fired, such as a brick or tile.

Three samples were subjected to radiocarbon analysis; a fragment of a bone ring produced a result of AD 1310–1630; a piece of human femur gave AD 245–590; and a piece of charcoal from a fragment of terracotta with 'inscriptions' gave AD 975–1265 (which agrees with a TL date on the terracotta itself, AD 1350 + 125).

Nineteen new TL dates were obtained from Glozelian objects; they fall into four groups – the Iron Age/Gallo-Roman period; mediaeval; and modern (at least four, and probably six dates fall in the first half of the 20th century, which will come as no surprise to most archaeologists). Two of the latter are especially noteworthy, since they are tablets covered with Glozelian inscriptions and with a vitrified layer on top. They form part of a group of nine Glozelian objects, fired at a high temperature, that was found in one spot in the field by Morlet in 1929.

It is also noteworthy that despite the range of dates, no type of Glozelian object can be attributed to any particular phase. And it should be stressed that even if all the dates obtained so far are correct (and tests of TL on well-dated mediaeval and Gallo-Roman sherds from the region suggest that they may be), both methods are merely dating the raw materials, not necessarily the working of those materials.

It is known that the Gallo-Roman period is attested archaeologically in the region, but it is puzzling that, if the field were occupied in that period, absolutely no objects characteristic of the relevant culture (and no metalwork whatsoever) should be present. By contrast, mediaeval occupation is very evident in the region, and it is known that the field contained a mediaeval glassmaker's kiln, which could account for bricks/tiles from that period.

The Ministry of Culture therefore attributes what archaeological finds there were in the field to mediaeval times, and suggests that the Gallo-Roman dates (which come largely from the analyses undertaken in the 1970s) may have been assigned an excessively high age due to methodological factors. Both TL and radiocarbon have produced modern ages for material, while the fragment of a terracotta lamp found in the field had been broken and mended with a modern glue. Finally, as mentioned above, the geochemistry of the field makes it clear that the bone objects must have been buried there in recent times – they could not have survived more than a few decades in this acid soil.

The report's conclusions are thus that one must definitively reject the hypothesis of a prehistoric culture here; that the site has not produced the slightest evidence of Gallo-Roman occupation, other than the TL dates (whereas there are abundant remains of that period in the region). It therefore states that "l'hypothèse de manipulations modernes reste d'actualité" (Daugas *et al.* 1995: 259); but, reluctant to cry fraud, it hedges its bets by suggesting that perhaps there was an original collection of authentic material which was subsequently 'expanded' in order to increase its interest. This echoes the sentiment that the flagrantly fake Ice Age decorated cave of Zubialde, reported in Spain in 1991, may contain a couple of authentic drawings which then had a galaxy of ridiculous fakes added to them (Bahn 1996)!

Unfinished business for the archaeological scientist

If it is now accepted that the assemblage of remarkable objects from Glozel is not a coherent prehistoric assemblage – which we unhesitatingly do – and if it is further accepted that the 'writing' on the 'tablets' and the incised animals are modern, then one cannot escape the conclusion that they were concocted with intent to deceive. That was the view of Dorothy Garrod, and of other commentators at the time (Crawford 1927; Vayson de Pradenne 1930). There is no merit in avoiding the evident verdict that Glozel was a fraud, and that the entire collection was assembled, and in part manufactured, with intent to defraud. It follows that while such a collection might well include numerous genuine antiquities from other sites, and even possibly some genuine antiquities from the site itself, every piece in it must be viewed with that special suspicion which one reserves for fraudulent dealings. In particular, when fraud is in the air, not all testimonies are to be taken at face value.

But what is one to make of the extraordinary failure of the archaeological scientists back in the 1970s, and particularly the thermoluminescence specialists, to come to a clear conclusion on the matter? And of their continuing failure now to explain what went wrong? One of us (CR) vividly remembers the Archaeometry and Archaeological Prospection Symposium for 1975 held at Oxford at which a good number of professional archaeological scientists were evidently inclined, on the basis of a number of thermoluminescence dates, not only to uphold the authenticity of the assemblage (McKerrell *et al.* 1974, 1975, 1976), but in effect to belittle the views of those archaeologists who, on plain typological grounds, regarded the finds as fraudulent and questioned the implications of the thermoluminescence determinations (Renfrew 1975). There was no attempt by the archaeologists to question that TL dating was being carefully applied, and applied in good faith by competent scientists, but there was real concern that those scientists were, in some ways, out of their depth when it came to assessing the assemblage of finds as a whole. The episode is worth considering further, particularly because the apparent conflict which emerged at the time between the specific TL dates and the overall interpretation has never been resolved, although various archaeological scientists not immediately implicated with the TL dating have commented (Hall 1975, Aitken and Huxtable 1975, Peacock 1976).

As one of us (CR) wrote to his former Director of Studies (and current Editor of *Antiquity*) Glyn Daniel on Saturday March 23rd of that year:

"The Oxford Conference ended at midday today, and I thought I would write at once, before setting off to Greece early tomorrow morning.

On Thursday I arrived in time to hear Dr Mejdahl's presentation of his TL dates and of McKerrell's, followed by Stuart Fleming's. Mejdahl's three dates are 600, 730 and 680 BC. McKerrell's is now 280 AD. Fleming gives a date of 180 + 320 BC. In the discussion it was clear that the TL people feel that the dates are in good agreement.

Moreover, Fleming's tests seem to rule out re-radiation, and it was felt that the dates cannot be explained by high local radioactivity, or anything like that. Mejdahl showed a number of slides including the reindeer (which some Scandinavian biologist colleagues pronounce a 'genuine reindeer') and later a comparison of 'Old Semitic' and Glozel signs. He did not, however, pronounce too emphatically about the significance of these things, but there was throughout some tendency by the TL people to speak of 'genuine tablets'.

Immediately after, over sherry with Teddy Hall, I spoke with him and Mejdahl and Fleming, and my impression was that at that stage they were inclined to regard the Glozel material, or part of it, as genuine....

I gave my comments in the afternoon, quoting parts of your open letter, including your 4 possibilities, and your strictures that it is the archaeologists who should do the archaeology, not the scientists. I advanced my own view: 1) the TL analyses have to be accepted, 2) Glozel is a total fraud, 3) that the material for the tablets was indeed ancient and used by the faker to carve his nonsense signs. I also said that publication would be premature, and that speculation about iron age contacts seems so too."

The question then remains: what went wrong? Were the TL determinations themselves in error? Or had the fraudulent objects been made from ancient materials? Or had they been partially refired, or subject to re-radiation? We simply do not know. But given that, in the light of the investigations undertaken for the French Ministry of Culture, there is a well-argued consensus for the fraudulent nature of the Glozel finds, and thus the recent constitution of the assemblage (even if it may deliberately contain some ancient components), is it not now time that the TL specialists began to work out some of the answers? It is surely incumbent upon those who set out to investigate material which had been declared fraudulent nearly 50 years earlier, and who used their scientific techniques to declare it genuine, to explain to the archaeological and scientific world just exactly what went wrong.

Archaeological science has advanced a great deal since those relatively early days. There are now three Chairs of Archaeological Science in this country. With the enhanced maturity which all that should bring, is it not now time that this second Glozel affair – that of the brief but disturbing 'validation' of Glozel by the archaeological scientists in 1975 – was properly investigated? Of course the issue here is not what it was in 1927, namely fraud. But the 'inscribed clay tablets' which the TL specialists were invited to date were, in fact not of iron age date, nor of mediaeval date, they were manufactured in the 20th century. It is up to the archaeological scientist, asked to date an artefact whose authenticity is already doubted, to work out for himself that an ancient brick may bear a modern incision. The ghost of Glozel will not finally be exorcised until this second 'affaire Glozel' is decently disposed of.

Conclusion

Despite all the naive protestations and excuses of those who still cling tenaciously to a belief in Glozel, it really is appropriate to apply the principle of Occam's Razor: *i.e.* since it is proved that some of the objects are modern, since it is proved that the bones must have been recently introduced into the site, and since this extremely heterogeneous collection of disparate material does not belong to any known culture, and simply cannot span a period from the Palaeolithic (the date of 17,000 BP, the engravings of pseudo-reindeer) through the Neolithic to Gallo-Roman and mediaeval times, it is self-evident that the whole thing is a hoax or an imposture. It is profoundly sad that there are still people gullible enough to believe in this ill-assorted jumble of material, and to treat its crude carvings as beautiful works of art. The truth about Glozel was already clear in the late 1920s. The application of TL dating in the 1970s served only to muddy the waters and to encourage those who still clung to their belief in this phantom culture, this crude mirage – what Adam has called "la plus pitoyable mystification de l'histoire de l'archéologie". Seventy years on, it is time that the fraud was exposed and denounced once and for all, and that Dorothy Garrod should have her honour and reputation restored in the France she loved so much.

Bibliography

Adam, J-P. 1975. *L'Archéologie devant l'imposture*. Paris: Robert Laffont.

Adam, J-P. 1988. *Le Passé Recomposé. Chroniques d'archéologie fantasque*. Paris: Le Seuil.

Aitken, M.J. and Huxtable, J. 1975. Thermoluminescence and Glozel: a plea for caution. *Antiquity* 49: 223–226.

Bahn, P.G. 1996. Putting a brave face on a fake (review of book on the cave of Zubialde by J-M. Apellániz). *Cambridge Archaeological Journal* 6 (2): 309–310.

Chauveau, C. 1997. Les adorateurs de Glozel. *Science et Vie* No. 963 (December): 102–108.

Crawford, O.G.S. 1927. "L'affaire Glozel". *Antiquity* 1: 181–188.

Daniel, G.E. 1992. *Writing for Antiquity*. London: Thames and Hudson.

Daugas, J-P. *et al.* 1995. Résumé des recherches effectuées à Glozel, entre 1983 et 1990, sous l'égide du Ministère de la Culture. *Revue archéologique du Centre de la France* 34: 251–259.

Demoule, J-P. 1994. Glozel, in *Dictionnaire de la Préhistoire* (A. Leroi-Gourhan, Ed.), 2nd ed. Paris.

Fradin, E. 1990. *Glozel et ma Vie*. Dijon: Edition Archéologia.

Garrod, D. 1968. Recollections of Glozel. *Antiquity* 42: 172–177.

Hall, E.T. 1975. The Glozel affair. *Nature* 257: 355–356.

Liris, R. *et al.* 1994. *Glozel. Les Graveurs du Silence*. Orcines: Editions BCG Toscane.

McKerrell, H., Mejdahl, V., François, H., and G. Portal 1974. Thermoluminescence and Glozel. *Antiquity* 48: 265–272.

McKerrell, H., Mejdahl, V., François, H., and G. Portal 1975. Thermoluminescence and Glozel: a plea for patience. *Antiquity* 49: 267–272.

McKerrell, H., Mejdahl, V., François, H., and G. Portal 1976. Études sur Glozel. *Revue Archéologique du Centre* 57–58: 3–41.

Peacock, D.P.S. 1976. The petrography of certain Glozelian ceramics. *J. Archaeol. Science* 3: 271–273.

Ponsonnard, C. 1984. *Glozel par le petit bout de la lorgnette*. Le Mayet de Montagne: Les Amis de la Montagne Bourbonnaise.

Renfrew, C. 1975. Glozel and the Two Cultures. *Antiquity* 49: 219–222.

Torchet, N., Ferryn, P. and J. Gossart 1978. *L'Affaire de Glozel*. Marsat: Copernic.

Vayson de Pradenne, A. 1930. The Glozel forgeries. *Antiquity* 4: 201–222.

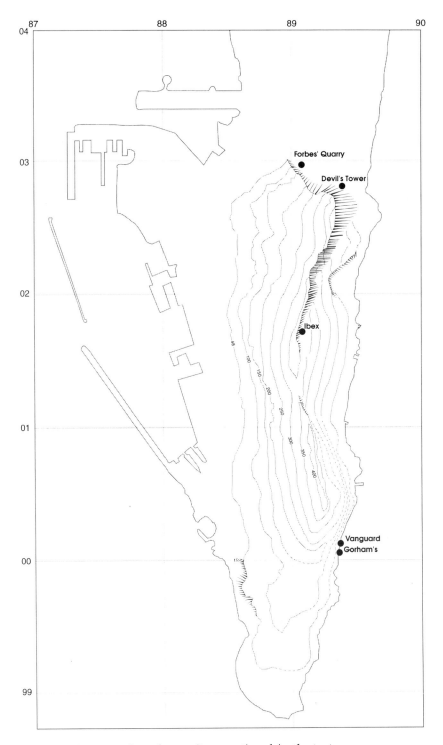

Figure 8.1: Gibraltar: Location of cave sites mentioned in the text.

8

Gibraltar Palaeolithic Revisited: New Excavations at Gorham's and Vanguard Caves 1995–7

C. B. Stringer, R. N. E. Barton, A. P. Currant, J. C. Finlayson, P. Goldberg, R. Macphail, P. B. Pettitt

Excavations at Gorham's and Vanguard Caves on Gibraltar between 1995 and 1997 have uncovered long sequences of deposits containing Middle and Upper Palaeolithic artefacts and other remains. This paper describes some of the preliminary findings and reports on new AMS radiocarbon dating results from each of these caves.

Introduction and background

Gibraltar is in a key biogeographical location, lying at the junction of the Atlantic and Mediterranean water masses and at the southern edge of the European continent, closest to Africa. The strait of Gibraltar forms a natural barrier for the movement of terrestrial organisms, including humans, between the two continents. During the Pleistocene, changes in climate and sea level must have altered the nature and effectiveness of the biogeographical barrier. Recent work in the Iberian peninsula has also raised intriguing issues about the coexistence of the last Neanderthals and the earliest modern humans in the region (Stringer and Gamble 1993, Carbonell and Vaquero 1996). Dating work at archaeological sites in northern Spain suggests that manufacturers of Upper Palaeolithic early Aurignacian industries (presumed *Homo sapiens*) were there prior to 38 kyr BP, while evidence from southern Spain and Portugal (Hublin *et al.* 1995, Vega 1993, Zilhao 1993) suggests that manufacturers of late Middle Palaeolithic (Mousterian) industries (*Homo neanderthalensis*) may have persisted there until *ca.* 30 kyr BP. The southern Iberian peninsula may thus have acted as a last refugium for the Neanderthals, from which they did not return. Sites in Gibraltar potentially have an important contribution to make to this debate. The Neanderthal finds from Forbes' Quarry and Devil's Tower are famous, the latter excavated by Dorothy Garrod between 1925 and 1926 (Rose and Stringer 1997). Less well known, however, are the impressive archaeological sites of Gorham's and Vanguard Cave, near present sea-level on the 'Governor's Beach', which are the subject of this paper.

Previous work on the Palaeolithic of Gibraltar

Despite the discovery of Neanderthal human cranial remains at Forbes' Quarry in 1848 (Busk 1865) and subsequently of a human milk tooth in Pleistocene deposits at the Genista cave No. 1 on the Windmill Plateau (Busk 1869: 128), no record of *in situ* Mousterian artefacts was found until 1919. In that year the Abbé Henri Breuil dug a trial trench through the talus slope of a small rockshelter at Devil's Tower (Breuil 1922). At his instigation Dorothy Garrod continued work there and in three short seasons between November 1925 and December 1926 she uncovered the now famous

Figure 8.2: Gibraltar caves: (entrance arches from left to right) Bennett's Cave, Gorham's Cave, and the double arches of Vanguard and Boat Hoist Caves (Photograph courtesy of the Natural History Museum).

Neanderthal child remains and an assemblage of Mousterian tools and other artefacts (Garrod *et al.* 1928). The publication of the excavation monograph stands as an important landmark in the history of Neanderthal studies and helped launch her long and distinguished research career (Clark 1989: 44).

Further excavations on the Palaeolithic of Gibraltar were undertaken by John Waechter, one of Dorothy Garrod's research students (Clark 1989: 144). His fieldwork in 1948 and between 1951–4 at Gorham's Cave on the east of the Rock demonstrated that a (lower) sequence of over 16 metres of sandy silts and breccias spanned much of the late Pleistocene and had a rich faunal and archaeological record from the Middle and Upper Palaeolithic (Waechter 1951, 1964). Conventional Gröningen radiocarbon dates on charcoal provided ages of *ca.* 28 kyr BP for layer D which contained Upper Palaeolithic artefacts and *ca.* 48 kyr BP for Layer G which contained Middle Palaeolithic tools (Waechter 1964: 219). A further phase of work at the site was subsequently carried out in 1989–91 by teams from the Natural History Museum and the British Museum and other collaborators, but artefacts recovered were largely from unstratified contexts.

Investigations at Gorham's and Vanguard Caves 1995–7

The present research project was initiated in 1995, following a preliminary season of reconnaissance and investigation at Ibex Cave (Rhodes *et al.* 1998, Barton 1998). The work involves the collaboration of a multidisciplinary team of specialists drawn from museums and universities in Britain, Gibraltar, Spain, Canada and USA. This paper provides a brief interim statement of some of our results up to 1997. At least one further season of work is planned in 1998.

Gorham's and Vanguard Caves are two adjacent caves facing on to the 'Governor's Beach' on the east coast of Gibraltar (Figs. 8.1 and 8.2). As mentioned above, only Gorham's Cave had been subjected to systematic exploration but this work had taken place over 40 years ago. The new project was concerned mainly with the upper units of the cave which cover the period of the Middle-Upper Palaeolithic transition. Re-examination of the archaeological deposits provided a unique opportunity for investigating high resolution changes during the crucial period in which Neanderthal populations were replaced by fully modern humans. It was anticipated that a sequence overlapping the one at Gorham's would be uncovered at Vanguard Cave (Goldberg and Macphail 1998).

Gorham's Cave

At Gorham's work so far has focused on exposed stratigraphic units towards the back of the cave covering three main time zones. The youngest, using correlation with previous Gröningen dates on charcoal from Waechter's Unit D (Waechter 1964: 219), covers the Upper Palaeolithic around 26–30 kyr BP. Initial results of new AMS dating work are given below (Table 8.1); the precise chronology of these units will continue to be clarified through dating work which is still in progress. The oldest covers the main Middle Palaeolithic sequence, which lies in and under units dated by a new

accelerator date on charcoal of 45,300±
1700 BP (OxA–6075), and above units
dated by Uranium-series determinations
to between 80–100 kyr. The third group
of units, which contain the youngest
Middle Palaeolithic and the earliest
Upper Palaeolithic were affected by
major collapse in 1996 but the section has
now been re-exposed and the units
comprehensively sampled for
radiocarbon and U-series dating.

The younger Palaeolithic units at
Gorham's have provided evidence of
dense concentrations of charcoal,
identified as combustion zones, which
also contain burnt bone but relatively
few diagnostic lithic artefacts. One of the
richest of these combustion horizons is in
context 9 (Figs. 8.3 and 8.4), for which
we now have four AMS radiocarbon
determinations that are statistically
identical and indicate an age range of
31–28 kyr BP (Table 8.1). The combustion
zone lies directly on a natural floor of
cemented limestone cobbles. Waechter
noted that in his Upper Palaeolithic
Layer D.I "the hearths were apparently
lined with flat water worn cobbles"
(1951: 85). The similarity of description
suggests that context 9 can be correlated
with Waechter's Layer D.I, although it
appears that he mistook the cobbles in
the floor for deliberate hearth lining. It is
particularly interesting also that the [14]C
dates for his Layer D (GrN–1455 – 28,700
±200 BP, and GrN–1363 – 27,860±300 BP)
are statistically indistinguishable from
those for context 9.

Amongst the identified bone in the
upper layers of the new excavations was
vertebral material from tuna fish. This is
an interesting discovery and if directly
linked with human activity, as seems
probable, implies a level of sophistication
in netting and sea fishing techniques
which may date back 28 kyr or earlier.

Gorham's Cave, Gibraltar: Areas I and II

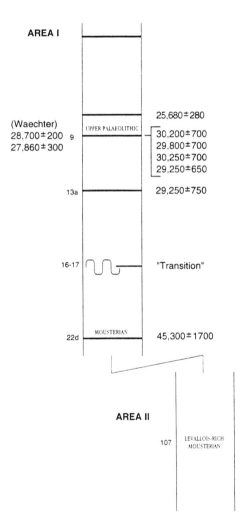

*Figure 8.3: Gorham's Cave: Schematic
section through the upper series of
sediments currently under excavation
(after Paul Pettitt).*

Table 8.1: AMS radiocarbon dates from Gorham's Cave

Context 7 (combustion zone)
OxA–6997 GORC 96 526, burnt bone (no ID) $\delta^{13}C = -21.2$ 25,680±280

Context 9 (combustion zone)
OxA–7074 GORC 96 511, charcoal, *Pinus* sp. $\delta^{13}C = -24.2$ 30,200±700
OxA–7075 GORC 96 512a, charcoal, *Pinus* sp. $\delta^{13}C = -27.3$ 29,800±700
OxA–7076 GORC 96 512b, charcoal, *Pinus* sp. $\delta^{13}C = -25.2$ 30,250±700
OxA–7077 GORC 96 514, charcoal, (no ID) $\delta^{13}C = -24.7$ 29,250±650

Context 13a (combustion zone)
OxA–7110 GORC 96 528, charcoal, *Pinus* sp. $\delta^{13}C = -24.4$ 29,250±750

Context 22 (combustion zone)
OxA–6075 GORC 93 240, charcoal (no ID) $\delta^{13}C = -25.2$ 45,300±1700

Figure 8.4: Gorham's Cave: The dark bands near the top of the stratigraphy record the Early Upper Palaeolithic zone radiocarbon dated to ca. 26–30 kyr. The base of the visible sequence records the Middle-Upper Palaeolithic transition for which dates are awaited. 50 cm scale (Photograph courtesy of the Natural History Museum).

The deposits of the main Middle Palaeolithic sequence offer substantial evidence of human activities in the form of lithic artefacts and residues of food processing activities (Fig. 8.5). The exceptional preservation of burnt organic material means that we should soon be able to provide a clearer idea of the wide range of edible plant foods available to the Neanderthals. Amongst the potential foodstuffs so far identified in the carbonised residues are wild olive (*Olea* sp.) and stone pine nut (*Pinus pinea*) (Carruthers and Gale, pers. comm.), both of which still grow wild in the area today. Of particular interest from the point of view of human activities was the discovery in one of these levels of large beach cobbles in amongst the spreads of charred nut shells and other organic remains. The existence of percussive damage on their extremities suggested they had been used in processing the foods. Evidence of meat eating in these pre–45 kyr BP levels comes mainly from ibex bones with cut-marks and from burnt tortoise bones.

Artefacts recovered from the Middle Palaeolithic levels conform to a Mousterian tradition characterised by the use of discoidal core technology and its variants (*cf.* Bordes

Figure 8.5: Large rounded "grinding" stones associated with carbonised plant remains in one of the Middle Palaeolithic levels at Gorham's Cave (Photograph courtesy of the Natural History Museum).

1950, 1961; Boëda 1988, 1993). The raw materials used are highly diverse but are mostly pebbles of apparently local origin (Barton 1998 in press). There may be exceptions to this pattern, however, as in the case of some of the honey-coloured, fine-grained cherts used in the manufacture of certain tools (Fig. 8.6). From our preliminary observations it appears that this material is not found locally on Gibraltar but may originate in SE Spain. Since the tools in the honey-coloured chert seem to be heavily re-sharpened, one of the possible implications currently being investigated, is that they represent heavily "curated" items imported from distance. Nevertheless, whether they constitute "local" raw materials (*sensu* Gamble 1993), *i.e.* lie within 40 km of the sites or lie beyond this hypothetical radius, has yet to be determined. A more relevant criterion may be the distance to the edge of the visible horizon, which in a northerly direction coincidentally lies 35–40 km away in the high Serranio de Ronda. An additional feature of interest is the presence of very large blade-like flakes in one of the lower Mousterian levels presently under investigation (context 107), which are of a "classic Levallois" blade technology (Fig. 8.6) (Mellars 1996: 80). From the size of these artefacts it is unlikely that the material on which they were made derives from immediately local sources.

We are still at an early stage of investigations into the Middle to Upper Palaeolithic transition at Gorham's. One level (contexts 16–17), unfortunately distorted by slumping or bioturbation, contained artefacts both characteristic of the Middle Palaeolithic (a flake from

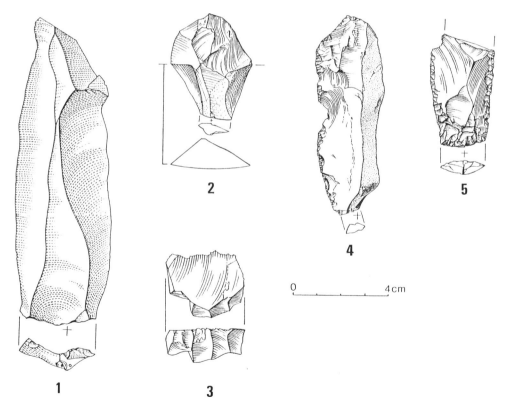

Figure 8.6: *Gorham's Cave/Vanguard Cave: Retouched tools and débitage including honey-coloured fine-grained chert.*

a discoidal core) and of the Upper Palaeolithic (a platform rejuvenation flake from a prismatic core) (Fig. 8.6, Table 8.1). So far, this is the only level that may be said to be 'transitional', although given the nature of the geological sequence at this point it is most likely that this is a mixture of at least two distinct archaeological deposits – that is to say a Middle and an Upper Palaeolithic assemblage, rather than a true transitional industry. Further AMS dates, notably on the remnants of a combustion zone may help establish the age of this horizon more closely, but for the moment we can only say that the transition at Gorham's took place somewhere between the dates for the oldest Upper Palaeolithic horizon at *ca.* 30 kyr BP, and the youngest clearly Middle Palaeolithic horizon at *ca.* 45 kyr BP. In order to provide as secure chronological controls as are possible, where available, pairs of charcoal and unburnt bone samples are measured in order to control for any potential systematic offset by material type. The resulting sequence, already clear and stratigraphically consistent, will provide an important framework for evaluating and interpreting the results of ESR, OSL and U-series dates on the same deposits. Further work will be concentrated in these units in 1998.

Vanguard Cave
A Mousterian discoidal core technology comparable to that of Gorham's has been recorded in a number of separate contexts at Vanguard Cave. The cave contains a sequence of over 17 metres of deposits which are mostly sands interspersed with finely laminated organic-rich silts and clay. Each of the archaeological levels has been systematically excavated and sampled for palaeoenvironmental and dating purposes (AMS, ESR, OSL and U-series techniques). Initial results reveal that except for the uppermost levels most of the units lie beyond the age range of AMS radiocarbon dating (Table 8.2). Ultimately, our preliminary results seem to indicate that the cave had filled to its present level by *ca.* 45 kyr BP, and so does not provide much overlap with the Upper Palaeolithic deposits at Gorham's Cave.

Table 8.2: AMS dates from Vanguard Cave

Top section, base of spit 3.
OxA–7389 VAN-S 96 377, charcoal (no ID) $\delta^{13}C = -25.5$ 45,200±2400

Unit 53
OxA–6891 VAN-S 96 285a, charcoal, *Juniperus/Tetraclinis* sp. $\delta^{13}C = -22.1$ 54,000±3300
OxA–6892 VAN-S 96 285b, charcoal, *Pistacea* sp. $\delta^{13}C = -22.6$ 46,900±1500

Unit 54
OxA–7127 VAN-S 96 347, charcoal, *Olea* sp. $\delta^{13}C = -24.4$ >49,400

Unit 55
OxA–6998 VAN-S 96 245, charcoal, *Olea* sp. $\delta^{13}C = -25.1$ 41,800±1400
OxA–7191 VAN-S 96 230, bone, *Sus* sp. $\delta^{13}C = -15.1$ 10,170±120
(*Note:* OxA–7191 has a low collagen yield and should be treated with caution: it is certainly an underestimate.)

The Alcove
OxA–7078 VAN-N96 351, charcoal, *Pinus* sp. (hearth) $\delta^{13}C = -23.9$ >44,100

Within the upper units of the cave (beneath Units 53–55: see Table 8.2) is a well-defined layer of ash and charcoal containing a concentration of broken and burnt mussel shells and associated quartzite flakes. The artefacts which are refittable indicate a limited knapping episode in which some of the resulting flakes were evidently then removed from the hearth area. Of particular interest is the presence of a chert sidescraper and one heavily utilised chert flake (Fig. 8.6), which must have been brought in to the site ready-made since there is no surviving evidence of their manufacture. The midden deposit also contains a number of coprolites deposited in and around the combusted areas. Examination, currently in progress, should reveal whether they are of human or other animal origin. To judge from the small number of artefacts, the limited selection of raw

Figure 8.7: Vanguard Cave: AMS radiocarbon dated hearth structure, 10 cm scale bars (Photograph courtesy of the Natural History Museum).

materials, and the existence of flake to core refits, it is highly probable that the lithic assemblage resulted from a single discrete episode of activity. The deposits provide exceptionally clear evidence for the exploitation of marine shellfish by Neanderthals. The uniformly large size of the shells suggests that they were obtained from a nearby estuarine source (P. Jeffery, pers. comm.), and may also imply a degree of selectivity, as one might expect to find in regularly eaten foods. Further work is now being carried out to determine the method of preparing the shellfish for consumption (Fernandez-Jalvo in prep.).

Lower down in the cave sequence are a series of well-defined occupation horizons which contain considerable quantities of Mousterian artefacts and bones. The area has been extended to reveal smashed bone, cut-marked bone and burnt bone, around combustion zones rich in charcoal and lithic artefacts. The activities represented seem again to be of a strictly limited duration, with artefacts being predominantly made on locally-obtained raw materials. The most numerically important species in the associated large fauna is ibex. Spatial analysis of these levels is currently in progress. Amongst the ideas to be tested is whether or not activities were focused on the combustion zones or were distributed much more haphazardly across the cave.

Finally, investigation of a small alcove on the north side of the chamber has yielded well-preserved hyaena (*Crocuta crocuta*) bones suggesting the possibility of denning activities. Also located in the same alcove was a small, sub-circular *in situ* hearth (Fig. 8.7). No artefacts were found in association, although an AMS date on pine charcoal from within the feature has confirmed its overall antiquity. Preliminary micromorphological analyses suggest that hearths were probably more abundant in the cave in the past but have been affected, and in some cases totally dismantled, by aeolian activity and sheetwash.

Conclusion

The excavations at Gorham's and Vanguard Caves are already beginning to yield significant results relating to the palaeontological, archaeological and palaeoenvironmental aspects of the Neanderthals and their modern human successors. The integration of new AMS and other dating results with sediments analysis should help us compare the sequences in both caves and to provide frameworks for situating human behaviour. For example, it would be interesting to know whether changes in sea level and resulting reconfiguration of the coastal plain were major factors responsible in the Neanderthal exploitation of highly local raw materials for toolmaking and the gathering of marine/estuarine foods. Using this information and comparing the archaeological evidence from the Middle and Upper Palaeolithic levels at the sites will help to place the Gibraltar finds in their European and Mediterranean contexts.

Acknowledgements

The authors would like to thank the following funding bodies for their support of the project: National Geographic Society, British Academy, Natural History Museum, Society of Antiquaries, NERC and Oxford Brookes University. The photographs were taken by Frank Greenaway (Natural History Museum). Hazel Martingell was responsible for the artefact illustrations and Gerry Black helped in the preparation of Figures 8.1 and 8.3.

Bibliography

Barton, R.N.E. 1998. Raw material exploitation and lithic use at the Mousterian site of Ibex Cave, Gibraltar. In C. Finlayson (Ed.), *Gibraltar during the Quaternary: the southernmost part of Europe in the last two million years*. Gibraltar Government Heritage Publications, Gibraltar. In press.

Boëda, E. 1988. Le concept Levallois et évaluation de son champ d'application. In Otte, M. (ed.), *L'Homme de Néandertal, Vol. 4: La Technique*, pp. 13–26. Liège: Etudes et Recherches Archéologique de l'Université de Liège.

Boëda, E. 1993. Le débitage discoïde et le débitage Levallois recurrent centripête. *Bulletin de la Société Préhistorique Française* 90 (6): 392–404.

Bordes, F. 1950. Principes d'une méthode d'étude des techniques et de la typologique paléolithique ancien et moyen. *L'Anthropologie* 54: 19–34.

Bordes, F. 1961. *Typologie du Paléolithique Ancien et Moyen*. Bordeaux: Delmas.

Breuil, H. 1922. Palaeolithic man at Gibraltar: new and old facts. *Journal of the Royal Anthropological Institute* 1 (ii): 46.

Busk, G. 1865. On a very ancient human cranium from Gibraltar. *Report of the 34th meeting of the British Association for the Advancement of Science, Bath 1864*, pp. 91–92.

Busk, G. 1869. On the caves in Gibraltar in which human remains and works of art have been found. *Transactions of the International Congress on Anthropology and Prehistoric Archaeology, Third Session (Norwich 1868)*, pp. 106–167.

Carbonell, E., and M. Vaquero (Eds.). 1996. *The last Neanderthals, the first anatomically modern humans: a tale about human diversity. Cultural change and human evolution: the crisis at 40 ka BP*. Spain: Universitat Rovira i Virgili.

Clark, G. 1989. *Prehistory at Cambridge and beyond*. Cambridge: Cambridge University Press.

Gamble, C.S. 1993. *Exchange and local hominid networks*. In C. Scarre and F. Healy (Eds.), *Trade and Exchange in Prehistoric Europe*, pp. 35–44. Oxford: Oxbow Monograph 33.

Garrod, D.A.E., Buxton, L.H.D., Smith, G.E., and D.M.A. Bate 1928. Excavation of a Mousterian Rock-shelter at Devil's Tower, Gibraltar. *Journal of the Royal Anthropological Institute* 58: 33–113.

Goldberg, P., and R. Macphail 1998. Micromorphology of sediments from Gibraltar Caves: some preliminary results from Gorham's Cave and Vanguard Cave. In C. Finlayson, (Ed.), *Gibraltar during the Quaternary: the southernmost part of Europe in the last two million years*. Gibraltar Government Heritage Publications, Gibraltar. In press.

Hublin, J-J., Barroso Ruiz, C., Medina Lara, O., Fontugne, M., and J.L. Reyss 1995. The Mousterian site of Zafarraya (Andalucia, Spain): dating and implications on the Palaeolithic peopling processes of Western Europe. *Comptes-Rendus de l'Académie des Sciences Paris*, 321, série II a: 931–937.

Mellars, P. 1996. *The Mousterian Legacy*. Princeton: Princeton University Press.

Rhodes, E., Stringer, C., Grün, R., Barton, R.N.E., Currant, A., and C. Finlayson 1998. Preliminary ESR dates from Ibex Cave, Gibraltar. In C. Finlayson (Ed.), *Gibraltar during the Quaternary: the southernmost part of Europe in the last two million years*. Gibraltar Government Heritage Publications, Gibraltar. In press.

Rose, E.P.F., and C.B. Stringer 1997. Gibraltar woman and Neanderthal Man. *Geology Today*, September-October: 179–184.

Stringer, C., and C. Gamble 1993. *In search of the Neanderthals*. London: Thames and Hudson.

Waechter, J. D'A. 1951. Excavations at Gorham's Cave, Gibraltar. *Proceedings of the Prehistoric Society* 17: 83–92.

Waechter, J. D'A. 1964. The excavations at Gorham's Cave, Gibraltar, 1951–1954. *Bulletin of the Institute of Archaeology of London* 4: 189–221.

Vega, L.G. 1993. La transicion del Paleolitico Medio al Paleolitico superior en el sur la Peninsula Iberica. In Cabrera-Valdès (Ed.), *El origen del Hombre Moderno en El Suroeste de Europe*, pp. 147–170. Madrid: Universidad Nacional de Educacion a Distancia.

Zilhao, J. 1993. Le passage du Paléolithique supérieur dans le Portugal. In Cabrera-Valdès (Ed.), *El origen del Hombre Moderno en El Suroeste de Europe*, pp.127–145. Madrid: Universidad Nacional de Educacion a Distancia.

9

The Evolution of the Balkan Aurignacian

Janusz K. Kozłowski

The review of the evolution of the Aurignacian in the Balkans shows this culture unit to have begun in that territory earlier than in other parts of Europe. However, its local origin could not be demonstrated. The Early Upper Palaeolithic ('Bachokirian') in the Balkans does not display any connections whatever with the local Middle Palaeolithic industries. The Aurignacian evolved further to its Middle Phase with a number of specific features which are different not only from the Italian Aurignacian but also from some middle Danube groups. The end of the Aurignacian was not synchronous over the whole territory of the Balkans. In some regions (Bulgaria, Istria, Peloponnese) Middle and Late Aurignacian groups co-existed with Gravettian and/or with other industries with backed bladelets.

Introduction

At the time when D. A. E. Garrod came to Sofia on 10th July, 1938, knowledge about the Early Upper Palaeolithic in the Balkans was limited to the results of investigations by a Bulgarian palaeontologist R. Popov in the Temnata Cave near Karlukovo (Popov 1931) and at Morovitsa near Teteven (Popov 1912). When Garrod studied materials from these sites she noticed a similarity in the finds from the Temnata Cave to "the earliest stage of the middle Aurignacian in Palestine" (Garrod *et al.* 1939: 52) and, at the same time, the presence of a "split-base *pointe d'Aurignac*" at Morovitsa. This made her inclined to believe that "this very scanty material can fairly safely be classified as Middle Aurignacian" (*ibid.*: 52).

The effect of the explorations carried out by Garrod in the Bacho Kiro Cave, from 27th of July to 8th August 1938, was that by the time she left Sofia by the Orient Express on 14th August it was already known that the evolution of the Aurignacian in the Balkans must have been much more complex than so far realised. The typical – in her opinion – Aurignacian material occurred in layers E, F and J in the Bacho Kiro Cave. The layers were separated by sterile layers G and H in Garrod's trial trenches. The comparison of the finds from Bacho Kiro with the documented sequence from Palestine confirmed Garrod's verdict ascribing finds from layer J to the Middle Aurignacian. But she hesitated whether the material from layers F and E could still be regarded as the Middle Aurignacian or whether it already belonged to the Late Aurignacian. Her doubts were caused by the fact that the fragment of a point found in layer F seemed to her "certainly too long and slender to be the upper part of a split-base *pointe d'Aurignac*" (Garrod *et al.* 1939: 62).

The excavations at the Bacho Kiro Cave took place at the same time as S. Brodar's (1938) publication of the results of investigations in the Potočka Cave which documented the presence of Aurignacian points in the north-west part of the Balkans. Thus, the state of knowledge at that time permitted Garrod to express a view that in the territories between the Near East and western Europe typical Aurignacian sites occurred that were later than the beginning of the Aurignacian and which contained "split-base *pointes d'Aurignac*".

After World War II, this state of knowledge remained unchanged for a long time except for the results of investigations by M. Brodar in high mountain sites in Slovenia, notably in the Mokriška Cave in the Alps. On that site, for the first time in the Balkans, a stratigraphic sequence was recorded where split-based points appeared earlier than the Mladeč points.

Commencing excavations in 1971 in the Bacho Kiro Cave, conducted together with B. Ginter and N. Sirakov (Kozłowski [ed.] 1982, Ginter and Sirakov 1974, Kozłowski and Sirakov 1975), I was guided by the results of Garrod's investigations in this cave which had revealed the exceptional importance of this stratigraphical sequence spanning from the Middle to the early Upper Palaeolithic. The results of excavations in the years 1971 to 1975 confirmed that our selection of the site had been correct, and that the site contributed significantly to the resolution of the problems of transition from the Middle to the Upper Palaeolithic. Geochronological data showed the particularly early age of the initial phase of the Upper Palaeolithic, and numerous other data evidenced a lack of continuity of cultural evolution between the Middle and the Upper Palaeolithic.

The seventies brought numerous important discoveries of the Aurignacian in the caves of Croatia and in open-air sites in Bosnia (Malez 1979, Montet-White 1996). In the eighties, once again following Garrod's tracks, we returned to Bulgaria and started investigations in the Temnata Cave, working in the same team together with H. Laville. Our investigations confirmed the early age of the Aurignacian in the eastern Balkans, and a much more complex nature of the evolution of the Late Phase of the Middle Palaeolithic than was originally assumed. Nonetheless, the concept of a hiatus between the Middle Palaeolithic and the Aurignacian remained unchanged. The 1980s saw interesting contributions to the knowledge of the Aurignacian also in the central part of the northern Balkans (Mihajlović 1992), in Volvodina – the territory which up till then had been a blank on the map of the Upper Palaeolithic.

The 1990s brought confirmation of the presence of the Aurignacian in Greece where only very few relics of this culture had been known. Even as late as 1995 C. Runnels stated that "the Aurignacian is extremely rare in Greece" (Runnels 1995: 714). In the early nineties, only one Aurignacian level from a fairly well-dated sequence in the Franchthi Cave (Perlès 1987) was available. A fairly rich open site of Elaiochori (Darlas 1989) and Aurignacian finds in mixed assemblages from open sites of Amalias, Kastron and Retunia in the western Peloponnese (Chavaillon *et al.* 1967, 1969) were also known. The first multilayer Aurignacian site in a well-dated sequence from a rock-shelter in the Klisoura Gorge was investigated as late as 1995 to 1996 (Koumouzelis *et al.* 1995, Koumouzelis and Kozłowski 1996). With the exception of Albania, the Aurignacian is known today in all the Balkan countries, but it is not uniformly distributed over the region. Multilayer sequences from Bulgaria enable us to determine the main developmental trends of the Aurignacian although its inter-site variability has yet to await complete reconstruction.

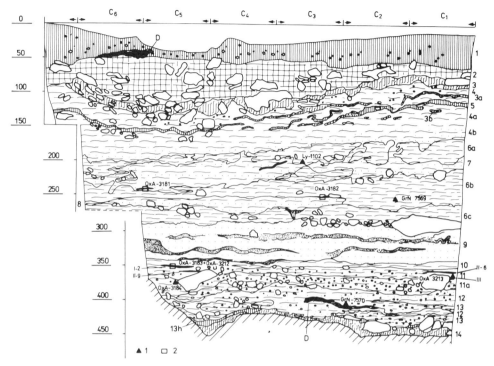

Figure 9.1: Bacho Kiro Cave: transversal section of the cave with position of ^{14}C samples. [1 = charcoals; 2 = bones]

Diachronic approach to the Balkan Aurignacian

The early dating of the basal Upper Palaeolithic in layer 11 in the Bacho Kiro Cave, namely to >43,000 years BP (GrN-7545), has evoked considerable interest as it makes layer 11 the oldest trace of the Aurignacian in Europe. Initially this date was accepted with some reservations; subsequently, comparable dates for the Aurignacian were obtained in [Mediterranean] Europe, notably from the Spanish caves of Arbreda and Castillo (Bischoff *et al.* 1989, Soler-Masferrer and Moroto-Genover 1993). At the same time, TL determinations from layer 4 in Temnata Cave, which reached more than 40,000 years BP (Ginter and Kozłowski 1992) were published.

In both Balkan sequences – Bacho Kiro and Temnata – the oldest Upper Palaeolithic industries dated at between 45 and 35 kyr BP are below the classical Aurignacian, dated in the range from 34 to 28 kyr BP. This sequence has been confirmed by the AMS dates obtained from these two Balkan sites (Hedges *et al.* 1994, Ginter *et al.* 1996). A comparison with the traditional radiocarbon determinations is given in Tables 9.1 and 9.2. In these sequences the oldest Aurignacian is represented by four phases of occupation (I-IV) from layer 11 in the Bacho Kiro Cave (Fig. 9.1) and three phases distinguished in layer 4, trench TD-I, in the Temnata Cave.

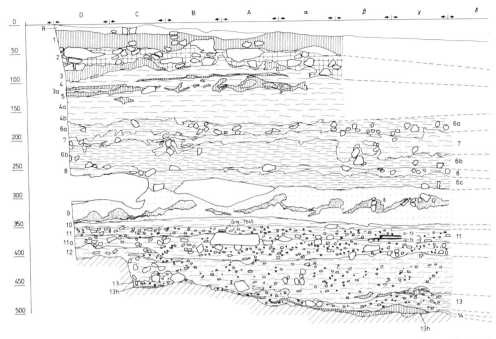

Figure 9.2: Bacho Kiro Cave: longitudinal section of the cave, with position of sample GrN-7545 and with hearths 14 and 13.

In the Bacho Kiro Cave, the oldest phase IV yielded one hearth (no. 14) located at the entrance to the cave. The next phase (level III) had two hearths (nos. 12 and 13), and the range of occupation moves further into the cave interior. The next level (II) yielded four hearths: no. 11 – located at the very entrance, directly underneath the cave wall, and nos. 7, 9, 10 – situated in the cave interior on the right, forming a semi-circle around hearth no. 8 which was partially covered by a large stone block. Another hearth (no. 6) is situated in the centre of the ante-chamber. This hearth is surrounded by a concentration of finds extending beyond the boundary of the trench. In the uppermost level (I) the occupation floor shifts still deeper into the cave interior, towards the right-hand part of the ante-chamber. This too extends beyond the trench boundaries; in this phase, three hearths (nos. 3, 4, 5) are situated near the large stone block sunk into level II. Near these hearths there is an extensive 'sweeping zone' ('zone de vidange'), no. 2 with postholes next to it; the postholes are probably traces of a tent-like structure. A hearth is situated closer to the cave centre (no. 1).

The stratigraphical position of sample GrN–7545, obtained from the middle of the trench (square metre B1), is identified with the upper part of layer 11 on the basis of its depth from the present ground surface. Subsequent analysis of the longitudinal profile has shown, however, a certain deformation of layer 11 in this place caused by a large limestone block located between layers 11a and 11 (*cf.* Fig. 9.2). Consequently, a charcoal sample obtained from above the block should be identified with the lower part of layer 11, probably with the level related to hearth no. 14, *i.e.* with occupation level IV.

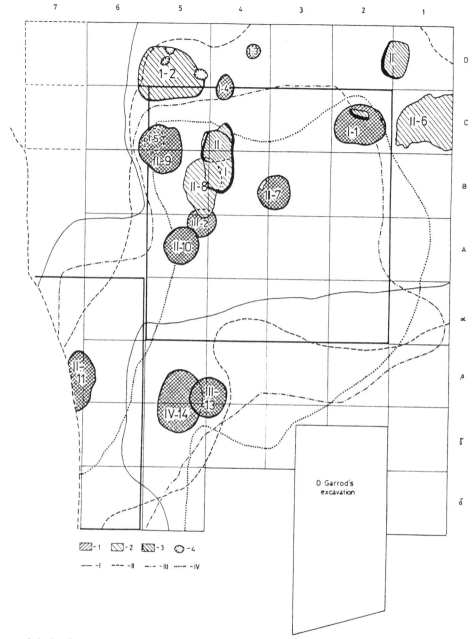

Figure 9.3: Bacho Kiro Cave: simplified map of layer 11. 1 – hearth; 2 – 'zones de vidange'; 3 – stone blocks; 4 – postholes. I–IV – maximum extension of finds in particular layers.

Sample OxA-3213 is a bone fragment from the C1 square metre, at a depth of 370 to 375 cm. Its position corresponds to the edge of the concentration of finds from level III (*cf.* Fig. 9.3).

Sample OxA-3183, obtained from square metre C5 at a depth of 355 to 358 cm, comes from hearth 2 in level I; from the same hearth a bone fragment is denoted as OxA-3212. This, however, could be an intrusion from layer 10 whose uneven base almost reaches the surface of hearth II-2.

The distribution of radiocarbon dates from layer 11, from >43,000 to 37,650 ± 1450 BP (if we disregard the OxA-3212 date of 34,800 ± 1150 BP), indicates a long formation process for this layer under weak natural sedimentation conditions. Particular occupation episodes of the cave were separated by long periods when the rubble sedimentation was minimal, and weathering processes fairly intensive in the conditions of a warm and wet climate. Similar climatic conditions had begun to develop already during the sedimentation of layer 11a. Although the periods of time separating particular episodes of cave occupation were fairly long, no major differences are observed in respect of lithic tool composition, the raw materials which were used or their procurement, or in the hunted fauna. The homogeneity of the culture of cave inhabitants over a period of about five thousand radiocarbon years is puzzling. The only change is the growing number of hearths, which may suggest that in the younger occupational phases the social organization became more complex, and the groups inhabiting the cave were more numerous. A tendency towards enlargement of activity areas and pushing their boundaries deeper into the cave interior can also be seen. The relation of peripheral hearths in horizons I and II to the well-delineated systems of central hearths is interesting. It is likely that the peripheral hearths may constitute the remnants of other, additional phases of settlement (sub-episodes in relation to phases I and II).

In the Temnata Cave the hearths located in the central part of layer 4 divide the layer into three complexes:

a) Complex C in the bottom part of layer 4, below the hearths. This complex yielded relatively few artefacts on which the date Gd-TL-256 was obtained.

b) Complex B with hearths in metres D1 and D2, in the middle part of layer 4: the profile showed that the features formed a sequence of three superimposed hearths, flat or slightly sunk into the palaeo-groundsurface, about 1 m in diameter. AMS ^{14}C dates OxA-5169, -5170 and -5179 (from 39,100 to 38,200 years BP) from these hearths and a TL date (Gd-TL-255) on a piece of burnt flint have been obtained.

c) Complex A in the top part of layer 4, located in square metres nearest to the cave entrance (B1, B2): unfortunately, this complex provided only one radiocarbon date loaded with a large error (Gd-2354).

From the point of view of palaeoclimate, the Early Balkan Upper Palaeolithic in the two Balkan sequences is distributed within a warmer oscillation (Fig. 9.4). The beginning of this warm oscillation in the Bacho Kiro Cave correlates with layer 11a, which yielded a scanty lithic inventory but with some Upper Palaeolithic features. The AMS date for this layer (OxA-3184 – 33,750 ± 850 BP) is too young, in disagreement with all the other dates from layer 11. In the Temnata Cave the warm episode begins with the sedimentation of layer VI on the talus (sector TD-II). The top part of this layer shows traces of pedogenesis. This colluvial layer contains faunal remains identified by J.L. Guadelli (pers. comm.) as: hyaena, *Mustella*, bear, deer, roe-deer, elk, more numerous ibex and abundant remains of bovids and large ruminants. Bison, horse and small ruminants were also well represented. This faunal composition is in agreement with the pollen spectra for this layer, containing predominantly grasses: 40% *Artemisia* and 20% Chenopodiacae. Layer VI contained the industry with transitional features between the Moustero-Levalloisian and the Upper-Palaeolithic substratum. This can be seen in the evolution of the Levallois technique towards the Upper Palaeolithic blade technique, and in the appearance of Upper Palaeolithic end-scrapers and burins (Ginter *et al.* 1996).

The warmer oscillation mentioned above begins, therefore, before the appearance of Upper Palaeolithic industries in layer 11 in the Bacho Kiro Cave and layer 4 in the Temnata Cave, probably as early as 50 to 45 kyr BP. The morphology of limestone debris and the fauna, especially rodents, in the occupation levels within layer 11 in the Bacho Kiro Cave indicate fairly warm and dry climatic conditions, persisting up to about 37 kyr BP.

Conditions during the sedimentation of layer 4 in the Temnata Cave (sector TD–I) can be interpreted in a similar way. The palynological data show that during that period as much as 70% of pollen belongs to pine, with some stenothermal trees (*e.g.* oak). The absence of *Artemisia* and the fact that monoletic spores do not exceed 10% (Marambat 1992) are characteristic. It is only in the final phase of the sedimentation of layer 4 that the proportion of pine drops to less than 10% and *Artemisia* re-appears (up to 15%). Such pollen composition was recorded in sector TD-V, in the top part of layer 4 (4a) where the AMS date of 33,000 ± 900 BP (OxA-5174) was obtained.

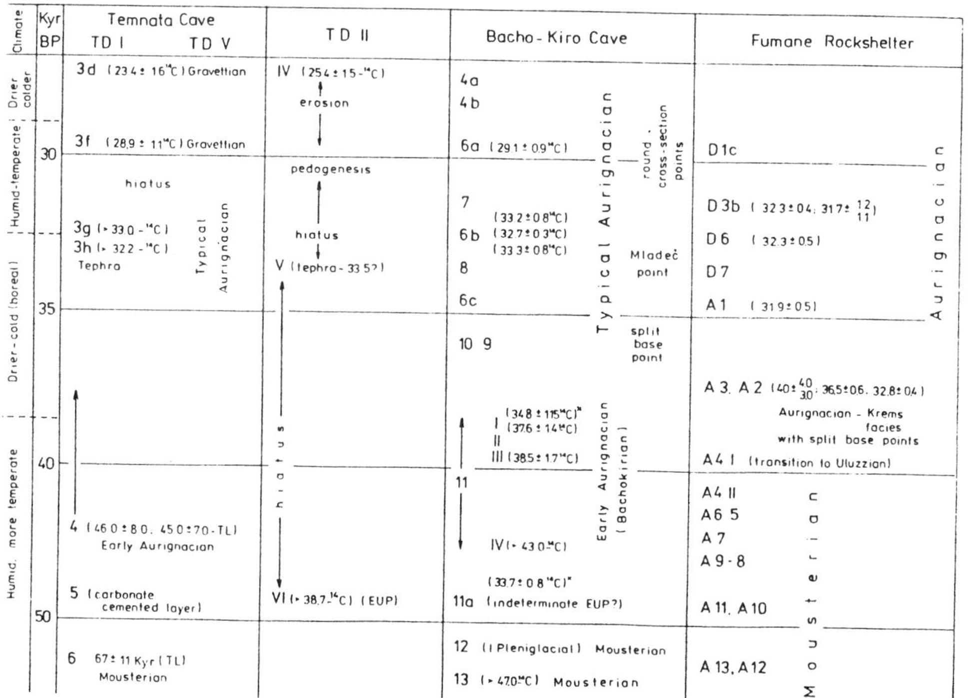

Figure 9.4: Synchronization of sequences of Bacho Kiro and Temnata caves, and Fumane rock-shelter.

Table 9.1: Radiocarbon dates of Bacho Kiro sequence

Lab. No.	Layer	Material	Date
Ly-1102	base 6a	bone	29,159±950
OxA-3181	base of 7	charcoal	32,200±780
GrN-7569	lower part of 6b	bone	32,700±300
OxA-3182	base 6b/boundary with 8	charcoal	33,300±820
OxA-3183	11, level I	charcoal	37,650±1450
OxA-3212	11, level I, boundary with 10	bone	34,800±1150
OxA-3213	11, level III	bone	38,500±1750
GrN-7545	11, level IV	charcoal	>43,000
OxA-3184	11a	bone	33,750±850
GrN-7570	13	bone	>47,000

Progressive cooling of the climate in the Bacho Kiro Cave took place during the sedimentation of layer 9 and especially layer 6c. When layer 6c was being deposited the climatic conditions became not only cooler but also wetter, evidenced by rodent spectra (Kowalski and Nadachowski 1982). The chronology of layer 9 and layer 6c can be based on the interval between the AMS dates of OxA-3183 and OxA-3182 (Table 9.1), that is in the range from 37 to 33 kyr BP. This period may correlate to the cool episode between the Kalabaki and the Krinides Interstadial (Wijmstra 1969).

The end of layer 4 sedimentation in the Temnata Cave was followed by the deposition of tephra, dennotated as layer 'v' in the cave's interior and layer 'V' on the talus. This tephra came from volcanic eruptions in the Flegrean Fields in Italy between 35,500 and 33,000 years BP. Such chronological position has been confirmed by radiocarbon determinations from the overlying layer 3g, above the tephra (Gd-4693 and Gd-4595). Layers 3g and 3h, containing typical Aurignacian, were deposited in medium-cool and dry climatic conditions (Table 9.2). This is confirmed by the domination of *Artemisia* together with Graminae and Centurae. Arboreal pollen such as alder, oak and hazel sporadically occur, indicating the presence of forest clusters.

Another climatic amelioration in the Bacho Kiro sequence can be seen in layers 6b, 7 and 6a. The grain-size composition and the degree of weathering of limestone rubble points to a warmer climate, while – at the same time – rodent spectra are indicative of fairly dry conditions persisting until the sedimentation of layer 6a. It is only at the end of this period that decidedly cold climate indices appear in microfauna: *Microtus oeconomus* and *Alopex lagopus*. In this part of the sequence in the Bacho Kiro Cave, a warmer episode correlates to the Krinides I Interstadial in the Greek pollen profiles (this is corroborated by the dates of *ca.* 32 kyr BP – GrN-7569 for the bottom of layer 6b, and OxA-3181 for layer 7), and subsequently a transition to permanently cold conditions takes place at the end of the Interpleniglacial (this is evidenced by the date of approximately 29 kyr BP for layer 6a – Ly-1102). Such cold and dry conditions persisted during the sedimentation of layers 4b and 4a in the Bacho Kiro Cave.

Table 2: Temnata Cave radiocarbon and TL determinations, and environmental conditions.

SECTOR TD-I			SECTOR TD-V			SECTOR TD-II		Glacial chronology	Isotopic chronology
Layer	Cultural attribution	Dates	Layer	Cultural attribution	Dates	Layer	Cultural attribution		
3a	Epigravettian	13600±200 (Ly-3439)* 20100±900 (Gd-4028)*	3a	Epigravettian	10880±370 (Gd-2488)*			IInd	
3b								PLENI-	2
3c	Gravettian					IVA	Gravettian	GLACIAL	
3d -	Hiatus		3d	Gravettian	21200±380 (Gd 2785)* 29700±700 (Gd 4231)*	IVB			
3f	Gravettian	28900±1400 (Gd 4223)*	Hiatus		Abandonment or erosion	H			
	Erosion Hiatus		3g	Evolved Aurignacian	> 33100 (Gd 4595)*	I A T	Erosion Illuviation	INTER	
			3h		> 32200 (Gd 4693)*	U S		PLENI-	
V	Tephras		Tephras			V			3
	Hiatus		3i	Aurignacian		Tephras		G	
4	Early Aurignacian	top A 31900±1600 (Gd 2354) B 46000±8000 (Gd-TL-255) 38200±1500 (OxA 5171)• 38800±1700 (OxA 5170)• 39100±1800 (OxA 5169)• C 45000±7000 (Gd-TL-256)	4a	Early Aurignacian top	33000±900 (OxA 5174)•	H I A T U S	Erosion Illuviation	L A C I	
			4b	Early Aurignacian base	36900±1300 (OxA 5173)• 38300±1800 (OxA 5172)•				
	Hiatus		5pg 4/3	Transitional industry		VIa VIb	Transitional industry >38700 (Gd4687)	A L	
5	Stalagmitic floor		5	Stalagmitic floor					
			5						
	Hiatus		5pg/8	Moustcrian					
			5pg						
6	Moustcrian	67000±11000 (Gd-TL-254)	6	Moustcrian					4

* C12 analysis, □ TL analysis, • AMS-C14 analysis

The warm episode corresponding to Krinides I Interstadial does not occur in the Temnata Cave: it can probably be correlated to the hiatus between layers 3g and 3f/3d. Layers 3f/3d yielded dates close to 29 kyr BP; the climatic context of these dates is distinctly cool and dry.

While in the Bacho Kiro Cave layers 6a, 4b and 4a, deposited after 30 kyr BP, still contain Aurignacian assemblages, in the Temnata Cave the layers dated to the same period (3f and the floor of 3d) reveal the earliest Gravettian assemblages (Ginter and Kozłowski 1992, Kozłowski 1996). As we shall show in this work, other Balkan regions (Croatia and Greece) have also supplied evidence of synchronicity of the Aurignacian and the Gravettian.

The oldest Balkan Aurignacian – the "Bachokirian"

Both Balkan sequences, in the Bacho Kiro and in the Temnata caves, show two similar tendencies:

1. The lowest Aurignacian layers are separated by a multi-aspectual hiatus from the Mousterian layers. This hiatus is seen in technology, retouched tool morphology, methods of lithic raw material procurement and, to some extent, the exploitation of the terrain around the camp.
2. In between the Mousterian and the Aurignacian there are levels poor in finds, with weakly-marked diagnostic features, such as layer 11a in the Bacho Kiro Cave and level C in layer 4, trench TD-I in the Temnata Cave. These levels can by no means

be regarded as 'transitional' from the Mousterian to the Aurignacian but rather as typologically dubious Upper Palaeolithic assemblages with low standardization of blade tools, with flake forms and notched-denticulated retouch (Drobniewicz *et al.* 1982: pl. XVI 10, 11). The latter features are in all likelihood not cultural features but the expression of the camp's function, or a discard pattern.

Examination of the inventories from Bacho Kiro layer 11 and Temnata layer 4 (notably levels A and B) revealed a fully-developed Upper Palaeolithic technology and morphology with a relatively low proportion of Aurignacian diagnostic forms. These are first of all (Figs. 9.5, 9.6):

a) atypical nosed end-scrapers, *i.e.* these are not high end-scrapers but blade end-scrapers with nosed fronts, *e.g.* in the Bacho Kiro Cave (Kozłowski 1982: pl. II, 13; pl. III, 2–10), and in the Temnata Cave (Ginter *et al.* 1996: Fig. 12: 4, 6, 7; Fig. 14: 4, 5, 7, 9).
b) Aurignacian retouched blades, frequently *appointé*, characterised sometimes by typical scaled retouch, *e.g.* Bacho Kiro (Kozłowski 1982: pl. VII, especially 15, 16; pl. VIII, 1–6), and Temnata (Ginter *et al.* 1996: Fig. 13: 3, 4; Fig. 15: 4–8).

It is not only the absence of such diagnostic features as typical carinated end-scrapers that contributes to the special character of these industries. There are also no carinated cores or burins, which appear in higher levels on the two sites (*i.e.* Bacho Kiro layers 6b, 7 and 7a, and Temnata 3g and 3h). A lack of typical Aurignacian bladelets and microretouched points at both sites cannot be overlooked, as this seems to be quite an important feature setting the Balkan assemblages apart from Italian ones (*i.e.* from the Apennine Proto-Aurignacian). It should be added that the absence of these tools in the Bacho Kiro Cave and the Temnata Cave is not the effect of methodological oversight, as all the material was carefully wet-sieved using fine sieves.

The differences in comparison to the later phases of the Aurignacian make us inclined to single out the oldest industries from the Bacho Kiro Cave and the Temnata Caves as a separate unit, denoted as the Bachokirian. The separate taxonomic position of this unit is based on the fact that the morphology of Aurignacian tools in these industries is not fully developed.

It should be stressed that there are some differences between lithic tools in Bacho Kiro layer 11 and Temnata layer 4, resulting from a different raw materials economy. Generally, the tools from the Bacho Kiro Cave are more heavily retouched and transformed, which is seen not only in the shape and dimensions of tools but also in large quantities of chips and small fragments (more than 80% of the total material excavated from layer 11). The tools in Temnata layer 4 are larger, with weaker retouching, without stronger traces of transformation or modification.

These differences are caused by the fact that in the Temnata Cave 60% to 80% of all artefacts are made from flint C, whose deposits are located in the Iskar valley near the locality of Kunino, only a few kilometres away from the site (Pawlikowski 1992). Flints imported from a distance of more than 60-100 km, from the territory of north-western and north-eastern Bulgaria, account for only about 20% to 30% and are represented in all major technological groups (cortical flakes including). Flints whose provenance has not been established (seven types) are present only as blades or retouched tools.

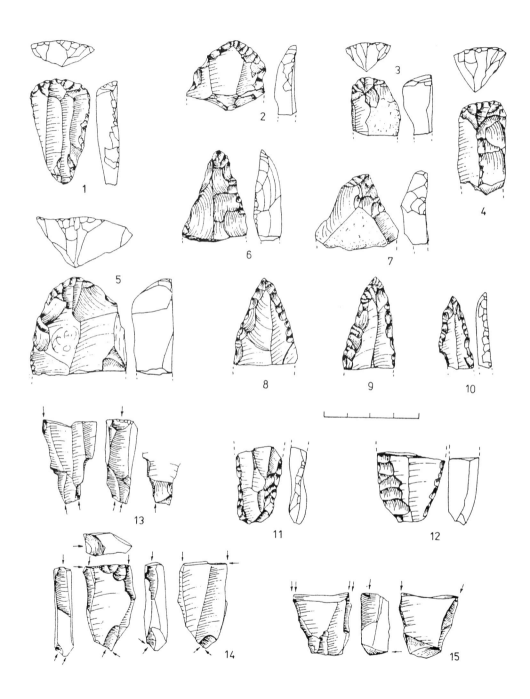

Figure 9.5: Bacho Kiro Cave, layer 11: selected end-scrapers, retouched blades and burins.

In the Bacho Kiro Cave almost 100% of artefacts were made from extralocal flints, supplied from a distance of sometimes more than 60 km. About 50% of these flints is the wax-chocolate type from north-eastern Bulgaria, *i.e.* from a distance of over 120 kilometres. Grey, opaque flints, probably from the basin of the Luda Kamchia river in eastern Bulgaria, *i.e.* over 60 km from Bacho Kiro, account for 25% of all flints. The provenance of other lithic raw materials is unknown, although brown and whitish opaque flints may have come from the Iskar river basin, more than 120 km to north-west.

The differing aspect of the 'Bachokirian' assemblages from the Temnata and the Bacho Kiro caves rests primarily in a more intensive tool reduction pattern used by the inhabitants of Bacho Kiro – the consequence of a greater distance from raw materials deposits. Some difficulties are encountered when the technologies of Temnata and Bacho Kiro are compared. They are caused by a very small proportion of cores in the Bacho Kiro Cave inventory (0.6% of the inventory, excluding chips and small fragments), which – in addition – represent strongly-reduced forms. The presence of cortical flakes in both caves (14% of all flakes in Bacho Kiro layer 11, and more than 30% in the Temnata Cave) shows that unprepared, cortical nodules of at least two types of flint were brought to the sites. The fairly high ratio of flakes with perpendicular or centripetal dorsal patterning indicates that cores were prepared and rejuvenated during reduction. Both industries used single- as well as double-platform blade cores. In the Temnata Cave inventory blade lengths have two distinct modes: between 3 and 5 cm and between 6 and 8 cm; in Bacho Kiro almost all blades are within the range from 2.5 to 5 cm although individual specimens reach the range of 6 to 7 cm. The absence of the second length mode is certainly the result of intensive transformation of blades into tools, and of making the blades shorter.

Summing up, we can say that the earliest industries from the caves of Bacho Kiro and Temnata display a mature Upper Palaeolithic technology (the volumetric concept of a blade core) with, at the same time, morphological forms of Aurignacian tools that are not fully developed. Assemblage variability was caused by the strong influence of raw material procurement strategies on the morphology of almost all tool groups via the tool reduction pattern.

The typical (Middle) Balkan Aurignacian

Inventories dated to the period between 34 and 28/29 kyr BP have been ascribed to this phase. Such industries were recorded in the sequences from the Bacho Kiro Cave (levels 9, 8, 7/6b, 7, 6a/7) and from the Temnata Cave (levels 3g and 3h).

The most important feature of these levels is the morphological development of Aurignacian tools manifested in the appearance of typical (both carinated and nosed) high end-scrapers made on flakes and chunks. Consequently, bladelets are present as the product of the shaping of end-scrapers. Sporadically, bladelets were microretouched; sometimes alternate retouch was used, producing shapes that resemble Dufour bladelets. Nonetheless, the assemblages in the listed levels are still dominated by end-scrapers, showing only a slight increase in burins (mainly in levels 7 and 4b in the Bacho Kiro Cave). Carenoidal burins are practically unknown. Levels

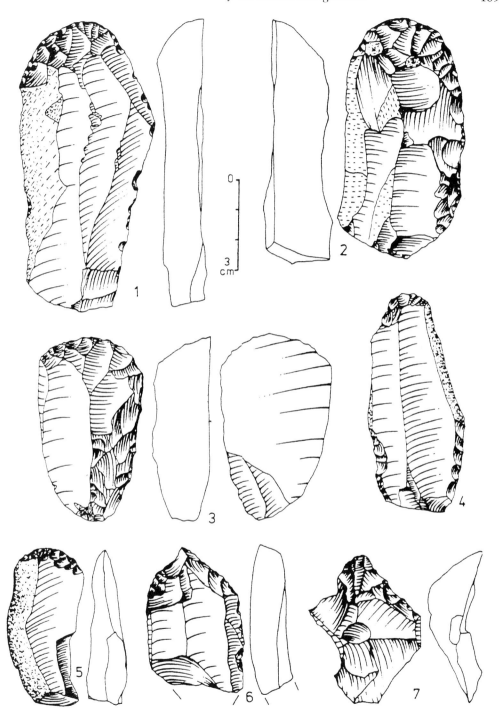

Figure 9.6: Temnata Cave, layer 4: selected end-scrapers, retouched blades and burins.

3g and 3h in the Temnata Cave may contain some mechanical admixtures from the Gravettian layers. On the other hand, a possibility that some of the bladelets with steep retouch could constitute an integral part of these assemblages – just as in the inventories from northern Italy (*e.g.* from Riparo Fumane: Broglio 1996) – cannot be excluded.

An essential element of the typical Balkan Aurignacian is the occurrence of bone points. In the Temnata Cave bone artefacts have not been preserved, but the upper levels of the Bacho Kiro Cave contain bone points which form a sequence similar to the classic western European model:

– layer 9 yielded a point with a split base (Kozłowski 1975: Fig. 18c);
– layer 8 yielded a fragment of a point, probably of Mladeč type (Kozłowski 1982: Fig. 10, 1);
– the level between layers 6a and 7 contained points with round cross-sections (Kozłowski 1982: Fig. 14: 1, 2).

A similar sequence is partly repeated in the north-western Balkan sites, notably in the Mokriška Cave where layer 7 contained points with split bases and layer 6 fragments of Mladeč-type points (Brodar and Osole 1979). The alleged co-occurrence of the two point types in the Potočka Cave (layer 7) is supported by the presence of only one specimen recorded among 50 Mladeč-type points, which has been probably erroneously ascribed to split-based points. A question can be posed: did the split-based points occur earlier than the typical Aurignacian – perhaps even contemporaneously with the Bachokirian – in the Balkans? Such points are absent in Bacho Kiro layer 11 yet, assuming the radiocarbon date of *ca.* 41 kyr BP from the lower level of the Istállóskö Cave is reliable, split-based points may have appeared in the middle Danube basin in the period corresponding to the Bachokirian.

When the sites of the typical (middle) Balkan Aurignacian – which besides Bulgaria is known mainly in Voivodina, Croatia and Slovenia – are examined it can be seen that this cultural unit shows fairly high homogeneity, seen in (Figs. 9.7-9.9):

1. the domination of end-scrapers over other tool types;
2. the presence of typical, carinated and nosed, end-scrapers, often made on flakes;
3. the presence of a large number of end-scrapers made on retouched blades;
4. the presence of retouched blades, mainly *appointé*, occasionally asymmetrical;
5. the appearance of side-scrapers, retouched flakes and notched-denticulated tools in greater number than in the early phase.

This homogenous character of the typical Balkan Aurignacian is partially obscured by functional differentiation of sites and, in some cases, by technological limitations imposed by the available raw materials.

Strong functional differentiation can be seen in the upper levels in the Bacho Kiro Cave, where two types of camp have been distinguished:

a) base camps with high proportion of flakes and waste from retouching and equal proportions of unretouched blades and retouched tools (levels 9, 7, 6a/7), or with ascendancy of retouched tools (levels 7/6b, 4b). Such proportions of major technological groups are typical of base camps located far away from raw material deposits.

b) short-term hunting camps whose existence is documented by individual blades and flakes (levels 4, 3b, 4b/6a), individual retouched tools (levels 5, 6b/8) sometimes in association with bone points and slabs of allochthonous rocks (level 8), individual retouched tools, blades and flakes (level 4a), or only waste from retouching and tool rejuvenation (levels 6c, 9/10).

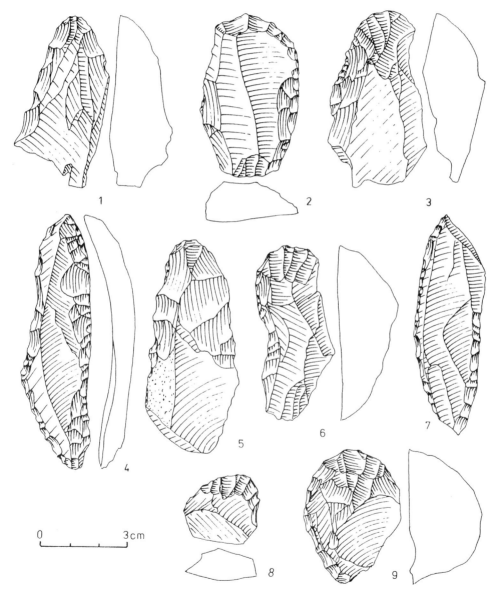

Figure 9.7: Šandalia II Cave, layer f: selected Aurignacian end-scrapers and retouched blades (according to M. Malez).

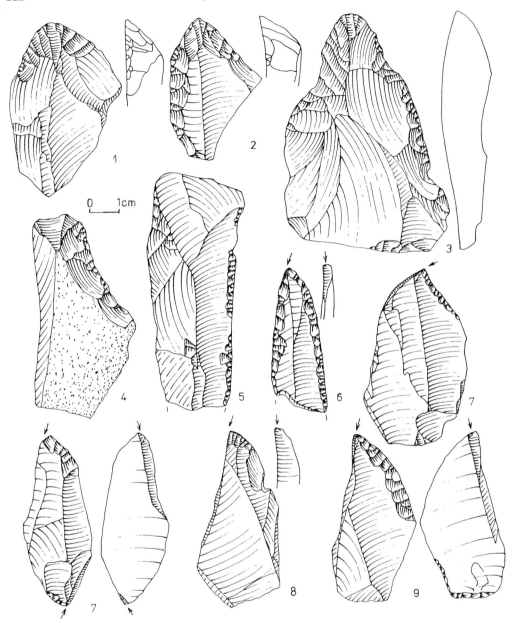

Figure 9.8: Lušcic, Bosnia: selected Aurignacian end-scrapers, retouched blades and burins (Collection of the Regional Museum at Sarajevo).

Base camps are fairly rare in other caves, with the exception of Šandalia II, layer f. In high-mountain caves in Slovenia, sites belonging to the short-term camps group are numerous. These are not only the sites of Mokriška and Špehovka with their poor inventories of a dozen or so lithic artefacts and several bone points, but also the Potočka Cave with 300 lithic artefacts to 101 bone points. The size of the inventory suggests that Potočka layer 7 is not a single camp but a series of brief sojourns of groups leaving behind inventories of a dozen or so stone tools and several bone points.

The example of the Potočka Cave, layer 7, shows how serious the influence of a lack of good raw material was on the morphology and dimensions of retouched tools. High-quality raw materials were unavailable in the Slovenian Alps. End-scrapers from poor quality local raw materials are exceptionally small in size. They are shortened by means of front rejuvenation, but some carenoidal features are nonetheless preserved. If sporadically larger retouched blades, often asymmetrical, appear in the Potočka Cave, they are characteristic of the typical Balkan Aurignacian (M. Brodar and S. Brodar 1983: Pl. I).

The biggest number of base camps representing the typical Balkan Aurignacian came from open sites, most importantly in the territory of Bosnia (Kamen, Luščič: Basler 1979, Montet-White 1996) and Voivodina (the complex of sites near Vršac, *e.g.* Črvenka and At: Mihajlović 1992).

D. Mihajlović (1992) believed that the sites near Vršac are a sequence of two types of the Aurignacian: level IIa at the site of At was correctly interpreted as displaying all the features of the typical Balkan Aurignacian, whereas the younger level IIb from the site of Črvenka is supposed to show the features of Krems facies, well-known from Banat (Magosanu 1978). However, our analysis has not confirmed this interpretation. Level IIb at the Črvenka site may indeed contain more core-like end-scrapers, but at the same time the proportion of retouched blades and burins is much higher. Retouched bladelets of Krems-Dufour type are missing. Such differences that exist between the two layers from the Črvenka and the At sites do not provide sufficient grounds to ascribe Črvenka level IIb to a separate taxonomic unit of the Aurignacian.

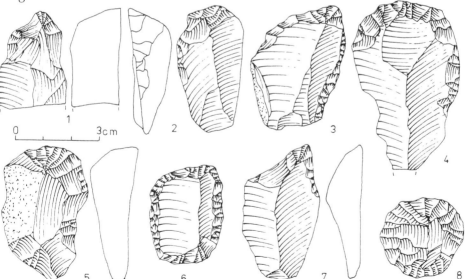

Figure 9.9: Vršac-Črvenka, Voivodina: selected Aurignacian end-scrapers, burins and retouched blades from layer IIb (according to D. Mihajlović).

The Late Balkan Aurignacian

When we follow the cultural situation in the Balkans after 29/28 kyr BP, we can see the geographic complexity of the distribution of various cultural units. Industries with backed pieces, described as the Gravettian, appear already in the period from 29 to 26 kyr BP The typical (Middle) Aurignacian vanishes from most of the Balkans in the period from 30 to 28 kyr BP.

The last Aurignacian radiocarbon-dated level 7a/7 in the Bacho Kiro Cave (Kozłowski [ed.] 1982) provided the date of 29,150 ± 950 BP (Ly-1102). It is followed only by level 4b – still within the same warm oscillation as level 6a/7 and level 4a in the next, cool episode, *i.e.* probably between 27 to 25 kyr BP. Levels 4b and 4 are unfortunately rather poor, with a smaller proportion of blades and blade tools which are gradually replaced by tools on flakes.

The only sequence in the northern Balkans where Aurignacian similar to the typical Balkan Aurignacian later than 25 kyr BP was recorded is level e in Šandalia II Cave, near Pula (Malez 1979). The date of 23,540 ± 100 BP from Šandalia is well-placed within the sequence between the date of 25,340 ± 170 BP for layer *f* with the Aurignacian, and a date of 21,740 ± 450 BP for the Gravettian layer *c*. Level *e* shows an ascendancy of end-scrapers, mainly short, flake ones with lateral retouch, carinated and nosed end-scrapers on chunks, and a few side-scrapers. When these artefacts are compared with finds from layer *f* it can be seen that blade tools decrease in number, especially Aurignacian retouched blades.

The recently-investigated sequence in Cave 1, from the Klisoura Gorge near Prosymna in the western Peloponnese, yielded a series of radiocarbon determinations placing the Late Phase of the Aurignacian around 20,060 ± 200 BP (Gd-10250) from layer 7a, but new dates on shells from the overlying layer 6a are older (23,800 ± 400 and 27,200 ± 500 BP: Gd-7994 and Gd-7996). This Late Aurignacian appears after the Middle Aurignacian layers dated between 28 and 32 kyr BP, and before the levels with some backed tool elements, with dates between 22 and 19 kyr BP (21,720 ± 90 BP: Gd-3877; 19,400 ± 100 BP: Gd-7641).

The Late Aurignacian in this sequence is unquestionably the effect of local evolution of the Middle Aurignacian. It is similarly characterised by the domination of end-scrapers on thick flakes or plaquettes; there are also steep scrapers with lateral retouch and steep and carinated end-scrapers with two or more fronts, sometimes almost discoidal. *Rabot*-type end-scrapers with either narrow flaking fronts or with broad, fan-like fronts appear. Splintered pieces are particularly numerous. There are, besides, bone points with oval cross-section reaching up to 10 cm in length, with a pointed or – less often – single-bevelled base (Fig. 9.10).

The whole Late Aurignacian industry, just like the earlier Aurignacian levels in Cave 1, Klisoura George, was based on local flints obtained from the deposit areas within a few kilometres' radius from the site. The only exception is marine shells, frequently perforated, supplied from the sea coast, at a distance of about 40 km from the site at that time.

In the uppermost Aurignacian levels certain backed elements appeared, first of all bladelets with concave blunted backs, sometimes double backed blades with occasional transversal retouch. These assemblages display a stronger blade style. These two facts provide the grounds for assuming that contacts with contemporaneous

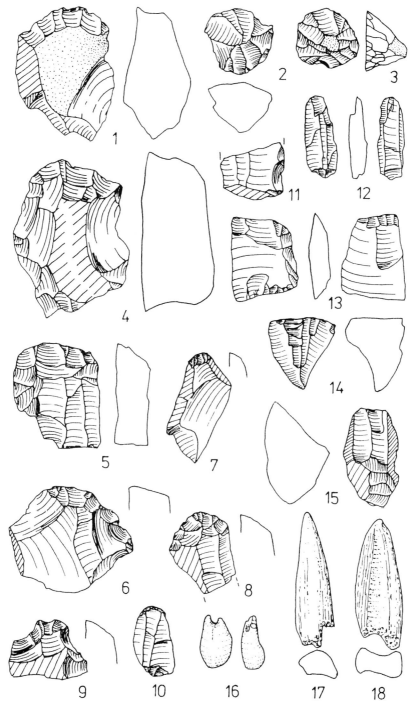

Figure 9.10: Klisoura, Cave 1, Peloponnese, Greece: selected tools from upper portion of Aurignacian layers (layer IIId).

Gravettian groups existed, or that the Aurignacian was undergoing transformation towards industries with microlithic backed pieces. Synchronicity of the highest Aurignacian levels in Cave 1 and the 'lithic phase II' with backed bladelets in the Franchthi Cave dated to 22,330 ± 350 and 21,480 ± 1270 years BP (Perlès 1987) can be the proof of co-existence, even in small territories, of groups whose cultural traditions were different. The distance from the Klisoura Gorge to the Franchthi Cave is only about 70 km.

Conclusions

The review of the evolution of the Aurignacian in the Balkans shows this culture unit to have begun in that territory earlier than in other parts of Europe. However, its local origin could not be demonstrated. The Aurignacian in the Balkans does not display any connections whatever with the local Mousterian substratum.

The Aurignacian evolved further to its Middle Phase with a number of specific characteristic features which are different from the Italian Aurignacian, and also from that of the Danube Basin.

The end of the Aurignacian was not a synchronous phenomenon over the whole territory of the Balkans. There is evidence to show that the Aurignacian occupied Istria and the Peloponnese as late as 25 to 20 kyr BP. In the period from 29 to 25 kyr BP, groups representing the typical (Middle) Aurignacian coexisted with the first Gravettian groups in the territory of Bulgaria. In the eastern Peloponnese, on the other hand, Late Aurignacian groups co-existed with industries with backed bladelets in small geographic areas. The effect of such co-existence was the mutual influence of the two cultures, expressed in the presence of backed bladelets in Aurignacian inventories and Aurignacian end-scrapers in early Gravettian assemblages.

Bibliography

Bishoff, J.L., Maroto, J., Soler, N., and J. Julia 1989. Abrupt Mousterian/Aurignacian boundary at ca. 40 ka bp: accelerator: radiocarbon dates from l'Arbreda Cave. *Journal of Archaeological Science* 16: 563-576.

Brodar, M., and F. Osole 1979. Nalazišta paleolitskog i mezolitskog doba u Sloveniji. In A. Benac (Ed.), *Pra istorija Jugoslovenskich Zemalja*. Sarajevo: Académie des Sciences.

Brodar M., and S. Brodar 1983. *Potočka zijalka*. Ljubljana: Slovenska Akademija.

Brodar, S. 1938. Das Paläolithikum in Jugoslavien. *Quartär* 1: 140-172.

Broglio, A. 1996. Le punte a dorso del Protoaurignaziano mediterraneo: I repertiti della grotta di Fumane. In A. Palma di Cesnola, A. Montet-White and K. Valoch (Eds.), *The Upper Palaeolithic (6) – Colloquia XI–XII*, pp. 237-248. Forli: A.B.A.C.O.

Chavaillon, N., Chavaillon, J., and E. Hours 1967. Industries paléolithiques d'Elide. *Bulletin de Correspondance Hellénique* 91: 151-201.

Chavaillon, N., Chavaillon, J., and E. Hours 1969. Industries paléolithiques d'Elide. *Bulletin de Correspondance Hellénique* 93: 93-151.

Darlas, A. 1989. I oriniakia lithotechnia tou Elaiochoriou Achaias. *Archaiologike Ephemeris* 128: 137-159.

Drobniewicz, B., Ginter, B., Ivanova, S., and N. Sirakov 1982. Middle Palaeolithic finds. In J.K. Kozłowski (Ed.), *Excavation in the Bacho Kiro Cave – final report*, pp. 81-116. Warszawa: PWN.

Garrod, D.A.E., Howe, B., and J.H. Gaul 1939. Excavations in the cave of Bacho Kiro, north-east Bulgaria. *Bulletin of the American School of Prehistoric Research* 15: 46-70.

Ginter, B., and N. Sirakov 1974. Rezultati ot raskopkite v pechterata Bacho Kiro prez 1973 g. *Archeologia* 2: 6-12.

Ginter, B., and J.K. Kozłowski 1992. The archaeological sequence. In *Temnata Cave – Excavations in Karlukovo Karst Area I, 1,* pp. 289-293. Kraków: Jagellonian University Press.

Ginter, B., Kozłowski, J.K., Laville, H., Sirakov, N., and R.E.M. Hedges 1996. Transition in the Balkans: News from the Temnata Cave, Bulgaria. In E. Carbonell and M. Vaquero (Eds.), *The Last Neanderthals, The First Anatomically Modern Humans,* pp. 169-200. Tarragona: Universitat Rovira i Virgili.

Hedges, R.E.M., Housley, R., Ramsey, C., and G. Van Klinken 1994. Radicarbon dates from the Oxford AMS system: *Archaeometry* datelist 18. *Archaeometry* 36: 337-374.

Koumouzelis, M., Kozłowski, J.K., Nowak, M., Sobczyk, K., Kaczanowska, M., Pawlikowski, M., and A. Pazdur 1995. Prehistoric settlement in the Klisoura George, Argolid, Greece (Excavations 1993, 1994). *Préhistoire Européenne* 8: 143-173.

Koumouzelis, M., and J.K. Kozłowski 1996. The prehistoric sites et the Kleisoura Canyon. *Archaiologia* 60: 57-62.

Kowalski, K., and A. Nadachowski 1982. Animal remains – Rodentia. In J.K. Kozłowski (Ed.), *Excavation in the Bacho Kiro Cave – final report,* pp. 45-52. Warszawa: PWN.

Kozłowski, J.K. 1983. L'Aurignacien dans les Balkans. In M. Otte (Ed.), *Aurignacien et Gravettien en Europe [UISPP 10, Nice],* pp. 273-284. Liège: ERAUL 13/1.

Kozłowski, J.K. 1982. Upper Palaeolithic assemblages. In J.K. Kozłowski (Ed.), *Excavation in the Bacho Kiro Cave – final report,* pp. 119-167. Warszawa: PWN.

Kozłowski, J.K. 1996. L'origine du Gravettien dans le Sud-Est européen. In A. Palma di Cesnola, A. Montet-White and K. Valoch (Eds.), *The Upper Palaeolithic (6) – Colloquia XI–XII,* pp. 191-202. Forlì: A.B.A.C.O.

Kozłowski, J.K. (Ed.) 1982. *Excavation in the Bacho Kiro Cave – final report.* Warszawa: PWN.

Kozłowski, J.K., and N. Sirakov 1975. Rezultati ot raskopkite v Pasterata Bacho Kiro prez 1974 g.. *Archeologia* 4: 33-41.

Magoseanu, F. 1978. *Paleoliticul din Banat.* Bucuresti: Academia Republici Socialiste Romania.

Marambat, F. 1992. Paléoenvironnements végétaux à Temnata – la séquence gravettienne et épigravettienne. In *Temnata Cave – Excavations in Karlukovo Karst Area, Bulgaria I, 1,* pp. 101-126. Kraków: Jagellonian University Press.

Malez, M. 1979. Nalazišta paleolitskog i mezolitskog doba v Hrvatskoj. In A. Benac (Ed.), *Praistorija Jugoslovenskih Zemalja 1,* pp. 227-276. Sarajevo: Académie des Sciences.

Mihajlović, D. 1992. *Orinjasienska kremena industrija sa lokaliteta Črvenka-At u blizinni Vršca.* Beograd: Centar za Arheološka Istrazivanija.

Montet-White, A. 1996. *Le Paléolithique en ancienne Yougoslavie.* Grenoble: Editions Jérôme Millon.

Pawlikowski, M. 1992. The origin of raw materials. In *Temnata Cave – Excavations in Karlukovo Karst Area, Bulgaria, I, 1,* pp. 241-288. Kraków: Jagellonian University Press.

Perlès, C. 1987. *Les industries lithiques taillées de Franchthi (Argolide, Grèce). Tome 1: Présentation générale et industries paléolithiques.* Bloomington: Indiana University Press.

Popov, R. 1912. Raskopki v Peshterata Morovitza. *Izvestija na Balgarskoto Archeologichesko Druzhstvo* 3: 291-295.

Popov, R. 1931. *Peshterata Temnata Dupka.* Sofia: Narodni Archeologicheski Muzei.

Runnels, C. 1995. Review of Aegean Prehistory: IV. The Stone Age of Greece from the Paleolithic to the Advent of the Neolithic. *American Journal of Archaeology* 99: 699-728.

Soler-Masferrer, N., and J. Maroto-Genover 1993. Les nouvelles datations de l'Aurignacien dans la Peninsule Ibérique. In L. Bánesz and J.K. Kozłowski (Eds.), *Aurignacien en Europe et au Proche Orient (Actes du XIe Congrès International des Sciences Préhistoriques et Protohistoriques, 2),* pp. 162-173. Bratislava: Archeologicky Ustav SAV.

Wijmstra, T.A. 1969. Palynology of the first 30 m of a 120 metre deep section in northern Greece. *Acta Botanica Neerlandensia* 18: 511-528.

118

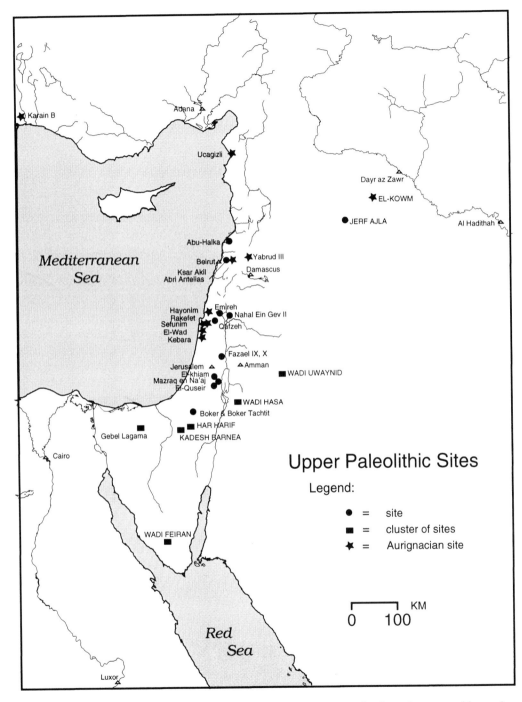

Fig. 10.1: Upper Palaeolithic sites in the Levant. Levantine Aurignacian assemblages in excavated areas are marked.

10

The Levantine Aurignacian:
60 years of research

A. Belfer-Cohen and O. Bar-Yosef

Dorothy Garrod and René Neuville:
Pioneering studies and conceptual framework
The Upper Palaeolithic sequence of the central and southern Levant, from the
Lebanese mountains in the north to the Judean Desert, was first studied and described
by the two prominent pioneers of Levantine prehistory, namely, Dorothy A.E. Garrod
and René Neuville. They were not alone in studying the prehistory of the region
during the "Golden Days" of archaeology between the two World Wars, but they
were the ones who created the basic framework of the local prehistoric sequence, in
particular that of the Upper Palaeolithic. Garrod and Neuville endeavoured to
incorporate all of the data available at that time, compiling information not only from
their excavations but also from other sites (Table 10.1, Fig. 10.1), *e.g.* Emireh and
Kebara caves, excavated by Turville-Petre (Bar-Yosef and Callander 1997), and the
sites excavated in Lebanon and Syria such as Ksar Akil (by Doherty and Ewing;
Ewing 1947) and Yabrud (Rust 1950). They both came up with a detailed scheme of
the various prehistoric entities, their main characteristics, the sites and layers from
which they were recovered, and their place in the chronological sequence of the
Upper Palaeolithic. This basic framework remains to this very day. Although many
modifications were introduced over time, it is still the "common ground" for any
attempt to define anew the Levantine Upper Palaeolithic sequence according to the
finds of current research.

Both Garrod and Neuville began digging in mandatory Palestine in 1928 and
both had to stop during the war years (1939–1945). Yet, it can be stated unequivocally
that Garrod's influence was of a greater magnitude. She was a professional
archaeologist, dedicating all of her time to prehistoric investigation, whereas Neuville
was pursuing a diplomatic career while he did archaeology. Furthermore, Garrod
continued her research in the region during the 1950s, publishing syntheses and
digging cave sites in Lebanon in Ras el Kelb (Garrod and Henri-Martin 1961) and the
Adlun sites (Garrod and Kirkbride 1961). Neuville, however, died in 1951, the year
his major volume was published.

Table 10.1: Neuville and Garrod's sequence of the Upper Palaeolithic (after Bar-Yosef 1970: 23, Copeland 1975: fig 10)

PHASE	FLINT TOOLS	SITES AND LEVELS		KSAR AKIL LEVELS
VI - Kebaran	Numerous truncated and pointed bladelets	Kebara B Hayonim C Nahal Oren 9	1 4	Kebaran
V - Atlitian	Polyhedral and truncated burins	El-Khiam E El-Wad C Nahal Ein Gev I	6 7	Levantine Aurignacian C
IV - Upper Antelian	Aurignacian endscrapers, few El-Wad points	Erk-El Ahmar B El-Wad D, Hayonim D Kebara D, El-Khiam F El Quseir C	8 9 10	Levantine Aurignacian B
III - Lower Antelian	Aurignacian endscrapers, many El-Wad points	Erk El-Ahmar D El-Wad E Kebara E	 13-11	 Levantine Aurignacian A
II - Unnamed	Pointed blades, endscrapers, burins	Erk El-Ahmar E, F Qafzeh D	15	Ksar Akil Phase B
I - Emiran	Emireh points, Levallois tec., Blades	El-Wad F, G Et-Tabban B Qafzeh E	21 25	Ksar Akil Phase A

Garrod and Neuville were trained, like their contemporaries, in the same schools of Old World archaeology. Garrod studied in Oxford and later with Abbé Henri Breuil, while Neuville studied in Paris. Close contacts between the leading professors in the two countries were responsible for their adopting similar approaches for classifying and defining phases or cultures within prehistoric sequences. In books and papers from the early part of the twentieth century, scholars rarely expressed explicitly the goals of their research. Often it was either implicit in the published results or mentioned only succinctly. Garrod, in her book on the Upper Palaeolithic of Britain (Garrod 1926), briefly mentioned the two aspects of her goals in prehistoric research: to identify the geographic distribution of cultural entities in a continent or continents in order to "reconstruct the migrations of the Palaeolithic culture."

Already during the years when Garrod excavated in Mt. Carmel and Neuville worked in the Judean Desert caves and rock-shelters (Fig. 10.1, Table 10.1), both published their suggested classification of Upper Palaeolithic assemblages (Garrod and Bate 1937; Neuville 1934). Though they both introduced minor changes through the years, the basic framework remained the same (see Bar-Yosef 1970; Copeland 1975; Gilead 1991).

The criteria for sub-dividing the Upper Palaeolithic in the Levant were derived from the criteria used for this period in Europe. The main concern was typological, and the dominant attribute was the presence of a 'fossile directeur'. This meant that special attention was paid to particular tool-types which were considered as typical for that specific prehistoric entity, aside from other more common tool-types such as endscrapers, burins, retouched artefacts, *etc.* Garrod and Neuville included among the 'fossiles directeurs' tools that were the typical 'guide fossils' of the French Upper Palaeolithic such as the Châtelperronian knives and the Font-Yves points (even though Garrod acknowledged that the latter were rather rare in the French sites). At the same time, both recognised the presence of special local forms that were not encountered in Europe and resembled, in some cases, the African types. An example is the triangular point with basal bifacial retouch which Garrod first named after the African Tabelbalat point, but later suggested renaming with the local name after Emireh cave (Neuville 1951: 70).

Following the original French subdivision Garrod identified each of the Upper Palaeolithic phases by giving them a cultural label. It should be remembered that all of the Upper Palaeolithic sequence in Europe was first subdivided into Early, Middle and Late Aurignacian (Breuil 1912), followed by the Solutrean and the Magdalenian. It was later recognised that the Early Aurignacian is better referred to as Châtelperronian and the Late Aurignacian became the Gravettian (Davies, this volume). Peyrony, tracing the blade industries, redefined the sequence as the persistence of two technological traditions – Perigordian (including the Châtelperronian and Gravettian) and Aurignacian (*e.g.* Bordes 1968). Bordes contributed to this scheme by demonstrating that the Châtelperronian is technologically and typologically the later evolution of the Mousterian of Acheulian Tradition.

Garrod's first scheme for the Levant began with the 'Lower Aurignacian' followed by the 'Middle Aurignacian.' She named the next phase as 'Atlitian' after Atlit, at the time a train station on the coastal plain in front of the Mt. Carmel caves. The 'Kebaran' designated the final Upper Palaeolithic stage before the Mesolithic period, which was represented culturally by the newly discovered Natufian culture (Garrod 1932).

Neuville's subdivision was first published in 1934, and Garrod tried to fit her data into his scheme while making several minor changes according to her own observations. Hence, the basic sequence accepted by both was as follows:

Phase I – A transitional phase from the Mousterian. The 'guide fossil' was the Emireh point that was produced on Levallois or triangular points, with sporadic appearance of blade elements, endscrapers and burins. The key sites were et-Tabban B, Qafzeh E and el-Wad F.

Phase II – This stage, identified by Neuville in the Judean Desert, had a limited geographic distribution. It is characterised by Châtelperron points and a few Font-Yves ones, which were later named el-Wad points (see below). It should be pointed out that Garrod did not find this phase in Mt. Carmel. It was identified in Erq el-Ahmar F, and perhaps in Qafzeh D.

Phase III – Typified by numerous Font-Yves (*i.e.* el-Wad) points and increasing
frequencies of other Aurignacian elements. According to Garrod and Neuville,
this is an early Aurignacian stage. The key assemblages were Erq el-Ahmar D,
Qafzeh C and el-Wad E.

Phase IV – A late Aurignacian stage with a dominance of carinated and nosed
endscrapers and a near total disappearance of the Font-Yves (*i.e.* el-Wad) points.
Key assemblages were Erq el-Ahmar B and el-Wad D.

Phase V – Characterised by an increase in the number of burins and other items made
on crude flakes. The number of Aurignacian items dwindles and microliths
appear for the first time. Key assemblages were el-Wad C and el-Khiam E.

Phase VI – Dominated by a plethora of various microliths, endscrapers on blades and
dihedral burins. The key assemblages were Kebara C and el-Khiam D.

During the ensuing years, Garrod made some changes to incorporate sites from
Lebanon into the diachronic framework. Her scheme was based on the character of
the assemblage as a whole rather than on the presence or absence of particular tool-
types. Every stage in the sequence was given a name and was considered as
representing an independent cultural entity (Garrod 1954). She also became aware of
the local nature of the lithic industries and thus replaced most of the European
terminology used by Neuville and herself with local names.

Hence, the first Upper Palaeolithic manifestation (Phase I) was named "Emiran,"
as Garrod realised that the assemblage retrieved by Turville-Petre in Emireh cave, as
he saw it, had a special configuration (Garrod 1955). Typical tool-types of this
industry are Emireh points, as well as endscrapers and some burins. The débitage is
a mixture of both flake and blade elements. She noted, according to her technological
criteria, the presence of the Levallois technique together with blade production
techniques and blade cores. Convex backed blades were considered as reminiscent of
Châtelperronian knives. In addition to Emireh cave, Garrod included in this entity
Yabrud II layer 7 and the assemblages from Abu-Halka cave in Lebanon.

Neuville's phase II was considered by Garrod (1957) as poorly defined and thus
did not justify the introduction of an independent stage within the regional Upper
Palaeolithic sequence.

The "Middle Aurignacian" (chronologically correlated with phases III and IV of
Neuville's scheme) was later named by Garrod (1957) as "Lower and Upper Antelian"
after the sites in Wadi Antelias, Lebanon, which include Abri Antelias, Abri Bergy and
Ksar Akil. These phases are typified by the presence of carinated and nosed
endscrapers, prismatic burins and retouched blades. The main difference between the
two stages of the "Antelian" lies in the changing frequencies of Font-Yves (el-Wad)
points. These slender items, shaped as points by an intermittent retouch along the
lateral edges and the tip, were numerous in the Lower Antelian, whereas they almost
disappear in the Upper Antelian.

The next entity had, according to Garrod, a very local character (not found in
either the Lebanese or Syrian sites), and thus she named it "Atlitian" (phase V of
Neuville). The Atlitian industry was dominated by burins, whether polyhedral
(possibly bladelet cores) or on truncations (Garrod and Bate 1937, Neuville 1951).

The final entity (phase VI) was named Kebaran by Garrod, who recognised the uniqueness of the microlithic industry uncovered by F. Turville-Petre in his one season of excavations at Kebara Cave. The industry was characterised by high frequencies of microliths, many of which were shaped as backed bladelets with an oblique truncation later called the Kebara point (Besançon *et al.* 1975–77).

Yet even with all these modifications, Garrod retained the basic assumption that the various prehistoric entities represented a unilinear sequence, and that all of the cultural evolution represented by this sequence occurred locally in the Levant.

The 1960s: Modifications and the impact of the 1969 London conference

In the following years, new excavations and publications revealed the need for further modifications in the basic scheme compiled by Garrod and Neuville. First there came new interpretations of the Upper Palaeolithic entities and their interrelationships. Returning to the site of El-Khiam terrace in the Judean Desert, first excavated by Neuville, J. Gonzalez-Echegaray concurred with Garrod's cultural terminology (Gonzalez-Echegaray 1964, 1966), though later he introduced some modifications (Gonzalez-Echegaray 1978).

Gonzalez-Echegaray's main point was that the Emiran was a local phenomenon while later on, intrusive elements, mainly the Aurignacian, arrived via migration from some centre in Russia or Anatolia. These were incorporated into the local tradition, creating a unique entity which differs from the Aurignacian of Western Europe.

In 1969 a small but historically important conference took place in the Institute of Archaeology in London. It was organised by R. Solecki and was sponsored by the Wenner Gren Foundation. The participants included most of the active Levantine Palaeolithic archaeologists at the time (O. Bar-Yosef, F. Bordes, M. Brezillon, L. Copeland, F. Hours, C. McBurney, J. Perrot, A. Ronen, B. Schroeder, G. Sieveking, R. Solecki, D. de Sonneville-Bordes, J. Waechter, and the latter's students I. Azoury and M. Newcomer). The aim was to agree on a common typological type-list for the Upper and Epi-Palaeolithic. The collections chosen to be used for creating these type-lists were those from the site of Ksar Akil, kept at the Institute of Archaeology, University of London. This site yielded about 18 metres' depth of Upper Palaeolithic deposits, rich in artefacts and bones. At that time, both Azoury and Newcomer were working on their theses, but no detailed studies had been published. It was acknowledged by most of the Levantine prehistorians that Ksar Akil represents the most complete sequence available for the Levantine Upper Palaeolithic (Copeland 1975).

F. Hours had prepared a preliminary type-list, which also benefited from Hours' discussions with J. Tixier, who then began to re-excavate Ksar Akil with this in mind. The final type-list which emerged by consensus from the conference was published in *Paléorient* (Hours 1974). The decrees of the London conference were widely accepted, as can be judged from the published proceedings of yet another symposium that took place several years later, in 1973, at the Department of Anthropology, Southern Methodist University, Dallas (Wendorf and Marks 1975). Indeed quite a few of the participants, while basing the fuller descriptions of the industries on both old and new collections, employed the new terminology.

L. Copeland (1975, 1976) and others re-defined the various criteria used by Garrod and Neuville and tried to examine them in the light of the data accumulated since the publications of the pioneer schemes. In accordance with the trend first suggested by Garrod, local names were given not only to the cultural entities as a whole but also to the various "guide fossils" (for example the 'el-Wad' point which replaced the Font-Yves point). Copeland accepted the interpretation that certain 'Emiran' assemblages such as el-Wad F and E were mechanically mixed (see also Bar-Yosef and Vandermeersch 1972). However, after examining the Ksar Akil material, where the earliest layers are characterised by chamfered pieces (*chanfreins*), she suggested the existence of a northern and southern facies of the transitional 'Emiran' phase.

Thus Ksar Akil became the type site of the Levantine Upper Palaeolithic, presenting in a sequence both lithic entities, known from other sites, as well as unique assemblages, known only from either Ksar Akil or at the most from other neighbouring sites in Lebanon. Indeed, the lowermost Upper Palaeolithic layers 25–15 were considered unique and thus were labelled Ksar Akil Phases A, equated with the Emiran, and B, which today could be considered as Early Ahmarian (Copeland 1975, Ohnuma 1988). These were followed by what was agreed in the London meeting to be named Levantine Aurignacian A, which seems to be present only in Lebanon (Ksar Akil layer 13–11) and characterised by el-Wad points and flat-faced carinated burins, or "Ksar Akil" burins. Both Azoury and Copeland proclaimed that this industry is not Antelian and rather is unique to Ksar Akil (Azoury and Hobson 1973; Copeland 1976:45).

The next stage, Levantine Aurignacian B, appears in layers 10–8 in Ksar Akil and is considered on typological grounds to be equivalent to phases III and IV of Neuville and both Antelian stages of Garrod. The first radiocarbon dates of the Upper Palaeolithic layers in Ksar Akil were obtained from these layers. A date of 28,840±380 BP was obtained from shells collected from strata which cover the top of layer 9, layer 8 and the bottom of layer 7 (Vogel and Waterbolk 1963). AMS dates that range from 29/30,000 to 26/27,000 BP, obtained from the renewed excavations by Tixier and his team, are quite compatible with the previous reading (Mellars and Tixier 1989). The industry is characterised by a rise in Aurignacian elements and the endscrapers outnumber the burins by as much as two times. There are many el-Wad points (up to 12%) and they differ slightly from those recovered in the preceding layers.

Levantine Aurignacian C (Ksar Akil levels 7–6) was considered as equivalent to the Atlitian (Garrod) or phase V (Neuville). The typological characteristics comprise prismatic burins and high frequencies of carinated endscrapers (mostly what seem to be keeled bladelet cores), while the nosed scrapers have disappeared. Many bladelets were collected in these layers.

With the extension of excavations and surveys, especially in the Negev and Sinai, a certain opposition to the proposed sequence was raised. For example, Marks (1976) claimed that this sequence (Copeland 1975) is valid only for the Lebanese sites and is not applicable for the whole of the Levant. According to his view, further supported by his excavations at Boker Tachtit, there were two basic facies during the early Upper Palaeolithic in the Levant: (1) a transitional phase which is present only in Lebanon

(Copeland's Ksar Akil phases A and B), and (2) the transitional phase observed at the site of Boker Tachtit, in the Negev Highlands (Marks 1983a).

The ensuing phase comprises all the entities including the assemblages with el-Wad points, carinated and nosed endscrapers, polyhedral burins, *etc.* These assemblages vary geographically, chronologically and probably also functionally. There is no place for a big scheme encompassing the whole Levant, except for a couple of valid general observations: (a) the el-Wad points as guide fossils are characteristic of early assemblages, and (b) thick and nosed endscrapers belong chronologically to the middle stage of the Upper Palaeolithic, and microliths and Dufour bladelets characterise assemblages of the later Upper Palaeolithic (Marks 1983b).

In 1976, Ronen proposed a general scheme for the Upper Palaeolithic industries of the western Galilee and Mt. Carmel, keeping the regional subdivision. The 12 assemblages he considered were subdivided according to lithic comparisons between them. Although he refers to the Ksar Akil sequence, the Israeli scheme is quite independent and self-contained. The earliest stage of the Upper Palaeolithic, following the Transitional Industry, is characterised by abruptly retouched blades and even bladelets. Technologically, more than half of the tools are on blades. The latter category contains a few Aurignacian elements, and some burins, with both the endscrapers and burins comprising less than 40% of the total tool component.

The middle stage of the Upper Palaeolithic is characterised by high percentages of Aurignacian elements and an increase in the percentage of burins as compared with the previous stage. The endscrapers and burins comprise *ca.* 50%-60% of the tools. Blade tools comprise only one-third of the tools.

In the latest stage, the endscrapers and burins comprise more than 80% of the tool component and the blade tools dwindle to less than 20%. Ronen suggested that an additional chronological subdivision is needed with the burins outnumbering the endscrapers in the latest phase and a decrease in the frequencies of Aurignacian endscrapers.

Most researchers dealing with the Levantine Upper Palaeolithic concur with Marks and Ronen that there is a geographic subdivision along the Mediterranean coastal ranges. There are no clear parallels to the Levantine Aurignacian A. Most of the assemblages in northern Israel are aligned with the Levantine Aurignacian B from Ksar Akil (levels 8–10), while some were assigned to the Levantine Aurignacian C (levels 6–7 at Ksar Akil). These assemblages are overlain in Ksar Akil by bladelet industries dated to *ca.* 22,000 years BP (Mellars and Tixier 1989). The dates of the Kebaran complex, once thought to represent the final stage of the Upper Palaeolithic sequence (*i.e.* phase VI of Neuville), are younger and fall between 19/18,000 and 13,000 BP (Byrd 1994).

As time went by, it became evident that the typical Aurignacian industries are absent from the semi-arid area of the southern Levant and that instead there is a dominance of blade industries, rich in el-Wad points and bladelets.

Garrod's contention that the "transitional industries" which occupy the early portion of the Upper Palaeolithic sequence evolved locally is supported by the evidence from Boker Tachtit (Marks 1983a). This is indeed the origin of the Ahmarian entity, defined in the southern Levant (Gilead 1981, Marks 1981) but found also in the north, always above the Mousterian and beneath later Upper Palaeolithic industries. This observation is supported by the evidence from Kebara and el-Wad where blade assemblages precede the Aurignacian ones.

There are a few assemblages in Lebanon and north Israel which are indeed Aurignacian or "Antelian" as proposed by Garrod (1957). They retained some of the most typical characteristics of the Aurignacian as it was originally defined, namely the nosed and carinated scrapers, the Aurignacian blades, Dufour bladelets and, to a lesser extent, the el-Wad (Font-Yves, Krems) points. Even some of the bone tools are reminiscent of the European forms, as is their raw material, such as using horn-cores and antlers for shaping points (Bar-Yosef and Belfer-Cohen 1996). It seems that most of the Aurignacian technological production resulted in ordinary and thick flakes as well as thick blades. The occasional thinner blades were rather an exception and most of them were shaped into tools, as can be seen from the low percentage of blades among the débitage compared to their high percentage among the tool blanks. The bladelets in these assemblages, generally twisted, were obtained from shaping the carinated scrapers.

From the 1980s to the present

Field work and laboratory studies that were done in the early 1980s presented us with some basic problems that need to be resolved: (a) the criteria used for defining 'lithic cultures' and 'traditions', (b) the radiocarbon chronology of the various assemblages, and (c) the geographic distribution of the Upper Palaeolithic industries across the Near East.

In the early 1980s, Marks (1981) and Gilead (1981, 1991) proposed to subdivide the Levantine Upper Palaeolithic into two major lithic traditions: a flake-dominated one, the Levantine Aurignacian, and a blade dominated one, the Ahmarian. The shortcomings of the basic criteria used for classifying assemblages into industries or traditions lay with the differential treatment of tools (retouched and secondary modified pieces) as opposed to débitage (which includes all the by-products, rejects, and non-retouched artefacts as well as the cores). Thus Gilead considered the ratio of blades/bladelets *versus* flakes in the débitage to be the decisive criterion. He also took into account the ratio between endscrapers and burins *versus* blade tools, *i.e.* retouched/pointed/backed blades, while ignoring the nature of the blanks of the aforementioned tools. Hence, according to his definitions the Levantine Aurignacian encompassed both northern sites such as Ksar Akil (levels 13–6), Hayonim D, Kebara E-D, and El-Wad E-D, and sites in the Negev and Sinai such as D14, 18, D22 (Arkov), D26, D 27, Ramat Matred I, G11, K9A, HHI, and Qadesh Barnea 602 (Gilead 1991).

Indeed defining the Ahmarian, a blade-orientated entity, was a major contribution to disclosing the Upper Palaeolithic lithic variability in the Levant. The impression that nearly all of the definable Ahmarian entities are geographically confined to the southern and eastern parts of the Levant is inaccurate. There are northern assemblages that bear the characteristics of the Ahmarian, such as those observed by Ronen (1976): Kebara Cave layer E (old excavations) and Units III and IV of the new excavations (Bar-Yosef *et al.* 1996); Qafzeh Cave layer E (old excavations) and layers 9–7 in the new excavations (Ronen and Vandermeersch 1972;

Bar-Yosef *et al.*, in preparation). It would be a mistake to lump all of the Ahmarian assemblages together. The recognition that there is variability among the Ahmarian assemblages is expressed in the definition of the Lagaman of northern Sinai (*e.g.* Bar-Yosef and Belfer 1977, Phillips 1994).

The Ahmarian seems to have evolved from the Emiran (the Transitional Industry). The excavations at Boker Tachtit (Marks 1983a) indicate that the dominant reduction sequence is not a typical Levallois one and that cores served for the reduction of blades. Emireh points were made from these triangular 'bladey' flakes, or so-called Levallois points, which have a bi-directional scar pattern (Volkman and Kaufman 1983). Similarly the et-Tabban B assemblage (in the Judean Desert) with the Emireh points is a non-Levallois industry.

The dates for the Emiran are earlier than the oldest Ahmarian readings. Boker Tachtit produced dates of 47/46 ka BP, while the first Ahmarian manifestations in Kebara (units III-IV) date between 43–36,000 BP (Bar-Yosef *et al.* 1996). In the Lebanon-Galilee area, the Ahmarian sequence is interrupted by the 'intrusion' of the Aurignacian, but in other areas the Ahmarian assemblages provide a range of 38,000 to 20,000 years ago. Hence, a partial contemporaneity of these two main industries is indicated. The 'why' and 'how' of such a phenomenon, though of utmost importance as a topic of investigation, is beyond the scope of the present paper.

It seems to us that the Ahmarian is indeed an independent entity, and that it differs considerably from the Levantine Aurignacian. However, the definition of the latter, originating at the London meeting (Copeland 1975) and adopted by Gilead (1981, 1991) and others, seems now to produce an impossible hybrid.

First, there are sound arguments why we should divide this entity at least into two, a division that is supported by the geographic distribution of the sites pertaining to each of the sub-divisions. The first group is the 'original' Levantine Aurignacian assemblages from the central Levant in Lebanon, the Anti Lebanon mountains and Galilee. The most reliable radiocarbon dates, from the Levantine Aurignacian levels of Kebara, indicate a range of 36/34–29/27,000 BP (Bar-Yosef *et al.* 1996, Bar-Yosef and Belfer-Cohen 1996). The second cluster of assemblages, which cannot be considered as Aurignacian, includes the Arkov/Divshon group 'flakey' entities. The radiocarbon dates range from 30,800 BP in Qseimeh II to *ca.* 17,000 BP in Ein Aqev (Phillips 1994) including Boker BE level 1.

In addition we should consider the typological and technological aspects of the whole lithic assemblage (tools and débitage alike), as well as other components such as the presence or absence in these layers of bone and antler artefacts and their shapes. The overall composition of the two clusters is shown in Table 10.2.

Table 10.2: General frequencies of blank types and tools.

Region	North and Central Levant	Southern Levant
Tool Blanks	Baldes=Flakes	Blades<Flakes
Bladelets	many	nearly none
Ratios	Endscrapers>Burins	Endscrapers<Burins
Aurignacian chars (*)	++++	——————

(*) = Aurignacian retouch, nosed, shouldered and carinated endscraper.

It should be mentioned that in 1976, Marks observed: "It is abundantly clear, however, that the term Levantine Aurignacian should not be applied to the Boker Area BE, and the Ein Aqev East assemblages, if it is also applied to such assemblages as Hayonim D, and el-Wad, D and E" (Marks 1976: 72).

The six sites in southern Jordan excavated by Henry (Coinman and Henry 1995) serve as an example that illustrates the apparent confusion when one tries to place any Upper Palaeolithic assemblage into the 'straight-jacket' definitions of either a 'flakey' (Levantine Aurignacian) industry or a 'bladey' (Ahmarian) one. When discussing the assemblages, Henry and Coinman state that the so-called Levantine Aurignacian sites (Tor Fawaz J403 and Jebel Humeima J412) vary technologically and typologically from the descriptions of the 'Levantine Aurignacian' as defined by Gilead (Henry 1995: 195). The authors also state that their Ahmarian sites (Tor Hamar J431, Tor Aeid J432 and J440) are somewhat uncharacteristic and inconsistent with other early Ahmarian assemblages in the southern Levant (Coinman and Henry 1995: 165) or are "lacking important features that are typical of early Ahmarian assemblages" (Coinman and Henry 1995: 179, 181). Indeed, Henry (1995) cites his own version of the Levantine Aurignacian and Ahmarian definitions which differ from those suggested by Gilead in the first place: "*Levantine Aurignacian* assemblages are dominated by endscrapers and burins on thick blades. *Ahmarian* assemblages also primarily consist of endscrapers and burins, but El-Wad points and a substantial bladelet component distinguish these assemblages from those of the *Levantine Aurignacian*..." (p. 37: italics are ours).

The Atlitian or phase V of Neuville's original scheme was initially comprised of only two assemblages: El-Khiam E and El-Wad C. Though Garrod claimed that there is some resemblance to the Antelian/Aurignacian of the previous layers at El-Wad, the difference was great enough to justify the coining of a new entity whose main characteristic was the appearance of polyhedral burins and burins on truncation. Over time, more assemblages were incorporated into this entity. It has become apparent, though, that it has been treated as a chronological unit incorporating a number of assemblages lacking common denominators, except for the fact that they seem to be late in the Upper Palaeolithic sequence. The radiocarbon chronology for the general entity of the Atlitian is poorly known.

The assemblages incorporated in the Atlitian are: El-Wad C (where no systematic sieving was practised) in which polyhedral burins and carinated endscrapers comprise up to 80% of the tools (Garrod and Bate 1937); the El-Khiam E assemblages with high percentages of burins on truncations (mainly on retouched notches), and some bladelets (Gonzalez-Echegaray 1966); Nahal Ein Gev I, with few endscrapers (less than 5%), a dominance of burins on retouched truncations and *ca.* 5–10% of finely retouched bladelets (Bar-Yosef 1973; Belfer-Cohen *et al.*, in preparation). Also included among these assemblages is that of Fazael IX where the dominant tool is once again the burins on truncations, though they are shaped on more delicate blanks than those of Nahal Ein Gev I and El-Wad C (Goring-Morris 1980). The assemblage of Ksar Akil level 6, which is also considered as 'Levantine Aurignacian C', contains no carinated scrapers but is dominated by burins on retouched truncations. A unique characteristic of this assemblage, noted by Bergman (1987), is the existence of bladelet cores indicating the presence of a second reduction sequence for bladelet production. It should be noted that the carinated scrapers from El-Wad C are effectively similar to the bladelet cores from Ksar Akil 6. Other examples are Abri Antelias layer II, Yabrud III layers 2 and 3, and the sounding in B7 at Nahal Oren (Bar-Yosef 1970), which demonstrates the variability of the so-called 'Levantine Aurignacian C.' Given the paucity of the original characteristics of the Aurignacian in these assemblages, it would be best to abandon this taxon.

Other entities prior to the earliest appearances of Kebaran assemblages are dated at *ca.* 21,000 to 19,000 BP. Several sites, mainly in Jordan (*e.g.* Uwaynid 18, Jilat 9, or Wadi Hasa 618) (Garrard *et al.* 1988, Clark *et al.* 1988), are characterised by various backed microliths and the microburin technique. Elsewhere, other assemblages are dominated by tool categories of various finely retouched bladelets with no microburin technique such as Ohalo II, Fazael X, and perhaps Masaraq e-Naj, Ein Aqev East, Shunera XVI and Azariq XIII. Goring-Morris (1995) proposed the term Masraqan for this entity, which is geographically located in the southern Levant, including the Jordan Valley.

Since the 1960s, the Kebaran, or Neuville's phase VI, has been considered the first Epi-Palaeolithic entity, and thus discussion of it is beyond the scope of this paper.

Concluding Remarks

It seems that the time is ripe to make new modifications to the general scheme of the Upper Palaeolithic Levantine sequence. There is a need to re-state which assemblages can be considered as Aurignacian, while a new taxon must be coined to accommodate the 'flakey' assemblages recovered from the 1960s onwards in the southern and south-eastern areas of the Levant. We have to eliminate the confusing taxon "Levantine Aurignacian C" or the Atlitian. As demonstrated above, this classification has became a 'waste basket' for assemblages whose only common denominator is their 'flakey' appearance and late date in the Upper Palaeolithic sequence. There is also a need to subdivide the various Ahmarian assemblages into local variants as has been done for the North Sinai Ahmarian assemblages, *e.g.* the Lagaman.

But it seems to us that there is also an urgent need to re-examine the issue of the so-called 'guide fossils,' common to both the Ahmarian and Aurignacian complexes. It was most unfortunate that the el-Wad points and bladelets which are more common in Ahmarian assemblages, especially in the later ones, were first identified and declared as 'guide fossils' of the Aurignacian. A more detailed study may reveal the differences between these tool-types in Aurignacian and Ahmarian assemblages. As an example we can indicate that production technology of the Aurignacian Dufour bladelets is different from that of the bladelets recovered in Ahmarian assemblages, such as the Lagaman ones. Perhaps a clearer definition of carinated scrapers and nosed scrapers on thick flakes (not the narrow and keeled types) would conform better to the original European definitions. In addition, a better knowledge of the variety of bone and antler tools and especially the split-based point, which is now known from Kebara, Hayonim and El-Quseir caves, would be helpful. Bone tools were also produced by the manufacturers of other Upper Palaeolithic industries, but it seems that split-based points and ornaments of pierced deer teeth (like those of the

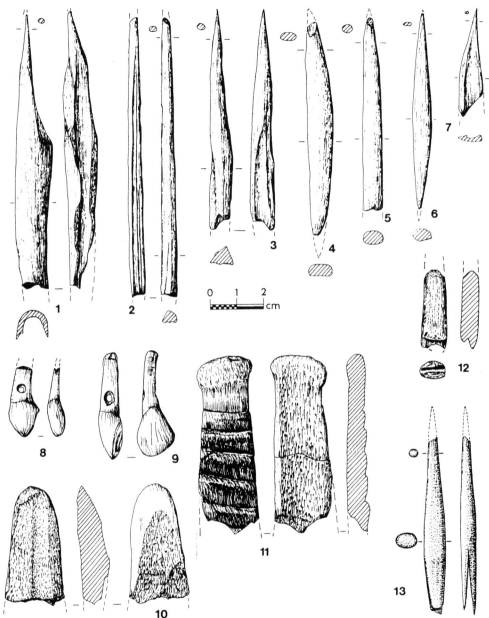

Figure 10.2: Levantine bone, antler and tooth objects from Hayonim Cave, layer D(1–12), and Kebara (13) (after Bar-Yosef and Belfer-Cohen 1996).

Aurignacian assemblages from Hayonim cave) indicate closer affinities to the European Aurignacian than any of the other bone objects (Figs. 10.2, 10.3).

With all this going on, it is still amazing to observe the insight of Garrod when she first defined the chrono-stratigraphy of the Levantine Upper Palaeolithic sequence. In her decision to consider the various entities as basically local phenomena, using

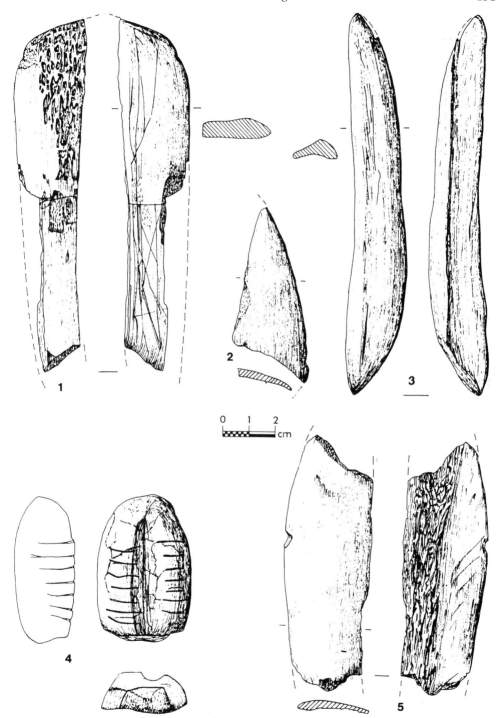

Figure 10.3: Bone tools and one "shaft-straightener" (4) from Hayonim layer D (after Bar-Yosef and Belfer-Cohen 1996).

local names and terms, and her assumption that their tempo and rate of evolution was locally tuned, she avoided the pitfalls of the Eurocentric attitude and tried to be objective in her interpretations. She provided the 'building blocks' of the study of Levantine prehistory which are still used today. Taking into consideration the quick tempo of changes and rapid accumulation of data sets in the Levant, Garrod's decisions are clear evidence for her ingenuity and foresight.

Bibliography

Azoury, I., and R. Hobson 1973. Comparing Palaeolithic Assemblages: Ksar Akil, a case-study. *World Archaeology* 4: 292–306.

Bar-Yosef, O. 1970. The Epi-Palaeolithic Cultures of Palestine. Ph.D. thesis, Hebrew University.

Bar-Yosef, O. 1973. Nahal Ein Gev I, preliminary report. *Mitekufat Haeven* 11:1–7.

Bar-Yosef, O., and B. Vandermeersch 1972. The Stratigraphical and Cultural Problems of the Passage from Middle to Upper Palaeolithic in Palestinian Caves. In F. Bordes (Ed.), *The Origins of Homo Sapiens*, pp. 221–225. Paris: Proceedings of the Paris Symposium 2–5 Sept. 1969.

Bar-Yosef, O., and A. Belfer 1977. The Lagaman Industry. In O. Bar-Yosef and J. L. Phillips (Eds.), *Prehistoric Investigations in Gebel-Maghara, Northern Sinai, Qedem 7*, pp. 42–84. Jerusalem: Monographs of the Institute of Archaeology, Hebrew University.

Bar-Yosef, O., and A. Belfer-Cohen 1996. Another Look at the Levantine Aurignacian. In A. Palma di Cesnola, A. Montet-White and K. Valoch (Eds.), *The Upper Palaeolithic (6) – Colloquia XI-XII (13th Congress, International Union of Prehistoric and Protohistoric Sciences, Forlì, 1996)*, pp. 139–150. Forlì: A.B.A.C.O.

Bar-Yosef, O., and J. Callander 1997. A Forgotten Archaeologist: The Life of Francis Turville-Petre. *Palestine Exploration Quarterly* 129: 2–18.

Bar-Yosef, O., Arnold, M., Mercier, N., Belfer-Cohen, A., Goldberg, P., Houseley, R., Laville, H., Meignen, L., Vogel, J. C., and B. Vandermeersch 1996. The Dating of the Upper Palaeolithic Layers in Kebara Cave, Mt. Carmel. *Journal of Archaeological Science* 23: 297–306.

Bergman, C.A. 1987. *Ksar Akil Lebanon.* Oxford: British Archaeological Reports International Series 329.

Besançon, J., Copeland, L., and F. Hours 1975–1977. Tableaux de préhistoire libanaise. *Paléorient* 3: 5–46.

Bordes, F. 1968. *The Old Stone Age.* London: Weidenfeld and Nicolson.

Breuil, H. 1912. *Les subdivisions du Paléolithique supérieur et leur signification.* Comptes Rendues Congrès Internationale d'Anthropologie et Archéologie Préhistorique, vol. 1, pp. 165–238. Geneva.

Byrd, B. 1994. Late Quaternary Hunter-Gatherer Complexes in the Levant between 20,000 and 10,000 BP. In O. Bar-Yosef and R.S. Kra (Eds.), *Late Quaternary Chronology and Paleoclimates of the Eastern Mediterranean*, pp. 205–226. Tucson and Cambridge: Radiocarbon and the Peabody Museum of Archaeology and Ethnology, Harvard University.

Clark, G.A., Lindly, J., Donaldson, M., Garrard, A., Coinman, N., Schuldenrein, J., Fish, S., and D. Olszewski 1988. Excavations at Middle, Upper and Epipalaeolithic sites in the Wadi Haxa, west-central Jordan. In A.N. Garrard and H.G. Gebel (Eds.), *The Prehistory of Jordan, vol. 1*, pp. 209–285. Oxford: British Archaeological Reports International Series 396.

Coinman, N.R., and D.O. Henry. 1995. The Upper Palaeolithic Sites. In D. O. Henry (Ed.), *Prehistoric Cultural Ecology and Evolution, Interdisciplinary Contributions to Archaeology*, pp. 133–214. New-York: Plenum.

Copeland, L. 1975. The Middle and Upper Palaeolithic of Lebanon and Syria in the Light of Recent Research. In F. Wendorf (Ed.), *Problems in Prehistory. North Africa and the Levant*, pp. 317–350. Dallas: Southern Methodist University.

Copeland, L. 1976. Terminological Correlations in the Early Upper Palaeolithic of Lebanon and Palestine. In *Deuxième Colloque sur la Terminologie de la Préhistoire du Proche-Orient (IX Congrès de Union Internationale des Sciences Préhistoriques et Protohistoriques, Nice, 1976)*, pp. 35–48. Nice: CNRS.

Gonzalez-Echegaray, J. 1964. *Excavaciones en la Terraza de "El Khiam" (Jordania): Vol. 1*. Madrid: Bibliotheca Praehistorica Hispana V.

Gonzalez-Echegaray, J. 1966. *Excavaciones en la Terraza de "El Khiam" (Jordania): Vol. 2*. Madrid: Bibliotheca Praehistorica Hispana V.

Gonzalez-Echegaray, J. 1978. Notes Toward a Systematization of the Upper Palaeolithic in Palestine. In L.G. Freeman (Ed.), *Views of the Past: Essays in the Old World and Palaeoanthropology*, pp. 177–191. The Hague: Mouton.

Ewing, J.F. 1947. Preliminary Note on the Excavations at the Palaeolithic site of Ksar 'Akil, Republic of Lebanon. *Antiquity* 21: 186–196.

Garrard, A.N., Betts, A., Byrd, B., Colledge, S., and C. Hunt 1988. Summary of palaeoenvironmental and prehistoric investigations in the Azraq Basin. In A.N. Garrard and H.G. Gebel (Eds.), *The Prehistory of Jordan, vol. 2*, pp. 311–337. Oxford: British Archaeological Reports International Series 396.

Garrod, D.A.E. 1926. *The Upper Palaeolithic Age in Britain*. Oxford: Clarendon Press.

Garrod, D.A.E. 1932. A New Mesolithic Industry: The Natufian of Palestine. *Journal of the Royal Anthropological Institute* 62: 257–269.

Garrod, D.A.E. 1954. Excavations at the Mugharet Kebara, Mount Carmel, 1931: The Aurignacian Industries. *Proceedings of the Prehistoric Society* 20: 155–192.

Garrod, D.A.E. 1955. The Mugharet el-Emireh in Lower Galilee: Type station of the Emiran industry. *Journal of the Royal Anthropological Institute* 55: 141–162.

Garrod, D.A.E. 1957. Notes sur le Paléolithique Supérieur du Moyen Orient. *Bulletin de la Societé Préhistorique Française* 55: 239–445.

Garrod D.A.E. 1966. Mugharet el Bezez, Adlun: Interim Report, July 1965. *Bulletin du Musée de Beyrouth* 19: 5–9.

Garrod, D.A.E., and D.M.A. Bate 1937. *The Stone Age of Mt. Carmel: Vol. 1*. Oxford: Clarendon Press.

Garrod, D.A.E., and G. Henri-Martin. 1961. Rapport préliminaire sur la fouille d'une grotte au Ras el Kelb, Liban. *Bulletin du Musée de Beyrouth* 16: 61–67.

Garrod D.A.E., and D. Kirkbride 1961. Excavation of the Abri Zumoffen – A Palaeolithic rock-shelter near Adlun, south Lebanon, 1958. *Bulletin du Musée de Beyrouth* 16: 7–46.

Gilead, I. 1981. Upper Palaeolithic Tool Assemblages from the Negev and Sinai. In P. Sanlaville and J. Cauvin (Eds.), *Préhistoire du Levant*, pp. 331–342. Paris: CNRS.

Gilead, I. 1991. The Upper Palaeolithic Period in the Levant. *Journal of World Prehistory* 5: 105–154.

Goring-Morris, A.N. 1980. Upper Palaeolithic sites from Wadi Fazael, Lower Jordan Valley. *Paléorient* 6: 173–191.

Goring-Morris, A.N. 1995. Complex Hunter/Gatherers at the End of the Palaeolithic (20,000–10,000 BP). In T.E. Levy (Ed.), *The Archaeology of Society in the Holy Land*, pp. 141–168. London: Leicester University Press.

Henry, D.O. 1995. *Prehistoric Cultural Ecology*. New York: Plenum Press.

Hours, F. 1974. Remarques sur l'utilisation de Listes-Types pour l'étude de Paléolithique Supérieur et de l'Epipaléolithique du Levant. *Paléorient* 2: 3–18.

Marks, A.E. 1976. Terminology and Chronology of the Levantine Upper Palaeolithic as seen from the Central Negev, Israel. In *Deuxième Colloque sur la Terminologie de la Préhistoire du Proche-Orient (IX Congrès de Union Internationale des Sciences Préhistoriques et Protohistoriques, Nice, 1976)*, pp. 49–76. Nice: CNRS.

Marks, A. E. 1981. The Upper Palaeolithic of the Negev. In P. Sanlaville and J. Cauvin (Eds.), *Préhistoire du Levant*, pp. 343–352. Paris: CNRS.

Marks, A.E. (Ed.) 1983a. *Prehistory and Paleoenvironments in the Central Negev, Israel: Vol. 3*. Dallas: SMU Press.

Marks, A.E. 1983b. Introduction: A preliminary overview of Central Negev Prehistory. In A.E. Marks (Ed.), *Prehistory and Paleoenvironments in the Central Negev, Israel: Vol. 3*, pp. 3–34. Dallas: SMU Press.

Mellars, P., and J. Tixier 1989. Radiocarbon-accelerator dating of Ksar 'Aqil (Lebanon) and the chronology of the Upper Palaeolithic sequence in the Middle East. *Antiquity* 63: 761–768.

Neuville, R. 1934. Le préhistorique de Palestine. *Revue Biblique* 43: 237–259.

Neuville, R. 1951. *Le Paléolithique et le Mesolithique du Desert de Judée*. Paris: Archives de l'institut de Paleontologie Humaine.

Ohnuma, K. 1988. *Ksar Akil, Lebanon*. Oxford: British Archaeological Reports International Series 426.

Phillips, J.L. 1994. The Upper Palaeolithic Chronology of the Levant and the Nile Valley. In O. Bar-Yosef and R.S. Kra (Eds.), *Late Quaternary Chronology and Paleoclimates of the Eastern Mediterranean*, pp. 169–176. Radiocarbon.

Ronen, A. 1976. The Upper Palaeolithic in Northern Israel: Mt. Carmel and Galilee. *Deuxième Colloque sur le Terminologie de la Préhistoire du Proche-Orient.(IX Congrès de Union Internationale des Sciences Préhistoriques et Protohistoriques, Nice, 1976)*, pp. 153–186. Nice: CNRS.

Ronen, A., and B. Vandermeersch 1972. The Upper Paleolithic Sequence in the Cave of Qafzeh (Israel). *Quaternaria* 16: 189–202.

Rust, A. 1950. *Die Hohlenfunde von Jabrud (Syrien)*. Neumunster: Karl Wachholtz.

Turville-Petre, F. 1932. Excavations at the Mughâret El-Kebarah. *Journal of the Royal Anthropological Institute* 62: 270–276.

Vogel, J.C., and H.T. Waterbolk 1963. Groningen Radiocarbon Dates IV. *Radiocarbon* 5: 163–202.

Volkman, P.W., and D. Kaufman 1983. A reassessment of the Emireh point as a possible type fossil for the technological shift from the Middle to the Upper Palaeolithic in the Levant. In E. Trinkaus (Ed.), *The Mousterian Legacy*, pp. 631–644. Oxford: British Archaeological Reports International Series 167.

Wendorf, F., and A.E. Marks (Eds.) 1975. *Problems in Prehistory: North Africa and the Levant*. Dallas: SMU Press.

11

The Genesis and Age of Mousterian Paleosols in the Carmel Coastal Plain, Israel

Avraham Ronen, Alexander Tsatskin and Stanislav A. Laukhin

Garrod was the first to have recorded a Mousterian open-air site on the Carmel coastal plain, embedded in a red sandy paleosol. Since the 1970s, additional find spots have been discovered in the same red loam, normally 0.5–1.0 m thick, with Levallois-Mousterian artefacts of Tabun C-B type. The most complete Mousterian pedocomplex, ca. 4 m thick, was recently discovered in a quarry near Kibbutz Habonim on the Carmel coastal plain. The pedocomplex is situated between two layers of sandstone and contains four sub-units ranging from red loam (Unit IV at the base) to vertisol (Unit II, upper), indicating an increasingly humid interval between the two sandstone layers. Mousterian artefacts occur in all the soil units and especially in the vertisol. Radiothermoluminescence (RTL) dates place the basal sandstone in Oxygen Isotope Stage 6, the pedocomplex in OIS 5–4 and the upper sandstone in OIS 3.

Introduction

A note in Nature of 1935 signalled, for the first time, the presence of stone artefacts in a red loam on the coastal plain of Mount Carmel (Garrod and Gardner 1935). The discovery was made in the Atlit quarry (Fig. 11.1), from where sandstone blocks were transported to build the port of Haifa (Garrod and Gardner 1935). Interestingly, this quarry was opened after the originally planned location, a limestone cliff on Mount Carmel some 3 km to the east, was ruled out because it contained the prehistoric caves of Tabun, Skhul and El-Wad (Garrod and Bate 1937, McCown and Keith 1939). The Atlit quarry finds, qualified as Mousterian, shed new light on the Quaternary geology and prehistory of the East Mediterranean coastal plain.

The Atlit finds could not be replicated for almost four decades. There has never been found a red loam exposed on the Carmel coastal plain, let alone a loam with Mousterian artefacts in it. Even four years of meticulous archaeological survey of the Mount Carmel area (1963–1967) failed to yield such finds (Olami and Ronen 1977; Ronen and Olami 1978, 1983; Olami 1984). Hence, there appeared some concern that Garrod's and Gardner's finds were perhaps not Mousterian, or were not *in situ*.

The picture changed rapidly when, in the early 70s, construction of the Haifa-Tel Aviv highway began on the Carmel coastal plain. Numerous North-South roadcuts along the major sandstone ridge on the Carmel plain exposed a layer of red loam between two sandstone beds. In several locations, the red loam contained perfectly *in situ* Levalloiso-Mousterian artefacts (Farrand and Ronen 1974, Ronen 1977). This is an exemplary case of a layer which has been completely covered by later deposits. The ridge in question is the continuation of the Atlit quarries, so that there can be no doubt that this is the Mousterian-bearing red loam identified in Atlit and briefly described by Garrod and Gardner in 1935. In that note the impression is given of a single find spot, but Garrod's recently-discovered diaries (Smith *et al.* 1997) specifically mention that during the research, between 4th and 7th April 1935, artefacts were in fact found in six locations along the quarry exposure (Jane Callander, pers. comm.).

The major ridge on the Carmel coastal plain is one of a series of narrow, elongated N/S-running ridges found on the coastal plain of Israel, roughly parallel to the present shoreline of the Mediterranean. Several red loam (Hamra) paleosols are buried within the sandstone layers on- and off-shore. The largest portion of the coastal stratigraphical sequence lacks chronological markers, let alone for two or three marine fossils (Issar 1971). Hence authors widely disagree on the chronological framework (Avnimelech 1962, Issar 1971, Neev *et al.* 1987). Pedological studies had focused on post-depositional processes which lead to the formation of sandstone, hamra and

Figure 11.1: The Atlit quarry, April 1935. E.W. Gardner standing below the Mousterian soil, photographed by Dorothy Garrod (courtesy Jane Callander).

vertisol, as well as on catenary relationships between them (Yaalon and Dan 1967, Karmeli *et al.* 1968, Wieder and Yaalon 1983). Dan and Yaalon (1968) inferred that present-day hamra-vertisol catena is basically similar to buried paleohamra occurrences.

Stratigraphical studies based on archaeological remains as markers of a relative chronology indicated the presence of at least 8 paleosol horizons of different ages. Five of the paleosols furnished artefacts ranging from the Epipalaeolithic through Lower/Middle Acheulean (Ronen 1975a, 1975b, 1977, 1979, 1983; Farrand and Ronen 1974; Boenigk *et al.* 1985; Ronen *et al.* n.d.; Brunnacker *et al.* 1982). Recent attempts at stratigraphical chronology of the coastal plain units, without reference to archaeological occurrences, have reached very similar results (Gvirtzman *et al.* 1984; Katsav and Gvirtzman 1994a, b).

Recently, direct dating of coastal plain sediments was attempted using various methods. The most efficient method appears to be thermoluminescence (Porat *et al.* 1994, Porat and Wintle 1994). A variant of this method, radiothermoluminescence, has been used to date the most complete Mousterian pedocomplex presently known on the Carmel coastal plain, that of Habonim quarry. Combined with archaeology and palaeopedology, these investigations form the subject of the present paper.

Materials and methods

The Habonim quarry is located on the major sandstone ridge along the Carmel coastal plain, *ca.* 1.5 km from the present shoreline and *ca.* 4 km from the foothills of Mount Carmel to the east (Fig. 11.2); its crest reaches 25 m amsl. Like elsewhere on the same ridge (Ronen 1975), below a thin topsoil three main stratigraphic horizons

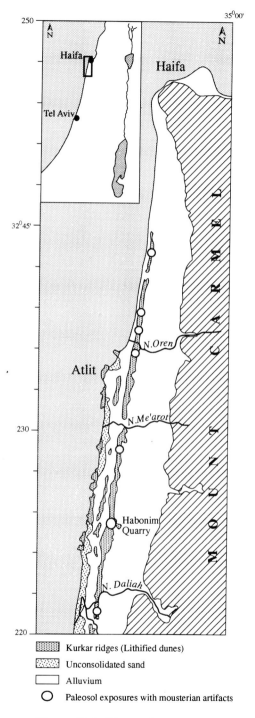

▦	Kurkar ridges (Lithified dunes)
▨	Unconsolidated sand
☐	Alluvium
◯	Paleosol exposures with mousterian artifacts

Figure 11.2: The study area in the Israeli Coastal Plain.

Figure 11.3: General view of Habonim quarry (Photo Ohad Zackheim).

are distinguished, from top to bottom (Fig. 11.3):

1. The Upper sandstone, *ca.* 4 m thick, dissected by numerous joints filled with bright-red clayey mass; sharp lower boundary.
2. The red loam (hamra paleosol), best preserved in a shallow depression about 100 m long, gradually tapering to the South and to the North; it consists of an AB and BCca horizon. The AB horizon (0.8 m thick) is a reddish-brown (2.5YR 4/4) sandy loam; massive to blocky; hard, slightly plastic; truncated at the upper contact; contains scattered 1 cm carbonate concretions that increase in abundance and size downward; gradual and clear boundary. The BCca horizon (0.4 m thick) is a brown (5YR 4/6) sandy loam; calcareous, with larger concretions at the lower contact with the Lower Kurkar layer. The paleohamra changes laterally into a complex dark-coloured sequence, which is analysed in detail further. The upper portion of hamra contained scattered flint implements (see below).
3. Lower Kurkar – sandstone *ca.* 2 m visible thickness, less cemented than the Upper Kurkar of layer 1.

Field observations were made using US Soil Taxonomy (1975) and The Israeli Soil Classification System (1979). The colour of paleosol horizons was designated according to Munsell Colour Charts. Organic matter was determined potentiometrically. Total calcium carbonate was measured by volumetric calcimetry. Particle size distribution was determined by the hydrometer method. The petrographic thin sections were described according to Bullock *et al.* (1985). Scanning electron microscope examination of the back-scattered electron images and microchemical determinations by EDAX were performed in the Geological Survey of Israel on GEOL 800. Mineralogical analyses were made by Fourier Transform Infra-red spectroscope (FTIR) in the Department of Structural Biology, the Weizman Institute of Science.

Samples for radiothermoluminescence (RTL) dating were taken at a depth of *ca.* 0.5 m in a freshly cleaned outcrop. The RTL measurements were made in the Radiochemistry Laboratory of Moscow State University following Vlasov and Kulikov's method (1989). The annual accumulation dose was calculated from the natural radioactivity of the sediments, measured in the laboratory.

Flint implements

Until now no archaeological excavation took place at Habonim quarry. Artefacts were found when cleaning the section, mostly located *in situ* in Unit II. A few finds came from unit III. The racloir of Fig. 11.4: 2 was found at the foot of the section, and could have originated in either Unit II or III. The small series found at Habonim includes cores, flakes and tools. Levallois products dominate with points (Fig. 11.4: 1), 'preferential' (Fig. 11.4: 3–6) and 'recurrent' flakes (Fig. 11.4: 5 and 6; see Boeda 1995), and cores (Fig. 11.4: 10). Cores (Fig. 11.4: 9, 10) and unmodified flakes (Fig. 11.4: 8) indicate, here as well as in the other red loam assemblages, local manufacture and maintenance. In the Mousterian series of the red loam, modification normally means brief retouching; in this context, the elaborate convergent racloir of Fig. 11.4: 2 is an exception. Beside this exception, the small Habonim series fits well into the Mousterian red loam industry (Ronen 1995). This industry is characterised as follows: there are but a few tool types, practically all fall into two groups – Levallois products and denticulated/notched/retouched items. The Levallois group dominates, reaching *ca.* 53%. Racloirs are practically absent and Upper Palaeolithic tools are very rare (Table 11.1). Cores are relatively numerous, of small size and strongly reduced (Fig. 11.4: 9 is typical). It may be remarked that the red loam is entirely devoid of stones of any kind, including flint; hence all the artefacts in the loam are manuports, and apparently, small nodules were used from the start. Flakes and tools are also of small size, on average. The peculiar composition of the red loam Mousterian is probably due to a particular function which remains unknown.

Paleosol catena

The red sandy loam paleosol (paleohamra) grades laterally into a 4.5 m thick soil-sedimentary sequence in an interdune depression at Habonim. In its middle portion, the sequence contains a dark-coloured vertisol (Fig. 11.3). The upper portion of the soil sequence, below the indurated Upper Kurkar, is complex and its genesis is not immediately obvious. Therefore, we tentatively divide the soil-sedimentary sequence at Habonim into four units, numbered I-IV from top downwards (Fig. 11.5):

Unit I encompasses a layer of loose clayey sand (1a) immediately beneath the indurated Upper Kurkar, overlying an immature gley paleosol (1b). The loose sand is 20–30 cm thick, yellow (10YR 7/8) with abundant fragments of land snails, occasionally complete shells; a 1 cm thick calcrete crust exists *ca.* 10 cm below the Upper Kurkar. This crust apparently impeded water penetration downward, and thus the snails were not dissolved in the course of the Upper Kurkar lithogenesis. The

Table 11.1: Mousterian of the Red Loam, Tool Types and Size.

Type	#	Size
Levallois flakes. typical	28	
Levallois flakes. atypical	7	
Levallois points	5	
Levallois points. retouched	1	
Pseudo- Levallois points	1	
Mousterian points		
Racloir. simple straight		
Racloir, simple convex	1	
Racloir. simple concave		
Racloir, convex-concave		
Racloir. double biconvex		
Racloir. convergent		
Racloir, transversal straight		
Racloir, transversal convex		
Racloir, transversal concave		
Racloir, on ventral face		
Racloir, abrupt retouch		
Racloir, alternate retouch		
Racloir, bifacial retouch		
Endscrapers		
Burins	2	
Awls	1	
Backed knives		
Natural backed knives		
Truncation		
Notches	10	
Denticulates	12	
Retouched and used	40	
Bifacial retouch		
End-notched piece		
Rabots		
Chopping tools		
Miscellaneous		
Total	108	

Cores (N=53)				
	Mean	Min.	Max.	S.D.
Length	44.9	25.5	77.0	14.0
Width	36.6	22.0	61.0	6.5
Thickness	16.5	9.0	38.5	6.3

Flakes (Unbroken , N=131)				
	Mean	Min.	Max.	S.D.
Length	45.2	24.6	95.0	16.4
Width	20.1	24.3	53.3	9.4
Thickness	9.3	4.0	17.0	3.6

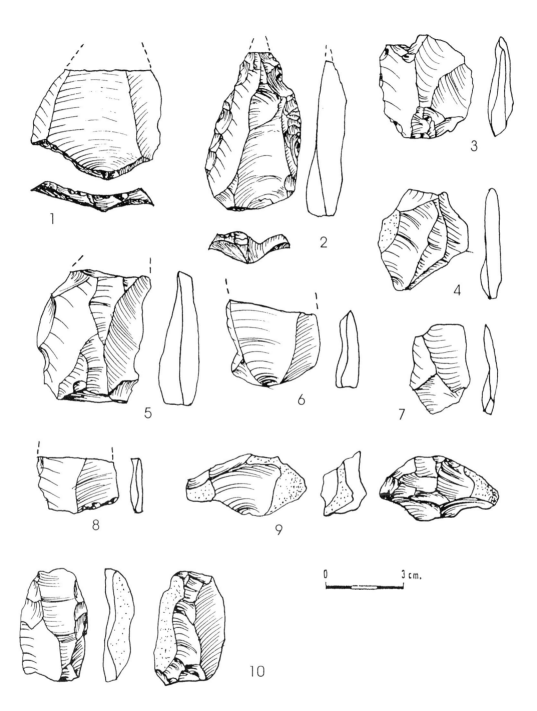

Figure 11.4: Habonim quarry lithic artefacts.

lower contact of 1a is clear. Sometimes narrow vertical cracks, 1–3 cm wide and *ca.* 50 cm long, filled with loose yellow sand, penetrate the underlying layer.

The paleosol 1b, 0.7 m thick, is a rather homogeneous horizon of greyish (5Y 5/1) sandy loam, with light olive grey (5Y 6/2) and yellow mottles; hard, slightly plastic, with blue-green root traces surrounded by yellow halo. Remains of land snail shells are common. The lower contact is gradual.

Unit II includes a paleosol horizon morphologically similar to surface vertisols in the area. This is a sandy clay loam 1.25 m thick, very dark-grey (5Y 3/1) grading to dark greyish-brown (2.5Y 3/2). It is hard, very plastic and sticky, with blocky structure superimposed by platy structure with a regular inclination towards the centre of the interdune depression. Slickensides and iron-manganese concretions; non-calcareous, though with scattered 0.5 cm carbonate concretions usually stained black (Mn?); few snail shells. The lower contact is gradual.

Unit III: Dark brown to yellowish-brown (10YR 4/6) sandy loam 0.75 m thick, plastic, less hard and slickensides less common than in Unit II. Massive and blocky structure on which platy peds, like those in Unit II above, are superimposed. The soil mass breaks to angular peds 1.5–2 cm thick, with faint Mn coatings on ped surfaces. In contrast to Unit II, the amount of carbonate concretions up to 1.5 cm in diameter with cavities inside substantially increases. The lower contact is gradual.

Unit IV consists of a well developed paleosol with an AB horizon and BCca horizon. The AB horizon is 1.0 m thick, reddish-brown to brown (7.5YR 4/6) sandy loam, quite friable and massive with rare Mn dendrite. The lower contact is sharp and stressed by large carbonate concretions up to 10 cm in size.

The BCca horizon is a 0.7 m thick friable brownish (10YR 6/6–6/8) sand with stony carbonate druses and occasional carbonate lenses. There are abundant burrows of earthworms 1–3 cm in diameter, filled with red soil material; gradual transition to the Lower Kurkar bed.

Thus, at least four morphologically different pedogenic units, partly overprinted, could be distiguished in the Mousterian interdune depression at Habonim (Fig. 11.5). These units are strikingly different in colour, texture, structure, abundance and character of secondary carbonates and/or ferro-manganese concretions. At the base, the sequence begins with a reddish sandy loam (Unit IV). The paleohamra grades upward to pedogenic units in which the general trend is a change from the reddish Unit IV to dark-brown Unit III, then to the olive-grey Unit II, with striking alteration of aggregation and increase in clay. Unit II reveals the mature vertic soil with slickensides and signs of mechanical replacement in the course of wet-dry cycles (note the different types of cracks superimposed). The paleovertisol grades upward to a horizon with pronounced gley features (Unit Ib), such as yellow mottles and Fe-Mn concretions. The gley paleosol of Unit I was eventually buried under a sandy layer (1a) without any signs of pedogenesis, apparently accumulated at a time of renewed dunes incursion in coastal areas. Although not cemented, the clayey sand layer of Unit Ia seems to be related to the Upper Kurkar.

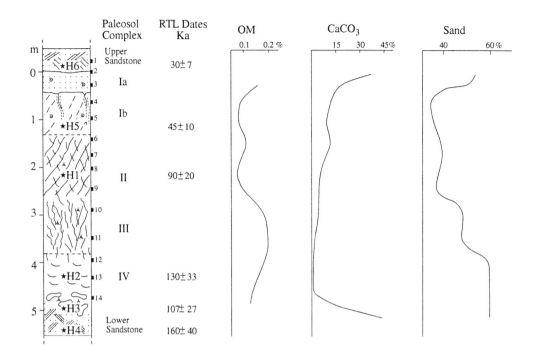

Figure 11.5: Mousterian pedocomplex of Habonim and its properties.

Analytical data

Various soil properties and RTL dates of the Habonim pedocomplex are plotted in Fig. 11.5. The clayey sand layer of Unit Ia contains 51.4% coarse sand and 46.2% of clay. It also contains 16.6% $CaCO_3$ and about 0.2% of organic matter. The calcrete pan shows a twofold increase in the amount of $CaCO_3$ (Fig. 11.5: Sample 2). FTIR analyses show that the calcrete pan is composed solely of calcite, whereas the Upper Kurkar contains both calcite and aragonite.

In the underlying gley of Unit Ib sand decreases to 35%, silt increases to 15% and clay is about the same as in 1a (50%). Thin sections show a heterogeneous distribution of sand and clay fractions. The sand is composed primarily of subrounded grains of quartz, feldspar, and biocalcite, ca. 0.2 mm median size. Sparitic calcite grains might have originated from the recrystallisation of foraminifera tests and algae remains. Occasionally grains of quartz, as well as of biosparitic calcite, have a clay coating. There are abundant nodules of micritic calcite, incorporating diffuse, tiny ferric segregations. Thick, disrupted ferric coatings cover the walls of some vertical planar voids, suggesting their precipitation in more aerated, oxidised areas of the soil. This suggests that soil-forming processes were controlled by periodically hydromorphic conditions. Environmental conditions were conducive for the existence of land snails, the carbonate shells of which were eventually recrystallised and embedded in the soil

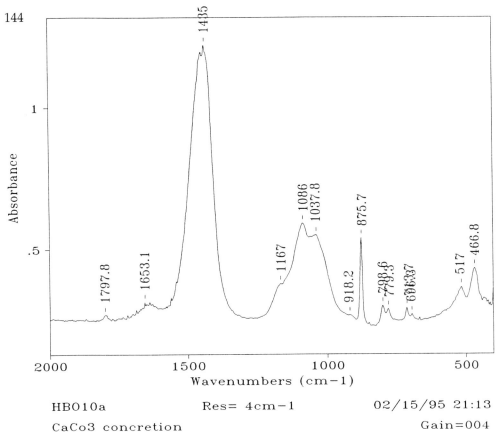

Figure 11.6: Mineralogical composition of a carbonate nodule from Unit II by Infra-red spectroscopy. The calcite peaks at 1435 cm⁻¹ and 875 cm⁻¹ dominate on the wave-number axis; 1086 cm⁻¹; splitted peaks at 798.6 cm⁻¹ and peak 517 cm⁻¹ characterise quartz; the peak at 1037.8 cm⁻¹ indicates admixture of clay.

mass. The final episode of soil formation took place under increased deposition of quartz sand and calcareous littoral materials.

The analytical data confirm that the paleosol in Unit I developed as a calcareous pseudogley (nazaz). In contrast to its modern counterparts, the morphological properties of our paleonazaz have not been fully preserved, which does not allow the recognition of the mature soil profile in the field. The presence of coated grains and the heterogeneous distribution of fine *vs.* coarse fractions suggest that the pedogenesis (at least in its final phase) might have occurred together with the accumulation and redistribution of sand, by either wind or run-off.

The underlying dark-coloured pedogenic horizon of Unit II has a particle-size distribution similar to the palaeonazaz of Unit Ib: 36 to 39% sand, 10%–12% silt and about 50% clay (Fig. 11.5). Although it is dark in colour, the amount of organic carbon does not exceed 0.15%; carbonates decrease to 4.90 % *versus* 16% in Unit I. In contrast to Unit I, a well-developed pedogenic fabric is recognised in thin sections of Unit II: for example, the microstructure is represented by complex blocky aggregates separated by numerous interconnected planar voids. The groundmass, largely composed of smectite, is characterised by strong birefringence. The aggregation of the material is close to that of Vertisols, where it results from alternations of swell-shrink processes. In contrast to unit I, in Unit II wind-blown marine organisms are very rare. The soil mass contains numerous micritic calcite nodules about 1 mm in size, which might have originated from the alteration of land snail shells. FTIR analysis of these nodules shows that they are composed of pure calcite, with the only peak at 875 cm^{-1} (Fig. 11.6). Manganese nodules, sometimes laminated and enriched with comminuted organic materials, are also common.

The paleosol in Unit II is a rather homogeneous, dark-coloured clayey loam, with cracks and slickensides, a complex pattern of microaggregation, abundant manganese and calcite nodules within the non-calcareous groundmass (Figs. 11.7 and 11.8). These features indicate that the paleosol in question is much more developed than that of Unit I, being similar to hydromorphic Vertisols of the wetlands in the Israeli Coastal plain. Like its modern analogues, the paleovertisol of Unit II is characterised by repeated expansion and contraction in wet-dry cycles, causing mechanical perturbations and slickensides formation.

In the brown-coloured Unit III, underlying the paleovertisol of Unit II, the amount of sand increases to 48% whereas clay slightly decreases to *ca.* 40%. There is a slight increase in organic matter, up to 0.36%, and a slight decrease in CaCO$_3$ to *ca.* 3.5% in the bulk sample, although carbonate concretions, according to field observations, are more abundant. In thin sections the well-sorted sand is embedded in the brownish clayey, decalcified groundmass. The soil mass contains various segregations of ferric oxides, as well as polygenetic calcite nodules incorporating fragments of clay coatings. The polygenetic calcite nodules might have originated from the alternation of carbonate leaching and episodes of clay illuviation.

Figure 11.7: SEM microphotography of a carbonate nodule in the clay groundmass of Unit II.

It should be stressed that by its genesis and lithology, the brown paleosol of Unit III is different from the overlying hydromorphic Vertisol of Unit II. However, both units are partly overprinted, and so the polygenetic nature of Unit III might have derived from the superimposition of processes substantially separated in time. In any case, the paleosol of Unit III contains *ca.* 10% more sand than the overlying vertisol, and demonstrates the features of reddening (rubefaction) of the soil mass due to the accumulation of finely dispersed ferric oxides. An important characteristic of this paleosol is evidenced by polygenetic concretions formed in the course of decalcification and translocation of clay. All these features allow us to identify the brown-coloured paleosol of Unit III as a semi-hydromorphic hamra soil.

The brownish-red AB horizon of the soil in Unit IV contains 60% sand, 35% clay and 5% silt. It is completely leached from carbonates and grades into a yellowish-brown BCca horizon, also strongly leached with only 0.75% of carbonates in its groundmass. In comparison, the Lower Kurkar contains more than 40% of $CaCO_3$ (Fig. 11.5). However, the BCca horizon of Unit IV shows the accumulation of large (5–8 cm thick) carbonate concretions (druses) in its base, as well as abundant biologically related features. The paleosol of Unit IV differs from the upper paleosols by its higher amount of sand, the lack of gley and the intensity of biological reworking. All these combine to suggest that during the formation of Unit IV, drainage has been good enough for a sandy loam to form in the depression.

Palaeopedological reconstructions

The paleosol catena in the interdune depression at Habonim demonstrates a complex, multiphase sequence of partly welded soils. Hence the so called "Mousterian paleosol" on the Carmel coastal plain is in reality a complex feature and not the single, monogenetic soil previously thought. The earliest phase of soil formation was the red sandy loam (hamra) of Unit IV, which included leaching of carbonates, rubefaction and intense bioturbations. Simultaneously, pedogenic reworking advanced, fine-grained materials accumulated and seasonal waterlogging intensified in the depression (Dan and Yaalon, 1967). This eventually led to the gley of Unit III. This episode might have been rather lengthy, as evidenced by the well-developed microfabric and, in particular, by the polygenetic nature of the calcite nodules. The latter show clear micromorphological signs of dissolution, recrystallisation and clay illuviation.

Later, the interdune depression partly filled with fine-grained materials (Unit II), which implies an increased sediment yield from the slopes of the dune. Swelling-shrinking processes of the expanding clays (up to 50% of the sediment) have led to the formation of a soil with distinct vertic features and abundant land molluscs. Under the conditions of seasonal ponding in heavier soils (contrary to the medium-grained soils of previous episodes), the processes of leaching and illuviation were reduced. The calcite nodules seem to originate primarily from the recrystallisation of snail shells. Manganese oxides precipitated under changing redox conditions. This was followed by intense slope and aeolian processes which filled and almost levelled the depression, forming Unit I. The increased rate of sediment accumulation in Unit I marks a new incursion of sand dunes into the area. Synsedimentary pedogenesis led

X-ray: 0–20 keV. Live: 9s, Present: 100s, Remaining: 91s, Real: 12s. 25% Dead.

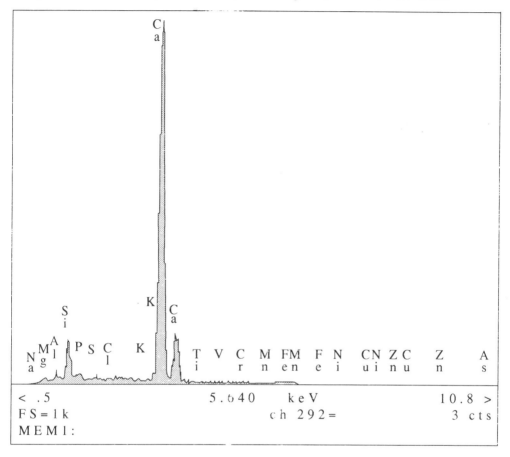

Figure 11.8: Elemental composition of the carbonate nodule in Fig. 11.7 with peak of Ca.

to the formation of gley soil, and favoured high biological activity (abundance of snails). The rate of aggradation could have been so high that, despite the surplus of water, the transformation of shells from aragonite to calcite was rather restricted. Moreover, in contrast to the poorly-drained vertisol of the previous Unit II, the sedimentary fabric of the calcareous gley of Unit I was not completely erased. Eventually, the pseudogley formation waned while the accretion of sand intensified, which resulted in the loose, friable sand of Unit Ia. Subsequently, the new coastal dunes had accumulated on top of the Mousterian soils and became transformed into sandstone (Upper Kurkar bed). The thin calcite crust at the top of Unit I, formed perhaps by water percolating through the sandstone, may have protected the loose sand of Unit 1a from calcification. Alternatively, layer 1a may have remained unconsolidated due to the constant percolation of water through the overlying sandstone bed.

Palynological material

The Habonim section is very poor in pollen remains. Only in one sample, from the base of Unit 1b, could one hundred grains be identified. Unit IV yielded 25 grains, and none could be found in the rest of the section (Aline Emery-Barbier, pers. comm.). At the base of Unit 1b the following taxa are present: 20% *Pinus*, 4% *Myrtus*, 3% *Pistacia*, 9% *Quercus coc.*, 1% *Olea*, 9% *Ephedra*, 48% NAP, and 3% pteridophytes. Surface samples contain numerous Carob tree pollen. The fact that Carob is absent from the Habonim assemblage argues against contamination. This small asemblage may be taken to indicate a higher humidity than at present, perhaps Interstadial conditions (Aline Emery-Barbier, pers. comm.). It may be noted that essentially the same taxa are present at the base of Unit IV, without *Olea* and *Myrtus* but with *Amygdalus*. Carob is absent here too.

Radiothermoluminescence dates

Preliminary RTL dates were measured in Moscow University (Fig. 11.5). The Lower Kurkar was dated to *ca.* 160 ka (Lab. no. 710), while the Upper Kurkar gave *ca.* 30 ka (Lab. no. 712). Unit I was dated to *ca.* 45 ka (Lab. no. 711), and the middle part of the Mousterian soil, Unit II, was dated to *ca.* 90 ka (Lab. no. 709). The dates are generally in agreement with the stratigraphy except for a reversal between the top of the Lower Kurkar (*ca.* 107 ka – Lab. no. 722) and the overlying hamra soil of Unit IV (*ca.* 130 ka – Lab. no. 721). The sample of Laboratory no. 722 was taken in the $CaCO_3$ concretions topping the Lower Kurkar; it is possible that younger carbonates were leached down to this horizon, which could explain the discrepancy. Additional dates are now in preparation.

The dates indicate an unexpected length of time for the Mousterian soil series. The Lower Kurkar may be assigned to Oxygen Isotope Stage 6, while the Upper Kurkar is dated to Stage 3. In a few places along the Carmel coastal plain the Lower Kurkar is capped by a beachrock *ca.* 10 m asl, in all likelihood from substage 5e (Ronen 1983). The soil units seem to have developed, then, through substages 5d-a and Stage 4. It may be inferred that the Epipalaeolithic red loam, the last to have formed on the Israeli coastal plain and not dated in the present study, dates to Isotope Stages 2–3.

Discussion

Our studies at Habonim quarry show that the "Mousterian red loam" is in reality a multiphase soil reflecting a long chain of environmental fluctuations, not necessarily close in time. Pedogenesis started with the leaching of carbonates and rubefaction of unconsolidated sands under conditions of relatively good drainage (Unit IV). Progressively the drainage deteriorated while more and more fine-grained material accumulated in the topographic low (Unit III). Eventually, under further impeded drainage, swell-shrink processes dominated in the vertisols of Unit II. The soil formation came to a halt under the massive encroachment of littoral sand and the formation of pseudogley of Unit I, apparently following sea level fluctuations. These sands later consolidated to form the Upper Kurkar. It should be stressed that the soil-forming episodes recorded in the Mousterian palaeodune depression at Habonim are not separated by non-soil sediments, hence the Habonim section and, by implication, the Mousterian red loam on the Carmel Coastal plain should be viewed as a pedocomplex.

The idea of pedocomplexes was first introduced in studies of European loess (Pecsi 1996), and recently developed for other loess areas including China (Kemp *et al.* 1995). Studying the Elbeuf I pedocomplex in France, Fedoroff and Goldberg (1982) found that the initial soil formation is characterised by brown forest soils with a typical Bt horizon on stable land surface. In the course of time, under the increased rate of aeolian dust input, the surface aggraded and pseudogley soils overprinted the earlier brown forest soils. In turn, this changed into soddy soils bearing cryogenic features. Thus, the Elbeuf I pedocomplex was shown to demonstrate a complex succession of pedogenic, sedimentary and cryogenic episodes relating both to the Eemian Interglacial and to Lower Weichselian Interstadials. Likewise, the Mousterian pedocomplex in the coastal dunes of Israel also shows an overprint of several successive pedosedimentary episodes. In spite of different environmental conditions, sedimentary regime and soil genesis, it is surprising that the East Mediterranean Mousterian soil complex as presented here is roughly correlative with the "Last Interglacial" pedocomplex of temperate climates.

Conclusions

The pedosedimentary record and RTL dates at Habonim site are rather consistent with the tentative correlation of the Mousterian pedocomplex with Oxygen Isotope Stages 5 and 4. The peak of human exploitation of the coastal environment falls in the later part of Stage 5, with the advent of swampy conditions. These were followed by environmental deterioration and the incursion of sand dunes which completely buried the Mousterian paleosols. The sand made the coastal plain unfavourable for prehistoric humans; during sand accumulation there is in fact no sign of human occupation on the coastal plain. In other words, the plain had virtually turned into a desert.

Acknowldegements

Ehud Galili (Israel Antiquities Authority) was the first to notice the section at Habonim quarry and we are grateful to him for having turned our attention to it in 1994. The research was supported by the Wolfson Family Charitable Trust for A. Tsatskin and by the Research Authority of the University of Haifa. Thanks are due to Steve Weiner (Weizmann Institute of Science) for kindly providing the FTIR facilities, and to Ms Anat Efenberger for assisting in field work. This is part of German-Israeli Foundation Project No I435–97.

References

Avnimelech, M. 1962. The main trends in the Pleistocene-Holocene history of the Israelian Coastal Plain. *Quaternaria* 6: 479–495.

Boëda, E. 1995. Levallois: A Volumetric Construction, Methods, a Technique. In H.L. Dibble and
    O. Bar-Yosef (Eds.), *The Definition and Interpretation of Levallois Technology*, pp. 293–304.
    Madison: Prehistory Press.
Boenigk, W., Brunnacker, K., Tillmanns, W., and A. Ronen 1985. Die Aolinite in der Nordlichen
    Kustemzone von Israel; Genese, Stratigraphie und Klimageschichte. *Quartar* 35/36: 113–140.
Brunnacker, K., Ronen, A., and W. Tillmanns 1982. Die jungpleistozanen Aolinite in der
    sudlichen Kustenzone von Israel. Ein Beitrag zur zeitlichen Klimaentwicklung. *Eiszeitalter
    und Gegenwart* 32: 23–48.
Bullock, P., Fedoroff, N., Jongerius, A., Stoops, G., and T. Tursina 1985. *Handbook for soil thin
    section description.* Wolverhampton: Waine Research.
Dan, J., and D.H. Yaalon 1968. The formation of the soils and landscape in the Sharon. *Ktavim*
    19: 69–94 (in Hebrew).
Dan, J., and D.H. Yaalon 1969. Catenary soil relationships in Israel, 1. The Netanya catena on
    coastal dunes in the Sharon. *Geoderma* 2: 95–120.
Farrand, W.R., and A. Ronen 1974. Observations on the kurkar-hamra succession on the Carmel
    coastal plain. *Tel-Aviv* 1: 45–54.
Fedoroff, N., and P. Goldberg 1982. Comparative micromorphology of two Late Pleistocene
    paleosols (in the Paris Basin). *Catena* 9 (3/4): 227–251.
Garrod, D.A.E., and E.W. Gardner 1935. Pleistocene Coastal Deposits in Palestine. *Nature* 135:
    908–909.
Garrod, D.A.E., and D.M.A. Bate 1937. *The Stone Age of Mount Carmel, vol. 1.* Oxford: Clarendon
    Press.
Gvirtzman, G., Shachnai, E., Bakler, N., and S. Ilani 1984. *Stratigraphy of the Kurkar Group
    (Quaternary) of the Coastal Plain of Israel.* Jerusalem: Geological Survey of Israel.
Issar, A., and L. Picard 1971. On Pleistocene shorelines in the Coastal Plain of Israel. *Quaternaria*
    15: 267–272.
Karmeli, D., Yaalon, D.H., and I. Ravina 1968. Dune sand and soil strata in Quaternary
    sedimenatry cycles of the Sharon coastal plain. *Israel Journal of Earth Sciences* 17: 45–53.
Katsav, E., and G. Gvirtzman 1994a. The origin of the Kurkar ridges in the Sharon (Central
    coastal plain, Israel). *Israel Geological Society Annual Meeting*: 52.
Katsav, E., and G. Gvirtzman 1994b. Stratigraphy of the Quaternary sequence of the coastal cliff
    of the Sharon (Central coastal plain Israel). *Israel Geological Society Annual Meeting*: 53.
Kemp, R.A., Derbyshire, E., Xingmin, M., Fahu, C., and P. Baotian 1995. Pedosedimentary
    reconstruction of a thick loess-paleosols sequence near Lanzhou in North-Central China.
    Quaternary Research 43: 30–45.
McCown, T., and A. Keith 1939. *The Stone Age of Mount Carmel. The fossil human remains from
    Levalloiso-Mousterian.* Oxford: Oxford University Press.
Neev, D., Bakler, N., and K.O. Emery 1987. *Mediterranean coast of Israel and Sinai; Holocene
    tectonism from geology, geophysics and archaeology.* New York: Taylor and Francis.
Olami, Y. 1984. *Prehistoric Carmel.* Jerusalem: Israel Exploration Society.
Olami, Y., and Ronen, A. 1977. Prehistoric sites on Mt. Carmel. *Quartar* 27: 147–151.
Pecsi, M. 1996. *Loess.* Berlin: Gebrueder Borntraeger.
Porat, N., Amit, R., and E. Zilberman 1994. IRSL dating of fault-related sediments at the Nahal
    Shehoret alluvial fan, Southern Arava, Israel. *Israel Geological Society Annual Meeting*: 84.
Porat, N., and A. Wintle 1994. IRSL dating of kurkar and hamra from the Givat Olga member
    in the Sharon Coastal Cliff, Israel. *Israel Geological Society Annual Meeting*.
Ronen, A. 1975a. The Palaeolithic archaeology and chronology of Israel. In F. Wendorf and A.E.
    Marks (Eds.), *Problems in Prehistory: North Africa and the Levant*, pp. 229–248. Dallas: Southern
    Methodist University.

Ronen, A. 1975b. Reflexions sur l'origine, la genese et la chronologie des gres dunaires calcifies dits 'première' et 'deuxième' chaines cotières sur le littoral Israelien. *Bulletin de la Société Préhistorique Française* 72: 72–77.

Ronen, A. 1977. Mousterian sites in red loam in the Coastal plain of Mount Carmel. *Eretz-Israel* 13: 183–190.

Ronen, A. 1979. Palaeolithic Industries. In A. Horowitz (Ed.), *The Quaternary of Israel*, pp. 296–307. London: Academic Press.

Ronen, A. 1983. Late Quaternary sea levels inferred from coastal stratigraphy and archaeology in Israel. In P.M. Masters and N.C. Flemming (Eds.), *Quaternary coastlines and marine archaeology: towards the prehistory of land bridges and continental shelves*, pp. 121–134. London: Academic Press.

Ronen, A. 1995. The Levallois Method as Cultural Constraint. In H.L. Dibble and O. Bar-Yosef (Eds.), *The Definition and Interpretation of Levallois Technology*, pp. 293–304. Madison: Prehistory Press.

Ronen, A., and Y. Olami 1978. *Athlit Map.* Jerusalem: The Archaeological Survey of Israel.

Ronen, A., and Y. Olami 1983. *Haifa-East.* Jerusalem: The Archaeological Survey of Israel.

Smith, P.J., Callander, J., Bahn, P.G., and G. Pinçon 1997. Dorothy Garrod in words and pictures. *Antiquity* 71: 265–270.

Soil Survey Staff. *Soil Taxonomy, 1975.* USDA Agriculture Handbook 436, US Government Printing Office, Washington.

The Israeli Soils Classification System, 1979. Division of Scientific Publications, Volcani Center, Bet Dagan.

Vlasov, V.K., and O.A. Kulikov 1989. Radiothermoluminiscence Dating and Applications to Pleistocene Sediments. *Physics and Chemistry of Minerals* 16: 551–558.

Wieder, M., and D.H. Yaalon 1983. Micromorphology of hamra soils. In D. Grossman (Ed.) *Between the Yarkon and the Ayalon*, pp. 27–34. Bar-Ilan University (in Hebrew).

Yaalon, D.H., and J. Dan 1967. Factors controlling soil formation and distribution in the Mediterranean coastal plain of Israel during the Quaternary. *Quaternary Soils, 7th INQUA Congress, 1965*, pp. 321–338.

Figure 12.1: Photograph taken by G. Henry Martin at Ras el-Kelb. Dorothy Garrod (centre) is showing the Rail Trench sounding to visitors who include (on the left) Pères Henri Fleisch and Maurice Tallon.

12

The Impact of Dorothy Garrod's Excavations in the Lebanon on the Palaeolithic of the Near East

Lorraine Copeland

The excavations carried out in the Lebanon by Dorothy Garrod between the years 1958 and 1963 had a tremendous impact on our understanding of the Lower and Middle Palaeolithic phases, not only of that country but also of those phases in Palestine (now Israel) and the rest of the Near East.

In retrospect one can see why Garrod, while working in coastal Palestine (at caves such as Tabun and Wad) in the 1920s and 1930s, had always regarded the regions immediately to the north with considerable interest. Her work at three Lebanese sites: Ras el-Kelb, Abri Zumoffen and Bezez Cave, which eventually took place three decades later, was a natural continuation and extension of her research into the Levantine Palaeolithic which had begun so fruitfully at Mount Carmel (Garrod and Bate 1937).

At that time, however, the date of the excavated materials of the Palestinian caves was not only frustratingly 'floating' in relation to that of Europe, but also the finds were not connected directly, as were those of Lebanon, to the marine chronological evidence (in the form of raised beaches, wave-cut abrasion-platforms, fossil dunes, *etc.*) of the Quaternary rises and falls of sea-level. Thus another approach to the establishment of a Palaeolithic chronology was denied her (Garrod 1962: 232 ff.). At the same time the coastal caves of Palestine and adjacent hilly terrain with which she was familiar were very similar to those located further north on the eastern Mediterranean littoral. Although it was known that many had been occupied during the Palaeolithic, only one had been extensively excavated: Ksar Akil, a rockshelter which proved to be of major importance. Located in a stream valley in much the same ecological situation as that of Tabun, it produced a sequence of Mousterian, Transitional Middle-to-Upper Palaeolithic, Aurignacian and Kebaran industries as well as a human skeleton, 'Egbert' (Ewing 1947). In collaboration with Père Henri Fleisch, the French Jesuit prehistorian, Garrod examined the extensive collections of flint artefacts held at the Université St.-Joseph in Beirut, where she observed artefacts instantly recognisable as being related to those in her "Upper Acheulean/Micoquian" (later re-named Yabrudian) levels at Tabun in level E. These had been recovered from a sounding by Père Gottfried Zumoffen at Adlun at the turn of the century (Zumoffen

1900). Garrod was aware of the remark by another eminent French archaeologist, E. Renan: "Si j'avais des fouilles à commencer en Phénicie – c'est Adloun que je choisirais." (St.-Mathurin 1983: 11). So, it was at Adlun that she resolved to work once her commitments in Europe had been completed. So that the Adlun excavations of 1958 and 1963 can be discussed together, we will begin with an account of the work at Ras el-Kelb.

Excavations at Ras el-Kelb

In 1957 Garrod was requested by Emir Maurice Shehab, the Director of Antiquities in Lebanon, to undertake a rescue excavation at the Mousterian cave site of Ras el-Kelb, located on the seashore at the foot of the Ras el-Kelb promontory 15 km north of Beirut, not far from Ksar Akil. The work took place in 1959.

This headland ends in a cliff which drops to sea-level, forming a barrier to north-south communications. In order not to destroy the famous commemorative *stelae* carved by Assyrians, Egyptians and later conquerors on the pass over the promontory, a pair of tunnels were in course of being pierced through the rock at its base to carry a new autoroute. This would inevitably destroy part of the Palaeolithic cave, whose mouth area had already fallen victim to the Australian railway-builders during the Second World War. The new tunnel had sliced off the rear of the cavity and Garrod's task was to investigate the remaining middle part of the cave, which could now be entered from inside the tunnel. She was also given permission to put down a sounding outside, along the railway line, where the sleepers were laid over the base of Palaeolithic deposit near what was once the mouth area (Garrod and Henri-Martin 1959). The occupation deposits were visible, filling the cave to its roof, exposed in the section of the railway cutting.

The excavations were carried out amidst the dust and noise caused by the dynamiting of the second tunnel. Garrod's co-excavator was Germaine Henri-Martin, an old friend and colleague, the daughter of Dr. Henri Martin, excavator of La Quina, a site in the Charente where Garrod had worked during her post-graduate days (later Garrod was to own a house next to the Martins', at Villebois Lavalette). They were joined at Ras el-Kelb by Suzanne de St.-Mathurin who was in charge of recording and administration. Very large numbers of faunal remains and flint artefacts were recovered from the cave; some layers were cemented into breccia so hard that it had to be extracted in blocks by use of pneumatic drills and these then had to be transported to the National Museum, Beirut, for breaking down and analysis. The excavation inside the tunnel ('Tunnel Trench') penetrated *ca.*2.5 m to the west and reached a depth of *ca.*3 m at an altitude of 7.10 m above sea-level (henceforth a.s.l.) Some 15 horizons (Units 0 to A) were distinguished, consisting of black hearth layers and calcareous lenses, some of which were brecciated, all being very rich in artefacts and faunal remains. A 'Storm beach' of shingle occurred near the floor between Units N and M at 7.70 m a.s.l..

Outside, the 'Rail Trench' sounding penetrated from *ca.*7.5 m to a depth of 5.30 m a.s.l. and consisted of five natural levels E-A. A pebble beach (Level E) was encountered on what seemed to be the floor of the cave, consisting of sand, shells and shingle, 40 cm thick. Artefacts occurred in its upper few centimetres, indicating that the cave was first occupied soon after the sea had retreated from the 5–8 m level, and when the sand was still unconsolidated. Subsequent levels, rich in artefacts, consisted of red bone breccias, hearths and calcareous layers, as well as traces of a storm beach at *ca.*6.40 m a.s.l. Correlations between the Rail and Tunnel beaches remain to be verified, since the central core of the cave remains unexcavated; the excavators suggested that Tunnel Units N/M linked with the beach in Rail C (Garrod and Henri-Martin 1959). Work at the site was stopped when dangerous cracks appeared in the cave roof. The flint material was given a preliminary sorting by St.-Mathurin in Beirut. Garrod and Henri-Martin published preliminary reports (1959, 1961) and Garrod discussed the results in other papers (Garrod 1958, 1962). In her opinion the material referred to the early Levalloiso-Mousterian of Layer C in Tabun, *i.e.* earlier than the Late Mousterian at Ksar Akil. It will be recalled that, at the time, the available ^{14}C dates indicated that the Levalloiso-Mousterian dated to *ca.*40,000 BC. It was suspected that these dates were too young, since Ras el-Kelb produced a ^{14}C date of more than 52,000 BC (Garrod 1962). Garrod considered that the industry appeared to be techno-typologically the same from top to base. Finds included human teeth, published as Neanderthal (Vallois 1962). Sadly, Garrod worked no more on the material except for brief sessions in the Beirut Museum in 1960 and 1961. After her death many seasons of study of the flint in the Beirut Museum were carried out by the present writer; although only half the levels had been examined when Lebanon's Civil War began, a detailed report is now published (Copeland and Moloney 1998; see also Copeland 1978).

As the study will indicate, the Levalloiso-Mousterian (or Levantine Mousterian) at Ras el-Kelb, which does (with certain exceptions) indeed seem to be similar from top to base of the levels studied, is distinctive both as to the techniques of debitage and as to the retouched tools. Typologically, it is characterised by near-absence of Levallois Points (the form so frequently seen in other Levantine sites), absence of bifaces and scarcity of blades, especially in the upper levels. Finely-retouched side-scrapers are the most numerous tool-types, and Mousterian Points and 'truncated-faceted flakes' were also well represented. These and the abundant unretouched flakes were struck from radially-prepared tortoise and Levallois bipolar cores, and are notable for the generally broad, oval shape in plan and by the centripetal ridges on their dorsal surfaces. No sign of the convergent core-reduction techniques seen at Kebara or Tabun B could be seen in any level. In the terminology of E. Boèda (Boèda 1995), the reduction techniques used at Ras el-Kelb would be described as linear, recurrent centripetal.

The date of Ras el-Kelb remains problematic even today. A conservative scenario would place the pebble beach in the Rail Trench as having been laid down in Oxygen Isotope Stage 5d, during the Last Interglacial transgression series. Although no *Strombus bubonius*, marker molluscs of the warm (erstwhile Tyrrhenian II) sea, were found in the sounding, their presence was found outside the cave on marine features referred to the Last Interglacial: Enfean in the terminology of P. Sanlaville (1977, 1998). Such a time-frame is supported by the presence at the southern Lebanese site of Naame, where the flint industry was typologically similar to that at Ras el-Kelb, and where the occupation deposits occurred overlying a beach at *ca.*8 m a.s.l. in which the

Strombus bubonius were present. The *Strombus* here gave Th–230 dates of *ca*.90,000 BC (Sanlaville 1977: 628–9).

As it happened, the work at Ras el-Kelb was of considerable interest to Garrod, even though it had delayed the start of work at Adlun. Not only was the industry of the 'broad oval' facies of Levalloiso-Mousterian which was clearly related to that at Tabun level C, up till then unknown elsewhere, but the finding of the earliest artefacts on a marine shingle beach on the cave floor provided a link between occupation by Palaeolithic man and the independently-constructed ice-age chronology of Quaternary sea-level transgressions and regressions. The evidence of these had been studied by geomorphologists and geologists such as Wetzel and Haller working in North Lebanon and many others. Père Fleisch had related to Garrod the advice he had been given by Père Teilhard de Chardin, to 'work with the sea' (Garrod 1962: 237) and he had subsequently done so with valuable results. For the first time in the Near East the relationships of specific industries to specific marine evidence had been worked out (Wetzel and Haller 1945; Fleisch 1956).

Excavations at Adlun

Adlun is a village between Tyre and Sidon located on a fossil marine platform *ca*.30 m a.s.l. At the foot of the dead cliff a marine terrace stretched toward the sea, and in the cliff was a rockshelter which Garrod named Abri Zumoffen after its finder, and a small cave (Zumoffen Cave); these sites were at *ca*.12–13 m a.s.l. A few metres to the south there opened the large cave of Bezez, whose mouth was at a slightly higher elevation, *ca*.15–16 m a.s.l. It was from the first-named site that Zumoffen had retrieved the 'Upper Acheulean/Micoquian' material similar to that at Tabun E, and also, as was now known, to the 'Jabrudian' (later 'Yabrudian') industry found in inland Syria by Rust (1950) underlying the Levalloiso-Mousterian. Moreover, the Adlun sites promised to reveal links with marine features and hence to a relative chronological 'fix'.

Abri Zumoffen

In 1958, accompanied by Diana Kirkbride as co-excavator, three trenches were excavated on the terrace in front of the rockshelter. With great difficulty, since much of the occupation deposit was consolidated into an intensely hard cement, a depth of 1.80 m was reached in Trenches A and B; in all, 21 distinct horizons were distinguished, following the geological layers. The lowest beach appeared to lie on an older, cemented soil or rockfall on what was presumed to be the limestone abrasion platform of a former sea-level; according to Zumoffen's description of 1900, this locale may have originally been inside a cave or larger rockshelter, later destroyed by quarrying. A later beach material seemed to post-date a rockfall (Garrod and Kirkbride 1961: 13). The industries found were of direct relevance to those at Tabun. The blade facies which, at Tabun E, was sandwiched between Yabrudian layers, occurred at Abri Zumoffen below Yabrudian and overlay a facies which Garrod called the Beach Industry, and which she regarded as a variant of the blade facies; the latter was now re-named Amudian, to mark its difference from the Pre-Aurignacian of

Yabrud I, and to record the earliest finding (by Turville-Petre at Zuttiyeh Cave in the Wadi Amud) of blades in a Yabrudian context (Garrod and Kirkbride 1961: 15; Garrod 1962: 242).

To Garrod's great satisfaction the Beach Industry was found to have penetrated to a depth of 30 cm a marine conglomerate at 12–13.5 m a.s.l., suggesting that the locale had been occupied soon after, or even during, a retreat of the sea. The facies was characterised by chopping-tools (and/or cores) mainly made in nummulitic flint deriving from local outcrops, but flakes and blade tools of Amudian type in grey, shiny flint were also present. The Amudian occurred above this in soil lenses which included intact hearths and faunal remains, separated by sterile calcareous bands; the cementation of the soils was attributed by F. Zeuner, who visited the site at Garrod's request, to the action of rain and sea-spray (Zeuner *et al.* 1961: 49). The Amudian was characterised by numerous nibbled blades, burins and backed knives and points, and almost no side-scrapers among the tools; in this it differs from the Pre-Aurignacian of Yabrud I, in which the main tool types are end-scrapers (Rust 1950). The unretouched (usually atypical but occasionally pointed) blades were apparently struck by non-Levallois methods, not always successfully, from prismatic cores of grey flint; the nummulitic flint was very little used. In the third Trench, C, *ca.*90 cm deep, the Amudian was found in connection with two different marine features: the basal layer 4 contained the Beach Industry in an intensely hard conglomerate which Garrod thought might be older than the beaches in Trenches A and B. This was overlain by a red clay with calcrete bands containing Amudian (layer 3); a second beach of pink marine sandstone overlay this (layer 2) which Garrod thought equated with the Lower beach in Trench A containing unabraded Amudian in vertical and horizontal positions (redeposited while the sand was still loose?). Layer 1 consisted of a hard grey breccia with Amudian, thought to relate to the Amudian layers 21–11 in Trenches A and B.

The Amudian was overlain by Yabrudian in Trenches A and B in hard red *terra fusca* soils, weathering out at the surface. The industry consisted of well-made bifaces, Quina and other side-scrapers and tools on heavy, non-Levallois blanks as well as a sprinkling of Amudian types on blades.

In spite of the intractable nature of the deposits, the excavation season at Abri Zumoffen was richly rewarding, although the virtual destruction of Zumoffen Cave by the landlord (in a search for treasure) was a disappointment. The results of the work gave rise to considerable controversy, not only as regards the nature of the Amudian industry (in the case of its analogue, the Pre-Aurignacian of Yabrud I, it was dated as indisputably Upper Palaeolithic according to Bordes: 1955, 504) but also its relationship to the enveloping Yabrudian from which it differed techno-typologically so greatly. Its date and position in the marine chronological sequence was also hotly debated within the framework of the state of research at that time (*e.g.* Garrod 1958, 1962).

Garrod viewed the Amudian and Yabrudian flint industries as representing different tribes (1962: 242) and suggested that they had a symbiotic relationship, possibly including intermarriage. The matter is still discussed. Jelinek, who continued the excavation of Tabun at a later date, thought, somewhat differently, that a "single basic technology may characterise both" the Amudian of Tabun Ea (his bed 48B) and the Yabrudian (Jelinek 1975: 310) and that the Amudian was a "specialised aspect of the Yabrudian" (Jelinek *et al.* 1973: 174). Much later, when the present writer came to study the Adlun material, she also suggested that special activities were carried out in the shelter area which might have formed an annexe, contemporary with the occupation of Bezez Cave (Copeland 1983: 244). I pointed out that the 'Upper Palaeolithic' blades were technically unlike those of Europe and (as Garrod had already noted) the retouched tools only superficially resembled the Chatelperronian, in the case of the backed knives, or the Aurignacian in the case of the end-scrapers and burins. (The Adlun burin was a special notched type made on a prismatic core; Garrod and Kirkbride 1961: 23). In any case, Garrod completely rejected the opinion of Bordes, as mentioned above, pointing out that the Amudian at Tabun, just as the Pre-Aurignacian at Yabrud, was found *below* deep Mousterian layers, and probably preceded the French Upper Palaeolithic of Würm III by at least 50,000 years (Garrod 1962: 248). In the preliminary report Garrod followed the view prevailing at the time and regarded the Adlun beaches as pertaining to the end of the Last Interglacial, with the Yabrudian as occurring at the start of the Würm glaciation (Garrod and Kirkbride 1961: 44; Zeuner *et al.* 1961). In the spring of 1963 the team worked again briefly at Abri Zumoffen while waiting for the Lebanese Department of Antiquities to excavate the historic and recent layers at Bezez Cave. What remained of Zumoffen Cave was examined and mapped and Trench B was lengthened to join with its deposits.

Bezez Cave

Once the Palaeolithic layers came to light in Bezez the Garrod team took over and excavated there for nearly three months. As Garrod describes in her preliminary report (1966), a series of 5 trenches were opened the length of the cave; three Palaeolithic phases were distinguished, an Acheuleo-Yabrudian at the base, overlain directly by Levalloiso-Mousterian, with Upper Palaeolithic in pockets and on wall breccias; Neolithic artefacts and much rubble filled a large central swallow-hole located under an aven or chimney, into which some of the deposits had been sucked down, their relative stratigraphic positions intact. Tragically, only a few weeks into the season, Garrod suffered what we must now understand to have been her first heart attack. She was unable to attend the dig for some days but was present in a chair overseeing proceedings for the rest of the time, apparently recovering towards the end of the season.

Nevertheless she was delighted with the results: an archaic form of Acheuleo-Yabrudian similar to that in Tabun Ed was found in direct contact with a marine beach at 15–16 m a.s.l. and also cemented to the walls and sill in hard breccias (level C). This level contained varying amounts, depending on spatial location across the cave floor, of choppers, Quina *racloirs* and other typical side-scraper types (*cf.* the transverse 'rocking-chair' form), as well as well-made bifaces and other more archaic-seeming bifaces (these occurred mainly in Trench M, on and in the beach of 15 m at the back of the cave). The overlying Mousterian was less easy to relate to Tabun but, while it was clearly unlike that of Tabun C or Ras el-Kelb, it appeared to resemble that in Tabun D or perhaps B; however, a large sample of Mousterian which included some classic Levallois cores also occurred in layers at the cave rear, disturbed by rodent burrows as well as by (according to Sweeting 1983) the karstic effects below the cave floor of dropping sea-level. The much smaller Upper Palaeolithic sample seemed to represent an Aurignacian industry similar to that of some levels at Ksar Akil. Garrod regarded the Yabrudian on the beach as having been laid down as the sea retreated from the 15–16 m transgression level, which she dated to the end of Tyrrhenian II, the end of the Last (Riss-Würm) Interglacial (Garrod 1966: 8).

Thus the excavation in Bezez confirmed the industrial succession at Tabun E-D and, although no dates were available, promised to provide some eventually from the samples collected. Unfortunately, Garrod's health deteriorated steadily and she was no longer able to study the material; some of the faunal and sediment samples (breccia blocks; shells including vermets) were lost and have not been found. During her last few years she permitted the present writer to study the Adlun Palaeolithic collections in London, in connection with a Diploma in Archaeology course at London University. Eventually, supported by the British School in Jerusalem, I was able to study the greater part of the finds in Beirut as well and to prepare a report for inclusion in the final publication; this came eventually to be edited by D. Roe (1983).

By this time great changes had taken place in our understanding of the Tyrrhenian I-III marine sequence and its relevance to the dating of archaeological materials. Not only had the theory of drifting continents emerged and the oxygen isotope deep-sea core chronology been published, but TL and other sophisticated new dating methods had been invented which suggested that the Palaeolithic industries were older than we had thought. Nevertheless, the relative succession of these was just as established by Garrod (with later refinements): Acheulean, Yabrudian with Amudian (now combined under the term 'Mugharan Tradition' by Jelinek, 1981), Mousterian, Emiran, Aurignacian, Kebaran, Natufian. It seems pointless, therefore, to describe the various positions taken before *ca.*1970 regarding which raised beach pertained to which Tyrrhenian phase, since the arrangements and the terminology depended on author. Garrod's thoughts on the subject in 1962 are tabulated in her Figure (1962: 249) "Correlation Table for the Tyrrhenian Shore-lines in the Eastern Mediterranean". In my copy of this article she has written in some additions: "Yabrudian (Archaic)" and "Bezez Cave" on the line for the Tyrrhenian II shoreline.

Advances since 1969 in understanding the chronology

Of considerable importance for Lebanon was the work of P. Sanlaville, who, following a ten-year study of Lebanese Quaternary shorelines, proposed a chronology which took into account that altitude above sea-level was not a criteria as to age, and that some marine features could be polychronic, *i.e.* the sea may have risen more than once to the same level. The old rule 'the higher the older' could no longer be maintained. Sanlaville's first interpretation of the situation at Adlun placed the highest (15–16 m) beach at Bezez in his Enfean I (Riss/Würm) Transgressive stage, at the start of the last Interglacial. The Acheuleo-Yabrudian occupation would have started during the earliest retreat phase. He suggested that the various marine conglomerates at Abri Zumoffen of 10–13 m could refer to the Enfean II, mid-interglacial, phase (Sanlaville 1977: 704–707). In spite of the absence of *Strombus* in the excavation itself, these molluscs were present close by in heterometric conglomerates similar to those at Abri

Zumoffen, and seen at similar or lower altitudes in many locales along the coast (Fleisch and Sanlaville 1967; Fleisch *et al.* 1973).

Besides many other factors to do with the analyses of the flint artefacts, it was this scheme which the present writer took into account in the interpretation of the Adlun situation; I suggested that the Bezez and Zumoffen occupations had been contemporary or closely successive in the series of marine retreats during the Enfean, and that they represented different (here spatially-separated) facies of the same industrial complex which occurred, vertically, in the stratigraphic column at Tabun (Copeland 1983: 244).

However, these ideas have since been affected by the results of further research. The back-dating of the Tabun Mugharan Tradition industries from the Last Interglacial to prior to it, has taken place by stages as new dating methods came on line. This allowed a new look to be given to Adlun. Bar-Yosef criticised the attribution of the higher Bezez beach with its Acheuleo-Yabrudian on grounds of altitude to the Enfean (1989: 599). For him, a pre-Enfean placement (Stage 7–6) for that industry would correspond better to Tabun E dating. This would then allow for the Zumoffen beaches to refer to the first (Enfean I: sub-stages 5e-d?) transgression instead of the second, Enfean II, and in this case the Mousterian coastal occupations (which occur linked with *Strombus* at many sites) would have taken place after Enfean IIa and or IIb, sub-stages 5c-a. As each series of dates were published, they were found unacceptable by some workers (*e.g.* Farrand 1994). It is worth noting that ESR dates for teeth from Garrod's Tabun collections contributed to the debate (Grün *et al.* 1991).

In a recent review of present knowledge, with all its imponderables, Sanlaville has presented two alternative scenarios: one places the beaches at Adlun as representing a pre-Enfean, Stage 7 transgression to *ca.*20–22 m a.s.l. This would be possible given the U/Th dates for the *Strombus* beaches with Mousterian of *ca.*90 kyr BP. The second hypothesis is based on the latest 'bombshell' – the publication of even earlier TL dates for Tabun E (and by extension Adlun) by Mercier *et al.* (1995) to before the Penultimate Glacial, *i.e.* to *ca.*332 kyr BP for Tabun Ed/Units X-XI. If this date were to be accepted, the beaches at Adlun could refer to Stage 9, perhaps the transgression to 30–40 m evidenced along the coast and, significantly, at Adlun above Bezez Cave; this advance may be part of his Jbailian II ('Mindel-Riss') transgression to over 30–32 m (Sanlaville 1977: 783–4; Sanlaville 1998). The occupations would have occurred in Stage 8. It is to be noted that Sanlaville does not separate the various beach deposits at Adlun by a climato-sedimentary cycle, as suggested by Bar-Yosef; the latter's suggestion is partially supported by the curiously un-Yabrudian like assemblage at Bezez in Trench M.152 on the beach at the back of the cave, in which *racloirs* formed only 27.5% of the tools (Copeland 1983: 150–152). Can one have an Acheuleo-Yabrudian with so few *racloirs*? Could this assemblage represent something older? Or does its composition refer to variations in spatial distributions across the cave floor, something seen, although vertically, at Tabun?

One can only surmise what Garrod would have thought of the latest datings, which include determinations of 306–270 kyr for Tabun Ea-D/UnitsXI-X. Mercier *et al.* remark that the Amudian in XI is dated for the first time (and Garrod would be surely pleased with this) to over 300 kyr BP, and suggest that its position in Stage 9 is not incompatible with the position of the similar industry at Adlun in beach deposits during a retreat of the sea (*ibid.*: 506). The Mousterian of Tabun C/Unit I occurred after a long gap, at the end of Stage 7 or start of Stage 6 (*ibid.*: 508); these datings are not incompatible with some new, older, determinations for the French Mousterian.

Before leaving the subject of Adlun, I would like to record a vivid personal experience; I participated as a novice at the Bezez dig and one day was permitted to keep an eye on the workmen excavating a Mousterian layer while Garrod and Kirkbride showed visitors around. As the artefacts were slowly prised from the black layer, it dawned on me that I was looking at implements made by a Neanderthal which had not seen the light of day for over 44,000 or more years. I resolved then and there to study Palaeolithic prehistory – something that could not have been achieved without the constant help and encouragement of Garrod and Kirkbride, then and in the future years.

The Transitional Middle/Upper Palaeolithic industry

On one of Garrod's last trips to London she visited the London Institute of Archaeology where we examined, together with Ingrid Azoury and Mark Newcomer, the as yet unpublished but crucially important Upper Palaeolithic assemblages excavated long before at Ksar Akil and Antelias Cave. The material was being prepared for publication by John Waechter, who had recruited me to aid in the sorting and marking. Readers will find an account of the vicissitudes suffered by this material (including the capture of the excavator, Ewing, by the Japanese during World War Two and the loss of most of the records) in my preface to Ksar Akil Volume II (Bergman 1987). The artefacts from the so-called Transitional (Middle to Upper Palaeolithic) layers XXV-XX were of particular interest to Garrod. It was she who had first proposed that a transitional phase had taken place in Palestine which occurred before the Aurignacian, for example at El-Wad F and El-Emireh caves, and which she dubbed 'Emiran' (Garrod 1952, 1955); included were the then little-known assemblages from north Lebanon at Abu Halka and Ksar Akil, to be discussed below. This proposal was criticised on the grounds that the Palestinian assemblages were disturbed 'mixes' of Middle and Upper Palaeolithic artefacts rather than genuinely (*i.e.* techno-typologically) transitional.

On seeing the materials from Ksar Akil levels XXV-XX and Abu Halka IV e (under study by Azoury (Azoury 1986) and from Antelias Cave level V, studied by myself (Copeland 1970), Garrod immediately realised that the assemblages were unlike those in Palestine, even though both groups contained examples of the 'type-fossil', the Emireh Point (*cf.* Bordes 1961: Plate 10, 1). A characteristic tool was the chamfered blade, unknown in Palestine. The assemblages in question occurred between Mousterian and Aurignacian at Ksar Akil, and below the Aurignacian at Antelias and Abu Halka. Briefly (as interpreted later by this writer), Middle Palaeolithic debitage techniques were used to fashion elongated Levallois points and blades on which were fashioned Upper Palaeolithic tool types such as burins and end-scrapers. Thus the transitional aspect occurred "on the same piece of flint" (Copeland 1970: 114). While the 'Levallois' attribution was later questioned by, for example, Marks and Kaufman (1983), the fact remains that the 'Abu Halka cores' and other

unilaterally-prepared core types present were indubitably Middle Palaeolithic, and
had been in use since its start, for example in Tabun D and Abu Sif (see Bordes 1961:
Plates 102 and 103). The assemblages were also 'transitional' in another sense; at Ksar
Akil the tools and techniques of reduction developed upward through the levels into
a more representative Upper Palaeolithic industry (Ohnuma 1988). Unfortunately
Garrod proved unable to follow this up, and soon her health broke down, she entered
hospital, and died in 1968.

A great deal of ink has been spilt since on the subject of the Transitional
industry; it is a subject which promises to run and run, for two reasons. Firstly due
to its relevance (perhaps more so in the recent past than today) to the debate about
the origins of Modern (Cro-Magnon) man in relation to Neanderthal man, and
secondly it continues to intrigue prehistorians searching for the reasons for cultural
change.

On the first count, the subject is in the domain of palaeoanthropology and
beyond the scope of this paper; specialists have noted that the 'Levantine corridor' is
a special case, and evolutionary developments appear to have been more complicated
than those occurring in Western Europe (Bar-Yosef 1994: 28). Furthermore, the
Lebanese Palaeolithic is not directly involved; the only fossil skeleton known (from
Ksar Akil 17: Egbert/Egberta) presents few problems. The young person was found
by Ewing in what is now known as an Ahmarian (or Ksar Akil Phase B) level,
occurring between the Emiran (Transitional: Ksar Akil Phase A in Azoury's
Terminology) and the Aurignacian (Bergman 1987); certain other fragmentary remains
have not been clearly identified as to race (Nishiaki and Copeland 1992: 121–123).

Nevertheless, Garrod had devoted much time and reflection to the subject
(Garrod 1962); the controversial skeletons (Neanderthal or *sapiens sapiens*?) were
recovered thanks to her work at the Mount Carmel caves. I think she would not have
been so much surprised as amused to follow the succession of classifications and re-
classifications of the available fossils through the years; she always advised me to "set
up a hypothesis, see if it could be knocked down, accept this and move on; this is
how science works". Concerning cultural change, one discovery (admittedly following
re-classifications of human fossils) which also need not have come as a surprise, was
that the Levalloiso-Mousterian industries in the Levant were used by both
Neanderthals (*e.g.* at Amud and Kebara) and modern humans (*e.g.* at Skhul and
Qafzeh), in contrast to the earlier beliefs that the industries were race-specific (Bar-
Yosef 1989: 604). As Garrod well knew, cultural adaptations and symbiotic
relationships characterise human communities to this day (*cf.*, for example, the rapid
adoption of hunting on horses by the North American Indians, or the cohabitation of
Bantu and Pygmy in the Congo). This distances somewhat the connection between the
subject of human origins and the question of a Transitional phase or industry but
makes it the more puzzling.

On the second count, Garrod would surely have been prepared to take her own
advice and change her mind concerning the Transitional industry in Palestinian sites.
She was not one to hold to entrenched positions, as were many of her contemporaries,
who seemed to think that it was humiliating to have mistakenly interpreted some
aspect of the Palaeolithic. To this day, no sign has been found in Israel or Jordan of
assemblages containing one of the Lebanese 'Transitional' type-fossils: the *lames à*

chanfreins of Haller (1947) at Abu Halka, the chamfered blades of Newcomer (1970) at Ksar Akil. Was there a gap in occupation after the Mousterian in Israel? This may not be so if the transitional phase in Israel is represented by the site of Boker Tachtit in the Negev (Marks and Kaufman 1983) unless the lowest level is an already Upper Palaeolithic assemblage, as the retouched tool-types suggest (Bar-Yosef 1994: 40–41). It is to be noted that typical specimens of the other type-fossil, the Emireh Point, do occur at Boker Tachtit.

Other workers are still searching for transitional material. At Jerf Ajla near Palmyra in Syria, where it was suggested that transitional material had been present (Schroeder 1966) the latter has recommenced his excavations (Schroeder pers. comm., 1997). The same phase has been under study in Jordan, for example at Wadi Aghar, thought by Henry (1995) to contain a Transitional/Early Ahmarian industry.

However, perhaps the most unexpected recent development has been the discovery at the spring mound of Umm el-Tleil at El-Kowm Oasis in Syria of a phase cautiously called *'Intermédiaire'* by the excavators, Boèda and Muhessen (1993). The material occurs below Aurignacian and overlies a deep series of Mousterian layers; it consists of three facies (levels II'base, III2a and III2b) in which different reduction techniques seem to have been used, although all are designed to produce blade forms; however, instead of the bladelet debitage characteristic of the Ahmarian, there are numerous miniature Levallois points. Tools consist of elongated Levallois-like points ('Umm el-Tleil Points'), burins and end-scrapers. Since the retouched tools are Upper Palaeolithic, has the transitional stage already been passed here? Umm el-Tleil, which will surely join Ksar Akil as a key site for the Near Eastern Palaeolithic, brings up many interesting questions and emphasises once again that the last words have not been written on the question of a Middle to Upper Palaeolithic Transitional industry.

Garrod did not hesitate to propose changes to the then current French terms and schemes for classifying the Levantine Palaeolithic. Albeit at the suggestion of the Abbé Breuil (Garrod 1937), Mousterian industries in the Levant were termed 'Levalloiso-Mousterian' to reflect the unusual prevalence of Levallois techniques there. The terms 'Upper and Lower Antelian' were proposed to replace the 'Aurignacian', or Phases 4 and 3, of Neuville (1951). These terms and the linear scheme held until 1981 when further research led I. Gilead to propose the name 'Ahmarian' for technically blade-oriented assemblages which seemed to be contemporary with the Aurignacian (the latter was characterised by flake technology), especially in the Southern Levant (Gilead 1981). This stemmed in part from the then-fashionable emphasis on technology at the expense of typology. Although this idea was at first adopted by most workers (*e.g.* Bergman 1987), a trend in the other direction was soon detectable (Goring-Morris 1989) whereby Garrod's original scheme was somewhat rehabilitated. More recently, as Bar-Yosef and Belfer-Cohen (1996: 143) state concerning the Ahmarian/Aurignacian debate: "We feel that the overall picture requires a return to the more comprehensive old model that demonstrated the variability between assemblages in terms not only of lithic technology but also of lithic typology."

From the above review it can be seen that Garrod was in her day at the forefront of Palaeolithic research in the Near East, and that her ideas continue to be discussed today.

I would like to end by expressing my deeply felt gratitude to Garrod for her unfailing kindness to me, a complete amateur when I first met her. It was she who introduced me to flint typology, which she had, in her turn, learned 'the hard way' from the Abbé Breuil; she used to relate how he had made her identify tool-types, placed in a bag, by feel alone. She gave me my first lessons in flint drawing and the 'history of prehistory'. Even after her death, when I had what I thought was an original brilliant idea, I would discover from the literature that she had already thought of it. Her long archaeological experience, beginning in the era "when it was bliss to be alive", her intuition and perceptive wisdom are greatly missed today.

Bibliography

Azoury, I. 1986. *Ksar Akil, Lebanon. A technological and typological analysis of the Transitional and Early Upper Palaeolithic levels of Ksar Akil and Abu Halka. Volume I, levels XXV-XII.* Oxford: British Archaeological Reports International Series 289.

Bar-Yosef, O. 1989. Geochronology of the Levantine Middle Palaeolithic. In P. Mellars and C. Stringer (eds.), *The Human Revolution: Behaviour and Biological Perspectives on the Origin of Modern Humans*, pp. 589–610.

Bar-Yosef, O. 1994. The contributions of Southwest Asia to the Study of the Origin of Modern Humans. In M. Nitecki and D. Nitecki (Eds.), *Origins of Anatomically Modern Humans*, pp. 23–66. New York: Plenum Press.

Bar-Yosef, O., and A. Belfer-Cohen 1996. Another look at the Levantine Aurignacian. In A. Palma, A. Montet-White and K. Valoch (Eds.), *Colloquium XI, Section 6 'Upper Palaeolithic', Acts of the XIIIth Congress of U.I.S.P.P.*, pp. 139–149. Forlì: Edizioni ABACO.

Bergman, C. 1987. *Ksar Akil, Lebanon: A technological and typological analysis of the later Palaeolithic levels of Ksar Akil. Volume II: Levels XIII-VI.* Oxford: British Archaeological Reports International Series 329.

Boèda, E. 1995. Levallois: un concept volumétrique, des méthodes, une technique. In O. Bar-Yosef and H. Dibble (Eds.), *The Definition and Interpretation of Levallois Technique*, pp. 93–116. Philadelphia: Prehistory Press.

Boèda, E., and S. Muhesen 1993. Umm el-Tlel (El-Kowm, Syrie): Etude préliminaire des industries lithiques du Paléolithique moyen et supérieur, 1991–1992. *Cahiers de l'Euphrate* 7: 47–91.

Bordes, F. 1955. Le paléolithique inférieur et moyen de Jabrud (Syrie) et la question du Pre-Aurignacian. *L'Anthropologie* 59 (5/6): 486–587.

Bordes, F. 1961. *Typologie du Paléolithique Ancien et Moyen.* Bordeaux: Delmas.

Copeland, L. 1970. The Early Upper Palaeolithic Flint Material from Antelias Cave, Lebanon: Levels VII-IV. *Berytus* 19: 99–149.

Copeland, L. 1978. The Middle Palaeolithic of Adlun and Ras el-Kelb (Lebanon): First results from a study of the flint industries. *Paléorient* 4: 33–57.

Copeland, L. 1983. The Palaeolithic Stone Industries. In D. Roe (Ed.), *Adlun in the Stone Age: The excavations of D.A.E. Garrod in the Lebanon, 1958–1963*, pp. 89–366. Oxford: British Archaeological Reports International Series 159.

Copeland, L. 1986. Introduction to Volume I. In A. Azoury, *Ksar Akil, Lebanon. A technological and typological analysis of the Transitional and Early Upper Palaeolithic levels*, pp. 1–24. Oxford: British Archaeological Reports International Series 289.

Copeland, L. 1987. Preface and Introduction to Volume II. In C. Bergman, *Ksar Akil, Lebanon: A technical and typological analysis of the Later Upper Palaeolithic levels of Ksar Akil. Volume*

II: Levels XIII-VI, pp. i-iv, & 1–15. Oxford: British Archaeological Reports International Series 329.

Copeland, L., and N. Moloney (Eds.) 1998. *The Mousterian Cave Site at Ras el-Kelb, Lebanon.* Oxford: British Archaeological Reports International Series 706.

Ewing, J.F. 1947. Preliminary Note on the Excavations at the Palaeolithic Site of Ksar Akil, Republic of Lebanon. *Antiquity* 21: 186–196.

Farrand, W. 1994. Confrontation of geological stratigraphy and radiocarbon dates from Upper Pleistocene sites in the Levant. In O. Bar-Yosef and R. Kra (Eds.), *Late Quaternary Chronology and Paleoclimates of the Eastern Mediterranean. Radiocarbon* 14: 33–154.

Fleisch, H. 1956. Dépôts préhistoriques de la côte Libanaise et leur place dans la chronologie basée sur le Quaternaire Marin. *Quaternaria* 3: 101–132.

Fleisch, H., and P. Sanlaville 1967. Nouveaux gisements de *Strombus bubonious* LMK au Liban. *Comptes-Rendus Sommaire des Séances de la Société Géologique de France, Fasc. 5,* p. 207.

Garrod, D.A.E. 1937. The Near East as a Gateway to Prehistoric Migration. In G. MacCurdy (Ed.), *Early Man,* pp. 33–40. Philadelphia: Academy of Natural Sciences Symposium of March, 1937.

Garrod, D.A.E. 1952. A Transitional Industry from the Base of the Upper Palaeolithic in Palestine and Syria. *Journal of the Royal Anthropological Institute* 82: 121–132.

Garrod, D.A.E. 1955. The Mugharet el-Emireh in Lower Galilee: type station of the Emiran industry. *Journal of the Royal Anthropological Institute* 85: 1–22.

Garrod, D.A.E. 1958. The ancient shore-lines of the Lebanon and the dating of Mt. Carmel Man. In *Hundert Jahre Neanderthaler,* pp. 182–184. Utrecht: Kemink en Zn..

Garrod, D.A.E. 1962. The Middle Palaeolithic of the Near East and the Problem of Mount Carmel Man. *Journal of the Royal Anthropological Institute* 92: 232–259.

Garrod, D.A.E. 1966. Mugharet el-Bezez, Adlun (Lebanon): interim report, July, 1965. *Bulletin du Musée de Beyrouth* 19: 5–10.

Garrod, D.A.E., and D.M.A. Bate 1937. *The Stone Age of Mount Carmel, I.* Oxford: Clarendon Press.

Garrod, D.A.E., and G. Henri-Martin 1959. Fouilles à Ras el-Kelb, Liban, 1959. *Actes du 16ᵉ Congrés Préhistorique de France,* Monaco, 1959.

Garrod, D.A.E., and G. Henri-Martin 1961. Rapport préliminaire sur la fouille d'un grotte à Ras el-Kelb, Liban, 1959. *Bulletin Musée de Beyrouth* 15: 61–68.

Garrod D.A.E., and D. Kirkbride 1961. Excavation of the Abri Zumoffen, a Palaeolithic Rock-shelter near Adlun, South Lebanon, 1958. *Bulletin Musée de Beyrouth* 16: 8–46, Plates, Plans.

Gilead, I. 1981. Upper Palaeolithic tool Assemblages from the Negev and Sinai. In J. Cauvin and P. Sanlaville (Eds.), *Préhistoire du Levant,* pp. 331–343. Paris: Editions du CNRS.

Goring-Morris, A. 1989. Developments in Terminal Pleistocene hunter-gatherer socio-cultural systems: a perspective from the Negev and Sinai deserts. In I. Hershkovitz (Ed.), *People and Culture in Change,* pp. 7–28. Oxford: British Archaeological Reports International Series 508.

Grün, R., Stringer, C. and H. Schwarcz 1991. ESR dating of teeth from Garrod's Tabun Collection. *Journal of Human Evolution* 20: 231–248.

Haller, J. 1946 (1942–43). Notes de Préhistoire Phénicienne: L'Abri de Abou Halka (Tripoli). *Bulletin Musée de Beyrouth* 6: 1–20.

Henry, D. 1995. *Prehistoric Cultural Ecology and Evolution.* New York: Plenum Press.

Jelinek, A. 1975. A Preliminary Report on some Lower and Middle Palaeolithic assemblages from the Tabun Cave, Mount Carmel, Israel. In F. Wendorf and A. Marks (Eds.), *Problems in Prehistory: North Africa and the Levant,* pp. 297–317. Dallas: SMU Press.

Jelinek, A. 1981. The Middle Palaeolithic in the Southern Levant from the perspective of the Tabun Cave. In J. Cauvin and P. Sanlaville (Eds.), *Préhistoire du Levant*, pp. 265–280. Paris: Editions CNRS.

Jelinek, A., Farrand W., Haas, G., Horowitz, A. and P. Goldberg 1973. New Excavations at the Tabun Cave, Mount Carmel, Israel, 1967–1972: a preliminary report. *Paléorient* 1: 151–183.

Marks, A., and D. Kaufman 1983. Boker Tachtit: the artefacts. In A. Marks (Ed.), *Prehistory and Paleoenvironments in the Central Negev, Israel, 1*, pp. 69–126. Dallas: SMU Press.

Mercier, N., Valladas, G., Valladas, H., Jelinek, A., Meignen, L., Reyss J., and J. Joron 1995. TL Dates of Burned Flints from Jelinek's Excavations at Tabun and their Implications. *Journal of Archaeological Science* 22: 495–509.

Neuville, R. 1951. *Le Paléolithique et le Mésolithique du Désert de Judée*. Paris: Archives de l'Institut Paléontologie Humaine 24.

Newcomer, M. 1970. The Chamfered Pieces from Ksar Akil (Lebanon). *Bulletin of the Institute of Archaeology, London* 8: 177–191.

Nishiaki, Y. and L. Copeland 1992. Keoue Cave, Northern Lebanon and its place in the context of the Levantine Mousterian. In T. Akazawa, K. Aoki and T. Kimura (Eds.), *The Evolution and Dispersal of Modern Humans in Asia*, pp. 107–129. Tokyo: Hokusen-Sha.

Ohnuma, K. 1988. *Ksar Akil, Lebanon: A technological study of the Earlier Upper Palaeolithic Levels of Ksar Akil: Volume III, levels XXV-XIV*. Oxford: British Archaeological Reports International Series 426.

Roe, D. (Ed.) 1983. *Adlun in the Stone Age: The excavations of D.A.E. Garrod in the Lebanon, 1958–1963*. Oxford: British Archaeological Reports International Series 159.

Rust, A. 1950. *Die Hohlenfunde von Jabrud (Syrien)*. Neumunster: Karl Wachholtz Verlag.

Sanlaville, P. 1977. *Etude géomorphologique de la région littorale du Liban*. Beirut: Université Libanaise, 3 volumes.

Sanlaville, P. 1998. Les Dépôts de Ras el-Kelb dans leur cadre stratigraphique et chronologique régional. In L. Copeland and N. Moloney (Eds.), *The Mousterian Cave Site of Ras el-Kelb, Lebanon*. Oxford: British Archaeological Reports International Series 706.

Schroeder, B. 1966. The Lithic Material from Jerf Ajla: a preliminary report. *Annales Archéologiques Arabes de Syrie* 16 (2): 201–213.

Sweeting, M. 1983. The Geological Setting. In D. Roe (Ed.), *Adlun in the Stone Age*, pp. 11–23. Oxford: British Archaeological Reports International Series 159.

Saint-Mathurin, S. 1983. Preface. In D. Roe (Ed.), *Adlun in the Stone Age*, pp. xi-xvi. Oxford: British Archaeological Reports International Series 159.

Turville-Petre, F. 1927. *Researches in Prehistoric Galilee, 1925–1926 and a report on the Galilee skull*. Bulletin of the British School of Archaeology in Jerusalem XIV.

Vallois, H. 1962. La dent humaine levalloiso-mousterienne de Ras el-Kelb, Liban. *Folia Primatologica*, vol. Jub. Schultz, pp. 155–162. Karger, Basel.

Wetzel R. and J. Haller 1945. Le quaternaire côtier de la région de Tripoli (Liban). *Notes et Mémoires de la Section Géologique, Délégation Générale de France au Levant, Beyrouth 4*, pp. 1–48.

Zeuner, F., Cornwall, I. and D. Kirkbride 1961. The Shore-line Chronology of the Palaeolithic of Abri Zumoffen Rock-Shelter, near Adlun, South Lebanon. *Bulletin Musée de Beyrouth* 16: 49–59.

Zumoffen, G. 1900. *La Phénicie avant les Phéniciens*. Beirut: Imprimerie Catholique.

13

The Early Upper Palaeolithic in the Zagros Mountains

Deborah I. Olszewski

D. A. E. Garrod's research in the Middle East began in the 1920s in the Zagros region. From there, she turned her attention to the Levant, with brief forays elsewhere, such as into the Balkans. Throughout the three decades or so that she worked in the Middle East, her views on the classification and origins of Middle Eastern Upper Palaeolithic traditions underwent modification, most particularly in her use of the term "Aurignacian" and her notions regarding the origin area for the Aurignacian. In this paper, the Upper Palaeolithic of the Zagros, as it is known from excavations subsequent to Garrod's work there, is described and compared to analogous industries of the Levant and Central Europe. It is concluded that the Zagros Upper Palaeolithic is a facies of the Aurignacian, which should be classified as the Zagros Aurignacian. This facies is a development from the local Middle Palaeolithic, one of many such local developments into early Aurignacian facies throughout Western Eurasia. Although these conclusions are contrary to Garrod's stance of the 1950s, aspects of her theoretical position are present in other research paradigms currently in vogue.

Introduction

Investigations by D. A. E. Garrod (1930) in the late 1920s in the Zagros region of the Middle East led her to comment on the origins and development of the Aurignacian Upper Palaeolithic (Garrod 1937: 36–39). Her observations were based, in part, on her characterisation of one of the industries of this region as Aurignacian ("Upper Aurignacian"). This was the assemblage from the cave of Zarzi in southern Kurdistan (Garrod 1930: 22). She theorised that the Aurignacian originated in the East, and concluded:

> "If the theory of an Eastern origin for the Aurignacian of Palestine is correct, we should expect ultimately to find that culture in the Zagros, most probably in immediate succession to the Levalloiso-Mousterian."   (Garrod 1937: 37)

Garrod subsequently excavated a number of important cave sites in the Levant and, by the 1950s, had substantively modified her position on the origin area of the Aurignacian, as well as on the issue of whether Middle Eastern industries were Aurignacian (Garrod 1953, 1957). She continued to remark on the widespread distribution of the Aurignacian in general, which she attributed to the movement of peoples, and drew attention to tool types she considered representative of unique elements of the Aurignacian. Based on her understanding of the Ewing excavations at Ksar 'Akil in Lebanon and her work at el-Wad in Palestine, she concluded:

> "... that the Aurignacian is a relatively late arrival in Palestine and the Lebanon by comparison with its position in Europe and that the direction of its diffusion must therefore have been from West to East. This would contradict my own earlier opinion that it originated in the Middle East..."   (Garrod 1953: 32)

One might well ask today which of Garrod's positions on the Aurignacian, if either, have stood the test of time, as Solecki asked and attempted to answer some decades ago (Solecki 1958: 36). Certainly, there are issues raised by the fact that subsequent work in the Zagros has resulted in the classification of the assemblage from Zarzi as Epipalaeolithic rather than Upper Palaeolithic (Braidwood and Howe 1960, Braidwood *et al.* 1961, Hole and Flannery 1967, Olszewski 1993b, Smith 1986, Wahida 1981). Additionally, radiocarbon dating of Aurignacian assemblages throughout western Eurasia has added an absolute chronological framework unavailable to Garrod. Finally, the interpretation of the meaning of typological and technological characteristics of chipped stone industries has been subject to at least two major paradigms, the cultural group model and the function/reduction model.

This paper examines the various positions taken by Garrod on the Aurignacian in the light of studies since 1960 on the Upper Palaeolithic industries of the Zagros Mountains. The Upper Palaeolithic of the Zagros is first described, and then briefly compared to contemporary industries from the Levant and from Central Europe. A discussion of the status of the Zagros Upper Palaeolithic is the final section. In this latter section, Garrod's research and observations are assessed against the paradigms that currently underlie archaeological research on the early Upper Palaeolithic in the Middle East.

The Zagros Upper Palaeolithic

Although Garrod (1930: 14) initially described the industry from the site of Zarzi in Iraq as "an Upper Palaeolithic industry of Aurignacian type," which was characterised by small, narrow elements less than 10 cm in length, and which included Gravette points, gravers (*i.e.* burins) and small scrapers, as well as a small quantity of geometric elements in the upper levels, many researchers now regard this industry as more appropriately placed within the Epipalaeolithic tradition. Garrod, herself, eventually recognised that the Zarzi assemblage was relatively late, being typologically similar to the "Mesolithic" (Garrod 1953: 22). The definition of a Zagros Upper Palaeolithic industry, therefore, must be based on the assemblages from explorations at other sites in the region, the majority of which were excavated several decades after Garrod had turned her attention to sites in the Levantine area of the Middle East.

Perhaps the foremost of the sites investigated after Garrod's work at Zarzi is Shanidar Cave in Iraq, where Solecki uncovered a sequence that included Middle Palaeolithic (Layer D), Upper Palaeolithic (Layer C) and Epipalaeolithic (Layer B) industries, as well as a recent to Neolithic deposit (Layer A) (Solecki 1958, 1–2). The

Table 13.1: Comparisons of Upper Palaeolithic Assemblages from Warwasi Rockshelter and Shanidar Cave.

	Warwasi P-Z		Warwasi AA-LL		Shanidar Cave C	
	N	%	N	%	N	%
End-scrapers	110	9.6	76	7.7	55	20.3
Burins	239	20.8	70	7.0	67	24.7
Borers	23	2.0	32	3.2	2	0.7
Backed Pieces	12	1.0	2	0.2	2	0.7
Notches/Denticulates	193	16.8	228	23.0	34	12.5
Truncations	23	2.0	14	1.4	2	0.7
Sidescrapers	49	4.3	242	24.3	30	11.1
Microliths	330	28.7	105	10.6	15	5.6
Multiple Tools	16	1.4	23	2.3	34	12.5
Retouched Pieces	136	11.8	188	18.9	5	1.8
Other Tools	17	1.5	4	1.3	25	9.2
Grand Total	1148		993		271	

tool assemblage from Shanidar Cave Layer C was described as a blade and burin industry, which includes a number of burin and end-scraper subtypes, as well as sidescrapers, chisels, perforators, points, various retouched and backed blades, notches/denticulates, truncations and *varia* (Table 13.1) (Solecki 1958: 46–50; typologically regrouped in Olszewski and Dibble 1994: 69). The microlithic component has some examples of Font Yves points and Dufour bladelets. Although Solecki described the Shanidar Cave C industry as blade-based, the debitage is dominated by flakes (Solecki 1958: 105).

In recent years, the Upper Palaeolithic assemblages from the Braidwood and Howe excavations at Warwasi in Iran (Braidwood and Howe 1960, Braidwood *et al.* 1960) have been analysed. The Warwasi assemblage can be subdivided into an earlier (Levels AA-LL) and a later (Levels P-Z) phase of the Upper Palaeolithic based on the increase of bladelet debitage and microlithic tool types through time (Olszewski 1993a, Olszewski and Dibble 1994: 69–70). The earlier Upper Palaeolithic at Warwasi is characterised by sidescrapers, notches/denticulates, and retouched pieces, with lesser frequencies of microliths, end-scrapers, and burins (see Table 13.1). The microlithic component contains examples of Font Yves points (analogous to el-Wad points) and Dufour bladelets. These tools are preferentially manufactured on flake blanks (72.4%), with blade[let]s comprising 25.4%, and the remainder (2.2%) on shatter and cores. The debitage is dominated by flakes (Olszewski and Dibble 1994: 70). The later Upper Palaeolithic includes microliths (again including Font Yves points and Dufour bladelets), burins, and notches/denticulates, with less common retouched pieces, end-scrapers, and sidescrapers. Blade[let]s are a more significant component of tool blanks (59.5%) than earlier in the sequence, with flake blanks at 37.9%, and other blanks at 2.6% (Olszewski 1993a: 189). The debitage is primarily bladelet in its composition.

Other Upper Palaeolithic assemblages include those from sites in the Khorramabad region of Iran. These have not been published in detail, but are reported to contain numerous backed pieces and "retouched rods" (Hole and Flannery 1967:

157). There are also a number of Gar Arjeneh points, which are analogous to Font Yves and el-Wad points. Examination by the author in 1992 of some of the materials from Yafteh Cave and Gar Arjeneh in the Khorramabad suggest that the Yafteh Cave assemblage is typologically similar to Warwasi P-Z, while the Gar Arjeneh materials are reminiscent of Warwasi AA-KK. The typological differences in the assemblages between Yafteh Cave, Gar Arjeneh, Warwasi, and Shanidar Cave, are preliminary indicators of significant variability within the Upper Palaeolithic of the Zagros. Some of this variability is clearly chronological, as at Warwasi, and perhaps also the differences between Gar Arjeneh and Yafteh Cave. Other aspects of this variability are probably related to site function and duration of occupation at particular sites.

The Upper Palaeolithic sequence in the Zagros region presently appears to document an industry which in its earlier phases contains a flake-based debitage that through time becomes increasingly dominated by bladelets. The typological content is initially reminiscent of the Middle Palaeolithic, with numerous sidescrapers and notches/denticulates. These types of tools, however, are contextually associated with end-scrapers, burins, and low frequencies of microliths, thus giving these early assemblages a characteristic Upper Palaeolithic appearance. The later Upper Palaeolithic assemblages are typically microlith- and burin-dominated, in conjunction with a high frequency of bladelet debitage.

Comparisons

There are several industries from two regions to which the assemblages of the Zagros Upper Palaeolithic can be readily compared. These are the Levantine Aurignacian, the Ahmarian, and the non-Ahmarian of the Levant, and the various Aurignacian facies of Central Europe.

The Levant

The Levantine research by Garrod and her colleagues was an essentially unilinear approach that explained the development of the Upper Palaeolithic as an evolution from one type of industrial tradition to another (Garrod 1957; Neuville 1934). It was divided into six successive phases, beginning with the Emiran (Phase I), followed by a local Upper Palaeolithic (Phase II), then two phases of the Aurignacian (Phases III-IV), then a non-Aurignacian Upper Palaeolithic (Phase V), and ending with the Kebaran (Phase VI) (Gilead 1989: 231). Although recognising the Aurignacian affinities of Phases III-IV, by the 1950s Garrod felt that the Levantine industries of this type were sufficiently distinct from their European Aurignacian counterparts to warrant a new name, the Antelian (Garrod 1957: 440).

Paradigmatic shifts in Levantine research since Garrod have resulted in the recognition of at least two, and possibly three, partially coeval Upper Palaeolithic traditions. The two most commonly cited are the Levantine Aurignacian and the Ahmarian (Gilead 1981, Marks 1981), while the third, the non-Ahmarian (Belfer-Cohen 1995, Coinman 1998: 56–57), is an outgrowth primarily of recent research in the southern Levant. Despite Garrod's call for the use of the term Antelian, the consensus of a symposium held in London in 1969 led researchers in the Levant to retain the use of the term Aurignacian, modifying it as the Levantine Aurignacian. Ahmarian assemblages have been radiocarbon-dated as early as about 37,000 uncalibrated BP in the Negev (Marks 1992: 15) and as late as 20,000 uncalibrated BP in west-central Jordan (Coinman 1993: 17); assemblages of the Levantine Aurignacian tradition appear no earlier than about 32,000 uncalibrated BP (Marks 1992: 16). Non-Ahmarian assemblages in the southern Levant have not yet been radiocarbon-dated.

The distinctions between the Levantine Aurignacian and the Ahmarian have been amply documented elsewhere (Gilead 1981, 1989, 1991; Marks 1981). Briefly, Levantine Aurignacian assemblages are characterised by a primarily flake debitage and a tool blank component that is approximately equally distributed between flakes and blade[let]s (Belfer-Cohen and Bar-Yosef 1981: 25–26). The tool component includes typical French Aurignacian tools such as Aurignacian blades, nosed scrapers, carinated scrapers, and Font Yves (el-Wad) points. There are also microliths, consisting of several types of retouched bladelets (Belfer-Cohen and Bar-Yosef 1981: 27). Although there have been attempts to classify a number of assemblages in the southern Levant as Levantine Aurignacian (*e.g.* Gilead 1989), current evidence suggests that the Levantine Aurignacian is confined to cave and rockshelter sites of the Mediterranean forest areas of northern Israel and Lebanon; sites in the southern Levant do not incorporate the fundamental Aurginacian tool types and technology to any significant degree (Belfer-Cohen 1995: 247; Coinman n.d.).

Ahmarian assemblages, on the other hand, are dominated by blade[let] debitage and by tools manufactured on blade[let]s (Gilead 1991: 121–125). Tools include numerous pointed, retouched and backed blades and bladelets, especially el-Wad points in the earlier phases (Gilead and Bar-Yosef 1993: 271; Phillips 1988) and Ouchtata bladelets/points in the later phases (Coinman 1993, Olszewski *et al.* 1998). These types of assemblages are widely distributed in the Levant, occurring in the Sinai, Negev, southern Jordan, and as far north as Lebanon (Ksar 'Akil). The majority of these sites known to date are open-air locales; however, an increasing number of rockshelters have been recently documented (Coinman and Henry 1995; Olszewski *et al.* press).

The non-Ahmarian assemblages of the southern Levant (referred to in some cases as Levantine Aurignacian by researchers such as Gilead 1991) incorporate moderate to high frequencies of end-scrapers, burins, and flakes. The most numerous microlithic tool is the Dufour bladelet, although bladelet tools in general are relatively rare. A few researchers, such as Coinman (1998: 41), regard these assemblages as potentially representative of functional differences within a broader Ahmarian tradition.

Comparison of the Zagros Upper Palaeolithic to the Levantine Aurginacian and Ahmarian traditions shows a closer fit of the earlier phase of the Zagros Upper Palaeolithic assemblages with the characteristics of the Levantine Aurginacian. Both groups have a flake debitage, tools manufactured on both flakes and blade[let]s with the Zagros assemblages from Warwasi heavily dominated by flake blanks, and several of the key tool types such as nosed, shouldered, and carinated scrapers, Font Yves points (el-Wad points), Dufour bladelets, and a substantial quantity of sidescrapers. The rarity of classic Aurginacian scrapers and Aurignacian blades in the Zagros is likely due to the small dimensions of most elements in these assemblages, where the majority of available raw material is in the form of small-sized nodules. The later phase of the Zagros Upper Palaeolithic does not appear to closely resemble either the Levantine Aurignacian or the Ahmarian, although these later Zagros assemblages contain carinated scrapers and carinated burins (as in Aurignacian assemblages) and a heavily bladelet dominated technology/typology (as in the Ahmarian).

Central Europe

Research in Central Europe has documented an extensive Aurignacian presence, particularly in the Austrian-Moravian area (Garrod *et al.* 1939; Hahn 1970, 1972; Oliva 1992: 37; Svoboda *et al.* 1996: 114). Some of these assemblages are as old as 38,000 uncalibrated BP, although most date after 33,000 uncalibrated BP. There are also indications of early Aurignacian-like industries, such as the Bachokirian in the Balkans, that are older than 43,000 uncalibrated BP (Kozłowski 1979, 1982). One notable feature of all the Aurignacian assemblages here is the high degree of typological variability between geographic clusters of assemblages (Oliva 1992: 44–47).

The earliest assemblage, the Bachokirian, contains Aurignacian elements in small quantities, but is described as principally composed of retouched and "pointed" blades (Kozłowski 1979: 96; see Kozłowski, this volume, also). There is also a moderate sidescraper component. This assemblage is further described as a well-developed laminar technology (Kozłowski 1988a: 13); in this case, blades are defined using the standard of "length is equal to or greater than twice the width" of the blank. Upper Palaeolithic blade technology, however, can be defined on the basis of blanks that possess parallel sides (prismatic blades); using this latter definition, many of the described blade tools and debitage of the Bachokirian could be considered flakes.

The later assemblages, particularly in the Austrian-Moravian area, appear to separate into two major typological groupings, one that emphasises scrapers, the other, burins. There is additional variability between assemblages that include primarily nosed/shouldered scrapers and others with primarily carinated scrapers (Oliva 1992: 44–45). Assemblages also appear to vary in the importance of blade blanks for tools and within the debitage, with some assemblages containing up to about 50% blades. Late sites contain bladelets, usually not backed, and abundant burins (Svoboda *et al.* 1996: 115).

Comparison to the Zagros Upper Palaeolithic suggests that the early Zagros Upper Palaeolithic assemblages bear some resemblance to the Bachokirian. This case is strengthened if Upper Palaeolithic blade technology is defined as a prismatic blade technology, because the Bachokirian would thus possess far less "true blade" technology (Olszewski and Dibble 1993). In this event, both the Bachokirian and the early Zagros Upper Palaeolithic have considerable quantities of flakes and tools on flakes. Additionally, a number of the convergent sidescrapers of the early Zagros Upper Palaeolithic are essentially similar to the "pointed" blades of the Bachokirian (*e.g.* Kozłowski 1979: Fig. 8). Both assemblages contain small numbers of Dufour bladelets and Font Yves points, as well as carinated end-scrapers. The later Upper Palaeolithic of the Zagros compares relatively favourably with the burin dominated Aurignacian assemblages of Central Europe. Moreoever, in the Zagros, retouched bladelets, especially Dufour bladelets, are a considerable component of the tool assemblage; in this respect, the later Zagros Upper Palaeolithic assemblages are more reminiscent of the "Krems" Aurignacian (*e.g.* Hahn 1970, 1972), than they are of the various Moravian Aurignacian facies (*e.g.* Oliva 1992: 46).

The status of the Zagros Upper Palaeolithic

Research and theoretical stances greatly influence the manner in which the lithic assemblages of Eurasia are regarded and conceptualised in the modelling of ancient human behaviour. Paramount among these are the paradigms that mould the discipline's views and guide the majority of researchers to adhere to one or another classification and interpretation scheme. This was as true during the days of Garrod's research as it is today. The Zagros Upper Palaeolithic is considered below in the light of these paradigms, which in turn influence origin hypotheses and naming conventions, as well as modifications of expert opinion over time.

Paradigmatic Issues

At the heart of modern debate on the "meaning" of lithic assemblages is a fundamental dichotomy that has been argued for decades: whether variability in lithic assemblages represents traditions of stone artefact manufacture, or can be explained on the basis of function or raw material reduction attributes which in themselves may or may not be linked to traditional methods of stone artefact manufacture (Bordes and de Sonneville-Bordes 1970; Binford and Binford 1966; Dibble 1987, 1991; Goring-Morris 1996; Henry 1996; Kaufman 1995; Neeley and Barton 1994). Both paradigms are keyed to explaining the differences between lithic traditions: in the former instance, regarding such differences as stylistic indicators of different groups of people, and in the latter, differences generated by activity sets, by mobility, by availability and quality of raw material, and by the nature of lithic reduction processes themselves.

If some aspects of lithic variability are indeed stylistic markers, then the recognition of either similarities or differences between assemblages or groups of assemblages warrants the separation of these entities into various distinctly "named" industries. In some cases, these appear to be geographically separate populations, *e.g.* the "Krems" *versus* the "ordinary" Aurignacian (Hahn 1970, 1972), or the Levantine Aurignacian *versus* the Ahmarian (Gilead 1989); in other cases, these may be chronologically separate populations, *e.g.* the Aurignacian *versus* the Epiaurignacian of Moravia (Oliva 1992: 49–50). Adherence to the "culture" paradigm highlights typological and/or technological similarities or differences between assemblages when these are present to a degree considered sufficient. If differences are stressed, then this results in a "splitter" approach to lithic analysis and interpretation. If similarities are stressed, then the "lumper" approach is followed.

The second major paradigm, that geared towards function or towards processes of lithic reduction, recognises differences between assemblages or groups of assemblages, but tends to emphasise the inherent variability expected to be present within lithic traditions. These differences are expected to reflect lithic tasks, aspects of mobility, and raw material constraints. They may or may not be linked to recognisably different groups of people; in most cases, it is assumed that these lithic differences are not stylistic and therefore not tied to specific groups in the archaeological record. The "naming" of lithic industries in this paradigm is thus an archaeological construct rather than a semblance of past cultural reality.

Lithic analysis and interpretation would be relatively uncomplicated, although still hotly-debated, if the choice were simply between the culture paradigm or the function/reduction paradigm. Both paradigms, however, contain cross-cutting variables, especially with regard to the recognition of raw material constraints and levels of mobility. Determination of the strength of each variable in each of the paradigms, therefore, inevitably predisposes the researcher to adopt either a "splitter" or "lumper" approach to assemblages. Once a "name" is applied, then it is predictably human that each named entity, *sui generis*, becomes real, whether interpreted as a "culture group," an activity, or a set of technological processes. Such classification schemes and outcomes are a by-product of the Western industrial world view (Barton 1991).

Classification of the Zagros Upper Palaeolithic or "What's in a Name?"
As outlined above, there can be much at stake in a "name" as it is applied to the archaeological record. In the case of the classification of the Zagros Upper Palaeolithic, the first choice is between an emphasis on difference or on similarity to existing named archaeological entities, especially to the assemblages classified as variants of the Aurignacian. Historically, the Aurignacian was defined on the basis of assemblages from Western Europe, and most particularly, from France. It has been described as containing blades, often with scalar (or Aurignacian) retouch, end-scrapers on Aurignacian blades, carinated end-scrapers, burins (which increase in frequency over time and include carinated varieties such as busked burins), rare strangled blades in its earliest phases, variable frequencies of Dufour bladelets, and Font Yves points (Bordes 1973: 155–157). Bone implements, especially points, are often another feature of these Aurignacian assemblages.

The French definition of the Aurignacian has been extended to include assemblages, as noted previously, throughout Central Europe and into the Levantine region of the Middle East. Across this large area, researchers have noted the heterogeneity of Aurignacian assemblages both spatially and chronologically. Such heterogeneity implies that specific tool types recognised as components of Aurignacian assemblages will vary greatly in frequency. A corollary to this is the variable frequency of blade[let]s in these assemblages because these depend to some degree on the extent of carination, *e.g.* carinated end-scrapers and carinated burins, present in an assemblage. Those assemblages characterised by high frequencies of carinated elements are likely to have relatively high frequencies of bladelets which are the result of the laminar removals from carinated elements; many of these bladelets are then retouched (*i.e.* into Dufour bladelets).

Solecki (1958: 3, 15, 21, 139) clearly recognised the similarities of the Zagros Upper Palaeolithic to the Aurignacian of Europe and the Levant, although he also noted that the assemblage from Shanidar Cave differed in some respects (Solecki 1958: 24). Research on the assemblages from Warwasi (Olszewski and Dibble 1993) and the summaries presented above, also highlight the overall similarity, and the differences, of this Zagros assemblage to Aurignacian assemblages. Given the perceived heterogeneity of the Aurignacian of Europe and the Levant, it is probable that the differences between the Zagros Upper Palaeolithic and the European/Levantine Aurignacian are a reflection of facies rather than tradition differences. In this instance, the similarities appear more persuasive than differences, which can be explained by factors such as geographic and chronological separation, as well as raw material constraints.

It is for these reasons that the Zagros Upper Palaeolithic should be classified as a variant of the Aurignacian (the "lumper" approach), in this instance, representative of a geographical facies, the Zagros Aurignacian (Olszewski and Dibble 1993). It appears to have its closest resemblance to the Aurignacian facies of Central Europe, where parallels for the early phase in the Zagros can be found with the Bachokirian (itself an industry with Aurignacian affinities) of the Balkans, and for the later phase in the Zagros, with the burin/carinated element-dominated Austrian/Moravian facies. The Zagros Aurignacian, especially in chronological trends, appears to share fewer similarities with the Levantine Aurignacian.

Origins of the Zagros Aurignacian
Of all the Early Upper Palaeolithic issues, the most controversial concerns the origins of the Aurignacian because this tradition has been linked by many recent researchers to the advent of anatomically modern humans (*Homo sapiens sapiens*) and their subsequent spread throughout much of Western Eurasia. The debate about the appearance of modern humans is complex, and variously includes arguments based on morphological traits of hominid fossils (*e.g.* Liebermann 1995, Rogers 1995, Stringer 1989, Wolpoff 1989), on mitochondrial DNA (*e.g.* Stoneking and Cann 1989), on stone and bone artefacts or the appearance of art (*e.g.* Harrold 1989, Kozłowski 1990, White 1989), or on combined assessments of palaeoanthropological and archaeological data and paradigmatic biases (*e.g.* Clark and Lindly 1989, Harrold 1991).

In general, two paradigms prevail. The first argues that the Aurignacian tradition is the product of anatomically modern humans and is carried throughout Western Eurasia as anatomically modern human groups migrate (*e.g.* Kozłowski 1988a, 18; 1988b, 231; Otte 1990, 147; Svoboda 1992, 34). This presupposes one origin area for the Aurignacian, which is commonly believed to be somewhere outside of Europe, perhaps in Anatolia (*e.g.* Otte 1990, 147). Pinpointing this area has been problematic for several reasons including the failure to establish a direct link between anatomically modern human fossils and early Aurignacian artefacts, archaeologically poorly-known regions, *i.e.* Anatolia, and the relatively late radiocarbon dates of Aurignacian facies outside of Europe, for example, the 32,000 uncalibrated BP date for the Levantine Aurignacian compared to the >43,000 uncalibrated BP date at Bacho Kiro and the 37,000–40,000 uncalibrated BP dates for the Spanish sites of L'Abreda Cave, Abric Romaní, and El Castillo Cave (Bischoff *et al.* 1989: 570; 1994: 546; Kozłowski 1979: 79; Bernaldo de Quirós and Cabrera Valdés 1992: 59; Marks 1992: 16).

The second paradigm stresses the polycentric origin of the Aurignacian. Its adherents often emphasise the material culture record, especially in the context of the spatially expansive extent of the Aurignacian and the nonsynchronous appearance of technological change (*e.g.* Oliva 1992: 48–49; Straus 1990: 276); others also argue for mosaic biocultural evolution (Clark and Lindly 1989). In this paradigm, the Aurignacian arose from various local traditions across Eurasia. Its appearance is not due to an immigration of anatomically modern humans, but represents a tradition eventually associated with the anatomically modern human form. Its local origins can be seen in the Mousterian-like elements present in early Aurignacian stone assemblages (*e.g.* Straus 1990: 292). Moreover, both the archaeological contemporaneity of early radiocarbon dates from the Aurignacian of disparate regions of Europe and the "late" appearance of the Levantine Aurignacian could be explained by polycentric, mosaic, origins. The development of a tradition that is similar in appearance over such a broad geographic area, as well as its time depth, is undoubtedly a reflection of a technological threshold achieved by many populations. This situation is analogous to the later, widespread, microlithisation of many traditions across Western Eurasia, a phenomenon that few, if any, have argued is the result of a single origin area and consequent migration of population.

At the sites of Shanidar Cave and Warwasi Rockshelter in the Zagros region, the stratigraphically earliest Zagros Aurignacian assemblages contain Mousterian-like elements, principally in the form of convergent sidescrapers. It might be argued that the levels with these Middle Palaeolithic elements are "mixed" because they immediately overlie Mousterian occupations at these sites and were excavated in arbitrary increments (Olszewski and Dibble 1994: 73). The appearance of similar elements in other early Aurignacian-like industries such as the Bachokirian in the Balkans, and in the Aurignacian of the Franco-Cantabrian region (Straus 1990: 292) and the Levantine Aurignacian (Belfer-Cohen and Bar-Yosef 1981: 29), however, suggests that the presence of Mousterian-like elements in the early Zagros Aurignacian reflects a local developmental sequence from the Middle to the Upper Palaeolithic. In the Zagros, this transition also includes aspects specific to the Zagros region such as heavy reduction indices, diminutive radial cores, and truncated-faceted pieces. It is my belief that the local development of the Zagros Aurignacian reflects one origin area among many (polycentric paradigm).

Radiocarbon dates for the Upper Palaeolithic of the Zagros are, unfortunately, rare, and processed using the solid carbon method common to the 1960s and earlier. The earliest of these dates range between 35,000 and >40,000 uncalibrated BP. If the Zagros is but one of many origin areas for the Aurignacian, then establishing whether or not this phenomenon is earlier rather than later is somewhat of a moot point. This development rather should be studied within the regional context of the Zagros and compared to analogous ecological situations, such as may have been present throughout areas of southcentral and central Europe.

A Retrospective on D. A. E. Garrod's Views on the Aurignacian of the Middle East
It is clear that Garrod's various views on the Aurignacian reflect a transition from a "lumper" to a "splitter" classificatory approach. In the 1920s and 1930s, she recognised the Aurignacian affinities of the assemblages of both the Zagros and the Levant, thereby adopting a "lumper" approach, which she held until the early 1950s (Garrod 1953: 24–29). By the late 1950s, however, her stress on the differences between the Upper Palaeolithic industries of the Middle East and Europe led her to advise Ralph

Solecki to name his Zagros Aurignacian-like assemblage from Shanidar Cave, the "Baradostian" (Garrod 1957: 446; Solecki 1958: 109), while she herself recommended the name of "Antelian" rather than Aurignacian for two of the Levantine Upper Palaeolithic stages (Stages III and IV) (Garrod 1957: 440). Although she did not use the term, the notion of Aurignacian facies is implicit in her 1950s work in the Levant. Today, both her "lumper" and her "splitter" views could be easily accommodated within current classificatory paradigms.

It is equally clear that Garrod's assessment of the Aurignacian throughout her career was one which linked this tradition to specific people, or in modern parlance, her views are those of the culture paradigm (Garrod 1937, 1953: 34–35). Her work speaks often of the spread of the Aurignacian or of Aurignacian immigrants. Thus, her concern with "the" origin area of the Aurignacian. The elusiveness of this single origin area remains to this day; current researchers vary in their choices from *terra* relatively *incognito*, such as Anatolia, to areas with early radiocarbon dates, such as the Balkans or Spain. Paralleling Garrod's position of the 1950s, few modern culture paradigm adherents see the traditional Middle East (the Levant or points farther east) as "the" origin area.

In preceding sections I have emphasised viewpoints, such as the recognition of the Zagros Upper Palaeolithic as a facies of the Aurignacian, an adherence to a paradigm more tightly allied to function/reduction, and a belief in a polycentric origin for the Aurignacian, which are contrary to many of Garrod's perspectives. These differences reflect my assessment of the archaeological record, which includes much data not available to Garrod, and my disinclination to see stone industries as representative of traceable groups of ancient people. Although modern researchers do not interpret the development of Upper Palaeolithic traditions as a unilinear sequence, it should not go unremarked, that were Garrod to maintain today her stance of the 1950s, she would find herself at home with many notable modern researchers. That many of her ideas have modern currency is a fitting tribute to a remarkable career.

Acknowledgements

I would like to extend special thanks to Frank Hole for allowing me to examine materials from Yafteh Cave and Gar Arjeneh (housed at Yale University), and to Harold Dibble, who facilitated my research on the Upper Palaeolithic and Epipalaeolithic materials from Warwasi Rockshelter, and who shared in many long discussions about the Aurignacian. A grant from the American Philosophical Society made possible the study of the assemblages from Warwasi Rockshelter Levels P-Z. The entire lithic collection from Warwasi Rockshelter is housed at the University Museum, University of Pennsylvania.

Bibliography

Barton, C.M. 1991. Retouched Tools, Fact or Fiction? Paradigms for Interpreting Palaeolithic Chipped Stone. In G.A. Clark (Ed.), *Perspectives on the Past: Theoretical Biases in Mediterranean Hunter-Gatherer Research*, pp. 143–63. Philadelphia: University of Pennsylvania Press.

Belfer-Cohen, A. 1995. Problems in Defining a Prehistoric Culture: An Example from the Southern Levant. In M. Otte (Ed.), *Nature et Culture*, Colloque de Liège, pp. 245–57. Liège: Etudes et Recherches Archéologiques de l'Université de Liège.

Belfer-Cohen, A., and O. Bar-Yosef 1981. The Aurignacian at Hayonim Cave. *Paléorient* 7 (2): 19–42.

Bernaldo de Quirós, F., and V. Cabrera Valdés 1992. Early Upper Palaeolithic Industries of Cantabrian Spain. In H. Knecht, A. Pike-Tay and R. White (Eds.), *Before Lascaux. The Complete Record of the Early Upper Palaeolithic*, pp. 57–69. Ann Arbor: CRC Press.

Binford, L., and S. Binford 1966. A Preliminary Analysis of Functional Variability in the Mousterian of Levallois Facies. *American Antiquity* 68 (2): 238–95.

Bischoff, J.L., Ludwig, K., Garcia, J.F., Carbonell, E, Vaquero, M., Stafford, Jr., T.W., and A.J.T. Jull 1994. Dating of the Basal Aurignacian Sandwich at Abric Romaní (Catalunya, Spain) by Radiocarbon and Uranium-Series. *Journal of Archaeological Science* 21: 541–51.

Bischoff, J.L., Soler, N., Maroto, J., and R. Julià 1989. Abrupt Mousterian/Aurignacian Boundary at c. 40 ka bp: Accelerator [14]C Dates from L'Abreda Cave (Catalunya, Spain). *Journal of Archaeological Science* 16: 563–76.

Bordes, F. 1973. *The Old Stone Age*. New York: McGraw-Hill Book Company.

Bordes, F., and D. de Sonneville-Bordes 1970. The Significance of Variability in Palaeolithic Assemblages. *World Archaeology* 2 (1): 61–73.

Braidwood, R., and B. Howe 1960. *Prehistoric Investigations in Iraqi Kurdistan*. The Oriental Institute of the Unviersity of Chicago Studies in Ancient Oriental Civilization No. 31. Chicago: University of Chicago Press.

Braidwood, R., Howe, B., and E. Negahban 1960. Near Eastern Prehistory. *Science* 131: 1536–1541.

Braidwood, R., Howe, B., and C. Reed 1961. The Iranian Prehistoric Project. *Science* 133: 2008–2010.

Clark, G.A., and J.M. Lindly 1989. The Case of Continuity: Observations on the Biocultural Transition in Europe and Western Asia. In P. Mellars and C. Stringer (Eds.), *The Human Revolution*, pp. 626–676. Princeton: Princeton University Press.

Coinman, N.R. 1993. WHS 618 - Ain el-Buhira: An Upper Palaeolithic Site in the Wadi Hasa, West-Central Jordan. *Paléorient* 19 (2): 17–37.

Coinman, N.R. 1998. The Upper Palaeolithic of Jordan. In D.O. Henry (Ed.), *The Prehistoric Archaeology of Jordan*, pp. 39–63. Oxford: British Archaeological Reports International Series 705.

Coinman, N.R., and D.O. Henry 1995. The Upper Palaeolithic Sites. In D.O. Henry (Ed.), *Prehistoric Cultural Ecology and Evolution*, pp. 133–214. New York: Plenum Press.

Dibble, H.L. 1987. The Interpretation of Middle Palaeolithic Scraper Morphology. *American Antiquity* 52 (1): 105–17.

Dibble, H.L. 1991. Mousterian Assemblage Variability on an Interregional Scale. *Journal of Anthropological Research* 47 (2): 239–57.

Garrod, D.A.E. 1930. The Palaeolithic of Southern Kurdistan: Excavations in the Caves of Zarzi and Hazar Merd. *Bulletin of the American School of Prehistoric Research* 6: 8–43

Garrod, D.A.E. 1937. The Near East as a Gateway of Prehistoric Migration. In G.G. MacCurdy (Ed.), *Early Man*, pp. 33–40. Philadelphia: J.B. Lippincott Company.

Garrod, D.A.E. 1953. The Relations Between South-West Asia and Europe in the Later Palaeolithic Age. *Journal of World History* 1: 13–38.

Garrod, D.A.E. 1957. Notes sur le Paléolithique Supérieur du Moyen Orient. *Bulletin de la Société Préhistorique Française* 54: 439–45.

Garrod, D.A.E., Howe, B., Gaul, J., and R. Popov 1939. Excavations in the Cave of Bacho Kiro, N.E. Bulgaria. *Bulletin of the American School of Prehistoric Research* 15: 46–87.

Gilead, I. 1981. Upper Palaeolithic Tool Assemblages from the Negev and Sinai, in the Negev. In J. Cauvin and P. Sanlaville (Eds.), *Préhistoire du Levant*, Colloques Internationaux du CNRS No. 598, pp. 331–42. Paris: Editions du CNRS.

Gilead, I. 1989. The Upper Palaeolithic in the Southern Levant: Periodization and Terminology. In O. Bar-Yosef and B. Vandermeersch (Eds.), *Investigations in South Levantine Prehistory*, pp. 231–54. Oxford: British Archaeological Reports International Series 497.

Gilead, I. 1991. The Upper Palaeolithic Period in the Levant. *Journal of World Prehistory* 5 (2): 105–54.

Gilead, I., and O. Bar-Yosef 1993. Early Upper Palaeolithic Sites in the Qadesh Barnea Area, NE Sinai. *Journal of Field Archaeology* 20: 265–80.

Goring-Morris, N. 1996. Square Pegs into Round Holes: a Critique of Neeley & Barton. *Antiquity* 70: 130–35.

Hahn, J. 1970. Recherches sur l'Aurignacien en Europe Centrale et Oriental. *L'Anthropologie* 74: 195–220.

Hahn, J. 1972. Das Aurignacien in Mittel- und Osteuropa. *Acta Praehistorica et Archaeologica* 3: 77–107.

Harrold, F.B. 1989. Mousterian, Châtelperronian and Early Aurignacian in Western Europe: Continuity or Discontinuity? In P. Mellars and C. Stringer (Eds.), *The Human Revolution*, pp. 677–713. Princeton: Princeton University Press.

Harrold, F.B. 1991. The Elephant and the Blind Men: Paradigms, Data Gaps, and the Middle-Upper Palaeolithic Transition in Southwestern France. In G.A. Clark (Ed.), *Perspectives on the Past: Theoretical Biases in Mediterranean Hunter-Gatherer Research*, pp. 164–82. Philadelphia: University of Pennsylvania Press.

Henry, D.O. 1996. Functional Minimalisation versus Ethnicity in Explaining Lithic Patterns in the Levantine Epipalaeolithic. *Antiquity* 70: 135–36.

Hole, F., and K. Flannery 1967. The Prehistory of Southwestern Iran: A Preliminary Report. *Proceedings of the Prehistoric Society* 33: 147–206.

Kaufman, D. 1995. Microburins and Microliths of the Levantine Epipalaeolithic: a Comment on the Paper by Neeley & Barton. *Antiquity* 69: 375–81.

Kozłowski, J.K. 1979. Le Bachokirien - La Plus Ancienne Industrie du Paléolithique Supérieur en Europe. In J.K. Kozłowski (Ed.), *Middle and Early Upper Palaeolithic in the Balkans*, pp. 77–99. Krakow: Jagellonian University.

Kozłowski, J.K. 1982. *Excavation in the Bacho Kiro Cave, Bulgaria: Final Report*. Warsaw: Paristowowe Wydarunietwo Naukowe.

Kozłowski, J.K. 1988a. L'Apparition du Paléolithique Supérieur. In J.K. Kozłowski (Ed.), *L'Homme de Neanderta, Vol. 8: La Mutation*, pp. 11–21. Liège: Etudes et Recherches Archéologiques de l'Université de Liège No. 35.

Kozłowski, J.K. 1988b. The Transition from the Middle to the Early Upper Palaeolithic in Central Europe and the Balkans. In J.F. Hoffecker and C.A. Wolf (Eds.), *The Early Upper Palaeolithic. Evidence from Europe and the Near East*, 193–235. Oxford: British Archaeological Reports International Series 437.

Kozłowski, J.K. 1990. A Multiaspectual Approach to the Origins of the Upper Palaeolithic in Europe. In P. Mellars (Ed.), *The Emergence of Modern Humans*, pp. 438–437. Ithica, N.Y.: Cornell University Press.

Liebermann, D.E. 1995. Testing Hypotheses about Recent Human Evolution from Skulls: Integrating Morphology, Function, Development, and Phylogeny. *Current Anthropology* 36 (2): 159–97.

Marks, A.E. 1981. The Upper Palaeolithic in the Negev. In J. Cauvin and P. Sanlaville (Eds.), *Préhistoire du Levant*, Colloques Internationaux du CNRS No. 598, pp. 343–352. Paris: Editions du CNRS.

Marks, A.E. 1992. The Early Upper Palaeolithic: The View from the Levant. In H. Knecht, A. Pike-Tay, and R. White (Eds.), *Before Lascaux. The Complete Record of the Early Upper Palaeolithic*, pp. 5–21. Ann Arbor: CRC Press.

Neeley, M., and C.M. Barton 1994. A New Approach to Interpreting Late Pleistocene Microlith Industries in Southwest Asia. *Antiquity* 68: 275–88.

Neuville, R. 1934. Le Préhistorique de Palestine. *Revue Biblique* 43: 237–259.

Oliva, M. 1992. The Aurignacian in Moravia. In H. Knecht, A. Pike-Tay and R. White (Eds.), *Before Lascaux. The Complete Record of the Early Upper Palaeolithic*, pp. 37–55. CRC Press.

Olszewski, D.I. 1993a. The Late Baradostian Occupation at Warwasi Rockshelter, Iran. In D.I. Olszewski and H.L. Dibble, *The Palaeolithic Prehistory of the Zagros-Taurus*, pp. 189–206. The University Museum Symposium Series Volume V, University Museum Monograph 83. Philadelphia: The University Museum, University of Pennsylvania.

Olszewski, D.I. 1993b. The Zarzian Occupation at Warwasi Rockshelter, Iran. In D.I. Olszewski and H.L. Dibble, *The Palaeolithic Prehistory of the Zagros-Taurus*, pp. 207–236. The University Museum Symposium Series Volume V, University Museum Monograph 83. Philadelphia: The University Museum, University of Pennsylvania.

Olszewski, D.I., Coinman, N.R., Clausen, T., Cooper, J., Fox, J., Hill, J.B., al-Nahar, M., and J. Williams. 1998. The Eastern Hasa Late Pleistocene Project: Preliminary Report on the 1997 Season. *Annual of the Department of Antiquities of Jordan* 42: 1–21.

Olszewski, D.I., and H.L. Dibble 1994. The Zagros Aurignacian. *Current Anthropology* 35: 68–75.

Otte, M. 1990. Les Processus de Transition du Paléolithique Moyen au Supérieur. In C. Farizy (Ed.), *Paléolithique Moyen Récent et Paléolithique Supérieur Ancien en Europe*, pp. 145–49. Nemours: Mémoires du Musée de Préhistoire d'Ile de France No. 3.

Phillips, J.L. 1988. The Upper Palaeolithic of the Wadi Feiran, Southern Sinai. *Paléorient* 14: 183–200.

Rogers, A.R. 1995. How Much Can Fossils Tell Us about Regional Continuity? *Current Anthropology* 36 (4): 674–76.

Smith, P.E.L. 1986. *Palaeolithic Archaeology in Iran*. The American Institute of Iranian Studies Monographs Vol. 1. Philadelphia: The University Museum, University of Pennsylvania.

Solecki, R.S. 1958. *The Baradostian Industry and the Upper Palaeolithic in the Near East*. Ph.D. thesis. New York: Columbia University.

Stoneking, M., and R. Cann 1989. African Origin of Human Mitochondrial DNA. In P. Mellars and C. Stringer (Eds.), *The Human Revolution*, pp. 17–30. Princeton: Princeton University Press.

Straus, L.G. 1990. The Early Upper Palaeolithic of Southwest Europe: Cro-Magnon Adaptations in the Iberian Peripheries, 40 000 - 20 000 BP. In P. Mellars (Ed.), *The Emergence of Modern Humans*, pp. 276–302. Ithica, N.Y.: Cornell University Press.

Stringer, C.B. 1989. The Origin of Early Modern Humans: a Comparison of the European and non-European Evidence. In P. Mellars and C. Stringer (Eds.), *The Human Revolution*, pp. 232–244. Princeton: Princeton University Press.

Svoboda, J. 1992. The Complex Origin of the Upper Palaeolithic in the Czech and Slovak Republics. In H. Knecht, A. Pike-Tay and R. White (Eds.), *Before Lascaux. The Complete Record of the Early Upper Palaeolithic*, pp. 23–36. Ann Arbor: CRC Press.

Svoboda, J., Locek, V., and E. Vlcek. 1996. *Hunters Between East and West. The Palaeolithic of Moravia*. New York: Plenum Press.

Wahida, G. 1981. The Re-excavation of Zarzi, 1971. *Proceedings of the Prehistoric Society* 47: 19–40.

White, R. 1989. Production Complexity and Standardisation in Early Aurignacian Bead and Pendant Manufacture: Evolutionary Implications. In P. Mellars and C. Stringer (Eds.), *The Human Revolution*, pp. 366–390. Princeton: Princeton University Press.

Wolpoff, M. 1989. Multiregional Evolution: The Fossil Alternative to Eden. In P. Mellars and C. Stringer (Eds.), *The Human Revolution*, pp. 62–108. Princeton: Princeton University Press.

14

The Zarzian Industry
of the Zagros Mountains

Ghanim Wahida

The Zarzian industry of the Zagros mountains appears to reflect a much more complicated cultural phenomenon than the simple model provided for it in the past.

Being an Iraqi prehistorian, it has been a great pleasure to me to contribute this paper in memory of Professor D. A. E. Garrod. In 1928 Garrod managed to penetrate Iraqi Kurdistan to excavate Zarzi and Hazar Merd caves, and that alone attests the magnitude of her achievements. Her excavations opened a new chapter in Iraqi prehistory, only widened much later by other workers. After Kurdistan, Garrod worked in Palestine, and her pioneering work in both areas revealed the importance of the cultures of the Near East during the Middle and Upper Palaeolithic periods.

As a true inheritor of Zarzi, I had the pleasure to re-excavate the site in 1971, in an attempt to evaluate the two-fold division of the Zarzian industry created by Garrod. While I was at there, the village sheikh and some workmen happily remembered Garrod, but still could not believe that she was only looking for *asti* (flints)! I wonder if my excavation had managed to make them change their minds: that there was no gold at Zarzi. Garrod named the cave after the nearby village of Zarzi, perhaps for simplicity; the villagers refer to it as *Kaunakouter* (pigeon roost). Garrod's personal [bound] copy of her famous report, *The Palaeolithic of Southern Kurdistan: excavations in the caves of Zarzi and Hazar Merd*, occupies a prominent space in my library; it gives me great pleasure every time I look at it.

Introduction

Garrod's excavation of Zarzi cave in Iraqi Kurdistan in 1928 (Figs 14.1, 14.2, 14.33) revealed the presence of geometric forms (scalenes and lunates) from the uppermost part of her layer B (50–150 cm: the Zarzian deposit), while backed blades and microlithic bladelets, among other tool types, were found throughout the deposit (Garrod 1930). This apparent subdivision of the microlithic levels has created a major problem in the definition of the Zarzian industry. The term 'Zarzian' has since been assigned in a general sense to the late Upper Palaeolithic industries of the Zagros mountains, subdivided into 'earlier' and 'later' phases depending on the occurrence of geometric forms. It has also been suggested that the later phase is to be divided

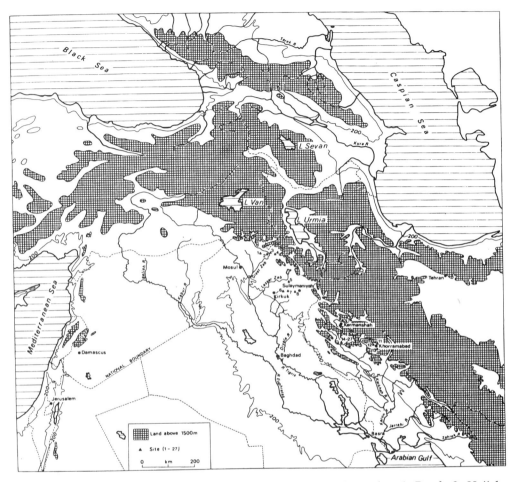

Figure 14.1: Map of Upper Palaeolithic sites in the Zagros Mountains: 1. Barak; 2. Hajiah; 3. Shanidar; 4. Babkhal; 5. Zarzi; 6. Turkaka and Kowri Khan; 7. Palegawra; 8. Hazar Merd; 9. Warwasi; 13. Gar Arjeneh; 14–17. Various sites in the Hulailan Valley (Mortensen 1975).

Figure 14.2: The natural amphitheatre and river valley of Zarzi: arrow shows cave position, and the village of Zarzi is visible on the left.

Figure 14.3: A view of the cave in the hillside.

into sub-phases on the basis of various geometric elements and other artefacts (Braidwood and Howe 1960). The ambiguity has remained, although several Zarzian and Baradostian sites have been excavated in the last four decades, and it is still difficult to define exactly the meaning of the term 'Zarzian'.

Many names have been used to designate the microlithic assemblages of the Near East. In the Caspian region of Iran such material is termed 'Epipalaeolithic' (McBurney 1968), in the Caucasus 'Late Upper Palaeolithic' (Zamiatnin 1957, Bader 1961), and in Palestine 'Kebaran' (Garrod 1937), 'Micro-Kebaran' (Kirkbride 1958) and 'Gravettian' (Ewing 1947).

Table 14.1: Principal Components Analysis for three Zagros sites: all tool types. Factor loadings for each tool type. Values above 0.5 or below –0.5 are shown in **boldface***; values between 0.1 and –0.1 are omitted.*

	Factor 1	Factor 2	Factor 3	Factor 4
Burins	.21	**–.68**		–.34
End-scrapers	.46	.34	**–.70**	
Backed blades	**.61**	**–.63**		
Backed bladelets	**–.80**	.48		–.17
Trimmed pieces	**.80**	–.16	.40	.14
Notched pieces	.44	**–.62**	–.31	.11
Drills	**.56**	**.55**	.46	.23
Scalene triangles	.16	**–.72**	.17	.27
Trapezes	**.68**	.46	.11	.20
Lunates	.30	**.78**	.10	
Isosceles triangles	**.80**	.20		**–.53**
Rectangles	**.93**	.22		
Lozenges	.40			**.81**
Shouldered points	**.80**	.20		**–.53**
Discoidal scrapers	**–.49**	.43	**.57**	
Core scrapers	–.13	**–.56**	**.73**	

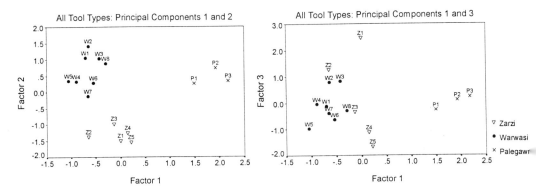

Figure 14.4: Principal Components Analysis for three Zagros sites: all tool types. Scatter diagrams of scores for each assemblage. The first two components account for 59% of total variance, the first three 71%.

In this paper, the stratigraphical, typological and chronological aspects of the Late Upper Palaeolithic industries of the Zagros mountains (the Zarzian) are discussed, in an attempt to try to define the meaning of the term 'Zarzian'. A discussion of an earlier industry, the 'Baradostian' of the Zagros, is included in order to evaluate the possible relationship between the two industries.

It is not always possible to provide full details of the stratigraphical, typological and chronological aspects of some late Upper Palaeolithic assemblages; one reason is the lack of radiocarbon determinations from many sites, which makes the construction of an absolute chronology difficult. In other cases, the stratigraphical deposits were not clearly identified, and the provenance of many artefacts was not clearly marked.

The opinions discussed in this paper were derived mainly from the author's re-excavation of Zarzi in 1971, together with a re-examination of published and unpublished materials from the Zagros Mountains. This culminated in my Ph.D thesis from Cambridge University in 1975.

Methods of analysis

In order to evaluate the problem of the two-fold division of the Zarzian, two different approaches to analysing flint industries were employed on existing Zarzian materials. The first method might be described as a traditional archaeological approach. Moreover, the assumption was made that each site could be taken as a whole, or else that relatively little cultural or chronological subdivision of the individual sites was called for. This reflects the way scholars have previously studied the two Upper Palaeolithic industries of the Zagros. The results have demonstrated, as will be made clear, significant industrial variability between these assemblages.

The second approach made use of multivariate statistics. Each assemblage from the multi-assemblage sites from which I had data for individual assemblages (Palegawra, Warwasi and Zarzi) was treated separately and their inter-relationships studied. The objective was to establish both the extent to which typological overlaps occur between sites and the 'behaviour' of the various tool-types which may be present, *i.e.* how far the latter exhibit mutual associations, as this may assist in the eventual recognition of tool-kits related to specific activities.

The various alternatives of data and method with which I have experimented give remarkably consistent results (it is not possible to display any of these in detail, for reasons of space). Two principal components analyses are shown for the three sites (Figs. 14.4, 14.5, and Tables 14.1, 14.2); the first is based on all tool categories in my type-list, whereas in the second some rare types are either omitted or grouped together to reduce the effects of sampling error. Each of the sites proves to be internally fairly consistent, and distinct from the others. Average-linkage cluster analysis entirely separates the three sites. When data from other sites are added, Pa Sangar and Shanidar B fall between Palegawra and Zarzi, whereas Warwasi remains clearly distinct from the rest.

These conclusions undoubtedly complicate any strict classification of late Upper Palaeolithic industries in the Near East. Moreover, the stratigraphical, typological and chronological evidence from Zarzian and Baradostian sites may now permit us not only to question but to revise the restrictive and misleading picture usually offered for the Zarzian in particular, and for the Upper Palaeolithic sequence in general. Admittedly the evidence is by no means complete; nevertheless, it serves at least to put such views in their right perspective.

Table 14.2: Principal Components Analysis for three Zagros sites: omitting notched and trimmed pieces, and shouldered points; grouping non-scalene microliths. Factor loadings for each tool type. Values above 0.5 or below –0.5 are shown in **boldface***; values between 0.1 and –0.1 are omitted.*

	Factor 1	*Factor 2*	*Factor 3*
Burins	**.55**	**–.57**	
End-scrapers	**.58**	.45	**–.53**
Backed blades	**.87**	–.32	
Backed bladelets	**–.91**	–.14	–.26
Drills	.34	**.78**	.42
Scalene triangles	**.50**	**–.54**	.40
Non-scalene microliths	.33	**.89**	
Discoidal scrapers	**–.57**	.17	**.70**

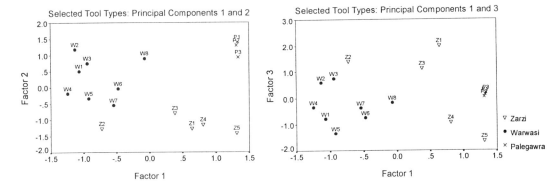

Figure 14.5: Principal Components Analysis for three Zagros sites: omitting notched and trimmed pieces, and shouldered points; grouping non-scalene microliths. Scatter diagrams of scores for each assemblage. The first two components account for 68% of total variance, the first three 83%.

The situation in the Iraqi Zagros

Before the re-excavation of Zarzi, the so-called Zarzian industry was represented in three groups of sites:-

A) *sites with an earlier Zarzian phase only:* **Barak, Hajiyah** and **Babkhal** rockshelters, **Hazar Merd** cave, and **Turkaka** and **Kowri Khan** open-air sites in the Chemchemal plain.

B) *sites with an earlier and a later phase:* **Zarzi** and probably **Shanidar** cave.

C) *one site with a later phase only:* **Palegawra** rockshelter.

Group A

The Zarzian phase of group A sites (Barak: 100 implements; Hajiyah: 200 implements; Babkhal: 250 implements; the Hazar Merd sample is too small, and is therefore excluded) is marked by "various burins, scrapers, microlithic tools and the usual cores" (Braidwood and Howe 1960: 60). In the estimation of the excavators – based entirely on morphological grounds – these small and somewhat disturbed samples may represent a separate Zarzian phase. Their argument is based on the lack of normal backed blades, geometric microliths, and the scarcity of notched pieces. On the other hand, the three samples from the rockshelters (Barak, Hajiyah and Babkhal) resemble to a striking degree the surface collections from the two open-air sites of Turkaka and Kowri Khan, again according to the excavators.

The material from Turkaka (1600 tools) included a small number of backed bladelets, and neatly-made thumbnail and discoidal scrapers; also a few, but fairly well-made, steep scrapers and burins of the simple-angled and especially polyhedral forms were collected (Braidwood and Howe 1960: 55). Microlithic and non-microlithic notched blades and flakes were abundant. The cores were generally of an irregular pyramidal form, derived from pebbles. According to the collectors, the material was typologically Zarzian, either a seasonal camp or a site representing a single stage in

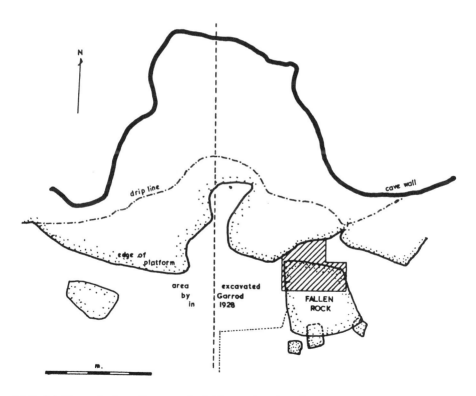

Figure 14.6: (a) Ground plan of cave and platform, showing the areas excavated in 1928 and 1971: the broken line indicates Garrod's line α-β on her Fig. 5, running roughly north-south. (b) Grid plan of the 1971 excavations, showing the area of excavation outlined by a heavy line.

the development of the Zarzian tradition, or a phase between the Zarzian and that of Karim Shahir, M'lefaat and Gird Chai (Braidwood and Howe 1960: 56). The normal backed blades and geometric microliths are missing.

The material from the Kowri Khan open-air site (500 tools) was said to have contained a few 'neat' endscrapers and a significant quantity of well-made burins, part of which represent the intermediate stage between polyhedral burins and steep scrapers. A good number of irregular, non-microlithic pebble cores were found together with a few poor, irregular discoidal and thumbnail scrapers, and irregular pyramidal pebble cores. Neatly-retouched discoidal and thumbnail scrapers, backed blades and geometric microliths are missing. The industry was considered to correspond typologically to a particular portion of the Zarzian tool-kit. Conversely, the abundance of polyhedral burins might also suggest a Baradostian industry (*ibid.*).

Like the material from the rockshelters of group A, the assemblages of the open-air camps lack the usual backed blades and geometric microliths. The absence of these tool types might be due either to the specialised exploitation of the hunting and gathering resources near these rockshelters and open camps, or to the attribution of this to a phase before the introduction of backed blades and geometric elements. The latter might also explain the absence of trapezoids and rectangles towards the top of Zarzi itself. Backed bladelets replaced backed blades in the Zarzian tradition at Pa Sangar rockshelter in the Zagros of Iran, as will shortly be made clear, and at Warwasi (also in Iran) no backed bladelets over 9 mm in width were found.

Group B

At Zarzi the new industrial sample is rather small, owing to the limited area left for excavation (Figs. 14.6, 14.8) and also to the fact that Palaeolithic material becomes less abundant further away from the cave mouth. In fact, Palaeolithic material was almost absent from the second half of square 3C (Fig. 14.7). As the 1971 excavations added no new tool types to those recovered either by Garrod or from other Zarzian assemblages in the Zagros area, I shall refrain from giving detailed descriptions of the categories involved. Instead, an account of the whole assemblage, including material from Garrod's and my own excavations, will be given below, together with drawings of some of the categories excavated in 1971 (Figs. 14.10–14.16).

Excavational techniques employed by different workers at different sites, or at the same site, may alter the results drastically. For example, during the course of excavation, the use of fine sieves greatly affects the percentages of the various tool types, and especially of microliths (also the number of bones, shells, seeds, *etc.*). With due respect to Garrod, while digging at Zarzi the present author picked up 48 tools from the surface of the old excavation dump, including one backed blade, 6 backed bladelets, 2 endscrapers, 2 discoidal scrapers, and 37 notched and trimmed blades and flakes. The typologist can also create problems, as various elements or attributes in the definition of tool types are subjective: for example, utilisation wear occurring on the edge of a blank might well classify it as a retouched tool, and *vice versa*. Similar errors might easily happen when shallow notches and trimmed pieces are classified; the definition of angled burins, as opposed to other types (those on breaks, for example), can be to some extent subjective.

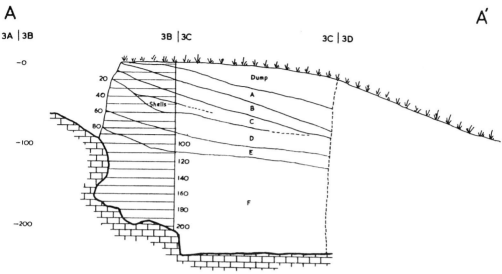

Figure 14.7: The A-A' section showing the south face of the main cutting in squares 3B and 3C.

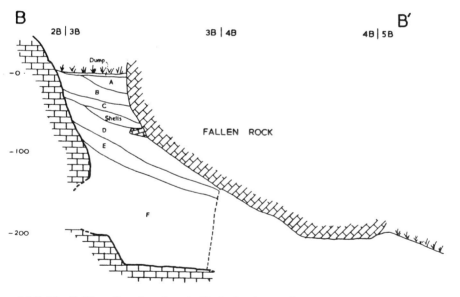

Figure 14.8: The B-B' section showing the limited volume of sediments available for excavation along the north-south face of the cutting.

With respect to Garrod's (1930) sub-division of the microlithic levels, the new excavations may now provide a better understanding of the sequence of events which may have led to the development of geometric elements, than did her simple model (geometrics only from the uppermost part of her layer B), and subsequently refined by Wahida (1981).

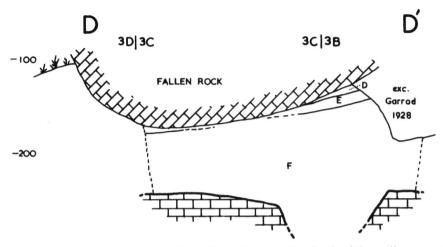

Figure 14.9: The D-D' section (north cutting), showing the depth of Garrod's excavations.

First, a word should be said about the uneven nature of the cave platform, as this may provide a better understanding of the depositional processes and the spread of Palaeolithic material to the east of the cave mouth. Initially, my excavations in square 3B were removed in 10 cm spits, owing to Garrod's (1930) description of her layer B's deposits as a white calcareous soil. During excavation of this square, I came to realise that natural layers did exist, and when square 3C was dug, only attributions to these natural layers were used. It is clear from Figures 14.7–14.9 that the excavated area of squares 3B and 3C was deeper (2.30 m depth) than that excavated by Garrod immediately outside the cave (50–150 cm depth). These marked differences in height seem to have had an effect on the eastward distribution of the material culture, especially when layer F was accumulating in both squares. It is, therefore, apparent that the platform in front of the cave was bare rock when the Zarzi fisher-hunter-gatherers arrived at the site. It was only when most of layer E (in both squares) had developed that the platform outside the cave was covered with deposits.

It would appear that a group of fisher-hunter-gatherers (fish bones appeared later in the sequence, in spit at 25–40 cm depth) had periodically occupied the cave, sometime before 15,000 BP. They seem to have left no finished tools (at least not on this part of the platform), as their early presence, detected in spits at 230–190 cm depth, was marked only by a small amount of débris. Animal bones (very few from both excavations in comparison to tools) appeared slightly later in the sequence, i.e. in spits between 200–190 cm depth. The five bones recovered from the one-metre thick deposits of layer F, square 3C, came from the upper part of the layer. Snail shells were totally lacking in layer F, square 3C, and made their appearance much later, in spits 160–150 cm, square 3B, where they were found in abundance.

The overall picture which emerges from this rather scanty evidence may indicate either a sporadic occupation of the site, or that cultural development may have been very slow. It is perhaps more likely that the uneven nature of the platform, before the deposition of layers E and above, may have been responsible for giving a totally different picture from what was happening inside the cave.

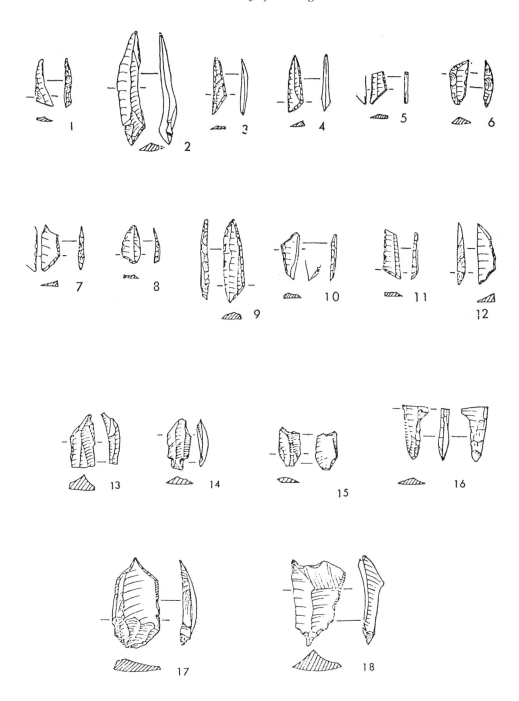

Figure 14.10: Zarzi tools, 1971: scalenes (1–12), microburins (13–16) and drills (17, 18).

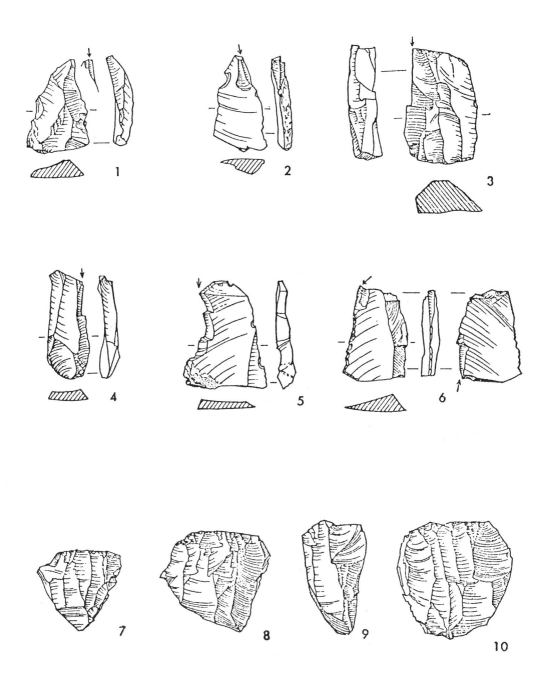

Figure 14.11: Zarzi tools, 1971: angled burins on flakes (1–3) and blade (4), rejuvenated burin (5), multiple burin (6) and single-platformed cores (7–10).

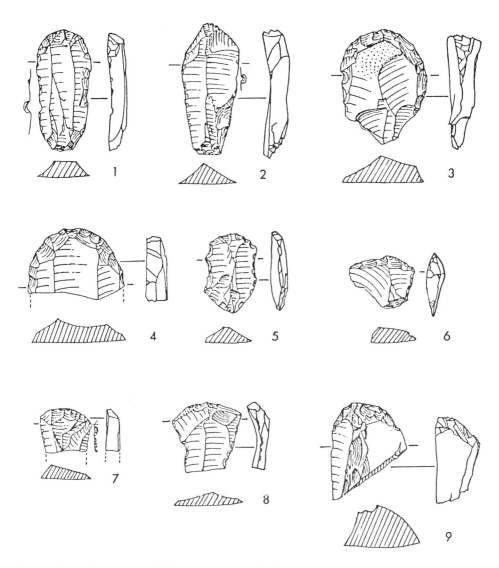

Figure 14.12: Zarzi tools, 1971: end-scrapers (1–9).

Although finished tools first appeared in spit 190–180, they were totally lacking in the overlying spit. From spits 170–160 and above, cultural developments seem to have gathered momentum: the number of artefacts and cores increased steadily from 6.19% in layer F to 19.47% in the thinner overlying deposits of layer E. Spit 90–80 recorded the highest number of tools (20.2%), although it should be noted that most of its deposits belonged to layer E. Layer D, square 3C, produced the highest number of tools and cores (39.82%); a situation which was perhaps the result of depositional processes. Table 14.3 shows the distribution of tools and cores in squares 3C and 3B.

Table 14.3: Inventory of Zarzi

Tool types	Garrod material		Wahida material	
	Nº	%	Nº	%
Burins	19	3.01	13	5.46
Microburins	1	0.15	5	2.1
End-scrapers	128	20.2	17	7.14
Backed blades	38	6.0	5	2.1
Backed bladelets	93	14.7	66	27.73
Trimmed pieces	88	13.9	34	14.28
Notches, Denticulates	196	31.9	68	28.57
Drills	4	0.63	2	0.84
Scalenes	31	4.9	16	6.72
Lunates	4	0.63		
Shouldered points	2	0.31	2	0.84
Discoidal scrapers	24	3.8	5	2.1
Core/round scrapers	5	0.78	5	2.1
Total	633	100	238	99.98

Only one animal bone was found in spit 200–190; bone quantities remained insignificant until spit 110–100, where they registered higher figures. Surprisingly, animal bones were totally lacking in layer E, square 3C, but 35 were recovered from spit 90–80, square 3B, which was nearer the cave. Snail shells appeared in spit 160–150; their numbers increased substantially through time, and especially in layer C, squares 3B and 3C, where a compacted, concentrated mass of shells was found covering a wide area (marked "shells" on sections A-A' and B-B': Figs. 14.7, 14.8) (Wahida 1981).

It was in layer E and above that we really began to see an increase in material remains, especially the number of tools, bones and snail shells. Moreover, it may not have been a pure coincidence that a change in the flora at Zarzi begins to be apparent in layer D and above (see later): very sparse and sporadic oak appeared, succeeded by intermittent lilac and almond. Pine also appeared and increased in the more recent layers. It should be noted here that trees appear to have been totally lacking in the two lower layers (F and E, with 529 identified pollen grains) (Leroi-Gourhan in Wahida 1981). The total flora is certainly that of a very dry steppe. The publication by this writer (1981) of two buckthorn seeds from Zarzi gave the impression to some authors of a new emphasis on non-traditional foods (Smith 1986). However, the two samples (both from square 3C) to have yielded seeds originally contained *many* plant species, but all remains and notes (excepting the buckthorn) went missing in the laboratory.

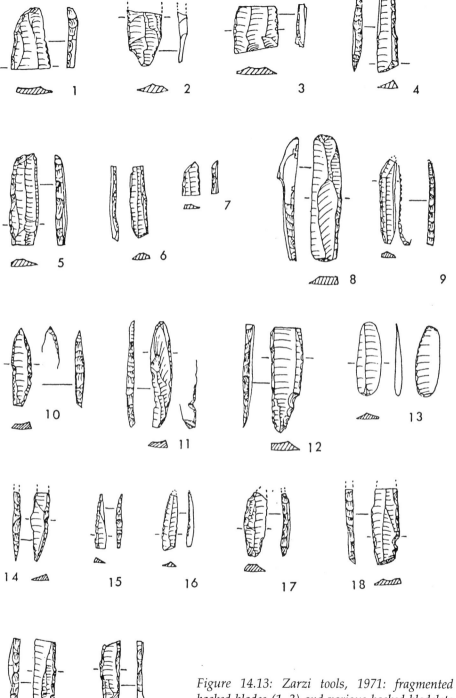

Figure 14.13: Zarzi tools, 1971: fragmented backed blades (1–3) and various backed bladelets (5–20).

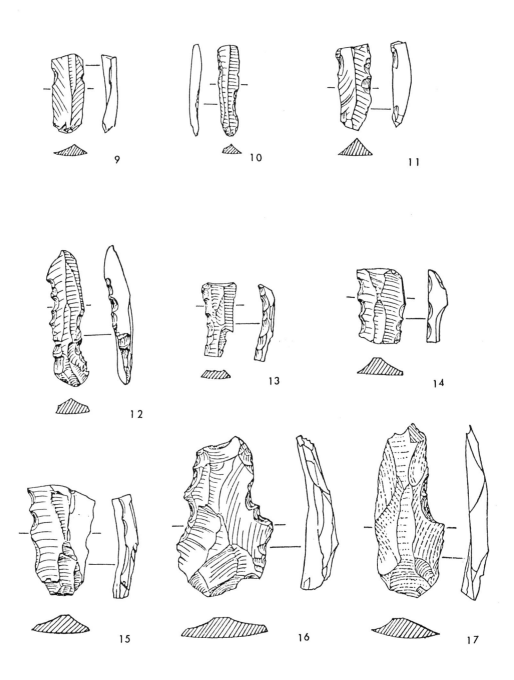

Figure 14.14: Zarzi tools, 1971: parallel notches (9–12), continuous notches and denticulates (13–15), irregular notch (16), and wide and deep notch (17).

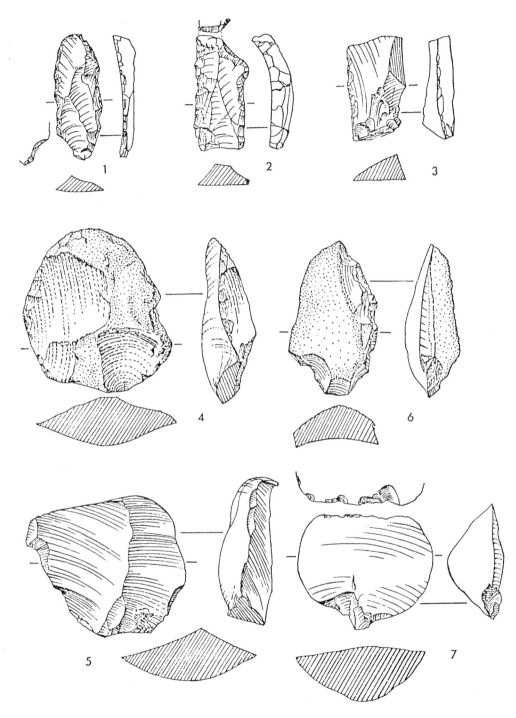

Figure 14.15: Zarzi tools, 1971: non-diagnostic implements made on flint and other, friable, materials (1–7).

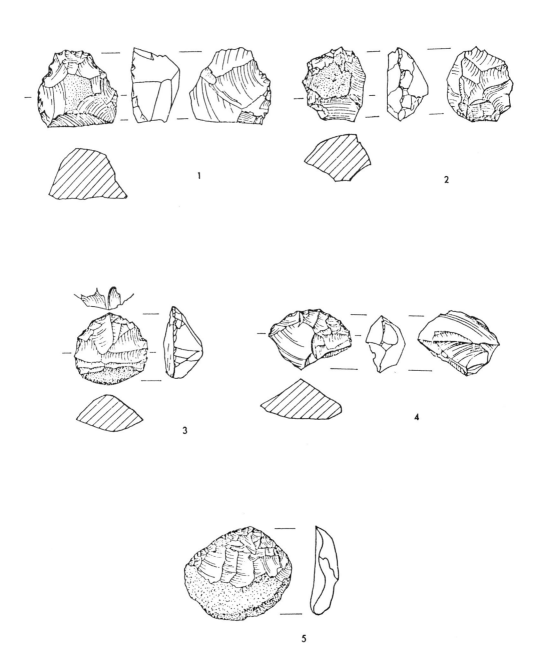

Figure 14.16: Zarzi tools, 1971: cores and round scrapers: limited retouch (1, 2) and round scrapers (3–5).

Table 14.4: Distributions of scalenes at Zarzi (1971).

Square 3B	Spits of 10 cm		Square 3C	Natural layers
0–30	[recent]		B	2
30–40	1		C	1
60–70	1		D	3
80–90	3		E	0
90–100	3		F	0
110–120	1			
120–230	0			6
	9			

It would seem, therefore, that during these technological developments, coupled perhaps with environmental improvements, tools of geometric form were first developed at Zarzi (scalenes and a few lunates: see Table 14.4 and Fig. 14.10). They were present in layer D, square 3C, but were definitely present before that, in spit 100–90, square 3B. The single scalene found in spit 120–110, square 3B, seems unlikely to belong to the top part of layer F, while those from spit 100–90, same square, could derive from layers D, E or F. Given the small number of artefacts from the whole of layer F, material is more likely to have derived from the overlying layers D and E. Thus, while it is certain that no geometrics occurred below the top few centimetres of layer F, it is possible that none occurred below layer D (see Fig. 14.7). Nevertheless, layer D is deeper than the uppermost part of Garrod's layer B, where geometrics have been found.

The importance of Zarzi lies not only as the key site of the Zarzian industry: the sequence of events described above shows for the first time the gradual development of geometrics at the site. I consider this development to have occurred within a framework of cultural change, perhaps pioneered by the Zarzi fisher-hunter-gatherers towards the end of the Palaeolithic era. Therefore the idea of a two-fold division of the Zarzi industry, implying a replacement of groups, is not supported by the actual evidence.

Shanidar (the Zarzian). At Shanidar, although the excavation is incomplete, and the stratigraphy has been complicated and sometimes destroyed as a result of rockfalls, pits, *etc.*, a possible interpretation of the stratigraphical and chronological characteristics is that the earlier phase of the Zarzian may have occurred in the upper part of the Baradostian layer C, but was considered by Solecki to have been intrusive from the basal part of layer B2. In fact, this idea was first suggested by Braidwood and Howe (1960: 155) on the basis of the available material from Zarzi, and from material found in layers B and C at Shanidar. Solecki's idea of intrusion may have been influenced by the geological stratigraphy of the cave, as well as the apparent 15,000 year hiatus between the Baradostian and Zarzian industries; however, industrial variation is independent of the geological deposits (Wahida 1975). It seems likely that if at least some of the material (without geometrics) came from the upper part of layer C, *e.g.* backed blades and bladelets, notched and denticulated pieces, end- and thumbnail-scrapers, worked bones, *etc.*, then that which was considered by the excavator to have been intrusive from the lower part of layer B2 might actually have been *in situ*. Thus there may have been a greater degree of continuity than was originally suggested.

The Zarzian of Shanidar B2 (less than three feet of deposits) was said to be marked by "several types of gravers, backed blades and bladelets, elongated triangles and sub-triangles or scalene points, notched blades, several 'Gravette' type points, and other flint types" (Solecki 1961: 418). In addition to scalene triangles, the industry also included trapezoids, lunates and rectangles.

Solecki's subdivision of the Zarzian layer B into B1 ('Protoneolithic') and B2 (Zarzian) is based upon "perceptible stratigraphic divisions coupled with a cultural or artefactual distinction which have been confirmed by ^{14}C dating" (Solecki 1961: 416). In layer B1, which has been dated at 10,600 ± 300 BP (Solecki and Rubin 1958), querns, mortars and hand rubbers were found in addition to chipped flint implements, as well as a number of 'luxury' items, such as beads, pendants and inscribed slates (Solecki 1961, 1963).

However, this writer found no major change in the chipped flint industry of layers B2 and B1, detecting continuity and cultural development rather than distinction between the two assemblages. Solecki's subdivision of layer B was based exclusively on the presence of ground stone implements and some 'luxury' items. A situation similar to that of Shanidar may be found at a number of caves and rockshelters, such as Zarzi, Palegawra, Ghar-i-Khar and Warwasi.

Shanidar (the Baradostian). The Baradostian industry of layer C, while comparatively poor in quantity, includes several types of gravers, perforators, scrapers of several types, points, notched blades, retouched blades and flakes, and a few worked bones (Solecki 1955). A ^{14}C date from the top part of layer C (two feet below the contact of layers B and C) was 28,500 ± 1500 BP (*ibid.*), while that from the bottom part of the layer, also two feet above the contact of layers C and D, was older than 34,000 BP (*ibid.*).

Thus, it would appear that there is an apparent chronological gap at Shanidar of about 15,000 years between the end of the Baradostian and the beginning of the Zarzian, a hiatus that Solecki attributed to the severe climate in the Zagros mountains at the time of the Würm maximum in the Alpine sequence of glaciation (Solecki 1955).

Palaeobotanical records from western Iran suggest a cool, dry climate prevailing for the whole Upper Palaeolithic period, *i.e.* from 40,000 BP until 14,000 BP, with an even more severe climate after 35,000 BP. The lower temperatures during Würm glacial times may be held partly responsible for the scarcity of trees in the Zeribar area, but dryness must also have been a major limiting factor for tree growth (Van Zeist and Bottema 1982); trees, including oak, were present by *ca.* 12,400 BP (see later) (Solecki and Leroi-Gourhan 1961).

Excavated caves in western Iran, however, showed no such hiatus between the Baradostian and the Zarzian. Even if Shanidar were abandoned for some reason, occupation and cultural development must have continued elsewhere, leaving no chronological or typological gap between the Baradostian and Zarzian industries. I tend to agree with Hole (1966: 291) that the "data from Shanidar are complicated by a stratigraphic hiatus of uncertain cause, and that the differences rather than possible continuities are also emphasised by some of the published drawings of tools in which the full range of assemblages is not shown".

Group C

The excavations at Palegawra revealed what seemed to be two archaeological zones. The upper one (0–60 cm depth) was a mixed deposit of Upper Palaeolithic implements and pottery from different periods. The major Palaeolithic material came from the lower zone at the rockshelter, *i.e.* 60–130 cm depth.

The industry was said (Braidwood and Howe 1960) to be generally marked by large numbers of backed blades and bladelets, various large and small end, round and other scrapers, simple angled and polyhedral burins, coarse scrapers, different forms of drills and fabricators, microburins, notched blades and flakes, and microlithic geometric forms. In the assemblage are bone tools, shell beads, pendants of teeth or stone, and a grooved abrading stone. A few celts came from a depth of 80–100 cm, and a fragment of quern from below 1 m depth.

I had the opportunity to work on the material in Chicago and Baghdad in 1970 and 1971. In all, 16 backed blades were found throughout the deposits, and 91 geometric elements, both normal and microlithic, were also present, with concentrations at depths between 60–90 cm and 90–120 cm; they were found in the upper zone as well (0–60 cm depth). The geometrics comprise an important component of the Palegawra assemblage, and include scalene triangles, trapezoids, lunates, rectangles, isosceles triangles and one parallelogram.

Four ^{14}C determinations for Palegawra were provided by the excavators; they range from 14,350 to 10,590 BP. The radiocarbon chart shows clearly that this fully-developed backed blade and geometric Zarzian phase is two thousand years older than that of Shanidar B2.

The situation in the Iranian Zagros

Although, only five Zarzian sites have been excavated or tested on the Iranian slopes of the Zagros until now, with radiocarbon dates available from only one site, the situation there seems to be rather different from that described above. While the earlier phase of the Zarzian has been found in Iran, in the lower Unit 1 of Warwasi (Olzewski 1993), this situation has not been found elsewhere. Geometrics which marked the later phase in Iraq were present throughout, apart from Warwasi Unit 1; surprisingly, backed blade elements occurred in the Baradostian and were either replaced with backed bladelets in the Zarzian (excepting Ghar-i-Khar), or did not occur at all in either assemblage from Iran. According to Hole and Flannery (1967), however, this apparently late Zarzian seems to have developed directly out of the late Baradostian, at least at Pa Sangar and Warwasi. Another important point is that the two phases in the Zarzian material of Warwasi (see below) seem to be very different from the assemblages discussed above: here backed bladelets comprise most of the assemblage.

Warwasi (700 implements)

According to Howe (pers. comm.), the deposits above the Mousterian levels contained Baradostian and Zarzian, with no difference in soil colour between the industrial levels. Pure Zarzian assemblages came from levels C-H (20–80 cm depth), while the levels below I-K/L (80–120 cm depth) contained a transition from Baradostian to Zarzian (perhaps a mixed deposit); the Baradostian occurred in levels M-T/W (120–200 cm depth). As in Shanidar B1 and the upper levels of Palegawra (0–60 cm depth), the upper 0–20 cm depth at Warwasi contained Zarzian implements mixed with pottery, *etc.*.

The Zarzian industry at Warwasi is marked by the normal and microlithic-sized end- and round-scrapers, some burins, various microlithic backed bladelets and scalene triangles (Braidwood 1960). While backed blades are completely missing, the assemblage does include a few lunates and trapezoids among the geometric forms.

The claimed Zarzian industry of Warwasi levels A-H was not only comparatively small, but essentially of microlithic appearance. Of the 700 tools studied by the author at Chicago, 523 specimens are microlithic. The characteristic form comprised elongated and obliquely truncated backed bladelets, with straight backs and retouched tips in many cases; in the whole group, curved backed pieces were the most predominant tools. None of the blades exceeded 9 mm in width (for further details on these characteristics, see Olzewski 1993).

The Baradostian assemblage comprises many types of burins, various end, round and steep scrapers, and worked and utilised implements (Braidwood 1960). Together with comparable material from Shanidar C, the Baradostian of Warwasi may, according to Braidwood, date back to about 25,000 to 30,000 years ago.

In the so-called 'transitional' levels between the Baradostian and the Zarzian, I found tools such as polyhedral burins, various end and discoidal scrapers, notched blades and flakes. Braidwood (*ibid.*: 695) suggested that the three stages of Mousterian, Baradostian and Zarzian may point to an uninterrupted continuum: a point which I would support (see also Olzewski 1993).

Ghar-i-Khar

The deposits of this deep cave yielded a sequence of lithic industries, including Mousterian and Baradostian, followed by Zarzian levels (Smith 1966, 1986); the deposit ended with an industry probably belonging to the aceramic Neolithic period. The Baradostian industry is said to include (*ibid.*) a number of burins, including those with multiple facets, end and round scrapers, backed blades, occasional backed bladelets, and notched and strangulated blades. There was also a number of bone tools.

According to the excavator, there was no discernible stratigraphic break between the zones representing Baradostian occupation and those in the overlying metre of deposits. Also, there was no clear indication of cultural discontinuity: backed blades, retouched blades and certain scraper types continued alongside new tool types such as truncated backed bladelets, 'Gravette-like' points, curved backed bladelets, triangles, microburins, chipped stone implements (axes?), grinding stones and bone awls (*ibid.*). Smith tentatively linked these cultural elements with some phase or phases of the Zagros Zarzian industry.

Although the material is too sparse for definite conclusions to be drawn (personal observation), Ghar-i-Khar seems to have produced normal backed blades and a few geometric scalenes and trapezoids. The presence of these tool types would tentatively link this assemblage with those found at Zarzi, Palegawra and Shanidar B2.

Pa Sangar
According to Hole (1966), the deposits of this rockshelter yielded two flint industries belonging to the Upper Palaeolithic period, with no apparent intervening stratigraphic and chronological gap. The earlier industry was assigned to the Baradostian, and the later one to the Zarzian.

The Baradostian. The Baradostian industry in general (in comparison with the Mousterian) shows a great increase in the number of tool types and a heavy emphasis on the manufacture of blades. Hole and Flannery (1967) divided it into three stages: early, middle and late; it is generally characterised by backed blades, slender (Arjeneh) points, various retouched bladelets, endscrapers, sidescrapers, and blades with steep retouch on one or both edges ('retouched rods': Hole and Flannery 1966). Burins of the simple type continued, while those of the polyhedral forms appeared and peaked in the later Baradostian (*ibid.*). [14]C determinations obtained from Yefteh cave showed that the Baradostian ranged from 21,000 BP to '>40,000 BP', with most samples falling between 29,000 BP and 38,000 BP. It should be noted here that these samples were obtained from the lower metre of deposit; the cave contained two metres of Baradostian materials.

The Zarzian. The Zarzian deposit at Pa Sangar lay on top of a late Baradostian layer. Many tools belonging to the late Baradostian, *e.g.* several types of retouched blade, polyhedral burins and a few 'retouched rods', continued in the Zarzian period, and suggest a direct development from the Baradostian to the Zarzian (Hole and Flannery 1967). Other tool types, such as end and round scrapers, increased in number but decreased in size; 'Arjeneh points' were no longer present. Notched blades, microburins and geometric forms, including scalenes, lunates and trapezoids, appeared in the Zarzian for the first time. Surprisingly, backed blades, present in the Baradostian, were replaced by backed bladelets in the Zarzian.

Mar Gurgalan Sarab
The material from layers D-E at Mar Gurgalan Sarab seems to suggest, according to Mortensen (1975: 4; 1993), a possible Baradostian tradition. The inventory was said to include notched blades, retouched flakes, burins, borers, end-scrapers, backed bladelets, and retouched microliths and blades.

The Zarzian. Layers B-D at Mar Gurgalan Sarab revealed an industry belonging to a geometric Zarzian tradition. The inventory included lunates, triangles, trapezoids, single-shouldered points, retouched blades and flakes, burins, notched blades, borers, end-scrapers, backed and truncated bladelets, and microburins (*ibid.*); the normal backed blades are missing.

Mar Ruz

The collected implements from the platform of the cave yielded a large number of notched or denticulated blades, small end-scrapers, backed bladelets and burins; two single-shouldered points were also found among the implements (Mortensen 1974). The *excavated* material of layer B at Mar Ruz produced notched and retouched blades, small scrapers, burins and microbladelets, of which a few were obliquely-truncated (Mortensen 1975, 1993). Mortensen mentions the presence of geometrics at Mar Ruz (*ibid.*), but made no reference to them in the inventory.

Four other caves and rockshelters, and nine open-air sites containing late Upper Palaeolithic (Zarzian) flints were discovered in the Hulailan valley of Iran during the 1974 survey (Mortensen 1975, 1993). Admittedly, the material is too small for specific conclusions to be drawn, but occasionally single-shouldered points, though with no backed blades or geometric elements, were found.

Summary

It would appear that the Zarzian of Pa Sangar, Ghar-i-Khar and Warwasi developed directly out of the late Baradostian, a phenomenon which does not seem, according to Solecki's reports, to have occurred at Shanidar. It may be concluded that, apart from the apparent stratigraphical division of the Iraqi Zarzian suggested by Zarzi and possibly Shanidar (both Iraq) and Warwasi (Iran), there are major typological differences, not only between the two phases, but also within each phase at different sites. The following observations may be summarised from the data presented above.

In Iraq:

(a)   A non-backed blade and non-geometric industry was found at Barak, Hajyah and Babkhal rockshelters, and also at Turkaka and Kowri Khan open-air sites.

(b)   A backed blade industry without geometrics may be present at Zarzi, layer F and the lower part of Garrod's layer B, and possibly in the upper part of Shanidar C (C-B2).

(c)   A fully-developed backed blade and geometric industry was found at Zarzi, layers B-E and the upper part of Garrod's layer B, Palegawra and Shanidar B2.

In Iran:

(d)   A non-backed blade and non-geometric industry, with single-shouldered points, was found at Mar Ruz cave, and at Dar Mar and Saimarreh D open-air sites.

(e)   A non-backed blade and possibly non-geometric industry was present in Warwasi Unit 1.

(f)   A non-backed blade geometric industry was found at Pa Sangar, Warwasi (Units 2 and 4) and Mar Gurgalan Sarab caves.

(g)   A fully-developed Zarzian industry with backed blades and geometric forms was present at Ghar-i-Khar cave.

Thus, the industry of Iraq's type (a) is present in Iran's type (e), while the industry of type (b) appears to be absent in Iran. The industry of Iraq's type (a) seems to lack the single-shouldered points present in type (d) of Iran.

The industries discussed above, despite their marked typological differences, have all been assigned by their excavators to a Zarzian tradition. In my view, this categorisation is too general and could profitably be further narrowed. More ^{14}C determinations would certainly be helpful; nevertheless, the following conclusions may be suggested.

If backed blades and geometrics are taken to be characteristic elements of the Zarzian in both its phases, then industries (a), (d) and (e) which lack both elements are not Zarzian, and an alternative classification is required. On the other hand, the entirely microlithic and non-backed blade assemblages of Warwasi appear to differ from industries (b) and (c) in Iraq, and (d) in Iran to a lesser extent (as it has no shouldered points). The Ghar-i-Khar material of type (g) in Iran seems to be the only counterpart to Iraq's industry (c): backed blades and geometrics were both present.

It is suggested that the term 'Zarzian' may be tentatively defined on the basis of Zarzi, Shanidar B2, Palegawra and Ghar-i-Khar as an essentially backed blade and geometric complex with microlithic elements, *i.e.* as the industries of types (c) and (g) above. The industries which lack one of these characteristic elements should perhaps be assigned to another phase/facies of the Zarzian when the overall assemblage does not differ markedly from the wider Zarzian tradition. Pa Sangar, Mar Gurgalan Sarab and Mar Ruz caves produced no backed blades, and the Warwasi assemblages are essentially microlithic. A strictly monothetic approach would probably conflict with the industrial variability occasioned by chronological and possible seasonal changes in habitat or activities. Palaeobotanical records from Zarzi (Wahida 1981), Shanidar (Solecki and Leroi-Gourhan 1961), Palegawra (Braidwood and Howe 1960) and the lake districts in Iran (Van Zeist and Bottema 1982) demonstrate clear regional variation in the late Pleistocene environment. Fisher-hunter-gatherers at this critical period in human history – an era of climatic change and rapid cultural development – had to respond to different environments in the course of their movements in the Zagros Mountains and the plains below. Varied habitats are likely to have called for differing responses from their occupants: hence a polythetic system of classification is more realistic for the late Upper Palaeolithic industries in the Near East. Furthermore, the scarcity of sites unfortunately prohibits the more precise identification of synchronous variants; consequently, the most satisfactory definition at present is one based on the requirement that a reasonable proportion of certain tool types should be found, without insisting on the presence of every one. The Warwasi material, for example, does not seem to fit into a restricted view of the Zarzian, but is acceptable as a member of a "Zarzian culture group", to use the terminology of Clarke (1968: 666).

Thus it would appear that the definition of an 'earlier' Zarzian phase characterised by backed blades, and a 'later' one with additional geometrics, is perhaps true in a basic stratigraphic sense at Zarzi and Warwasi, but not in a typological one; this definition stemmed from Garrod's original excavation and is commonly applied by scholars to the late Upper Palaeolithic industries. Comparable results have not been found at any other Zarzian site in the Zagros mountains.

An important point, casting further doubt on the idea of an 'earlier' and 'later' Zarzian tradition, is that backed blade tools which have been used as diagnostic elements of the Zarzian in both its phases (especially the 'earlier') can no longer be regarded as characteristic elements solely of the Zarzian: a belief originally based upon the absence of backed blades in the Baradostian of Shanidar, and upon the then-current lack of a sufficient number of excavated sites. As shown above, more recent excavations in Iran have revealed the occurrence of backed blades in the Baradostian of Yefteh, Gar Arjeneh, Ghar-i-Khar and Pa Sangar. At the latter site, these elements were common in the Baradostian and were replaced with backed bladelets in the Zarzian. At Warwasi and Mar Gurgalan Sarab, backed blades were totally absent in the geometric and non-geometric Zarzian assemblages.

Thus I propose to reject the old definition of an 'earlier' and 'later' Zarzian, frequently used in the literature for the late Upper Palaeolithic industries, as it is meaningless at Zarzi, Warwasi and elsewhere: tool-types (including geometrics) were developing over time as a matter of course. Such a distinction remains to be established, although should the inventories of types (a) and (d) of Iraq and Iran be proved to be earlier than Zarzi and later than the Baradostian, the term 'earlier' Zarzian could perhaps be applicable to these hypothetical inventories. Meanwhile, we shall continue to use Garrod's (1930) term 'Zarzian' for the later Upper Palaeolithic complexes of the Zagros mountains, as we do not have sufficient evidence to abandon it. The Zarzian has been defined in this work to include industries characterised by the presence of at least one of the following tool types: backed blades, microlithic bladelets, geometric forms, shouldered points, small core scrapers, microlithic drills and microburins, although the last may well have been the by-product of geometric manufacture. It should be noted that backed blades and notched pieces may occur in the Baradostian as well.

As for the possible development of the Zarzian from the late Baradostian, in the absence of the final Shanidar report I believe that the present evidence in the Zagros points to a possible evolutionary development of a single Upper Palaeolithic industry identified in two stages, rather than to two unconnected industries. This development appears to have been slower in its earlier stages, *i.e.* during the Baradostian period, becoming more rapid in its closing stages, the Zarzian.

It can be demonstrated from at least three sites that the appearance of geometric forms and microburins was largely coincident with climatic improvements in the Zagros. These sites are Zarzi, Palegawra and Shanidar B2; unfortunately, no palynological records are available from the other sites in the Zagros, and only one Iranian site provided ^{14}C determinations (Yefteh). At Zarzi, geometrics *appear* to be absent in the basal layer F, before the arrival of trees in the area (Wahida 1981); moreover, only scalenes and a few lunates were uncovered in the upper levels. At Palegawra, not far from Zarzi, and dated to *ca.* 14,350 BP, charcoal remains of oak, tamarisk, poplar and conifers suggest greater climatic improvements than at Zarzi (Braidwood and Howe 1960); in addition to scalenes, many lunates, trapezoids, and fewer isosceles and rectangular forms were present in the deposits at Palegawra. In Shanidar layer B2, which is even younger than Palegawra (*ca.* 12,400 BP), similar geometric forms to those of Palegawra were found in more improved climatic conditions: a scrub savannah had already begun to develop, and oak (*Quercus*) had reached 6% (Solecki and Leroi-Gourhan 1961). Geometrics were not only becoming noticeably variable in form, but also frequent in number.

Prehistorians are accustomed to working within well-defined temporal boundaries for industries, but this can prove restrictive, and was derived from historical models. We must consider Upper Palaeolithic cultures as representative of a complex and cohesive series of events brought about by a variety of factors over a long period of time: techno-typological developments, ecological variants, environmental changes, raw material quality and availability, seasonality, settlement patterns, human skills and their transmission across generations, and social organisation, all operating in a much wider arena than the archaeologically-known 'immediate vicinity of a cave" or a 'single catchment'. The contemporary ecosystem must have included the mountains as well as the foot-hills of the Zagros mountains (Wahida 1981).

We can now propose that the lithic assemblages of these groups constituted one basic Upper Palaeolithic industry. The Baradostian, I believe, did not cease at a particular date, or when one or more new tool types had been developed; nor did the Zarzian end in Shanidar B1, or in the upper layers of Palegawra, Zarzi, Warwasi, Pa Sangar, Ghar-i-Khar, Mar Ruz and Mar Gurgalan Sarab. Rather, this single Upper Palaeolithic industry developed into those associated with the Epipalaeolithic and early Neolithic assemblages of the Zagros. Evidence for such developments, hitherto neglected, may be found in the lithic material and in the 'luxury' and other items (querns, mortars, hand rubbers, beads, pendants, *etc.*) found in the upper levels, or even within pure Zarzian contexts at some sites.

The old notion that Palaeolithic hunters had lived in caves while Neolithic farmers constructed villages in the open needs, I believe, serious revision (see Wahida 1975, 1981). Although the idea of 'base camps' and 'transitory stations' has been more recently developed, prehistorians still seem reluctant to break with the idea that caves were the permanent 'houses' of hunters. More attention, I believe, should be given to open-air sites, since they are abundant when looked for, *e.g.* Hulailan (Mortensen 1974, 1975). Prehistorians should also abandon what I may tentatively term the 'hit-and-run' type of excavation, designed earlier in the century for rapid techno-typological information, and when the nature of hunting and gathering was of less concern.

Bibliography

Bader, N.O. 1961. The relations between the Upper Palaeolithic cultures of the Crimea and the Caucasus [O Sootnoshenii kul'tury verkhrevo Paleolita i mesolita kryma i kavkaza]. *Sovyetakaya Arkhelogiya* 4: 9–25.

Braidwood, R.J., and B. Howe 1960. *Prehistoric Investigation in Iraqi Kurdistan.* Chicago.

Clarke, D.L. 1968. *Analytical Archaeology.* London: Methuen.

Ewing, J. 1947. Preliminary note of the excavations at the Palaeolithic site of Ksar Akil, Republic of Lebanon. *Antiquity* 21: 186–196.

Garrod, D.A.E. 1930. The Palaeolithic of Southern Kurdistan: excavations in the caves of Zarzi and Hazar Merd. *Bulletin of the American School of Prehistoric Research* 6: 8–43.

Garrod, D.A.E., and D.M.A. Bate 1937. *The Stone Age of Mount Carmel, vol. 1.* Oxford: Clarendon Press.

Hole, F. 1966. The Palaeolithic culture sequence in Western Iran. *Proceedings VI UISPP Congress, Prague 1966*, pp. 286–292.

Hole, F., and K. Flannery 1967. The Prehistory of Southwestern Iran: A Preliminary Report. *Proceedings of the Prehistoric Society* 33: 147–206.

Kirkbride, D.V.W. 1958. A Kebaran rock shelter in Wadi Madamagh, near Petra, Jordan. *Man* 58: 55–58.

McBurney, C.B.M. 1968. The cave of Ali Tappeh and the Epi-Palaeolithic in N.E. Iran. Appendix on the bone sewing needles from Ali Tappeh by Rosemary Payne. *Proceedings of the Prehistoric Society* 34: 285–413.

Mortensen, P. 1974. A Survey of Prehistoric Settlements in Northern Luristan. *Acta Archaeologica* 45: 1–47.

Mortensen, P. 1975. Survey and Soundings in the Holailan Valley, 1974. *Proceedings of the 3rd Annual Symposium on Archaeological Research in Iran (Teheran 1975)*, pp. 1–12.

Mortensen, P. 1993. Palaeolithic and Epipalaeolithic Sites in the Hulailan Valley, Northern Luristan. In D.I. Olzewski and H.L. Dibble, *The Paleolithic Prehistory of the Zagros-Taurus*, pp. 159–186. The University Museum Symposium Series Volume V, University Museum Monograph 83. Philadelphia: The University Museum, University of Pennsylvania.

Olzewski, D. 1993a. The Late Baradostian Occupation at Warwasi Rockshelter, Iran. In D.I. Olszewski and H.L. Dibble, *The Paleolithic Prehistory of the Zagros-Taurus*, pp. 187–206. The University Museum Symposium Series Volume V, University Museum Monograph 83. Philadelphia: The University Museum, University of Pennsylvania.

Olzewski, D. 1993b. The Zarzian Occupation at Warwasi Rockshelter, Iran. In D.I. Olszewski and H.L. Dibble, *The Paleolithic Prehistory of the Zagros-Taurus*, pp.207–236. The University Museum Symposium Series Volume V, University Museum Monograph 83. Philadelphia: The University Museum, University of Pennsylvania.

Smith, P.E.L. 1966. Research in the Prehistory of Central Western Iran. *Science* 153: 386–391.

Smith, P.E.L. 1986. *Palaeolithic Archaeology in Iran*. American Institute of Iranian Studies Monographs: I. Philadelphia: The University Museum.

Solecki, R.S. 1955. Shanidar Cave, a Palaeolithic site in Northern Iraq, and its Relationship to the Stone Age Sequence of Iraq. *Sumer* 11: 14–38.

Solecki, R.S. 1961. Shanidar Cave: A late Pleistocene site in northern Iraq. *Rep. 6th Intern. Congr. Quatern.*, pp. 413–422. Warsaw.

Solecki, R.S. 1963. Prehistory in the Shanidar Valley, Northern Iraq. *Science* 139: 179–193.

Solecki, R.S., and A. Leroi-Gourhan 1961. Palaeoclimatology and Archaeology in the Near East. *Annual of the New York Academy of Science* 95: 729–739.

Solecki, R.S., and M. Rubin 1958. Dating of Zawi Chemi, an early village site at Shanidar, Northern Iraq. *Science* 127: 1446.

Van Zeist, W., and S. Bottema 1982. Vegetational History of the Eastern Mediterranean and the Near East during the last 20,000 years. In *Palaeoclimates, Palaeoenvironments and Human Communities in the Eastern Mediterranean Region in Later Prehistory*, pp. 277–321. Oxford: British Archaeological Reports International Series S133.

Wahida, G. 1975. *A Reconsideration of the Upper Palaeolithic in the Zagros Mountains.* Unpublished Ph.D. thesis, University of Cambridge.

Wahida, G. 1981. The Re-excavation of Zarzi, 1971. *Proceedings of the Prehistoric Society* 47: 19–40.

Zamiatnin, S.N. 1957. Paleolit zapadnovo zakavkaz'ya [The Palaeolithic of the Western Transcaucasus]. *Sbornic Musea Antropologii i etnografii A.N./S.S.S.R.* 17: 463–479.

15

"Twisting the kaleidoscope"
Dorothy Garrod and the 'Natufian Culture'

Brian Boyd

The latter part of the twentieth century has seen a gradually increasing concern on the part of individuals, social and political institutions and, particularly, the media, to mark anniversaries, to commemorate to the very day, month, and year culturally significant events and times, the births and deaths of great figures and the founding of great places. At the time of writing Jewish people around the world are marking the 50th anniversary of the creation of the State of Israel: the latest round of US-brokered Arab-Israeli peace negotiations has faltered, and the immediate political future of Israel and the Palestinian-administered territories remains uncertain and unclear. Attempting to form a clear picture of the political map of the region, with its various ethnic and social groups and competing factions, has been described recently as 'shaking the kaleidoscope', an analogy coincidentally used by Dorothy Garrod when discussing the nature of archaeological practice: 'New knowledge has given a twist to the kaleidoscope, and the pieces are still falling before the bewildered eye' (Saint-Mathurin 1969). In 1948, as the new state of Israel came into being, Garrod, as Disney Professor of Archaeology at Cambridge, was instrumental in securing for women full admittance to, and membership of, the University for the first time in its seven hundred year history.

Twenty years previously, in the late summer of 1928, she had arrived at Cambridge from Oxford to take up a research fellowship at Newnham College. Earlier that year she had paid her first visit to Palestine, a visit which allows us to mark another anniversary; more modest, politically, than those mentioned above, but of immeasurable importance in archaeological terms. In early April 1928 – exactly seventy years ago as I write – Dorothy Garrod and her team entered the Wadi en-Natuf in the Judean Hills and commenced excavations in a cave 1 km south of the Palestinian village of Shukba. There she discovered, for the first time in a stratified deposit, the Levantine Mesolithic, subsequently termed 'the Natufian' or 'the Natufian Culture'. Over the next six years, Garrod directed a remarkable series of excavations on Mount Carmel, in the Wadi el-Mughara, which laid the foundations for the Levantine prehistoric sequence still largely in use today. More importantly, she framed a set of archaeological and historical questions which – with some amendments – continue to define and characterise the nature of prehistoric archaeology in the region.

Garrod's work on the Middle to Upper Palaeolithic Levant is dealt with elsewhere in this volume. What follows here is a consideration of (a) the historical context of her pioneering research into what she initially termed 'Mesolithic Palestine', (b) how the current state of archaeological knowledge on the 'Natufian Culture' continues to be very largely shaped by the types of questions framed by Garrod's and others' early research agendas, and (c) how such questions may be reworked and carried forward within a different historical programme, one which breaks with normative research traditions and instead actively seeks new forms of knowledge, new ways of thinking.

Archaeology in 1920s Palestine

The Palestine which Dorothy Garrod encountered in 1928 was one in the midst of fundamental social and political transformation, largely brought about by the discourse of British imperial control. The Balfour Declaration of 1917, followed by the British Mandate (1922–9), had facilitated the first waves of immigration of both Jews and Arabs into Palestine: 'British census reports show that the increase in Jerusalem's population between 1921 and 1933 by immigration amounted to 20,000 Jews and more than 21,000 Arabs' (Gilbert 1996: x). Details of the subsequent religious and political tensions are well known and need not be reiterated here.

At the time of Garrod's first visit, archaeological research in Palestine was dominated by historical and theological perspectives, characterised by the work of scholars such as William Foxwell Albright who helped pioneer what rapidly became known as 'biblical archaeology' (Albright 1949). Since 1865, the majority of survey and excavation carried out in the region had been organised and financed by the (British) Palestine Exploration Fund, although several important expeditions were undertaken by the American Palestine Exploration Society (established 1870) and by German and Austrian archaeologists (*ibid.*: 23ff). 'Prehistoric archaeology', however, did not exist in any formal sense. Certainly, survey work had taken place in the Galilee and elsewhere (*e.g.* Karge 1917), and the French Dominican and Jesuit Fathers – Morétain, Vincent, Mallon and others – had carried out some surface collections and preliminary cave soundings since the late 1800s. This work, and that of Zumoffen in Lebanon (Zumoffen 1900), suggested that evidence for earlier prehistoric (*i.e.* pre-Neolithic) occupation of Palestine seemed likely, but it was not until 1925, with the work of F. Turville-Petre at the cave sites el-Emireh and el-Zuttiyeh in the Wadi el-Amud to the north-west of the Sea of Galilee, that the first systematic stratigraphic excavation of Palaeolithic deposits took place (Turville-Petre and Keith 1927), confirming the existence of the 'stone age' in Palestine.

Shukba 1928

> "As it will be convenient to have a name for this culture, I propose to call it Natufian, after the Wady en-Natuf at Shukba, where we first found it in place."
> (Garrod 1929: 222)

The archaeological material in the cave of Shukba, western Judaea, was in fact initially discovered by Father Alexis Mallon of the University of St. Joseph in September 1924, on a journey from Jemmala to Lydda (Garrod 1942). He published his observations, based on surface flint scatters, in the 'Mélanges de l'Université de St. Joseph' (Mallon 1925) and subsequently, according to Garrod, 'waived his rights as discoverer' (Garrod 1928: 182), although the precise nature of this agreement is unclear. The 1927–8 Annual Report of the British School of Archaeology in Jerusalem (B.S.A.J.) mentions that the Director of the School, J.W. Crowfoot, visited the cave in February 1928 and 'arranged for its excavation by Miss D.A.E. Garrod on behalf of the School', but no further details are given. Garrod later stated that it was Mallon himself who had 'generously suggested' that the British School should excavate the site (Garrod 1942: 1). Whatever the case, Garrod, with her recently awarded M.A. from Oxford, arrived in Palestine (via Iraq) later that same month and, along with her colleagues George and Edna Woodbury from the American School of Prehistoric Research, began planning the excavation of Shukba cave which subsequently took place from early April to mid-June. The work was funded by Lord Astor, Mr. H. Osborne O'Hagan and, principally, Mr. (later Sir) Robert Mond, Honorary Treasurer of the B.S.A.J.

The British School was, in 1927–8, in serious financial difficulties. The Director's report for that year makes for grim reading: 'it is only with the greatest difficulty that the general income of the School itself can be assured', and 'the government grant [a Treasury grant of £500 per year] has not been renewed, and the School now depends wholly on voluntary subscriptions'. These difficulties are reflected in the arrangments made for the publication of Garrod's Shukba excavations: 'for eventual definitive publications of Memoirs on the work at Shukbah, arrangements are being made with the American School of Prehistoric Studies' (as it transpired, the results of the excavations never appeared in monograph form: see below). By the following year, 1928–9, the School's financial position had worsened to such an extent that Crowfoot was obliged to report that, 'the School cannot be kept open beyond the next season unless more adequate funds are raised'.

Despite these difficulties, there does seem to have been a clear committment to the continuation of Garrod's excavations at Shukba. Both the 1927–8 and 1928–9 B.S.A.J. Annual Reports, as well as Garrod's 1942 publication of the excavation results, state that when the team left the site in the middle of June 1928, they did so with the intention of resuming work there the following spring. The reasons why this never actually happened are discussed later. First, some consideration of the Shukba excavations is required.

During the course of the two-month excavation, according to Garrod's first report for the Palestine Exploration Fund, the cave's main chamber (Chamber I) was effectively emptied of its archaeological deposits (she does contradict this in a later article). It appears that the stratification was complex and, as Garrod herself later admitted, 'rather difficult to interpret' (Garrod 1942: 2), but three archaeological layers were nonetheless discernable. Layer A ('Early Bronze Age to Recent') yielded numerous limestone fragments and, in one part of the cave, a number of hearths containing Early Bronze Age pottery sherds. Layer D was initially labelled 'Upper Mousterian' on account of its abundance of diagnostic lithic types, while Layer C, a 'stiff red clay', was a redeposited layer of material eroded from Layer D (Garrod 1928). It was Layer B, however, that proved to be the most significant in terms of the existing Levantine prehistoric sequence. This layer (80–300 cm thick), underlying the Early Bronze Age deposits, contained a microlithic flint industry associated with several hearths, burnt animal bones, polished bone artefacts, and the fragmentary remains of a number of human skeletons. The recent discovery of the Garrod archive in the library of the Musée des Antiquités Nationales, St. Germain-en-Laye, gives an insight into the first days of the excavation:

> "4th April... Drew plan of cave. 5th April. Trench started against E. wall... At 70 cm depth found skeleton of child, 165 cm from wall. It lay on its side with legs drawn up and hands behind head..."   (quoted in Smith *et al.* 1997: 270)

Lacking any comparable Levantine data, Garrod noted similarities between the Shukba Layer B material and that of the late Capsian 'kitchen middens' of North Africa (Garrod 1928: 183). The full archaeological significance of this microlith-dominated flint assemblage and its associated evidence did not become clear until the commencement of Garrod's excavations at el-Wad the following year (see below). Apart from two short, purely descriptive, interim reports (Garrod 1928, 1930a), the Shukba material was not published until 1942, by which time the map of the earlier prehistoric Levant had been substantially redrawn, largely by Garrod herself, and by the French Vice-Consul in Jerusalem and archaeologist René Neuville, whose work in the caves and rock shelters of the Judean Desert (Neuville 1934, 1951) also yielded much important Palaeolithic evidence. This work is discussed later.

Staying for the moment with 1928, Garrod left Palestine at the end of June. In September, she presented a paper on the Shukba excavations at a meeting of the British Association in Glasgow before spending the autumn and early winter period excavating cave sites in Iraq. She returned to Palestine in December to prepare for a second season at Shukba which, given the B.S.A.J.'s financial difficulties, was to be funded partly by the American School of Prehistoric Studies and partly by a further donation from Robert Mond. In the late autumn or early winter of 1928, however, a new major public works project at Haifa on the Mediterranean coast altered these plans, effectively curtailing further work at Shukba. According to the B.S.A.J. Annual Report for 1928–9, "a casual find revealed a rich Palaeolithic deposit in a cave near Athlit, and the Department of Antiquities, after preliminary reconnaissance with Mr. Lambert, most generously invited the British School of Archaeology in Jerusalem to undertake the exploration of it. Accordingly Miss Garrod postponed work at Shukbah, and devoted the whole season to Athlit". Even at this early stage (the report is dated 25 October 1929), the results of this one season of excavation were being hailed as being of 'the highest scientific importance'. The cave in question was, of course, the Mugharet el-Wad, Mount Carmel.

el-Wad 1929–32

The circumstances leading to the unintended cancellation of the Shukba project (the B.S.A.J. envisaged that this work would in fact recommence in 1930 despite the importance of the el-Wad excavations, source: Annual Report 1928–9), are now relatively well known. The latter part of 1928 saw the large-scale development of the port of Haifa, much of the required construction material being quarried from the cliffs of the Wadi el-Mughara ('Valley of the Caves'). E.T. Richmond, Director of the Department of Antiquities, stressing the anticipated importance of the archaeological deposits from the caves of el-Wad, ej-Jamal, et-Tabun and es-Skhul, entered into negotiations with the Department of Public Works. While these talks were in progress, permission was given for Richmond's deputy, Charles Lambert, to open five test trenches at el-Wad (November 1928), one in the outer chamber, and two on the terrace in front of the cave. Dorothy Garrod later wrote, 'although he never reached a completely undisturbed layer he was able to demonstrate the great importance of the cave as a prehistoric site. His most notable find was the carving in bone of Natufian date, which was the first example of Stone Age art to be discovered in the Near East' (Garrod and Bate 1937: 3–4). Equally, if not more important, however, was the discovery of a microlithic flint industry closely resembling that found at Shukba.

As a result of the perceived importance of Lambert's finds – the fragment of a carved long bone (depicting a cervid on one extremity), a pierced shoulder blade of a deer, and the remains of three human skeletons (Garrod 1930b), all in association with a microlithic industry – the Shukba excavations were abandoned after only one season (the site has not been re-excavated to this day), the funding re-diverted accordingly, and the first of seven seasons' extensive work at the Mount Carmel caves commenced in April 1929.

In the first season, Garrod was assisted by Elinor Ewbank and Mary Kitson Clark, students of Oxford and Cambridge respectively, and by two representatives of the American School of Prehistoric Research, Harriet Allyn and Martha Hackett. Given prevailing attitudes to women, particularly single women, in both Europe and the Levant at this time, Garrod's decision to have her excavation team composed largely of women – all her diggers were local Arab girls – was pioneering. According to the St. Germain-en-Laye Museum archive, only the heavy work was carried out by (Arab) men (Smith *et al.* 1997). Nevertheless, this practice was probably regarded as something unusual at the time, if William Albright's comments are anything to go by:

"Women often make the best archaeologists, as is attested by a growing list of women archaeologists. However, it is often wise to separate the sexes in excavating, since the presence of a mixed group in a camp far from a town greatly increases the expense of maintenance. In small expeditions it is difficult to mix the sexes unless the undertaking is very brief or is amply provided with funds.... Where expeditions are mixed it is highly desirable to have the director's wife present, both to provide a feminine social arbiter and to avert scandal – which has brought not a few expeditions to grief. Lady Petrie and Mrs. Garstang were invaluable members of their husbands' expeditions." (Albright 1949: 13)

During the first excavation season at el-Wad, a large pit containing, according to her first preliminary report, a collective burial of 'four adolescents and six children' (Garrod 1929: 221), was revealed in the outer chamber of the cave (Chamber I). Additionally, one other burial was revealed by a small sounding on the terrace in front of the cave. Garrod was also able to confirm the presence of the microlithic flint industry, which was found in situ associated with the large burial pit. In terms of stratification, the microlithic layer (B) at el-Wad lay between an Upper Palaeolithic level (C) and a disturbed layer (A) containing Bronze Age and later material. Bringing together the Shukba and el-Wad evidence, Garrod assigned her newly named 'Natufian Culture' (1929: 222) to a local manifestation of the 'Mesolithic' on the basis of the flint typology (predominantly crescent-shaped lunates, with backed blades, round and 'core-scrapers') and the absence of pottery (Garrod 1930a: 153). She believed the Shukba material to slightly pre-date that of el-Wad (*ibid.*).

Excavation of the cave (and of a 14 x 7 m trench on the terrace) continued in 1930, where Garrod (now a Research Fellow at Newnham College, Cambridge) was again assisted by Martha Hackett, and also from the American School of Prehistoric Research, Theodore and Donald McCown. At the end of the season, Garrod and Theodore McCown investigated a cave 15 km south of the Wadi el-Mughara:

> "In travelling by train from Haifa to Jerusalem, I had often noticed a cave lying in the cliffs to the east of the railway just south of the station of Zikhron Yakob... I went over there with Mr. Theodore MacCown [*sic*] and made a sounding. We were able to identify a Natufian layer...[and] I thought it very important that this site should be worked together with the Mugharet el-Wad, and the British and American Schools therefore asked Mr. Turville-Petre and Mrs. Baynes to undertake the excavation."   (Garrod 1932b: 267)

The cave – Mugharet el-Kebara – had been tested by Moshe Stekelis (Hebrew University, Jerusalem) in 1927, but he was unable to raise funds to carry out a full excavation. 1931, therefore, saw the third year of excavations at el-Wad cave and terrace running concurrently with Turville-Petre's first season at el-Kebara. Gradually, a fuller picture of the indigenous Mesolithic of Palestine was being built up. It became clear, by the close of the 1931 season, that el-Wad had provided the most complete prehistoric sequence yet known in the Levant, running from Middle through Upper Palaeolithic, to Mesolithic, Bronze Age and later (Garrod 1932a: 6). Refinement of Garrod's internal chronology for the Mesolithic came with the subdivision of Layer B at el-Wad into Upper (B1) and Lower (B2) Natufian. This division was based primarily on attributes of the flint industry. Specifically, the frequency of 'Helwan' retouch – oblique bifacial – on certain tools, notably lunates, was seen to decrease from from B2 (earlier phase) to B1 (later phase). Further, microburins appeared frequently in B1 but rarely in B2, while bone artefacts and 'art objects' proved more numerous in the earlier phase. Comparing her two sites, Garrod reversed her earlier opinion and concluded that Shukba Layer B corresponded with the later Natufian layer B1 at el-Wad (1932a: 7). The el-Kebara Natufian layer (B), with its microlithic industry and extraordinary worked bone assemblage (Turville-Petre 1932), she equated with el-Wad B2 (Garrod 1932a: 11).

Aside from assigning the Natufian material to the Mesolithic, very little in the way of interpretation of the phenomenon itself was put forward at this early stage. It does appear, however, from reading Garrod's preliminary reports, that certain assumptions regarding the nature of 'the Natufian Culture' were already beginning to be formed. Her reports on the 1930 and 1931 seasons at el-Wad for the American School of Prehistoric Research and the Palestine Exploration Fund (Garrod 1931a, 1931b, 1932a, 1932c), as well as Turville-Petre's el-Kebara article for the 'Journal of the Royal Anthropological Institute' (Turville-Petre 1932), discuss the large numbers of backed blades displaying 'a high degree of polish along the working edge' (*ibid.*: 272) recovered from the excavations, referring to them as 'sickle-blades'. Similarly, in the worked bone assemblages, one category of artefact was afforded special attention, despite there being only (at maximum) thirty examples from both sites: the 'sickle haft'. As early as her 1931 reports, Garrod was already arguing that the Mesolithic layer at el-Wad provided 'evidence for a primitive form of agriculture afforded by the large number of sickle-blades and hafts discovered' (Garrod: 1931a: 10) ('large number' refers to blades rather than hafts). She also noted that the flint sickle-blades displayed 'the peculiar highly polished edge produced by cutting straw' (*ibid*.: 9), and that one of the bone hafts held two flint blades in the groove running along one of its edges. She did later note, however, that these particular blades did not display any diagnostic polish (Garrod and Bate 1937: 37), raising the question as to their other possible uses.

Similarly, Turville-Petre (1932: 272) noted: "Probably the most important object found [at el-Kebara] was a grooved bone sickle-blade haft". The Director of the American School, George Grant MacCurdy, was similarly enthused enough to write: "discoveries of prime importance... these are of Mesolithic age and are the first of their kind to have been found anywhere in the world" (source: Director's report, April 1932). In terms of sheer artistic quality, the complete haft from el-Kebara is undoubtedly one of the most impressive and well-known Natufian artefacts. It measures 38 cm in length, and has an animal head carved on one end. This complete haft, along with an almost complete specimen, later led Garrod to suggest that the thirteen fragmentary examples from el-Wad – and the carved bone discovered by Lambert in his November 1928 sounding – were more or less similar artefacts to those from Kebara (Garrod and Bate 1937: 37). It is of some interest to note that whereas Garrod described the hafts in purely functional terms, Turville-Petre (1932: 272) ventured to suggest that they were "possibly ritual objects", a suggestion also put forward slightly later by René Neuville (1934).

So, the possibility of some form of 'primitive agriculture' in Mesolithic Palestine had been (very tentatively) suggested for the first time, predating Childe's support for the Levant as the geographical area for the origins of agriculture by some two years (Childe 1934). Garrod, although aware of Childe's theories, rarely refers to him in any of her works (as noted by Henry 1989). She was, however, clearly aware that such debates were taking place. In her first major synthesis of the results of the Shukba and el-Wad excavations (Garrod 1932c), in which she provisionally dated the Natufian to between 4000–5000 BC, she makes reference to a 1927 article by Peake and Fleure, advocating a Western Asian origin for agriculture. Summing up her current view of the Natufian, she concluded: "in the circumstances it may seem surprising that we get evidence of the practice of agriculture at such an early date among a people who possess no pottery and do not appear to have domesticated animals" (*ibid*.: 268).

By making such observations Garrod was, in effect, setting the research agenda for Levantine Mesolithic/Neolithic transition archaeology for decades to come. Before discussing this, however, we must turn to the early work of René Neuville, for without this we have only a partial view of the historical circumstances under which that archaeology developed. As mentioned earlier, the late 1920s and early 1930s saw the recognition of Natufian material at several sites in the southern Levant other than those excavated by Garrod. In terms of establishing the Levantine prehistoric sequence, the most significant are those excavated by Neuville (l'Institut de Paléontologie Humaine de Paris) in the Judaean Desert. Neuville, like Garrod, considered the Natufian to be a 'Mesolithic culture', characterised by a microlithic industry. Taking attributes of this industry, as well as stratigraphic observations from his cave/rock-shelter sites Erq el-Ahmar, Oumm ez-Zoueitina, Tor Abu Sif and el-Khiam, Neuville constructed a four-phase chronological scheme which became, with some reservations and refinements, the generally accepted model for the Natufian for the next thirty years (Neuville 1934). The principal characteristics of each phase of Neuville's scheme can be summarised as follows:

Natufian I: Large numbers of lunates with oblique bifacial retouch, backed bladelets, points, flat scrapers, lustred sickle blades, well-developed bone industry, art objects.

Natufian II: Smaller lunates, sharp decrease in frequency of oblique bifacial retouch, appearance of microburins, numerous burins, borers, discoidal scrapers, scalene triangles.

Natufian III: Even smaller lunates, less frequent and totally lacking oblique bifacial retouch, longer bladelets, microlithic scrapers, large number of microburins.

Natufian IV: Similar to Natufian III, appearance of notched arrowheads.

While Neuville was constructing this internal chronology for the Natufian, Garrod's el-Wad excavations continued with impressive results. The 1931 season had begun to uncover the now-famous 'veritable cemetery' of burials, several decorated, on the terrace. The British School of Archaeology in Jerusalem by now had been forced to abandon its premises and sell off many assets. The French Archaeological School of St. Stephen offered to place a room at the disposal of the B.S.A.J., which served as an office, and the library was moved to the American School of Oriental Research. By the following year, however, some financial improvement had occurred.

Two seasons of excavation at the Mount Carmel Caves took place in 1932. The first, in spring, was directed by solely by Theodore McCown and funded by the American School. In August, Garrod and McCown presented the results of the Mount Carmel excavations to the International Congress for Prehistoric and Protohistoric Studies held in London. For reasons I have been unable to ascertain, Garrod was unable to return to Palestine until the autumn/winter season (October-December), which was financed by a £450 grant from the Royal Society. Garrod herself, it appears, concentrated mainly on the excavation of Tabun, leaving the el-Wad work to her assistants, E. Kitson (Girton College, Cambridge, and University College, London) and T.P. O'Brien (U.C.L.), and R. Sears and A.H. Fuller (both of the American School). This latter pair removed the modern wall in the cave mouth in an effort to link the cave and terrace layers. Garrod subsequently reported that, apart from two Lower Natufian burials, "no objects of special interest were found" (Garrod 1934: 11). The 1932–3 annual report of the B.S.A.J. reported that material from the Mount Carmel excavations would be distributed, with the permission of the Department of Antiquities, to the British Museum, and the Universities of Oxford, Cambridge, Manchester, Glasgow, Toronto and McGill, Montreal.

Garrod and the 'Natufian Culture' after el-Wad

With the results of the Mount Carmel excavations, Garrod was now able to present, for the first time, a comprehensive overview of the 'Stone Age of Palestine' (Garrod

1934), in which she detailed the Levantine prehistoric sequence from its 'Tayacian' beginnings through to the Bronze Age and later. In this article, she reconfirmed that since no ceramics had been found in any known Natufian deposit, then the culture could be "truly described as Mesolithic, even though the presence of sickles points to the existence of some form of agriculture" (*ibid.*: 138). More elusive, however, was the question of Natufian origins. Garrod recognised that the Natufian was a local facies of the Mesolithic, but she clearly believed that its roots lay elsewhere:

> "Natufian art shows no Predynastic affinities, nor, in spite of certain superficial resemblances, can it be linked with that of the Magdalenian, to which it is inferior. In the matter of Natufian origins we have everything to learn, but it is a fairly safe guess that excavation in Anatolia would throw light on this problem."
> (Garrod 1936: 128)

For his part, Neuville argued (Neuville 1934: 251) that on the basis of lithic assemblages, the Natufian displayed a continuity from the Upper Palaeolithic.

By the time of the final publication of the Mount Carmel excavations in two large monographs (Garrod and Bate 1937), the internal chronology for the Natufian as constructed by Neuville was generally accepted. Garrod agreed that Neuville's 'Natufian I' corresponded with el-Wad B2 (Lower Natufian), but she appeared unconvinced by his placing of el-Wad B1 somewhere between Natufian II and IV:

> "In the main, Neuville's classification appears to be valid, but it needs to be confirmed, especially as regards the middle stages, by further excavation."
> (*ibid.*: 117)

These proved to be Garrod's last comments on the nature of the Natufian for twenty years. She published a short paper on the decorated skeletons from el-Wad (Garrod 1940), followed by the long-awaited report on the Shukba excavations (Garrod 1942), but these were purely descriptive accounts. Her next (and final) words on the subject were given at the Albert Reckitt Archaeological Lecture on 20 November 1957, and subsequently published in the *Proceedings of the British Academy* (Garrod 1957). In the interim period, a number of important developments took place which need to be recounted in order to understand Garrod's views in that final paper.

Changes to Neuville's chronology became necessary following the recommencement of his excavations at el-Khiam, when it was realised that the notched arrowheads, until then characteristic of his 'Natufian IV', also appeared in the previous phase. As a result, 'Natufian IV' came to be characterised by the appearance of pressure-flaking techniques, denticulated sickle blades, and a new type of arrowhead (Perrot, in Neuville 1951). More importantly, however, Neuville proposed that 'Natufian I' (which he, with some foresight, placed between the 10th and 12th millennia BP) witnessed the first appearance of cereal cultivation, followed in phases III and IV by the domestication of cattle, pig and goat (Neuville 1951: 217). The debate widened as the American archaeologist Robert Braidwood, working in other areas of the Near East, rejected Neuville's view, arguing that the Mesolithic economy was one based purely on the hunting of wild animals and the collection of wild cereals. He did, however, concede that the initial steps towards agriculture and domestication probably took place during this period (Braidwood 1956). [*Note:* it was later demonstrated that there was in fact no Natufian material from el-Khiam, the lithic industry being instead entirely consistent with a pre-pottery neolithic A (PPNA) assemblage (Perrot 1968)].

It was not until 1957, long after she had stopped working in Palestine, that Dorothy Garrod herself discussed the possibility that grain cultivation was first practised in the early Natufian. Noting the high proportion of [apparent] sickle blades from Natufian sites, and the care spent in adorning some of the hafts, she finally agreed with Neuville "in thinking that the Lower Natufian people were probably the first agriculturalists" (Garrod 1957: 216). She was also able to suggest, based upon the faunal evidence from Shukba and el-Wad studied by Dorothea Bate, that the domestication of the dog – but no other animal species – took place during this phase (*ibid.*: 224). Owing to a lack of recognisable evidence for substantial structures or houses, researchers tended to agree with her that cereal cultivation took place before sedentism and village life. As for the origins of the Natufian, Garrod had suggested Anatolia as a likely source. By 1957, with no evidence forthcoming to support this claim, she retracted, believing that "the Natufian makes its first appearance apparently full-grown with no traceable roots in the past" (1957: 225).

The 'Natufian Culture' after Garrod

The European consensus, then, by the late 1950s, was that the Natufian represented a Mesolithic gatherer-hunter 'culture' practising cereal cultivation with the beginnings of animal domestication. The use of the European nomenclature, despite the fact that both Garrod and Neuville recognised that the Natufian belonged to the Pleistocene, raises the issue of the profoundly European perspective on Levantine prehistory at this time. As we have seen, Europeans were carrying out the first professional archaeological research in the region, and the only comparable chronological and cultural framework available was that constructed for European prehistory. However, the imposition of a European perspective, and the fact that an independent Near Eastern framework had never been constructed (even today most of the terminology used to describe prehistoric periods, artefact classification, and so on, is closely based on the western European framework), may well reflect the effects of European political control in the region during the post-First World War British and French Mandates (Rosen 1991). In evaluating this stage in the history of Near Eastern prehistoric research it is important to recognise these factors, since they have a direct bearing on the current state of European involvement in the archaeology of the region.

Within ten years, archaeologists' view of the Natufian had changed, largely due to interpretations of the evidence from three major new excavations: Jericho (Kenyon 1952, 1959), Nahal Oren, the first Israeli-run Natufian excavation (Stekelis and Yizraeli 1963) and Mallaha (Eynan) (Perrot 1960, 1966). The first C14 dates for the pre-ceramic levels at Jericho assigned the stratigraphically earlier Natufian level at the site to between 8000–10,000 BP. Two dates subsequently obtained from charcoal samples taken from the Natufian level itself appeared to confirm this estimate (Kenyon 1959: 5–9; *note:* the Jericho PPNA dates were apparently available in 1958, but were not published until after the publication of the Natufian dates). Even more significant, the nature of the material evidence recovered from Nahal Oren and Mallaha seemed to demonstrate that it was these Mesolithic gatherer-hunters who in fact constituted the first settled communities, for it was at these sites that the first major structural remains were found in the form of large stone-built round 'houses'. One of the main figures at this time was the French archaeologist Jean Perrot, a pupil of Neuville's, who directed the excavations at Mallaha from 1959–61. His work was strongly influenced by the new perspectives coming from America, particularly those of Braidwood. The quality of the evidence from Mallaha was such that he found himself in a position where he was able to refine and revise the earlier perspectives of Garrod and Neuville. He argued for recognition of the Natufian as a "cultural and ethnic whole", as displayed in the homogeneity of its lithic, stone and bone industries, art objects and funerary practices (Perrot 1966). In addition, the economy of this cultural/ethnic group was, for Perrot, based not on cereal cultivation and animal domestication (there being no evidence from Mallaha to suggest this), but on hunting and gathering. On this premise, he proposed the replacement of the traditional term 'Mesolithic' with 'Epipalaeolithic' (*ibid.*: 483), to demonstrate the essential continuity of the economic and technological base from the preceding Upper Palaeolithic period.

By the late 1960s, then, we have a rather different picture for the Natufian: sedentary gatherer-hunters – the first settled communities – with indigenous origins. It is of interest to note that with Perrot's rejection of animal domestication in the Natufian, the apparently domesticated dogs of Shukba and el-Wad were, until relatively recently, referred to in the literature as wolves, despite no further faunal analysis being carried out.

Over the last twenty-five years, Natufian archaeology in Israel has been carried out, for the most part, by Israeli scholars, notably from the Institute of Archaeology at the Hebrew University in Jerusalem (principally O. Bar-Yosef, A. Belfer-Cohen and A. N. Goring-Morris) and the Zinman Institute at the University of Haifa (M. Weinstein-Evron, who is currently carrying out a new series of excavations at el-Wad), with significant contributions by F. R. Valla (C.N.R.S., Paris) and the American researchers D. O. Henry (*e.g.* Henry 1989) and A. E. Marks (*e.g.* Marks 1976). After Garrod's work in the region, large-scale British involvement effectively ended, with the exception of Eric Higgs' brief spell at Nahal Oren (Noy *et al.* 1973), following the end of Kenyon's excavations at Jericho. As Rosen rightly argues, the lack of a British presence in this field may well be "a reflection of (and reaction to) the colonial legacy and international politics" (1991: 314). Moreover, it is also equally a matter of British funding priorities. At the time of writing, the British Academy has 'merged' the British Schools of Archaeology in Jerusalem and Amman in a controversial 'cost-cutting' exercise.

Jean Perrot's general hypothesis has remained, with some refinements, the broadly accepted model for the Natufian. Throughout the 1970s, debate tended to concentrate on the refinement of definitions. In his unpublished Ph.D. thesis (1970), Ofer Bar-Yosef proposed a tighter definition for the Natufian. Alluding to the concept of a geographical 'core and periphery', he suggested a hierarchy of known sites on the following basis:

(a) Base camps: large sites in the *terra rossa* Mediterranean zone, containing a lithic industry characterised by lunates (crescent-shaped microliths which are still regularly regarded as the 'cultural marker' for the Natufian) and sickle blades, ground stone tools, stone-built structures, human burials and art objects.

(b) Seasonal camps: smaller sites, within a 50 km radius of the base camps, containing a similar lithic industry but lacking most of the other attributes. Seasonal camps in the semi-arid and arid zones, and in the Lebanese mountain area, were considered as having only tenuous links with the Natufian of the 'core' Mediterranean zone.

Further refinements came with the American archaeologist Donald Henry's (1973, 1974) development of an internal chronology for the Natufian, based upon features and attributes of its lithic assemblages. In 1975, presenting the most complete synthesis to date, François Valla, in an effort to escape the restrictions of Bar-Yosef's equation of the Natufian with Mediterranean zone base camps, suggested a more comprehensive and geographically extensive definition, at the same time stressing the need for further fieldwork in Syria, Lebanon, Transjordan and Egypt. Such work, he argued, would enable the recognition of the diversity of the Natufian "modes de vie probables" (1975: 123), as reflected in the lithic industries, and allow the construction of a more detailed chronology based upon developments within regional lithic assemblages. By the mid–1980s, Valla, in his major works on the typology and evolution of Natufian lithic industries (1981, 1984, 1987a), was able to present a tripartite chronology based not only on lunate attributes, but also on a quantitative and qualitative analysis of other lithic tool types, as well as radiocarbon dates. With a few minor adjustments, mainly the results of new fieldwork, the criteria put forward by Valla represent the currently accepted framework for Natufian chronology.

Twisting the kaleidoscope

As should be evident from the above, the current state of research into the Natufian is the result of a number of historical traditions – mainly British, French and Israeli – with some American processual influence figuring fairly prominently in several researchers' work (see Rosen 1991 for discussion of current 'paradigms and politics in the Levant'). Extensive fieldwork in the Negev, Jordan, Syria and, to a lesser extent, Lebanon, may have supplied a vast and rich data base, as exemplified in the 1991 Bar-Yosef and Valla edited volume, *The Natufian Culture in the Levant*, in which over fifty scholars contributed to this 'state of the art' corpus, but the *fundamental categories of research* have remained virtually unchanged for decades. Current research seems to involve little more than fitting new sites, new material evidence, into the long-established Natufian framework. There is little scope for innovative theoretical debate, despite some optimism in this respect:

> "Undoubtedly, much of the renewed research will arise from theoretical approaches that cannot be tested on the basis of the available data."
>
> (Bar-Yosef and Valla 1991: 7)

The nature and diversity of the Natufian data lend themselves to stringent theoretical analysis, and yet regardless of local, regional or intrasite diversity and variability, the current literature seems to be concerned with the same themes, the same issues. There is an over-riding emphasis on three principal questions: what is the Natufian? where do we look for its origins? what is the relationship between the Natufian and the subsequent Neolithic? That is, can we locate the origins of sedentism, animal domestication and agriculture in the later Epipalaeolithic Natufian (Perles and Phillips 1991)? This is Garrod's legacy, with which we are still struggling.

It is evident, then, that after 65 years of archaeological research on the Natufian in the Levant, the current literature is largely characterised by the same concerns as those set out by Dorothy Garrod, and others, in the 1930s. We have a vast database from which innovative research issues may be pursued, but this does not seem to be generally happening. What is required is a break from what may be termed the 'normative' research traditions which currently prevail. Normative research is cumulative, it accepts current forms of knowledge and seeks to add details, to fill gaps in that knowledge. As such, it emphasises and maintains *continuity* in research programmes. A critical evaluation of normative research would attempt to understand how the nature of current theoretical and practical (dominant) knowledge has been shaped by the, often unacknowledged, selection processes of past research traditions but, at the same time, would seek a break with current forms of knowledge which simply maintain continuity with those research traditions rather than seeking new forms of knowledge and new ways of thinking. This is the intellectual challenge facing us today. How may the traditional questions asked of 'the Natufian' be reworked and carried forward within a different historical programme, a programme which breaks with normative research traditions and instead actively seeks new forms of knowledge?

As a tentative example of this way of thinking, some basic preliminary steps towards the theoretical reorientation of traditional research themes may be suggested. What is initially required is a critical examination of the current principal areas of archaeological enquiry. Following those set out by Bar-Yosef and Valla (1991), these may be identified as:

1. Environment.
2. Settlement pattern.
3. Subsistence.
4. Artefact industries.

An archaeology which has at its heart the analysis of social practice, of knowledgeable human action and of how people engage practically with their world, cannot accept these normative categories in their traditional sense. I would suggest that they can be reworked by placing each in a perspective which recognises the fundamentally social nature of the world as understood by people (in the present as well as in the past). For example, 'environment' and 'settlement pattern' are far more than simply regional or local climatic conditions and the geographical distribution of 'sites'; they surely constitute the material conditions within which people lived, worked and built. At the heart of their analysis lies people's perceptions of landscape and how they may have inhabited the 'natural' and 'constructed' environments. Similarly, 'subsistence' cannot be reduced to the execution of a food procurement strategy. It is, rather, the social act of appropriating and transforming 'nature' (Ingold 1986). Again, the ways in which people perceived and drew upon the available resources in their landscape is an essential element in understanding their social worlds. Finally, artefact 'industries', and artistic representations, as *technologies*, are the medium for meaningful social action, for effective agency.

These are but some preliminary thoughts; there will be many other possibilities, other perspectives. The crucial point is that if we are to do justice to the legacy of those past pioneers who gave our discipline its initial momentum, we are *obliged* to carry forward their ideas in new analytical, interpretative, journeys – twisting the kaleidoscope – rather than relying on increasingly lifeless, single-view, models of the past.

Acknowledgements

I wish to thank Anna Belfer-Cohen for her constructive comments and criticism. I hope I have managed to address at least some of her concerns in the final version. Special thanks must go to Zoe Crossland for last-minute comments.

Bibliography

Albright, W.F. 1949. *The archaeology of Palestine*. Penguin.
Bar-Yosef, O. 1970. *The Epipalaeolithic cultures of Palestine*. Unpublished Ph.D. thesis. Jerusalem: Hebrew University.
Bar-Yosef, O., and F.R. Valla (Eds.) 1991. *The Natufian culture in the Levant*. International Monographs in Prehistory. Michigan: Ann Arbor.
Childe, V.G. 1934. *New light on the most ancient east*. London: Kegan Paul.
Garrod, D.A.E. 1928. Excavation of a Palaeolithic cave in western Judaea. *Quarterly Statement of the Palestine Exploration Fund* 60: 182–185.
Garrod, D.A.E. 1929. Excavations in the Mugharet el-Wad, near Athlit, April-June 1929. *Quarterly Statement of the Palestine Exploration Fund* 61: 220–222.
Garrod, D.A.E. 1930a. Fouilles paléolithiques en Palestine, 1928–1929. *Bulletin de la Société Préhistorique Française* 27: 151–160.
Garrod, D.A.E. 1930b. Note on Three Objects of Mesolithic Age from a Cave in Palestine. *Man* 30: 77–78.
Garrod, D.A.E. 1931a. Excavations in the caves of the Wady-el-Mughara, 1929–1930. *Bulletin of the American School of Prehistoric Research* 7: 5–11.
Garrod, D.A.E. 1931b. Excavations at the Mugharet el-Wad, 1930. *Quarterly Statement of the Palestine Exploration Fund* 63: 99–103.
Garrod, D.A.E. 1932a. Excavations in the Wady al-Mughara (Palestine), 1931. *Bulletin of the American School of Prehistoric Research* 8: 6–11.
Garrod, D.A.E. 1932b. Excavations in the Wady el-Mughara, 1931. *Quarterly Statement of the Palestine Exploration Fund* 64: 46–51.
Garrod, D.A.E. 1932c. A new Mesolithic industry, the Natufian of Palestine. *Journal of the Royal Anthropological Institute* 62: 257–269.
Garrod, D.A.E. 1934. The Stone Age of Palestine. *Antiquity* 30: 133–150.
Garrod, D.A.E. 1936. A summary of seven season's work at the Wady el-Mughara. *Bulletin of the American School of Prehistoric Research* 12: 125–129.
Garrod, D.A.E. 1940. Notes on some decorated skeletons from the Mesolithic of Palestine. *Annual of the British School at Athens* 47: 123–127.
Garrod, D.A.E., and D.M.A. Bate 1937. *The Stone Age of Mount Carmel*. Vol. 1. Oxford: Clarendon Press.
Garrod, D.A.E., and D.M.A. Bate 1942. Excavations at the cave of Shukbah, Palestine, 1928. *Proceedings of the Prehistoric Society* 8: 1–20.

Garrod, D.A.E. 1957. The Natufian culture: the life and economy of a Mesolithic people in the Near East. *Proceedings of the British Academy* 43: 211–227.

Gilbert, M. 1996. *Jerusalem*. London: Pimlico.

Henry, D.O. 1973. *The Natufian of Palestine: its material culture and ecology*. Unpublished Ph.D. thesis. Dallas: Southern Methodist University.

Henry, D.O. 1974. The utilization of the microburin technique in the Levant. *Paléorient* 2/2: 389–398.

Henry, D.O. 1989. *From foraging to agriculture: the Levant at the end of the ice age*. Philadelphia: University of Pennsylvania Press.

Ingold, T. 1986. *The appropriation of nature: essays on human ecology and social relations*. Manchester: Manchester University Press.

Karge, P. 1917. *Rephaim*. Publisher unknown.

Kenyon, K.M. 1952. Early Jericho. *Antiquity* 26: 116–122.

Kenyon, K.M. 1959. Earliest Jericho. *Antiquity* 33: 5–9.

Mallon, A. 1925. Quelques stations préhistoriques de Palestine. *Mélanges de l'Université de Saint-Joseph* 10: 191–192.

Marks, A.E. 1976. *Prehistory and palaeoenvironments in the central Negev, Israel. Volume 1: the Avdat/Aqev area, Part 1*. Dallas: Southern Methodist University.

Neuville, R. 1934. La préhistoire de Palestine. *Revue Biblique* 43: 237–259.

Neuville, R. 1951. *Le Paléolithique et Mésolithique du Désert de Judée*. Mémoires de l'Institut de Paléontologie Humaine, 24. Paris: Masson.

Noy, T., Legge, A.J., and E.S. Higgs 1973. Recent excavations at Nahal Oren, Israel. *Proceedings of the Prehistoric Society* 39: 75–99.

Perles, C., and J.L. Phillips 1991. The Natufian conference – discussion. In O. Bar-Yosef and F.R. Valla (Eds.), *The Natufian culture in the Levant*, pp. 637–644. International Monographs in Prehistory. Michigan: Ann Arbor.

Perrot, J. 1960. Excavations at Eynan (Ain Mallaha): preliminary report on the 1959 season. *Israel Exploration Journal* 10/1: 14–22.

Perrot, J. 1966. Le gisement natoufien de Mallaha, Israel. *L'Anthropologie* 70/5–6: 437–484.

Rosen, S.A. 1991. Paradigms and politics in the terminal Pleistocene archaeology of the Levant. In G.A. Clark (Ed.), *Perspectives on the past: theoretical biases in Mediterranean hunter-gatherer research*, pp. 307–321. Philadelphia: University of Pennsylvania Press.

Saint-Mathurin, S. de 1969. Nécrologie: Dorothy, Annie, Elisabeth, Garrod (5 février 1892–18 décembre 1968). *Syria* XLVI: 385–390.

Smith, P.J., Callander, J., Bahn, P.G., and G. Pinçon 1997. Dorothy Garrod in words and pictures. *Antiquity* 71: 265–270.

Stekelis, M., and T. Yizraeli 1963. Excavations at Nahal Oren: preliminary report. *Israel Exploration Journal* 13/1: 1–12.

Turville-Petre, F. 1932. Excavations in the Mugharet el-Kebara. *Journal of the Royal Anthropological Institute* 62: 271–276.

Turville-Petre, F., and A. Keith 1927. *Researches in prehistoric Galilee 1925–1926 and a report on the Galilee skull*. London: British School of Archaeology in Jerusalem.

Valla, F.R. 1975. *Le natoufien: une culture préhistorique en Palestine*. Paris: Gabalda.

Valla, F.R. 1981. *Les industries de silex de Nahal Oren et les stades du natoufien*. Troisieme Colloque sur la terminologie de la préhistoire au Proche-Orient. Mexico: UISSP.

Valla, F.R. 1984. *Les industries de silex de Mallaha (Eynan) et du natoufien dans le Levant*. Mémoires et Travaux du Centre de Recherche Français de Jérusalem, No. 3. Paris: Association Paléorient.

Valla, F.R. 1987. Chronologie absolue et chronologies relatives dans le natoufien. In O. Aurenche, J. Evin and F. Hours (Eds.), *Chronologies du Proche Orient/Chronologies of the Near East: relative chronologies and absolute chronology 16 000–4 000 B.P.*, pp. 267–294. Oxford: British Archaeological Reports International Series 379.

Zumoffen, G. 1900. *La Phénicie avant les Phéniciens*. Beirut.

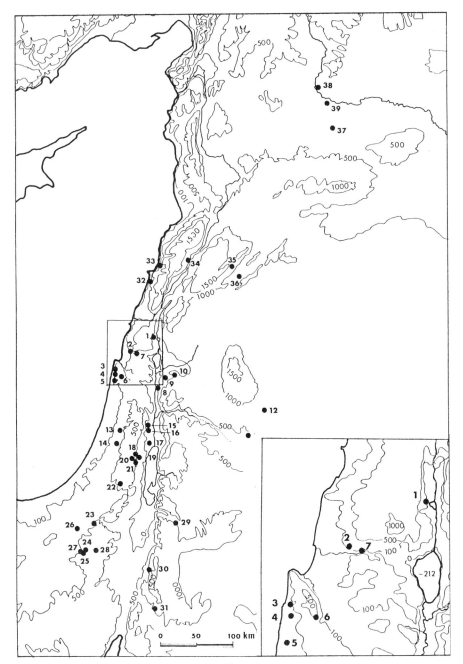

Figure 16.1: Map of main Natufian and Harifian sites.

1) *Mallaha (Eynan)*; 2) *Hayonim*; 3) *Nahal Oren*; 4) *el-Wad*; 5) *Kebara*; 6) *Rafeket*; 7) *Nahal Hillazon*; 8) *Wadi Hammeh 27*; 9) *Ain Rahub*; 10) *Taibe*; 11) *Azraq 18*; 12) *Khallat Anaza*; 13) *Shukba*; 14) *Hatoula*; 15) *Fazael*; 16) *Salibiyah*; 17) *Jericho*; 18) *Erq el-Ahmar*; 19) *Ain Sakhri*; 20) *Oumm ez-Zoueitina*; 21) *Tor Abu Sif*; 22) *Ira*; 23) *Rosh Zin*; 24) *Rosh Horesha and Saflulim*; 25) *Abu Salem*; 26) *Shunera*; 27) *Ramat Harif*; 28) *Maale Ramon*; 29) *Tabaqa*; 30) *Beidha*; 31) *Wadi Judayid*; 32) *Les Sables de Beyrouth*; 33) *Jiita*; 34) *Saaide*; 35) *Jabrud*; 36) *Jairoud*; 37) *El Kowm*; 38) *Mureybet*; 39) *Abu Hureyra.*

16

The Natufian: A Coherent Thought?

François R. Valla

The ideology of prehistoric populations is always difficult to grasp. It is hidden behind very varied types of behaviour, which express it in a partial and ambiguous fashion. Owing to the relative wealth of material which they left behind them, the Natufians have given us more access than have others to their mode of thought. However, this wealth also constitutes a handicap through the multitude of approach methods, and the impression of incoherence which results from it.

Without ignoring the hazards of such an attempt, one seeks to separate the meanings of the archaeological remains in terms of the ideas, whether conscious or not, which they seem to imply to those who elaborated them. To this effect, internal analysis and the pursuit of associations are used in order to extract the meanings carried by the evidence itself, and to keep interpretative intervention to a minimum.

Evidence is taken into account whose purpose is today considered as technical (flint industries) or as symbolic (marine shells and body ornaments), and then the more complex evidence, where there is no doubt that it is inextricably interlinked with values of different and complementary natures: burials, living areas, art.

It follows from this that Natufian society was promoting a certain type of hunting. Body ornaments reveal a binary mode of thought expressed through masculine (obvious) and feminine (discreet) symbols. Burials, the discovery of isolated human skulls and that of headless skeletons imply that the dead were a subject of contemplation for the living. The grave goods and the organisation of certain tombs seem to be linked to a complex thought which contrasts humans and dogs to the non-human world, animal and mineral, whilst maintaining links. There a possible opposition is disclosed between the village and the outside world. Yet the villages themselves remain too little known for their study to support research in this direction.

The figurative art is essentially plastic; the non-figurative art almost always takes the volume of the decorated object into account. It is proposed to reconcile these characteristics with a spatial perception tied to sedentism, for which the world would be centrally-organised. Conversely, the myths which probably accompanied this art seem virtually inaccessible.

Introduction

Distinguished in 1928 by Dorothy Garrod in the Shukba cave, the Natufian has never ceased to intrigue prehistorians since. Such as it is understood today (including the Harifian, which is a late development in the Negev), its occupation area stretches from the Middle Euphrates down to the Negev and to the Edom mountains, and from the Mediterranean to the oases of the Syro-Jordanian desert (Fig. 16.1). The human groups which frequented this region between *ca.* 12,500 and 10,200 BC (un-calibrated ^{14}C years) seem to have shared a certain number of cultural traits (of technological, but also symbolic, type), whose distribution to our eyes describes a "cultural sphere" and which justifies the common appellation "Natufian", despite the probable differences in the way of life owing to the extreme diversity of environments juxtaposed in this small region.

These two phenomena, cultural unity and diversity in ways of life, are the two essential traits which we must keep in mind for all approaches to the Natufian. The more especially as, despite its relative brevity for a prehistoric culture (about 2000 ^{14}C years), the Natufian cannot be taken for a static entity, but must, to the contrary, be seen as a complex spanned by multiple challenges through time as well as in space. Only the studies which take account of these challenges can give us the means to understand the changes which led to the culture of Jericho to the south (the Sultanian), and to that of Mureybet on the Middle Euphrates (the Mureybetian). It will nevertheless be difficult to do justice to this diversity within the framework of this paper. Interest will be taken particularly in that area conventionally called the "Carmel-Galilee centre", because it is there that the most significant changes arose, to which one refers when speaking of the Natufian; they accompany a tendency towards sedentism, which seems to have been considered as a model by the peripheral populations. The aim of this paper is to identify unity rather than diversity. Indeed, I should like to pursue the possible coherence of prehistoric people's thought from the multiplicity of approaches through which it is accessible to us: not just art and personal adornment, but also technical systems, organisation of living space and funerary practices, each of which offers us no more than a vivid and partial glimpse.

The Symbolic Investment of the Technological System

Traditionally, research has striven to recognise the technological characteristics of the Natufian, which one has depended upon in order to assign individual groups to that culture. Knapping of the flint has produced the determining criteria; we shall try to explore the symbolic side which accompanies and underlies these characteristics.

The Natufian flint industry is microlithic. This fact leads us to suppose that society was organised around a principal activity: hunting. Indeed, microwear specialists observe that Natufian microliths are almost always projectile weapon points (Buller 1983; Valla, Le Mort and Plisson 1991; Plisson, pers. comm.). Although part of lithic tool production has not been directly engaged in the process of provisioning from hunting, this still sufficiently dominated thought to direct almost all the set of practices bound up with flint knapping.

However, the analyses which aim to determine what the Natufians lived on do not demonstrate that the contribution from hunting had been as preponderant as the microlithic aspect of the industries could lead us to believe. The strontium-calcium ratio in the bones from the inhabitants of Carmel and Galilee indicates that the proportion of plant foods was considerable in the early and late phases of the Natufian, before diminishing slightly in the final phase in favour of meat (Sillen 1984, Sillen and Lee Thorp 1991). This was not always obtained by the techniques which bring weapon projectiles into play. After preliminary study of the Hayonim cave fauna, Tchernov concluded that a Natufian had probably as many chances of eating a bird's leg or a lizard's tail for his lunch, as of a piece of gazelle (Tchernov 1991). Where the site permitted it (Mallaha, Mureybet), a lot of fish were consumed (Cauvin 1977, Desse 1987). Trapping, for these small prey and for others such as rabbits and foxes, seems to have been more developed than in the preceding cultures of the Levant.

The maintenance of a comprehensively microlithic system of flint exploitation suggests, nevertheless, that the Natufians continued to accord a particular prestige to the hunting of medium-sized mammals. The social value invested in the lunates could be a supplementary argument in support of the promotion of hunting: these projectiles are considered as characteristics of the culture; they are encountered in the whole cultural area of the Natufian, but with some apparently non-random discrete variations. These variations concern the dimensions of the objects, their proportions (more or less slender), and their mode of manufacture (with or without the microburin technique, and using one mode of retouch or another). They are temporally-related: the lunates become smaller and smaller, and increasingly rarely-worked by Helwan (oblique bifacial) retouch; are also tied to geographical zones: in the Negev, for example, the microburin technique is used more systematically than elsewhere; lastly, they are tied to the sites themselves: the Mallaha lunates retain a particularly squat appearance for probably more than a millennium (Valla 1984). These variations, which do not correspond to technical imperatives since the product remains virtually the same and seems intended for the same function and for similar operation, appear to be justified only as group customs. They would thus be of exclusively social origin, and at first sight especially surprising since they influence the attributes which were to be invisible once the tool (projectile) is hafted. It is probable that they express, in their way, the social value which society attributed both to these objects and, through them, to the activity in which they were involved, as well as the latter's product.

This analysis, if it is pertinent, lets us glimpse a fundamental aspect of Natufian thought: a thought which would promote hunting – and a particular hunting at that – beyond the actual part played by this activity in economic life.

Shells and bone ornaments

The microliths are just some of the manufactured objects which Natufian societies seem to have invested with a symbolic function. Another category of objects, shells, is present on almost all the sites. It is possible that these objects also had had a technical efficacy in the thought of people from that period: perhaps the act of wearing such and such a shell was considered as a sure means of dispelling certain dangers, but this remains unknown. For us, because this possible efficacy appears contrived, it passes to the background if not forgotten, and it is the symbolic function of the shells which seems essential. From this view-point, their presence in almost all of the Natufian assemblages can be understood as one of the marks of the common idea which was tying the groups together: the shells would be the expression of the same thought shared by the groups which were employing it.

The interest in shells and the act of investing them with a symbolic value are both traditional. Prehistoric peoples, like modern ones, seem to have made choices from the array of available forms. Two forms were preferred by the Natufians: *Dentalia* (tubular shells which dominate in frequency almost all the marine shell assemblages from this period) and *Columbella* sp., to which must probably be added *Nassarius* sp., cones, cowries, *Mitrella* sp. (and also *Theodoxus*, a small freshwater mollusc). Bivalves of *Glycymeris* or *Cardium/Cerastoderma* species are notoriously rare, although "their valves form the bulk of the shellbanks on the Mediterranean coast of Israel" (Mienis 1987: 164). However, in the late and final Natufian at Mallaha, the dominant forms are precisely those which elsewhere are secondary: *Melanopsis praemorsa buccinoidae*, which one can liken to the *Columbella* species, *etc.*, and *Unio terminalis*, a bivalve. But interpretation is complicated by the fact that we are dealing with freshwater molluscs, accessible near to the site and also edible (Mienis *ibid.*). Nevertheless, the presence of two groups of principal and clearly different forms, one of which is generally dominant whilst the other occurs in small quantities, is a phenomenon too widespread to be owing to chance. It can be accepted, without excessive boldness, that it expresses a pair of opposed and complementary values.

There is no doubt that a number of these shells have been employed as ornaments. One sometimes encounters them combined in complex ornaments in the tombs: head-dresses, necklaces, bracelets, "garters", ornaments sewn onto clothes(?) (Garrod and Bate 1937, Perrot *et al.* 1988, Reese 1982, Edwards 1991, Noy and Brimer 1980), especially, but not uniquely, in the early Natufian and in Carmel and Galilee. Thus we have positive proof, if it were needed, that they carried meaning; in several cases, they are associated with bone ornaments.

As seen for shells, the use of osseous materials (including teeth) in body ornaments is traditional in the Palaeolithic cultures of Eurasia. It is nevertheless hardly attested in the Levant before the Natufian (*cf.* Belfer-Cohen and Bar-Yosef 1981: 31, and Fig. 6; Albrecht 1988: 214). In this culture the bone ornaments are quite widespread: the majority derive from Carmel and Galilee, but some are also known in the neighbouring regions (Transjordan, Judaea), and on the Middle Euphrates (Moore 1975, Maréchal 1991). Sometimes they can be counted in hundreds, especially from the early Natufian. Several principal types can be identified: (1) pear-shaped pendants, of which one face is more or less flat and the other is convex; (2) pendants with a globular extremity, intended to be grouped in pairs (sometimes the pair is sculpted as a single piece), the "twin pendants" of Garrod; (3) the sectioned distal extremities of gazelle phalanges; (4) the tibio-tarsal extremities of partridge; (5) fox canines. Tubular beads are also encountered, but they are relatively numerous only at Mureybet.

With regard to their form, the first two types are very close: Garrod notes the transition from one to the other in the necklace from H-57 at el-Wad (Garrod and Bate 1937: 39); they probably derive from the same model, which could be red deer canines. For their part, types (3) and (4) resemble each other. Yet, despite their diversity, it is not possible to divide the bone ornaments into two large groups, as was the case for the shells. Rather, one is dealing with a single body of interchangeable objects since, in the region where they are abundant, their prevalence varies between sites: the "twin pendants" are known only at el-Wad.

This interpretation, fragile it is true, perhaps finds initial confirmation in the attested associations between bone and shell ornaments. All the types of bone pendant have sometimes been found associated with shells (always *Dentalia*). The associations are generally close; the loosest account for several ornaments, some in bone and the others in shell, on the same individual: H-33 at Hayonim wears a belt of fox canines and a *Dentalium* necklace (Belfer-Cohen 1988). Sometimes the same ornament combines the two elements. Thus at el-Wad, H-41 and H-57 wore head-dresses combining *Dentalia* and bird tibio-tarsi, H-23 wore an elliptical pendant in a *Dentalium* head-dress, and two bodies (H-23 and H-57) wore necklaces of "twin pendants" and *Dentalia* (Garrod and Bate 1937). Likewise, the belt from H-9 at Hayonim associates piriform pendants with *Dentalia* (Belfer-Cohen 1988, 1991), and a bracelet from Erq el-Ahmar combines gazelle phalanges, partridge tibio-tarsi and *Dentalia* (Neuville 1951, Pichon 1983). At Mallaha, H-6a and H-23 seem also to have retained mixed body ornaments, incorporating the sectioned phalanges of gazelle (Perrot *et al.* 1988). More interesting still, some cases are known where the very shape of bone ornaments has been exploited to form a mixed ornamentation: the best example of this is furnished by the sectioned gazelle phalanges into which a *Dentalium* has been introduced, known at Mallaha and at Wadi Hammeh 27 (Edwards 1991: Fig. 11, no. 12). The "twin pendants" which "do not hang well unless the pairs are separated in this way [by the *Dentalia*]" according to Garrod's prescription (Garrod and Bate 1937: 39), could be another example. In this case, one can almost ask oneself whether the bone component had not been conceived with a view to the final combination. Notwithstanding this, the association of *Dentalia* (but not the forms of *Columbella* type) with all types of bone ornaments is not in doubt. To summarise provisionally the lesson of the shell and bone ornaments, one can say that they show a view where two complementary aspects or elements are represented, one of which is expressed discreetly while the other is displayed.

A third material was exploited for personal decoration, in addition to shell and bone ornaments: stone body ornaments are always rare, but their frequency seems to increase with the final manifestations of the Natufian. With regard to their general appearance, one can recognise more or less piriform (or, exceptionally, globular) pendants, tubular beads and small annular, strung elements. The first two types are easily assimilated to the bone objects; the third seems to reproduce the small rings of *Dentalium* seen earlier. It is possible that the development of the use of stone, limited as it is, results from a weakening of inter-group relationships in the Natufian cultural zone. Perhaps there were deeper forces at work? At this stage it is difficult to say. We note, nevertheless, that stone introduces new choice criteria, such as the texture of the material or its colour.

The lessons of the burials

The ornaments introduced us to the funerary domain. Burials are numerous in the Carmel and Galilee region, and in its immediate periphery, to Judaea in the south, Azraq to the east, the Lebanese Beqaa to the north. They are spread throughout the whole duration of the Natufian and there is no uniformity. It is not our concern to offer a summary here (*cf.* Valla 1995 for a brief survey), but instead to consider some significant associations and the cases which permit us to enter into the thought of their authors.

The Living and the Dead

The first important fact is inhumation: the bodies are not destined for dispersal. This could be the sign of a certain idea of self, and of other people in general, but remains barely explicit. The dead are thus interred, but not just anywhere. They are buried in the "village", keeping them in touch with the group in a certain fashion. The link which unites the burials and the houses *can* be discussed (see also Boyd 1992). It is obvious that different situations have prevailed according to sites and periods. In Hayonim cave, in the early Natufian, the first burial had become hidden, and the skeleton cut again by the buildings. Afterwards, the tombs have been dug towards the back of the cave, beyond the circular structures. At Mallaha, floors and burials are tightly-interstratified at the site of at least one of the early Natufian houses. Later, in the late phase, the tombs are clearly in the fill. At Nahal Oren the cemetery is devoid of buildings, and would have been levelled before each inhumation (Noy 1989). Yet the place, rich in all sorts of objects, cannot be supposed to be totally set aside: a hearth is noted there, and some stone circles which suggest post-holes. These differences are not so surprising if one considers the duration of the period. In all cases, the desire to maintain a link between the former and current inhabitants of the village is everywhere attested.

Manipulation of skulls

Here I want to talk of the manipulation of skulls. Is this sporadically-observed phenomenon related to the above-mentioned behaviour? Two groups of actions can be mentioned, separated by a long period.

In the early Natufian of Mallaha two skulls are known (one intact, the other sectioned), each unequivocally resting on a different floor (Perrot 1966: 445; Valla 1988). One of the two is associated with material (gazelle horn-cores and a dog mandible) which presupposes a relationship with representations (let us call them a "myth", to simplify matters) which are also expressed in certain funerary practices, as shall be seen later. The presence of six skulls without post-cranial bones in a tomb from Erq el-Ahmar – still from the early Natufian – perhaps results from the same thinking (if the observation, which dates from 1931, is reliable) (Neuville 1951). It attests, in any case, the removal and the setting apart of skulls doubtless kept for a while with the manipulators themselves.

Much later, in the late or final Natufian, the inverse situation is encountered at Hayonim cave and terrace, and perhaps also at Nahal Oren. The skull has been removed from certain tombs, without one knowing of any retained or separately-buried skulls. Given the length of time which separates the two sets of actions, one cannot accept that any relationship exists between them, except the general ambience which tends to maintain a link between living and dead. Nevertheless the myth, to which I referred earlier regarding one of the floors from Mallaha, is also found behind a tomb from the Hayonim terrace, in a context where the removal of skulls is not unknown. That is not enough to demonstrate a fundamental relationship between this myth and the removal of skulls in the late-final Natufian, but does establish that the same minds could be acquainted with one and practise the other. The possibility, not to say probability, of a relationship (perhaps even consistency) cannot be discounted. On the other hand, the fact of finding similar associations together, on that which is best interpreted as a living floor within a semi-circular structure and in the tombs, corroborates the observations suggesting that the thought did not disconnect the living from the dead.

A Natufian Myth: Humans and the animal and mineral worlds
The most complete and, above all, the most obviously organised expression of the above-mentioned myth occurs in a tomb from Hayonim terrace (late Natufian). This tomb contained the remains of three individuals within two layers. In the lower level, two bodies were associated with two dogs and with two bony tortoise carapaces. One of the dogs, whose head adjoined that of one of the humans and whose left hind-paw was resting on the skull of the other human, testified to the consistency and organisation of the two inhumations. A stone was placed on the skull of each of the humans. A large block was pinning down the chest of one of them, who also had a stone with a cup-hole standing in front of his face. Lastly, a slab covered the thoraxes of the dogs (Fig. 16.2). In the upper level, the remains of an individual were associated with stones on the skull and on the chest, and with gazelle horn-cores. There are good reasons for thinking that the lower level has been organised with a view to the upper one. After an erosional episode, the whole had been re-covered by stones (Valla 1996).

Figure 16.2: Grave from Hayonim terrace: human and dog remains with stones.

Without pretending to reconstruct from these elements a myth lost for good (if not for an improbable transmission of thought between the Natufians and us), it is possible, *from a purely formal view-point*, to show that Natufians, consciously or not, established association/opposition relationships between the diverse elements employed in this tomb, whose significance (implicit or explicit) one is entitled to investigate. Five of these relationships are particularly clear. They comprise (1) humans and unmodified stones, (2) dogs and unmodified stones, (3) humans and dogs, (4) humans and gazelle horn-cores, (5) dogs and gazelle horn-cores. They are revealed by humans and dogs receiving equal treatment, in relation to the stones (which cover them or pin them down) and to the gazelles (not buried, but represented by a bone). At the abstract level, there is no doubt that the treatment imposed upon humans and dogs likens them to each other. Conversely, this conclusion is not invalidated by the several other examples, where human, dog and gazelle remains occur one with another, or all together (Mallaha tombs 104 and 10, floor 131: *cf.* Valla 1996).

That the gestures which liken the dogs to the humans result from a deliberate – in this sense – intention cannot be demonstrated on the basis of the all-too-scarce available evidence. One can only note the array of data which render this intention plausible, not to say probable. Firstly, the commensalism of the wolf (becoming the dog) probably led to the taming of certain animals by humans (Tchernov and Valla 1997); secondly, no other animal was buried at that time in the tombs; finally, the rarity of dog remains in the cooking waste leads us to suppose that these animals were not eaten, but that their corpses were removed to the outside of the village. All these indications agree, suggesting that dogs had acquired a different status to that of other mammals; their assimilation to humans through certain funerary acts did not simply acknowledge their presence in the village. The Natufians would have understood that the connection which they maintained with the animal world was already in the process of changing.

In the preceding paragraphs I considered the proximity of burials and dwellings in terms of the relationship of the human group to itself, from the view-point of the living and the dead. The examination of certain tombs subsequently led me to emerge from this plane, and to touch upon the connections of humans with the animal kingdom. The study of the funerary practices is not limited to the domains where it is perhaps most explicit. One saw that the tomb with dogs at Hayonim also establishes an opposition relationship between humans and the stones which pin them down. The case is not unique: it is encountered in other tombs from Mallaha (H-15, H-43, H-82, H-88) and el-Wad (H-62, H-12). At the abstract level, it conveys a contrast between the human and the inert. This time it is the connection between humans and the mineral world which is expressed. Yet this contrast is not left in this condition; a mediating element, the stone with cup-mark, interposes in the Hayonim tomb: inert in its material, but modified through working. Though objects of this kind are rare in the grave goods, we nevertheless have some examples (*cf.* the H-57 group and H-60 at el-Wad).

As in the case of the relationship established between men and dogs, one must ask oneself what the Natufians had in mind when they brought stones and humans together in the tombs, or introduced worked stones there. Did they intend to express an opposition between themselves and the surrounding world? Did they wish to say that this external world was also susceptible to being transformed and used? Or, as is probable, were these abstractions concealed under other levels of meaning?

Burials and sedentism

Responding to these questions will help us to answer another which is impossible to avoid, regarding the populations which show a strong tendency towards sedentism. Does the accumulation of tombs in the "villages" also signify something in terms of a possible dichotomy between the humanised space and the outside world? The myth presupposes a separation of this kind, if it is true that in likening the dogs to humans it takes account of their communal presence in the "villages". The abundance of burials in the Carmel-Galilee "centre" also encourages us to believe this: almost 150 tombs have been more or less summarily described there. It must then be accepted that to have been buried in the "villages" was the rule. This would suppose that the "peripheries", where burials were unknown, had developed a different conception of space to that which prevailed in the "centre". Indeed, the living space could not be identical there: the territory would need to be all the more wide-ranging, and mobility all the more extreme, as the resources are more deficient. The gathering together of the living and the dead in the same place would be pointless there if the groups moved away or dispersed during part of the year. The contrast between the practice which is observed in Carmel-Galilee and that from the peripheries could thus be understood as an argument in favour of a realisation of the uniqueness of the space humanised by the sedentary groups of the "centre". The erected monolith at Rosh Zin in the Negev (Henry 1976), which is perhaps the best expression of the symbolic rôle imparted to the "village", must then be understood as an attempt to render this rôle visible in an unprofitable environment, where the village could not effectively fulfil it.

Territory and the village

The outside world was probably contrasted with the humanised space of the village. The world was thus organised around a special point. Furthermore, the presence of tombs ensured that the village was not only understood as a point in space, but that it also served as a temporal reference point. From then on, two avenues present themselves to the study which attempts to grasp something of the representation of the world by the villages' inhabitants. The first will seek to identify the territories of which they could be aware; the second will examine the organisation of the village itself as a possible microcosm.

Along the first avenue, the study of the provenance of objects brought onto the sites permits the identification of three concentric ranges. Almost all the objects whose origin is identifiable could be derived from the nearby environment (flint, haematite). A second range could correspond to the Natufian zone of influence, within which circulated *Dentalia* from the Mediterranean, basalt, and probably other special stones; a third embraces the world outside the Natufian cultural area, from which spring several rarities: Red Sea *Dentalia*, shells from the Nile, obsidian. Unfortunately, this avenue does not lead to any means of accessing the collective representations of these increasingly removed ranges.

In theory, the study of "village" plans should permit us to arrive at both the way in which the Natufians understood the organisation of the world around them, and that in which they organised their society. In practice, it is as difficult to progress along this avenue, as along the previous one. Does the curvilinear form of the dwellings (circular, semi-circular or ovular) refer to an image of the world? With regard to the layout of villages, it is clustered in the Hayonim cave, where the constructed cells crowd close to each other, but is looser at Mallaha, where the buildings in the excavated area seem to be aligned with regard to the topography. Is it necessary to interpret the layering which results from it as the reflection of a stratified vision of the cosmos? Likewise, the organisation of the group, save the division implied by the presence of separated cells, is not very explicit. The fact that the cells would be united in Hayonim cave can be taken as the sign of familial ties between the occupants (Bar-Yosef and Belfer-Cohen, pers. comm.). The observed tendency at Mallaha, which could be general (Goring-Morris 1996: 422), to construct smaller and smaller cells doubtless signifies something concerning the mode of grouping of the inhabitants. But it must be admitted that in this domain the analyst is left to speculation; it is thus completely out of the question to formulate on this basis the slightest hypothesis upon the organisation of the group, and the fashion in which this would possibly reflect an idea of the organisation of the world.

At this stage, our research in Natufian thought founders on the opacity of the information, from which we are incapable of deciphering the most accomplished forms of thought which governed their development. How the Natufians integrated sedentism into their system of thought remains difficult to discern, despite some suggestive indications.

"Artistic" expression

We have reserved the domain of "art" until now, although this domain is usually considered as the place *par excellence* where ideology would be expressed. The art, in the sense of graphic or "plastic" (*i.e.* sculptural) expression – the only forms which have reached us – is relatively well-represented in the Natufian. Body ornamentation, mentioned before and to which we shall need to return, there incorporates both the choice of shaped volumes, and the rhythmic combinations of the bead/pendants, whenever these are preserved for us. There is also art which can be described as figurative, "realistic" or sometimes of schematic tendency, and geometric art.

It is not possible, from the existing publications, to draw up an exhaustive inventory of Natufian figurative art; besides, this is not our intention. This art adheres in a more or less realistic manner to subjects, including humans and animals, represented more or less completely. The head, the hoof, and the phallus are the preferred choice of elements for the partial representations.

This art possesses a certain number of notable characteristics. From the point of view of its conception, it is almost exclusively plastic/sculptural. The only possible exceptions would be two pendants from Wadi Hammeh 27 which have no real thickness, but which are nevertheless sculpted or carved in the bone, so that they are more plastic than graphic. The theme is never illustrated as it would be on a surface, but always exploits the volume. This manner of self-expression most probably reveals a conception of space: it has attained the strongest, and aesthetically the most accomplished, expression in the Mount Carmel region where, from the early to the late Natufian at least, a particular style was maintained which comprised the incorporation of the representation onto the end of an elongated object. This object could be a tool, like the knife handles from Kebara which end in an animal head (Turville-Petre 1932: Plate XXVII, figs. 1, 2) or certain hoof-shaped pestles from el-Wad. Sometimes it is simply a suitable blank – bone, flint nodule, *etc.* – of which one end, if not both, has been sculpted (Garrod and Bate 1937: plate XV, 4, no. 2, and plate XII, 2, no. 14; Noy 1991: fig. 5, 1 & 3; Weinstein-Evron and Belfer-Cohen 1993: fig. 3, nos. 1 & 2). Even when the work is intended to be decorative, this is not conceived as the simple covering of a surface: the volume was exploited, to such an extent that the representation would lose its character if one wanted to ignore it.

The representations never display more than one individual; not just any scene is represented. The subjects are never shown in action and no narrative discourse outlined. The only associations which can be cited bring together two representations, each isolated on the ends of a single blank. They are encountered on a phallic flint nodule from el-Wad (Weinstein-Evron and Belfer-Cohen 1993: fig. 3, no. 2), and two objects from Nahal Oren: one end of a bone carries a ruminant head and the other a possible human representation, and a limestone fragment where two hardly-identifiable heads are sculpted (Noy 1991). The meaning is never clarified by the work itself: for the sculptor and those whom he was addressing, the meaning had to be conveyed independently, doubtless through language. Only one sculpture is exceptional: a representation from Ain Sakhri, whose Natufian origin can be disputed but yet seems probable (Neuville 1933, 1951), shows a scene of humans copulating in a seated position.

These characteristics invite two observations. In the absence of all explicit discourse, Natufian art is identical to the previous or contemporary Palaeolithic art in the rest of Eurasia. The representations can be considered as "mythogrammes" (Leroi-Gourhan 1964b: 268; 1965: 221): they could only be understood with the aid of a verbal accompaniment, which is lost to us; stylistic analysis suggests that the figures were made to be identified as such by their users. The realism is "synthetic" ("expressionistic" according to the terms of Boas (1927) 1955: 351), and not "photographic" ("impressionistic": *ibid.*), *i.e.* it tends to perceive at a glance the elements of the subject judged essential by the given figurative tradition, free to effect the necessary "deformations" related to naïve observation. At the same time, this art is distinguished from Palaeolithic art by its refusal to be displayed on a surface according to the classical formula for graphic art. André Leroi-Gourhan suggested that the distribution of figures along certain routes in the caverns could be understood as a symbolic translation of the living space by the hunter-gatherers moving around in their territory (*op. cit.* 1965: 240). It is tempting to see the expression of a different spatial experience, linked to sedentism, in the recourse to sculptural/plastic expression by the Natufians.

From realistic art, one passes easily to more or less explicit schematic expressions. The blanks for these representations, and their realisation, can be of different kinds. Certain blanks have been chosen for their volume, which the decoration exploits, as in realistic art, *e.g.* a limestone figurine from Mallaha (Perrot 1966: fig. 23, no. 1), or incised flint nodules from el-Wad (Weinstein-Evron and Belfer-Cohen 1993: fig. 2, nos. 1–3); others can be likened to pebbles. The engraver took advantage of the general form of the stone and of the convexity of one face, but the reverse is left unmodified (Perrot 1966: fig. 23, nos. 2 & 3; Noy 1991: fig. 2, no. 6). This treatment recalls that of a certain figurative representation on bone (Noy 1991: fig. 5, no. 2).

The use of flat blanks is not frequent. The dimensions of these blanks, meanwhile, vary sufficiently for two of them, at Hayonim and at Wadi Hammeh 27, to be considered as non-portable (Belfer-Cohen 1991: fig. 9; Edwards 1991: 133). The engravings are of varying depth. Sometimes the juxtaposed motifs tend to occupy all the space. They are deployed in associations of curvilinear or rectilinear lines which can form closed figures (Perrot 1966: fig. 21, nos. 14 & 16; Edwards 1991; Noy 1991: fig. 2, no. 5); in these characteristics they approach decorations of more confirmed geometric tendency.

Geometric decoration most often appears either on suspensory objects or, more commonly, on bone or stone objects. One can distinguish two categories of blanks, depending on whether the surface is perceived as a cylindrical one which one seeks to emphasise, or as a flat one. In both cases the "rhythm" and symmetry are systematically exploited through the interplay of the ordered repetition of the same motif (Garrod 1942: plate IV, no. 2, top-right; Perrot 1966: fig. 15, nos. 9 & 10; Noy 1991: fig. 3; Belfer-Cohen 1991: fig. 6, nos. 6 & 7, fig. 7, nos. 1, 3 & 6; Edwards 1991: fig. 6, nos. 7 & 8). Usually the geometric aspect of the decorations derives more from the simplicity of repeated elements (series of strokes, interlocking lines), than from their strict geometry. Mention must be made of a motif reported at Hayonim and Kebara, which seems inspired by the appearance of basket-work (Campana 1991: fig. 3; Belfer-Cohen 1991: fig. 3, no. 1). One understands that the constraints particular to this type of work are considered by several authors as one of the causes which would have produced the commonplace geometric decorations starting from the Neolithic, but what seems most important here is the tendency to perceive the blank in volumetric terms and not as a two-dimensional space. The result is that the decoration is often centred along the longitudinal axis of the object, and not on a point on its surface. This choice is consistent with that which has been observed in the figurative art, and seems to relate back to the same spatial conception, in which the repetition of the motifs now incorporates time.

It is not very surprising that the study of Natufian art informs us more upon their way of perceiving space, than upon their mythology; it also informs us on their manner of expressing their thought, which it would be necessary to remember when one seeks to understand it. The next developments appear at Jerf el-Ahmar, on the Euphrates, during the PPNA (Stordeur *et al.* 1996). This fashion of self-expression, through "mythogrammes", is not in itself original; it is that of the whole Palaeolithic tradition. But it seems to us that it takes on a particular depth here which renders it more concentrated, and thus more allusive and more opaque than before. The recourse to pictograms could have been a means of deploying anew the mythical discourse, thanks to a more explicit mode of expression. Notwithstanding this, the thought carried by the Natufian "mythogrammes" remains essentially impenetrable to us. Yet, one cannot avoid questioning the meaning.

Figure 16.3: Hayonim terrace: small female figurine (red clay). (Twice actual size).

We accept, with Boas, that "c'est la fonction représentative qu'un objet peut assumer dans les contextes qui lui sont propres qui le rend, quel qu'il soit, utile ou non, interprétable comme art" (Severi 1991). Consequently, there is hardly any doubt that the objects which we have seen introduced into the tombs are akin to the art. Similarly, the horn-cores of *Bos primigenius* collected at Azraq 18 (Garrard 1991), one of which is perforated, probably possessed a "representative function". It is difficult to go much further into this domain, for want of information on the contexts and because, even when these exist, they are barely explicit. Also, objects such as ornaments and the associated shells cannot be set apart from the arena of symbolic representation.

Impenetrable as it is, Natufian art nevertheless includes a certain number of symbols which carry an obviated meaning (even if this could be concealed by embellishment owing to the interplay of mythic thought). These symbols all refer in a certain manner to fecundity or to the phenomenon of reproduction, which involves the aforementioned Ain Sakhri figurine, a small female figurine from Hayonim (Fig. 16.3), or the phalluses from el-Wad and elsewhere. That is neither surprising nor strange: the perpetuation of species, and of the world of which they are a part, is a universal preoccupation. On their part, ornaments would seem entirely dominated by the theme of sexual division. That is obvious for the shells, which unequivocally divide into male (*Dentalia*) and female (*Columbella* sp. *Nassarius* sp., *etc.*) forms. It is more than probable that bone ornaments obey the same logic if it is true that the piriform pendants are derived from red deer canines. Indeed, the symbolism of teeth in general, and of canines in particular (from red deer, but also from fox, *etc.*) is well-known (*cf.* Leroi-Gourhan 1964a: 28–29). At first sight, the masculine symbols are clearly commoner than the feminine ones, although it would still be necessary to beware of possible ambivalence (what do the *Dentalia* transformed into annular beads signify?), and not to pre-judge the wealth of mythic discourse in concluding too fast that society was dominated by its male half. Nevertheless the relative promotion of hunting suggests that the lithic scheme would accord quite well with a masculine domination, at least on the symbolic plane.

Death was very present in Natufian villages. Symbols which cannot but evoke it, human skulls or parts of skulls, were involved in the expression of myths, including those outside the funerary space comprised by the tombs. This does not contradict the insistence upon the symbols for the perpetuation of species. At least, by right of the hypothesis, one can ask if, conversely, these symbols do not penetrate as far as the burials with gazelle horn-cores. It would suffice in convincing oneself of it to admit that these bones here still have the symbolic value of life and masculinity which is so often theirs in the Eurasian tradition.

It has been seen that through a play of formal contrasts the myth secretly supposes an equivalence between humans and domestic animals. At our current level, this comparison could prove to be confirmed if we were permitted to see the dogs buried in the tombs as sacrificed animals, and provided that we could suppose that from this time, the sacrificed replace the sacrificer. One would be then entitled to conclude that the formal equivalence in treatment corresponds to a conscious comparison. Anyway, if it is true that the comparison of domestic animals to humans, conscious or not, results from the introduction of the former into the villages, the phenomenon returns us afresh to the living space and to the comprehension of a world henceforth divided between a humanised centre, with all that it contains, and the surrounding world, in which it participates but which is nevertheless different. In the tombs, the outside world is evoked by animal remains (gazelle, tortoise) which are also amongst the commonest of the meal leftovers, and by the stones which often pin the bodies down but which are likely to be transformed into useful objects. Like the village itself, do the tombs (at least the most sophisticated of them) represent a microcosm?

Conclusion

For seventy years, the Natufian has given rise to the gathering of numerous observations which refer to symbolic behaviour. The data are scattered across territories which do not support relationships *a priori*, except that they share the same cultural context. The result is an impression of disparity and incoherence. Long experience, and also our methodological presuppositions, lead us to believe that this impression does not correspond to reality. That is why we wanted to inquire into whether there were no bridges which would allow the data to be connected to each other. At the end of the inquiry, it seems to us that certain links can be established.

But the thought of prehistoric peoples is only expressed to us in a very indirect fashion, through difficult-to-read behaviour. The myths in which it was conveyed have disappeared with those who transmitted them; the "mythogrammes" which are left to us are nearly indecipherable. Moreover, it is known without any possible doubt that they are capable of reinvesting themselves with different meanings, according to the context in which they were implemented. All attempts at interpretation consequently run the risk of reflecting the ideas of the interpreter; conscious of this risk, we have nevertheless ventured some proposals.

The existence of a binary symbolism, which is expressed through objects generally invested with sexual connotations related to their form, cannot be called into question: it is incontestable in the body ornaments. The theme of procreation also seems to occur across certain artistic manifestations. Besides, it is too universal for one to be surprised to find it in the Natufian. In itself, the "finding" is nothing more than a banality. Here, this theme seems to be associated with that of death; that is not very original either.

More interesting to us seem the points where we believe we recognise a perception of space in connection with sedentism. It is impossible that the transition to sedentary life left unchanged the world-view of peoples until then devoted to mobility within a territory. The villages are still too poorly-known for their organisation to be easily interpreted. The interpretation is the more perilous since we have at our disposal very few points of comparison with the earlier hunter-gatherers in the region. At the very most, it is known that the curvilinear dwellings were probably traditional there. Perhaps the most explicit evidence in this respect is the multiple burial from the terrace at Hayonim, with its dogs, gazelle horn-cores, *etc..* The interment of dogs indeed represents a novelty which one has reasons to associate with a new spatial practice. The systematic recourse to plastic art/sculpture for representation and the integration of decorations within volumes on suitably-shaped objects seem to us to carry an originality which demands explanation. The fact is that the Palaeolithic tradition, without ignoring the sculpture, practised the graphic arts above all. On the other hand, the sedentary peoples of the Near East, from the Natufian onwards, have produced hundreds of animal and human figurines, while flat, painted or engraved decorations are rather exceptional. Likewise, the solutions adopted by the Natufians for volumetric decorations would be repeated and amplified *ad infinitum*, particularly on ceramics. We propose that these practices could be interdependent, through connection with a spatial conception henceforth centred upon the sedentary village. Obviously, the connection which we propose between two clear facts – the tendency towards sedentism on one hand, a preference for plastic art on the other – is for the moment nothing more than a hypothesis. This hypothesis seems to us in agreement with the type of revolution, that the Natufians could not avoid perceiving space in their own way. It would appear to account for the statistical reversal between graphic and plastic art which is observed from the Eurasian Palaeolithic art to that from the Neolithic, but remains, meanwhile, to be supported.

Acknowledgements

I should like to thank the editors of this volume for inviting me to contribute in honour of D. A. E. Garrod. Thanks are also due to O. Bar-Yosef and A. Belfer-Cohen for discussing the contents of this paper with me, and especially to W. Davies, who took on the difficult task of translating it from the French. The illustrations for this paper were prepared by D. Ladiray and M. Barazani (CRFJ, Jerusalem).

Bibliography

Albrecht, G. 1988. Preliminary results of the excavation in the Karain B Cave near Antalya, Turkey: the Upper Palaeolithic assemblages and the Upper Pleistocene climatic development. *Paléorient* 14 (2): 211–222.

Bar-Yosef, O., and F.R. Valla 1991. *The Natufian culture in the Levant.* Archaeological Series 1. Ann Arbor: International Monographs in Prehistory.

Belfer-Cohen, A. 1988. The Natufian graveyard in Hayonim Cave. *Paléorient* 14 (2): 297–308.

Belfer-Cohen, A. 1991. Art items from layer B, Hayonim Cave: A case study of art in a Natufian context. In O. Bar-Yosef and F.R. Valla (Eds.) 1991, pp. 569–588.

Belfer-Cohen, A., and O. Bar-Yosef 1981. The Aurignacian at Hayonim Cave. *Paléorient* 7 (2): 19–42.

Boas, F. 1927. *Primitive Art.* Oslo: H. Ascheloug and Co. (reprinted by Diver Publications, 1955).

Boyd, B. 1992. The transformation of knowledge: Natufian mortuary practices at Hayonim, western Galilee. *Archaeological Review from Cambridge* 11 (1): 19–38.

Büller, H. 1983. Methodological problems in the microwear analysis of tools selected from the Natufian sites of el-Wad and Ain Mallaha. In M.C. Cauvin (Ed.), *Traces d'utilisation sur les outils néolithiques du Proche-Orient*, pp. 107–127. Lyon: Maison de l'Orient.

Campana, D. 1991. Bone implements from Hayonim Cave: some relevant issues. In O. Bar-Yosef and F.R. Valla (Eds.) 1991, pp. 459–466.

Cauvin, J. 1977. Les fouilles de Mureybet (1971–1974) et leur signification pour les origines de la sédentarisation au Proche-Orient. *Annual of the American School of Oriental Research* 44: 19–48.

Desse, J. 1987. Mallaha: l'icthyofaune. In J. Bouchud (Ed.), *La faune du gisement natoufien de Mallaha (Eynan), Israël*, pp. 151–156. Paris: Mémoires et Travaux du Centre de Recherche Française de Jérusalem. Association Paléorient.

Edwards, P. 1991. Wadi Hammeh 27: an Early Natufian site at Pella, Jordan. In O. Bar-Yosef and F.R. Valla (Eds.) 1991, pp. 123–148.

Garrard, A. 1991. Natufian settlement in the Azraq Basin, eastern Jordan. In O. Bar-Yosef and F.R. Valla (Eds.) 1991, pp. 235–244.

Garrod, D.A.E., and D.M.A. Bate 1937. *The Stone Age of Mount Carmel, vol. 1.* Oxford: Clarendon Press.

Garrod, D.A.E., and D.M.A. Bate 1942. Excavations at the Cave of Shukbah, Palestine, 1928. *Proceedings of the Prehistoric Society* 8: 1–20.

Goring-Morris, A.N. 1996. The early Natufian occupation at el-Wad, Mt. Carmel, reconsidered. In M. Otte (Ed.), *Nature et Culture*, pp. 417–427. Liège: Études et Recherches Archéologiques de l'Université de Liège 68.

Henry, D.O. 1976. Rosh Zin: a Natufian settlement near Ein Avdat. In A.E. Marks (Ed), *Prehistory and Palaeoenvironments in the Central Negev, Israel, vol. 1: The Avdat/Aqev area, part 1*, pp. 317–347. Dallas: Southern Methodist University Press.

Leroi-Gourhan, A. 1964a. *Les religions de la préhistoire.* Paris: Presses Universitaires de France.

Leroi-Gourhan, A. 1964b. *Le geste et la parole: technique et langage.* Paris: Albin Michel.

Leroi-Gourhan, A. 1965. *Le geste et la parole: la mémoire et les rythmes.* Paris: Albin Michel.

Maréchal, C. 1991. Éléments de parure de la fin du Natoufien: Mallaha niveau I, Jairoud 1, Jairoud 3, Jairoud 9, Abu Hureira et Mureybet IA. In O. Bar-Yosef and F.R. Valla (Eds.) 1991, pp. 589–612.

Mienis, H. 1987. Molluscs from the excavation of Mallaha (Eynan). In J. Bouchud (Ed.), *La faune du gisement natoufien de Mallaha (Eynan), Israël*, pp. 157–178. Paris: Mémoires et Travaux du Centre de Recherche Française de Jérusalem 4. Association Paléorient.

Moore, A.M.T. 1975. The excavation at Tell Abu Hureyra in Syria. *Proceedings of the Prehistoric Society* 41: 50–77.

Neuville, R. 1933. Statuette érotique du désert de Judée. *L'Anthropologie* 43: 558–560.

Neuville, R. 1951. *Le Paléolithique et le Mésolithique du désert de Judée*. Paris: Mémoires de l'Institut de Paléontologie Humaine 24. Masson.

Noy, T. 1989. Some aspects of Natufian Mortuary Behaviour at Nahal Oren. In I. Hershkovitz (Ed.), *People and Culture in Change*, pp. 53–58. Oxford: British Archaeological Reports, International Series 508.

Noy, T. 1991. Art and decoration of the Natufian at Nahal Oren. In O. Bar-Yosef and F.R. Valla (Eds.) 1991, pp. 557–568.

Noy, T., & B. Brimer 1980. Adornment of Early Natufian burials. *Israel Museum News* 16: 55–64.

Perrot, J. 1966. Le gisement natoufien de Mallaha (Eynan), Israël. *L'Anthropologie* 70: 437–484.

Perrot, J., Ladiray, D., and O. Solivers-Massei 1988. *Les hommes de Mallaha*. Paris: Mémoires et Travaux du Centre de Recherche Français de Jérusalem 7. Association Paléorient.

Pichon, J. 1983. Parures natoufiennes en os de perdrix. *Paléorient* 9 (1): 91–98.

Reese, D. 1982. Marine and freshwater molluscs from the Epipalaeolithic site of Hayonim terrace, Western Galilee, Northern Israel, and other East Mediterranean sites. *Paléorient* 8 (2): 83–90.

Severi, C. 1991. [Anthropologie de l']Art. In P. Bonte and M. Izard (Eds.), *Dictionnaire de l'Ethnologie et de l'Anthropologie*, pp. 81–85. Paris: Presses Universitaires de France.

Sillen, A. 1984. Dietary change in the Epi-palaeolithic and Neolithic of the Levant: the Sr/Ca evidence. *Paléorient* 10 (1): 145–155.

Sillen, A., and J.A. Lee Thorp 1991. Dietary change in the Late Natufian. In O. Bar-Yosef and F.R. Valla (Eds.) 1991, pp. 399–410.

Stordeur, D., Jammous, B., Helmer, D., and G. Willcox 1996. Jerf el-Ahmar: a new Mureybetian site (PPNA) on the Middle Euphrates. *Neo-Lithics* 96 (2): 1–2.

Tchernov, E. 1991. Biological evidence for human sedentism in southwest Asia during the Natufian. In O. Bar-Yosef and F.R. Valla (Eds.) 1991, pp. 315–340.

Tchernov, E., and F.R. Valla 1997. Two New Dogs, and Other Natufian Dogs, from the Southern Levant. *Journal of Archaeological Science* 24: 65–95.

Turville-Petre, F. 1932. Excavations in the Mugharet el-Kebarah. *Journal of the Royal Anthropological Institute* 62: 271–276.

Valla, F.R. 1984. *Les industries de silex de Mallaha et du Natoufien dans le Levant*. Paris: Mémoires et Travaux du Centre de Recherche Française de Jérusalem 3. Association Paléorient.

Valla, F.R. 1988. Aspects du sol de l'abri 131 de Mallaha (Eynan). *Paléorient* 14 (2): 283–296.

Valla, F.R. 1995. The first settled societies – Natufian (12,500–10,200 BP). In T.E. Levy (Ed.), *The archaeology of society in the Holy Land*, pp. 169–187. London: Leicester University Press.

Valla, F.R. 1996. L'Animal "bon à penser": la domestication et la place de l'Homme dans la Nature. In M. Otte (Ed.), *Nature et Culture*, pp. 651–667. Liège: Études et Recherches Archéologiques de l'Université de Liège 68.

Valla, F.R., Le Mort, F., and H. Plisson 1991. Les fouilles en cours sur la terrasse d'Hayonim. In O. Bar-Yosef and F.R. Valla (Eds.) 1991, pp. 93–110.

Weinstein-Evron, M., and A. Belfer-Cohen 1993. Natufian figurines from the new excavations of the El-Wad Cave, Mt. Carmel, Israel. *Rock Art Research* 10 (2): 102–106.

242

Figure 17.1: Nina Frances Layard (1853–1935) aged 25. Portrait taken in San Francisco in 1878, soon after the fateful visit to New Zealand. (Copy from print, Layard-Whytehead MSS)

Figure 17.2: The Layard Family at Combe-Hay Rectory, near Bath, in 1873. (left to right) Back row: George Somes Layard, Nina Frances Layard, Clement Villiers Layard, Nellie Layard. Seated: Abel John Layard, Mrs Sarah Layard (née Somes), May Layard, Revd. C Clement Layard. Front, seated: Annie Layard. (Copy from print, Layard-Whytehead MSS)

17

Nina Frances Layard, Prehistorian (1853–1935)

Steven J. Plunkett

At Ipswich in 1906 Sir John Evans (1822–1908) remarked, *"the scientific world generally are indebted to Miss Layard for her discoveries of flint implements in the neighbourhood of Ipswich, who has proved that these things belong not to a pre-glacial but to a post-glacial period. That is something indeed for a lady to have done"* (Anon 1906). Nina Frances Layard, F.S.A., F.L.S., (Figure 17.1), whose formal work in prehistory spanned the years 1898–1935, was a pioneer in a man's world who made use of her intellectual and social advantages to define a permanent role for women in the advancement of archaeological research.

The Layard family in England (motto: *Perseverando*), of Huguenot extraction, could then boast two hundred years of distinguished service to the British Crown, and afforded to young Nina the living examples of her father's cousins Sir Henry Austen Layard (1817–1894), excavator of Nineveh (Layard 1851) and later Ambassador to Constantinople: Edgar Leopold Layard (1824–1900), Curator of the South Africa Museum, Cape Town, and later Governor of Fiji (Summers 1975, Roth and Hooper 1990): Sir Charles Peter Layard K.C.M.G. (1806–1893), a governor in Ceylon, whose collection of shells and minerals was bequeathed to the Imperial Institute, and Lady Charlotte Guest (later Schreiber) (1813–1895), translator of the *Mabinogion*, and collector of English ceramics and fans. Miss Layard was also aware of her near family relationship (through her father's mother, Louisa Port of Ilam Hall) to Mrs Delany (1700–1788), the botanical illustrator, who married a friend of Swift, and was a fashionable personality of the courts of Georges II and III (Johnson 1925)

Nina Layard, the fourth of seven children of an Evangelical Anglican clergyman (of the third successive generation educated at St John's College, Cambridge), was born at Stratford (Essex) in 1853. Until 1873 she grew up in the (then rural) vicarages of Harrow and Wembley. Her only formal education was received at a dame school in Willesden, though her brothers attended Harrow School, and the family mixed socially with Matthew Arnold, Charles Kingsley and Lady Cadogan. In 1873 they removed to Combe-Hay Rectory near Bath (Figure 17.2), where Nina conducted an increasingly solitary existence pursuing her interests of egg and shell collecting and her literary efforts which had been encouraged by Arnold.

Her first visits to Ipswich were probably made in the mid-1870s while her brother Villiers was a curate at St Margaret's Church. Her sister Nellie having married the proprietor of the Blue Cliffs Run in Timaru, Canterbury Settlement, New Zealand, Nina and Villiers travelled there in 1877–8 only to arrive to find their sister dead, and they returned across America via San Francisco and Utah (Woodhouse n.d.). Villiers (who was taught at Harrow by John Smith and Dean Farrar) had been an undergraduate at Corpus Christi, Cambridge (1868–1871), where he became fast friends with H.R. Whytehead, nephew of the brilliant but doomed Thomas Whytehead, accomplice of Bishop Selwyn in the early mission to New Zealand. After a brief chaplaincy at Corpus Christi College, Villiers returned to New Zealand as a curate, but drowned in 1885 in the loss of the *Otaki*. H.R. Whytehead married Nina's eldest sister, May, and became an eminent clergyman at Marlborough and Warminster. In 1890 another brother, Abel, died in Ceylon (Layard-Whytehead MSS).

Only in 1882, and quite by chance, did Nina become aware of the fossil kingdom (though she lived in the village which had been the home of William Smith, father of Palaeontology): this, and a friendship with a basket-maker living in a rock-shelter on the banks of the Bradford-on-Avon Canal, was the beginning of her prehistoric interests. She began collecting omnivorously in the Bath area, discussing her finds with the elderly Leonard Jenyns; she also collected in Ipswich, staying with her close friend Evelyn Garratt (daughter of Canon Samuel Garratt), where she came to know the inspirational curator and popular scientific lecturer, Dr. John Ellor Taylor (1837–1895). Under these mentors, her reading in Darwinian theory led to short studies which Taylor published in the *Science-Gossip Magazine*, and on 5 May 1890 – the year after she moved permanently to Ipswich – she became the first woman to have a paper accepted and read before the Victoria Institute, of which she had become an Associate in 1882 (Layard 1890a). With the encouragement of Captain Petrie and Sir G.G. Stokes she developed her theme, a critique of the theory of Rudiments, and in 1890 at Leeds she scored another first (Figure 17.3) by delivering her own paper to Section H of the British Association with Dr. Garson in the Chair (Layard 1890b). Her performance was followed by a lively, almost sensational discussion. Sir W.H. Flower and Sir J.W. Dawson took an interest in her work, and she delivered further addresses on the same theme to the Association annually until the Ipswich Meeting of 1895 (Layard 1895). On the latter occasion she also coordinated the local Ethnographical sub-Committee for Sir Edward Brabrook.

Figure 17.3: Miss Layard addressing the British Association at Leeds, 1890. (Caricature by Harry Furniss, Yorks Post)

Meanwhile she published two volumes of poetry (Layard 1890c, 1893), the former for Longmans with the help of Andrew Lang, which were greeted with national interest, and which display some Sapphic sentiments. These works produced encouraging contacts with George MacDonald, Francis Thompson,

Figure 17.4: Mary Frances Outram (1862–1935). This youthful portrait of c.1890 shows Miss Outram as Daisy Bates would have known her, and as Miss Layard first met her. (Ipswich Borough Museums)

and friends of Walter Pater's, and she continued to publish in *Longman's Magazine* in England and Harper's in New York from time to time. It was also in about 1895 that she met and fell in love with Mary Frances Outram (1862–1935), (eldest daughter of Sir Francis, a hero of Cawnpore, and granddaughter of Sir James, 'The Bayard of India'), who became her lifelong constant companion, fellow-worker and amanuensis (Figure 17.4). Nina Layard frequently visited and stayed in the Outram home at Pitlochry. Mary had travelled widely in Europe and the Middle East with her family, and was an accomplished water-colourist, authoress and lecturer with a special interest in Egypt and the Bible Lands. Until shortly before she met Nina Layard, Mary had been the particular friend and companion of Daisy Bates (Daisy O'Dwyer), the extraordinary and beloved white woman who later lived as a spiritual friend and physical healer among the natives of the Australian outback, and was known to them as *Kabbarli* (Bates 1936, 1938; Salter 1972: 6–8). The 'Outram girls' remained Bates's dear friends by correspondence through most of her outback years (Hill 1973: 19).

In 1898 Miss Layard began the work of systematic archaeological recording in Ipswich which has continued to the present day. Her first investigative excavations were at the Blackfriars and Whitefriars sites, and produced evidence of Prehistoric and Saxon occupation as well as mediaeval remains. Early in 1899 she was recruited for the Suffolk Institute of Archaeology, and in late July she gave two lectures to the Royal Archaeological Institute (Layard 1899a, 1899b) which in that year held its Annual Congress in Ipswich: Sir Talbot Baker said he had never heard the Institute addressed by a lady before. Her work was commended by, and discussed with, amongst others, Sir Henry Howorth, William St-John Hope, George E. Fox (excavator of Silchester) and J.T. Micklethwaite, and the hope was expressed (later amply fulfilled) that she would found a school of archaeology in the Town (Proceedings 1899, Anon 1899). From this point onwards she embarked fearlessly on a correspondence with leading archaeologists and antiquaries, which continued unabated until her death in 1935, which is preserved in entirety (letters received) with her papers in the Suffolk Record Office, Ipswich (Layard MSS), and from which much of the factual content of the present account is drawn.

Diaries of finds dating from 1900 onwards show that, while Miss Layard obtained a steady flow of artefacts from building sites and service trenches in Ipswich by offering small payments to labourers, her own time was devoted to searching for prehistoric materials in the Valley Gravels of the river Gipping (where Dr. Taylor had obtained palaeoliths and extinct mammalian remains in the 1880s) and in materials dredged from the peat bed of the river Orwell. Some discoveries of antler and human bones were displayed at the British Association in Glasgow, where they were admired by Boyd Dawkins and Robert Munro, and Miss Layard had the opportunity to hear Dr. Sturge describe his chronology of Stone Age Man. However, it was the chance gift of a superb large pointed hand-axe from Levington Road, in 1901, which led her to investigate the brickearths of the raised plateau on the north-east side of Ipswich, where in 1902 at Foxhall Road brickpits she made a momentous discovery of deposits containing numerous unrolled twisted ovate bifaces and associated evidences of an industry. The find was announced in a lecture by Sir Henry Howorth in Ipswich in May 1902 (Anon 1902), by which time Sir John Evans and Clement Reid had already become involved in an advisory capacity. In the same year the first of three accounts of the site was given to the British Association and was accepted for publication in the Journal of the Anthropological Institute (Layard 1903), of which Miss Layard became a Fellow in 1902 after ten years of membership.

The conduct of the excavations carried out in that year, and in the winter months of 1903–4 (Figure 17.5) and 1904–5, won for Miss Layard a good deal of respect in the scientific fraternity. Although nearly 50 when her serious prehistoric work began, her energy was unflagging. She convened an excavation committee, which included the Ipswich Corporation Museum, the Ipswich Scientific Society (an all-male preserve) and Sir John Evans, and by their joint funding (£5 apiece in each season) she was able to employ two workmen whom she trained to excavate to a grid system, systematically exposing and recording 'floors' and horizons and taking grid measurements and depth locations for every find. Although these data were never published in detail, many plans and diaries survive and await a modern reappraisal. Evans and Reid made occasional visits, as did Boyd Dawkins once, Dr. Henry Woodward identified osseous remains by post, and Arthur Smith-Woodward made visits to Miss Layard's home Museum to identify specimens. (Smith-Woodward remained a lifelong friend.) She showed that the implementiferous layers formed part of a silted fluviatile/lacustrine deposit overlying a thick layer of chalky boulder clay which had partially infilled an older elevated river valley across the plateau, and therefore that these industries, characterised as 'Acheulian', post-dated a major glaciation, at the extreme south-eastern margin of that boulder-clay deposit. The decided ogival twist on the edges of these implements modified Evans's own views concerning that feature.

Further interim reports delivered to the British Association in 1904 and 1906 were again published by the Anthropological Institute, and another, connected account was delivered to the Cambridge Antiquarian Society at the request of Professor Ridgeway at a meeting chaired by A.C. Haddon, who was an enthusiastic supporter of Miss Layard's work (Layard 1904b, 1906a, 1906b). She had, meanwhile, developed in other

Figure 17.5: Palaeolithic Excavations at Foxhall Road, Ipswich, 1903–4. Miss Layard (left) and a distinguished visitor at the west end of the pit excavated during the first year of formal work at the Ipswich Palaeolithic site, with Miss Layard's trained labourers Arthur Barker and F Fox. (Print from original plate negative held at Suffolk Record Office, Ipswich.)

fields of interest also, presenting a handsome paper on the mediaeval Pax instrument to the Royal Archaeological Institute at Howorth's request (Layard 1904a). In Ipswich from 1898 onwards she produced a regular monthly antiquarian column to the leading regional newspaper, the *East Anglian Daily Times*, many of her finds went on display in the new archaeological Museum at Christchurch Mansion, and in 1903 she was the moving force behind the erection of a memorial to the Protestant Martyrs of the Town (Layard 1902).

Miss Layard nurtured the hope of finding fossilised human remains, but never did so. This pursuit led to her next major excavation, at Hadleigh Road, Ipswich, where skeletons – apparently of a 'low type' (in fact posthumously deformed) – began to appear during road-widening operations late in 1905. After a short time it became apparent that she had stumbled upon a pagan Anglo-Saxon cemetery in undisturbed pasture, which was rapidly being destroyed as up to 200 labourers at a time were engaged in levelling the land as part of a sensitive Ipswich Corporation workfare scheme. Nothing daunted, throughout 1906 and January 1907 she worked, often at her own expense, wih a team of four of the 'unemployed' whom she trained to the task, to recover the burial goods and record the details of about 160 graves. She was assisted with interpretations by Anatole von Hügel, of the Cambridge Museum of

Archaeology and Anthropology, who was a cousin of Mary Outram's. Evans also gave her constant encouragement, and following her report to the British Association in August 1906 she was invited to submit a paper to the Society of Antiquaries. With work in full progress, she and Evans took the specimens to London in November, though members of the Ipswich Museum Committee sought to prevent this: Evans's proposal that she be permitted to read her own work was rejected, and the paper was delivered to the Antiquaries by Hercules Read: and on her return to Ipswich she found that the Corporation foreman had smashed up several graves. Nonetheless she worked the cemetery out, and so preserved the first substantial record of the outstanding Anglo-Saxon archaeology of the Ipswich district (Layard 1907a, 1907b; Plunkett 1994a, 1994b). From this episode arose a lifelong friendship with Reginald Smith, very fruitful in their later work. Earlier in 1906 she had been elected a Fellow of the Linnean Society – only the second year of women's Fellowship.

Progress by perseverance against prejudice remained necessary when, the Corporation having claimed the Anglo-Saxon finds, Miss Layard was effectively denied access to them for post-excavation study during 1907, even though she had earlier been promised a role as 'Amateur Honorary Curator' of collections found by her, in a room at Christchurch Mansion. A great debacle followed, in which the Museum's honorific President, Sir Ray Lankester, intervened on her behalf to insist that the Museum honour its promise. It was not until his second, and irate, intervention following a deliberate snub given to her at the Museums' Association Meeting at Ipswich in 1908, that her Honorary Curatorship was fully accepted; and though she and the official Curator, Frank Woolnough, were not on speaking terms for several months (Figure 17.6), she retained control of her room, and built there a substantial collection of local and comparative prehistoric materials, which (accompanied by talks and press articles) had a strong impact on popular awareness of the subject in the region (Plunkett 1994a). Meanwhile her Anglo-Saxon researches attracted the interest of George Payne, Professor Baldwin Brown, and E.T. Leeds.

Miss Layard found three sites for prehistoric research in 1908. In the earlier part of the year she was at work in the Lark Valley in West Suffolk, where she collected implements from a putatively Upper Palaeolithic industry. Her report on these to the British Association at Belfast (Layard 1908b) provided opportunities for collecting at White Park Bay and elsewhere. The chance discovery of rough 'implements' along the beach at Lough Larne led to a long correspondence with the veteran Irish antiquary, W.J. Knowles of Ballymena, and in the following year to a joint excavation with him on the raised beach in search of a context for the 'Older Series' of Irish implements (Layard 1909a). Some viewed these with scepticism, but in Ipswich she made discoveries of more permanent and original value, in the so-called Stoke Bone Bed. When the railway tunnel through Stoke Hill had been navigated during the middle years of the 19th Century, great quantities of fossil mammalian bones were discovered which were then studied by Joseph Prestwich. Miss Layard now obtained permission to expose a small section where bones were protruding, and in the following months collected a variety of faunal remains and also a small number of worked flints (Layard 1910c). The site had an abiding interest for her, and she was to return to it for a maturer consideration in 1919–20.

All these finds swelled her Museum, and she was already among the most established of East Anglian prehistorians when, at the end of 1908, W.A. Dutt (1870–1939), W.G. Clarke (1877–1925) and Dr. Allen Sturge (1850–1919) first convened the Prehistoric Society of East Anglia (Clarke 1919), of which she became a founding member. Her views were in many ways more orthodox, and her academic recognition and contacts more august, than those of some who coalesced in the formation of this Society. An intense interest developed in the later Edwardian period in the search for inter-glacial and pre-glacial evidences for Early Man, and the question of Tertiary – Pre-Palaeolithic – Man became an early preoccupation of the group. The support given by Sir Joseph Prestwich, Professor Rupert Jones and others, to the Harrisonian Eoliths, although repudiated by Boyd Dawkins and John Evans, was under-pinned in popular under-standing by introductions to

The · last · of · the · Martyrs

Figure 17.6: Miss Layard's opinion of Frank Woolnough, c.1907. (Caricature by John Shewell Corder of Ipswich (Private Collection))

human evolution promulgated by the Rationalist Press Association, in the widely-read works of Samuel Laing, Ray Lankester (1847–1929), and the Aldeburgh Rationalist, Edward Clodd (1840–1930), themselves connected with the circle of Sir Thomas Huxley (Clodd 1888, 1926; Laing 1889, 1892; McCabe 1932).

Miss Layard's role in the Society was not at first an official one – perhaps because her *bête noir*, Frank Woolnough, was the Secretary for Ipswich Meetings. Cambridge was ready to acknowledge her work. In 1909 she had meetings with Petrie and the Ridgeways at Professor McKenny Hughes' house, and a return delegation including Professors Ridgeway and Hughes, Baron von Hügel and Dr. Duckworth visited Ipswich to inspect her collections in October. Her brother George, a man of letters who wrote useful works on Sir Thomas Lawrence and Charles Keene (*cf.* Bibliography), lived at Felixstowe, and Mrs Layard and her son John had often assisted in her excavations. A year or two later John was received with open arms by

Dr. Pfeiffer at Weimar (author of *Die Steinzeitliche Technik* (Pfeiffer 1912)) in remembrance of the hospitality afforded to him in England by Miss Layard. Enthused by his boyhood experiences, John Willoughby Layard (1891–1974) was introduced to A.C. Haddon and studied at Cambridge, falling under the spell of W.H.R. Rivers. Rivers and he travelled together to Australia in 1914 intending to conduct researches in Melanesia. After a week Rivers abandoned him on the Isle of Atchin, and Layard lived alone among the natives of that monolithic culture for many months. His experiences there were the basis for one of the monumental works of twentieth century ethnology, *Vao – Stone Men of Malekula* (Layard 1942): he was a very considerable and gifted scholar in his own right, with the unorthodox brilliance characteristic of his family.

Miss Layard received recognition from various quarters at this time. In May 1910 she was elected a Vice-President of the Suffolk Institute of Archaeology – the first woman appointee since the foundation of 1848. London County Council invited her to conduct the excavation of a group of Anglo-Saxon burials discovered at Coulsden. Furthermore, when the Geologists' Association of London visited Ipswich in July 1910 they were deeply impressed by her work at Stoke Tunnel, observing that the greatest possible credit was due to her *"for the true scientific manner in which the work has been carried out and its results recorded"* (Slater 1911). They were less convinced by their visit to Reid Moir's site at Bolton and Laughlin's Brickyard. Given Moir's rising position in the new Prehistoric Society, it may be significant that Miss Layard chose to entrust her publication of the Stoke Tunnel finds not to their *Proceedings*, but to the Suffolk Institute of Archaeology.

In October 1909 James Reid Moir (1879–1944), a young amateur collector in Ipswich, had begun to find implements and other fractured flints in residual Crag basement bed deposits within buried channels in the London Clay, filled above with mid-glacial gravels. He won the support of the geologists William Whitaker and John E. Marr for the claim that his implements were of sub-Crag date, comparing them with finds made beneath the Norwich Crag by W.G. Clarke in 1905. A sub-Committee of the Prehistoric Society was formed late in 1910 to deliberate specifically on whether the flints showed deliberate or natural flaking (and not on the interpretation of the geological context). Miss Layard was co-opted with Dr. Sturge, W.G. Clarke, Lt-Col. Underwood (an erstwhile colleague of Lewis Abbott and Benjamin Harrison) and Frank Corner, and decided conclusively in favour of human intention (Sturge 1911b). Miss Layard was the last to be convinced, and it seems clear that she was swayed by the inclusion among the specimens studied of two (intrusive) genuine implements showing alternate edge-flaking. She took great care, comparing the British Museum's Harrison specimens and discussing conclusions with Reginald Smith, and she was well aware that Professor Bonney considered Moir's stratigraphy to be misinterpreted. On the given evidence, she was persuaded that all the flints showed fracture by human intention (Plunkett 1995).

The story of how Ray Lankester championed Moir's cause (now discredited) is told elsewhere (Moir 1935), but both Lankester and Miss Layard were impressed above all by the argument that, if flint fractures represented the primary evidence for human intention in identifying tools and industries, then the apparently systematic flaking of the sub-Crag and pre-Palaeolithic types required scientific explanation if they were to be negatively differentiated from those later types considered to be authentic. After decades of argument about 'chip and slide' theories this particular point holds true, despite A.S. Barnes's apparently scientific repudiation which, as Moir and the MacAlpine Woods recognised, was motivated by deep antagonism to Moir (PSEA MSS, Moir MSS), and reversed Barnes's own earlier findings and demonstrations (Schwartz and Beavor 1909). When, early in 1912, Moir announced the discovery of a seemingly modern type of human skeleton in boulder clay at Ipswich (a stratification which he later acknowledged to be mistaken (Moir 1912, 1916)), the anti-Eolith faction led by Boyd Dawkins ran eagerly into the arms of the Piltdown hoaxer to bring forward contrary evidence of the period of human evolution: Lankester was only cautiously appreciative.

Moir's results did not plunge Miss Layard into an assiduous quest for eoliths – quite the contrary. In April 1911, following a great storm which eroded part of the shore at Thorpe Ness, she was called as expert witness in a Treasure Trove enquiry held at Aldeburgh Moot Hall to determine the ownership of a mass of bronze coins and artefacts picked up on the beach by fishermen (Layard 1911a, 1911b). Although obviously stray losses, and items eroded from deposits on the cliff-top, the landowners and the Receiver of Wrecks sought custody of the finds. Miss Layard's sympathies lay firmly with the fishermen, and this was characteristic of her nature. The Christian beliefs with which she was imbued in childhood had led to a number of activities in social reform at a practical level. Early in the 1880s she had been involved with her father in the foundation of Temperance Coffee-Taverns in Bath, and she was similarly active in the creation of the Excelsior Club in Ipswich in 1900. Her poems published in 1890 had included several drawing attention to the plight of poor people exploited by commercial manipulation of alcohol and by radical politicians and trade unions. The labourers whom she habitually tipped for finds and the 'unemployed' whom she trained for archaeological work found her sympathetic and without side.

The increasing momentum of the Socialist movement in 1912 gave Miss Layard a new cause. She was appalled when the activist Ben Tillett invited his followers to pray for the death of Lord Devonport, and on 24 May she took the train up to London to be present at the Dock Strikers' rally at the Maritime Hall at the West India Docks. With bible in hand she mingled in the crowd, gathering groups of the strikers around her, and appealing to them to realise that reform, not Socialist revolution, would bring them a true hope of improving their lot. She spoke as a Christian, not to convert, but to appeal to humane instincts. Her reception was lively, but not entirely unappreciative. Over the summer of 1912 she spoke at meetings in Ipswich and spearheaded a campaign of letters in the press, replying to one challenge after another and always answering personal attacks in impersonal and reasoned terms. Late in the year she and her friends came together to re-establish the (New) Excelsior Club and coffee tavern in Ipswich, as a Conservative initiative in social welfare for the working classes (Layard 1912).

Her prehistoric work recommenced about a year later, though in the interim there were many visitors to her collections at home and in the Museum, including the young Miles Burkitt, whom she encouraged, and who always retained a personal respect for her. She did not take a large part in the Grimes Graves excavation of 1914, though she collected extensively there both before and afterwards, and her specimens were called upon for comparison. Reginald Smith desired examples of the Foxhall Road implements for the British Museum, and as the claypit was about to be sold for building purposes, he and Miss Layard jointly purchased two lots, and she conducted fresh excavations adjacent to her original pits. Some important stratigraphical clarifications were made (Smith 1921). Before the work was finished, War was declared, and Smith was so involved with packing up the British Museum collections that Miss Layard was left to her own devices. For the first two years of the War she and Miss Outram moved out of Ipswich to Rise Hall in nearby Akenham. Sir Ray Lankester, whose nerves were badly affected by the War, was at this time conducting a steady correspondence with Reid Moir. Lankester did not progress in the usual way from Vice-Presidency to Presidency of the Prehistoric Society of East Anglia in 1915 (though his friend Clodd served on the Committee from 1914–6), and the maintenance of the work of this Society, and that of the Suffolk Institute, was left in the hands of those who were not directly involved in the War effort.

Sir Grahame Clark has explained how Reginald Smith made use of the War years further to develop a wider-than-regional base for the Prehistoric Society, with his own eyes firmly fixed on the acquisition for the British Museum of the immense Sturge Collection (Clark 1985). Smith and Moir helped to lead the Society out of the War in a healthy condition and ready for the expanding interests of the 1920s. Miss Layard acted as their representative at Congresses in London during the War, but also took on the duties of Hon. General Secretary of the Suffolk Institute, with the amiable bachelor architect John Shewell Corder, in 1917–9. She corresponded with Lankester, taking a growing interest in the problem of flint fractures and the question of human intention. Lacking the opportunity to excavate, she instead conducted experiments which suggested that some implements were made with deliberate finger-grips, conjecturing that prehistoric Man would first make a clay 'squeeze' model of the tool and then imitate the form by flaking (Layard 1917b, 1919b). She also reproduced Professor Marcus Hartog's experiment showing that parrots, given small pieces of wood, would repeatedly shape them uniformly into convenient scratching-tools resembling small twisted ovates. Since her childhood, a parrot had always been kept in the Layard household. She was not unaware of the humorous side of the work (Figure 17.7), and entrusted the publication to *Knowledge* rather than to the mainstream journals (Layard 1917a).

At the end of the War her first exciting work concerned three bronze crowns which she obtained from the landlord of the Crown Inn at Mundford in 1918. With only Reginald Smith sharing her conviction that they were ancient, she set out to find the discovery spot on Cavenham Heath, and her researches into their origins continued for several years. In the meantime she was busy on other fronts, notably on a site yielding implements formed from pebbles, at Mundford (Layard 1919a). In 1918/9 and 1919/20 she served on the Committee of the Prehistoric Society, and in those *Proceedings* published her work of 1919–20 on the Stoke Tunnel site (Layard 1920). In 1919, with Reid Moir, E.T. Lingwood and others, she assisted at the excavation of Anglo-Saxon burial mounds on Brightwell Heath near Ipswich (Moir 1921).

Figure 17.7: Nina Layard with a tool-making parrot, c.1917. (Ipswich Borough Museums)

She and Miss Outram had taken lengthy holidays in 1919 – one highlight was a personal visit to Lily Greenwood, the child sweetheart of Hartley Coleridge, at Grasmere. Such living links with the past were for Nina inspirational: before the War she had obtained souvenirs of Miss Pigot, Byron's associate, from the Allenby family at Felixstowe. She also encouraged younger poets: during the War she befriended the young Geoffrey Faber during his periods of leave. In 1920 the ladies moved to Kelvedon (Essex), (giving up the Curatorship of the room at Christchurch Mansion a month after Frank Woolnough retired), and there they made close friends with the veteran Old Shireburnian poet, classicist and pageant-writer, James Rhoades. They wrote and performed their own village pageant, 'The Eyes of Kelvedon Bridge', with the help of the villagers, and on Sunday afternoons in the garden of their home, 'The Dowches', the villagers used to assemble for prayers and hymns accompanied by a brass band as Miss Layard called out the hymn numbers (pers. comm. Arthur Frost of Kelvedon).

At 67 Miss Layard had no thoughts of giving up her studies, and she and Miss Outram began to travel further afield. In July, having chatted to Hall Caine on the Channel crossing, they visited Professor Rutot at the Musée Royal de l'Histoire Naturelle at Brussels to investigate his evidences for the typology and industries of Early Man. (Rutot had been elected a corresponding Honorary Member of the Prehistoric Society back in 1912, when he lent his support to the sub-Crag implements: his system included Oligocene and Miocene evidences). Then they went on to Paris for a week to see the Abbé Breuil and the St. Germain Museum. Miss Layard's continuing energy is reflected in her election as Vice-President of the Prehistoric Society for 1920–1 and President for 1921–2, the year in which Dorothy Garrod became a Member. At the same time, she received a long-awaited accolade. A law was passed in 1920 obliging Societies with statutes precluding the admission of women to override those regulations. In 1921 the Society of Antiquaries of London avoided the possible withdrawal of their grant by admitting five statutory women Fellows, of whom Miss Layard was one. Three years later Maria Millington Evans, Sir John's widow, wrote to her:

> "They do not propose to admit any more. As one of their body put it 'an archaeological angel direct from Heaven would have no chance.' I regret this for Joan's sake... Of the five statutory women FSAs you will notice that only one (Miss Graham) lives in London – Of the other four the homes are Paris, Rome, Iraq, and Kelvedon! They seem to have been chosen as unlikely to attend."
>
> (26 Jan. 1924: Layard MSS)

Her inclusion in so select a group reflects the very high esteem in which her work was held.

Following her excavation of a Prehistoric cooking-place in Norfolk, which formed the subject of the Presidential Address to the Prehistoric Society (Layard 1922), Miss Layard's interests developed *in tandem* in Upper Palaeolithic and in Neolithic materials, and her outlook became more European. September 1923 was the occasion of a very extensive tour of French Cave sites, on which she and Miss Outram took whatever chances they got to scavenge specimens from the debris of excavations. Their visits to Laugerie Basse, Brantome, the Fourneau du Diable, Les Rebières, Les Eyzies and Le Moustier culminated in a meeting with M. Peyrony, and a banquet in the Abri at the Gorge d'Enfer, where they were in company with McGregor, Ami, and the Garrods. Their suitcases must have been heavy on the journey home, to judge from the quantity of specimens from those sites now in the Ipswich Museum.

The following spring she made a formal investigation of the late Neolithic site discovered by W.A. Bird at Canewden in Essex, which she reported to the Antiquaries (Anon 1924). In early August of 1924 there was another continental excursion. At the request of the Official Delegate of the British Association, Dr. Garson, Miss Layard attended and addressed the French Congress at Liège, and made the acquaintance of several important figures including de Mortillet, Desmaisons, Oppenheim, Fraipont, Servais and Hamal-Nandrin. It was at the latter's Museum and home that she had the first sight of the implements from the Neolithic mines and ateliers of Ste. Gertrude, Holland (discovered in 1881), and they did not return to England until they had travelled to see the site for themselves. In October 1924 she and Miss Outram were back in Holland to collect a range of specimens, to have them conveniently at hand in England for comparative purposes: the resultant paper was read in April 1925 before the Prehistoric and Royal Anthropological Societies jointly, and made a substantial contribution to the Prehistoric Society's *Proceedings* (Layard 1925a). Her excavator, Jean Rompelberg (provided by the Comte de Geloes), supplied further specimens in later years.

The announcement to the Antiquaries of the conclusion of the investigation into the Cavenham 'Crowns', was a moment of outstanding success (Layard 1925b). Excavations on the spot where they had been found proved beyond doubt a Roman context for what most archaeologists and antiquaries (especially Sir Hercules Read) who had seen them considered to be post-Mediaeval curiosities. In later years, the discovery of similar objects at Hockwold in Norfolk vindicated Miss Layard's findings completely, and her six years of searching enquiry and detective-work to convince a disbelieving establishment are easily overlooked.

There followed a move back to Ipswich for Misses Layard and Outram, but they found valuable work to do in Essex at White Colne, where in 1926 they discovered and excavated what appeared to be a late Palaeolithic industry, within clearly-defined stratigraphy which was elucidated by Moir. Sir Archibald Garrod was at that time for several months on the Committee of Ipswich Museum, and, in the wake of Miss Garrod's newly-published work on the Upper Palaeolithic in Britain, Nina and Dorothy had what they called a 'flint orgy' at Ipswich as they compared and discussed the forms. Abbé Breuil also offered his opinions, and in the paper which Miss Layard delivered to the Antiquaries in March 1927 the French terminology reflecting the fashionable classification of those forms is prominent (Layard 1927). (This was the year in which Dorothy Garrod followed in Miss Layard's footsteps by becoming Vice-President of the Prehistoric Society of East Anglia.) Miles Burkitt drew parallels with Miss Garrod's *Creswellian* material (see also Garrod biography, this volume), and Grahame Clark described the industry as *Mesolithic* (Clark 1932: 59–62): but Miss Layard's 'Solutrean' blade from the site has stood the test of time as a late Palaeolithic artefact.

Amid all this work there had also been time for a new volume of poetry in 1924, and the excavation of a Belgic cremation cemetery at Boxford, Suffolk (Anon 1926). After the White Colne publication, in her 75th year, the pace of her labours slowed, and Miss Layard began to consider unfinished work from years before, and to gather reminiscences perhaps with an autobiography in mind. She and Miss Outram were nonetheless busy in wet and cold weather for some weeks late in 1930 investigating the gravels at Mildenhall and recording the interesting stratigraphy of sections with multiple horizons. She remained active and lucid, and a few press articles from the early 1930s recall her first collecting experiences. In 1932, when the organisers of the First International Congress of Prehistoric and Protohistoric Sciences blatantly snubbed the Prehistoric Society of East Anglia by disregarding it, it was Mortimer Wheeler's appeal to Miss Layard at a chance meeting in London which induced Reid Moir to calm down and invite a delegation to Ipswich, which duly came (PSEA MSS, Moir MSS).

The two ladies moved house early in 1933 to East Bergholt (Figure 17.8), where they maintained a strict routine of morning prayers, with Miss Layard's personal maid of long service, Sarah Ferris, and a young resident cook-general, and received distinguished visitors for days at a time. As in her previous homes, Miss Layard constructed a small private Museum adjacent to the house, where she continued to deliver illustrated talks to large groups of visitors who were obliged to enter through an external door. From time to time there would be an excursion in Miss Layard's antique automobile to Ipswich or Frinton, Miss Layard herself driving (as she had done since the days of horse-drawn cars), usually very slowly and in the middle of the main roads, to the frustration of other motorists (pers. comm. Mrs E. Mann of East Bergholt).

In the following year it was arranged for Sir William and Lady Burton to purchase from her a vast collection of antiquarian paintings which she had acquired back in 1898, and to present them to the Ipswich Museum (Anon 1934). In this way, the work of one of Suffolk's foremost artist-antiquaries, Hamlet Watling (1818–1908), was preserved, and at her last public appearance Miss Layard recounted to a large audience at Christchurch Mansion her memories of a man who had given the decisive impetus to her archaeological career (Plunkett 1997). Her last winter was spent in a wrangle with Grahame Clark over the publication of her article describing investigations at Seacliff Cave in Scotland in 1905, and this was one disagreement in which Clark did not prevail. Miss Layard was very pleased to see the fruits of her busy correspondence with Graham Callander in print, with all the illustrations however unfashionable in style (Layard 1935), and she had the approval of Thomas Kendrick and Gordon Childe for her opinions. Childe, who had just then engineered the election of Breuil as President of the Prehistoric Society of East Anglia to ease its transition into the new Prehistoric Society, wrote warmly to her of the many times her name had arisen in conversation with his step-aunt Evelyn Garratt, the companion of her young days in Ipswich. In May 1935 her beloved Mary died, racked with arthritis, and Nina had little time to adjust to her loss before she herself succumbed after an operation in the following August. They were buried in the same grave in Kelvedon churchyard.

*

Since before the Great War Miss Layard had been a regular contributor at small gatherings and reading-groups, in which religious and philosophical matters were presented and discussed, and these forums continued to stimulate her thoughts and work throughout the 1920s, and generated a number of antiquarian contributions to the local press which appeared above her name (*e.g.* Layard 1921). Through these articles and draft papers it is possible to trace an emerging synthesis of ideas, in which the love and creative authorship of the Christian God is never lost sight of, but is rather progressively revealed by the scientific understanding of the material universe and the evidences of prehistory. This was the Paleyist Christianity of her old mentor Dr. Taylor, into which Miss Layard had matured through a life of devotion to science, from the Evangelical spirit of her childhood environment. It is an essential part of her legacy, that she lived and experienced within herself the transition from a pre-Darwinian religious consciousness to a type of 20th Century spirituality which is still valid – and that she made this transition through the study of prehistory.

If Nina Layard's achievements were to be reckoned only in terms of her contribution to archaeology, they would be remarkable enough. She had a knack for discovering new sites – when asked if she owed this to the patron saint of lost things, St Anthony of Padua, she replied, "I may perhaps owe more to St. Henry and St. Augustine" (meaning her cousin, the excavator of Nineveh). Certainly she began the systematic recording of archaeological finds in the Ipswich district which Ipswich Museum and the Suffolk Archaeological Unit continue to this day. Her researches were marked by a method more careful and modern, and a path of enquiry more focussed upon the elucidation of specific problems, than those of many of her

Figure 17.8: Nina Layard (left) and Mary Outram in their home, Hill House, East Bergholt, 1933. (Print, Author's Collection, from glass negative held at Ipswich Borough Museums)

contemporaries, and she was prompt in the publication of her findings. Her willingness to approach any authority and to weigh up the advice she received from various quarters with an open mind led to productive friendships and her admission into the highest circles of academic discourse. This network of connections was a decisive asset in the formative years of the Prehistoric Society of East Anglia, and brought a mature dimension to a forum where unorthodoxies and enthusiasms needed some restraint. In the same way it provided a bridge between the Victorian schools of Prehistory, and the new outlook which the Prehistoric Society of East Anglia began to develop during the 1920s.

Many of Miss Layard's excavations retain an important place in the history of prehistoric studies, and her records, especially at Foxhall Road, Stoke Tunnel and White Colne, still have considerable scientific value. Her interpretations have in many cases survived the rigours of later critical analysis. The Museum which she formed in Christchurch Mansion, and the collections to which she added throughout her later life, formed the core upon which Reid Moir and Guy Maynard built up the immense representative series at Ipswich Museum, which in the inter-war years was considered a reference study resource of international importance. It was, however, her original collections, lectures and press articles which first really engaged popular interest in prehistoric studies in Ipswich during the formative Edwardian decade, and which were the inspiration to the rising generation of collectors and scholars in East Suffolk – among them, perhaps, the Garrods. Melton, near Woodbridge, had been the home of several families closely involved with the study of the Pliocene-Pleistocene succession, including the Searles V. Woods and the Lankesters, and the Garrod memorials in Melton church testify to that family's attachment to the place and its traditions.

Nina Layard was a woman of her time, and although slight of stature and not strong in physical constitution, her resources of social confidence, manners and intelligence combined with an inner determination and spiritual resilience led her into fields of literary, intellectual and emotional expression where her contribution was accepted and valued. If she was not an institution, like Elizabeth Garrett Anderson of Aldeburgh, or had not the seafaring fortitude of Lady Brassey, she combined instead an intensity, vision and scientific vocation with a poetic spirit which in more immediate, intimate ways compelled the attention of those who knew her and worked with her. Her collections, her notes, and her correspondence are the material part of her legacy, and are a rich resource: her living legacy is in the part she played in the formation of prehistoric discourses and institutions, and in the work of those men and women whom she inspired.

Acknowledgements

I am grateful to the many people who have helped with my researches, but particularly I wish to thank Mrs Margaret Whytehead and Robert Layard Whytehead for access to valuable family archives, Lady Elspeth Layard, Mrs C. Scott-Barrett and Pat Millward for further information, and Mr and Mrs Arthur Frost (Kelvedon) and Mrs E Mann (East Bergholt) for personal reminiscences of Miss Layard. Continuing background research on Miss Layard's work is made possible through the courtesy of the Trustees of the British Museum, the staff of the Suffolk Record Office, Ipswich, and the Ipswich Borough Council Museum. I am particularly indebted to Dr. Mark White (Cambridge) for having proposed my name for authorship of this article.

Bibliography

Anon 1899. Royal Archaeological Institute – The Visit To Suffolk. *East Anglian Daily Times* 26 July 1899

Anon 1901. Excelsior Working Men's Club. *East Anglian Daily Times* 18 June 1901.

Anon 1902. Prehistoric Ipswich – Relics of the Oldest Inhabitants. *East Anglian Daily Times ca.* 20 May 1902.

Anon 1902. Suffolk Archaeological Institute – Lecture by Sir Henry Howorth, M.P.. *East Anglian Daily Times* 27 May 1902.

Anon 1906. An Anglo-Saxon cemetery at Ipswich. *East Anglian Daily Times* 13 Dec 1906.

Anon 1924. Flint Implements at Canewden. *Essex County Standard* 1 Mar 1924.

Anon 1926. Interesting finds at Boxford – many ancient cinerary urns unearthed. *East Anglian Daily Times* 22 Mar 1926.

Anon 1934. Enriching a Town's Treasure-House – Gifts to Christ Church Mansion. *East Anglian Daily Times* 2 Jan. 1934.

Anon 1935. Death of Miss Nina Frances Layard. *East Anglian Daily Times* 14 Aug. 1935.

Bates, D.M. 1936. My Natives and I (First chapters omitted from her book published as *The Passing of the Aborigines*). *Adelaide Advertiser*, 4 & 6 Jan 1936.

Bates, D.M. 1938. *The Passing of the Aborigines: A Lifetime Spent among the Natives of Australia*. London: John Murray

Blackburn, J. 1994. *Daisy Bates in the Desert*. London: Secker and Warburg.

Boswell, P.G.H. 1945. James Reid Moir, F.R.S. (1879–1944). *Proceedings of the Prehistoric Society* 11: 66–68.

Clark, Sir J.G.D. 1932. *The Mesolithic Age in Britain*. Cambridge: Cambridge University Press.

Clark, Sir J.G.D. 1985. The Prehistoric Society: From East Anglia to the World. *Proceedings of the Prehistoric Society* 51: 1–14.

Clarke, W.G. (ed.) 1915. *Report on the Excavations at Grime's Graves, Weeting, Norfolk. March-May, 1914*. Prehistoric Society of East Anglia Monograph. London: H.K. Lewis.

Clarke, W.G. 1919. In Memoriam: W. Allen Sturge, M.V.O., M.D., F.R.C.P. *Proceedings of the Prehistoric Society of East Anglia* 3: 12–13.

Clodd, E. 1888. *The Story of Creation: A Plain Account of Evolution*. London.

Clodd, E. 1895. *A Primer of Evolution*. London.

Clodd, E. 1926. *Memories*. London: Watts & Co.

Evans, J. 1956. *A History of the Society of Antiquaries*. London: Society of Antiquaries.

Furniss, H. 1890. Sketches at the British Association. *Yorkshire Post* 6 September 1890.

Garrod, D.A.E. 1926. *The Upper Palaeolithic Age in Britain*. Oxford: Clarendon Press.

Hill, E. 1973. *Kabbarli: A Personal Memoir of Daisy Bates*. Sydney.

Hughes, T. McK. 1872. Man in the Crag. *Geological Magazine* 9: 247.

Johnson, R.B. 1925. *Mrs Delany at Court and Among the Wits*. London: Stanley Paul & Co.

Keith, Sir A. 1912. The Ipswich Skeleton (Hunterian Lectures – Important Phases in the Evolution of Man). *The Medical Press*, 6 March 1912: 244–246.

Keith, Sir A. 1944. James Reid Moir. *Obituary Notices of Fellows of the Royal Society* 4: 733–745.

Laing, S. 1889. *Problems of the Future, and Essays*. London: Chapman and Hall.

Laing, S. 1892. *Human Origins*. London: Chapman and Hall.

Lankester, Sir E.R. 1911. On the discovery of a novel type of flint implements below the base of the Red Crag of Suffolk, proving the existence of skilled workers of flint in the Pliocene age. *Philosophical Transactions*, Series B, 202: 283–336.

Layard, Sir A.H. 1851. *A Popular Account of Discoveries at Nineveh*. London: John Murray.

Layard, G.S. 1892. *The Life and Letters of Charles Samuel Keene*. London.

Layard, G.S. 1894. *Tennyson and his Pre-Raphaelite Illustrators*. London.

Layard, G.S. 1897. *George Cruikshank's Portraits of Himself*. London.

Layard, G.S. 1901. *Mrs Lynn Linton: Her Life, Letters, and Opinions*. London.

Layard, G.S., and M.H. Spielmann 1905. *The Life and Work of Kate Greenaway*. London: A. & C. Black.

Layard, G.S. 1906. *Sir Thomas Lawrence's Letter-Bag*. London: George Allen.

Layard, G.S. 1907. *A Great 'Punch' Editor: Being the Life, Letters, and Diary of Shirley Brooks*. London: Isaac Pitman & Sons.

Layard, G.S. 1907. *Suppressed Plates, Wood Engravings, &c*. London: A. & C. Black.

Layard, G.S. 1922. *The Headless Horseman: Pierre Lombart's Engraving, Charles or Cromwell?* London.

Layard, G.S. 1927. *Catalogue Raisonné of Engraved British Portraits from Altered Plates*. London: Philip Allan & Co.

Layard, J.W. 1942. *Stone Men of Malekula – Vao*. London: Chatto and Windus.

Layard, N.F. [n.d.] Collections and Bequests. Archaeological and Palaeontological Collections presented to Ipswich Borough Museums 1882–1936.

Layard, N.F. MSS. Correspondence and Papers 1887–1935. (Suffolk Record Office, Ipswich, S 2/3/1 to 5)

Layard, N.F. 1890a. Rudimentary organs. *Victoria Institute, Tracts of the Philosophical Society of Great Britain.* Paper to be read at a Meeting of the Members and Associates, May 5 1890. (?Not in Transactions.)

Layard, N.F. 1890b. Reversions (text of paper to British Association). *Ipswich Journal* 13 Sept. 1890.

Layard, N.F. 1890c. *Poems.* London: Longman and Green.

Layard, N.F. 1893. *I and Myself, and other poems.* Ipswich.

Layard, N.F. 1895. Ultimate vital units (text of paper to British Association). *East Anglian Daily Times* 18 Sept. 1895.

Layard, N.F. 1896. Flaws in the theory of evolution. *East Anglian Daily Times* 4 May 1896.

Layard, N.F. 1897. *Songs In Many Moods.* (Ipswich)

Layard, N.F. 1899a. Remarks on Wolsey's College, and the Priory of St Peter and St Paul, Ipswich. *Archaeological Journal* 56: 211–215.

Layard, N.F. 1899b. Original researches on the sites of religious houses of Ipswich: with plan of excavation. *Archaeological Journal* 56: 232–238.

Layard, N.F. 1899c. Recent discoveries on the site of the Carmelite convent of Ipswich, and the old river quay. *Proceedings of the Suffolk Institute of Archaeology and Natural History* 10 (2): 183–188.

Layard, N.F. 1901a. *A Brief Sketch of the History of Ipswich School.* Ipswich.

Layard, N.F. 1901b. Notes on a human skull found in peat in bed of the river Orwell. *Report of the British Association for the Advancement of Science* (1901), pp. 789.

Layard, N.F. 1901c. Palaeolithic implement with alleged thong-marks. *Report of the British Association for the Advancement of Science* (1901), pp. 798.

Layard, N.F. 1901d. Horn and bone implements found in Ipswich. *Report of the British Association for the Advancement of Science* (1901), pp. 806.

Layard, N.F. 1902. *Seventeen Suffolk Martyrs.* Ipswich: Smith.

Layard, N.F. 1903. A recent discovery of Palaeolithic implements in Ipswich (text of paper to British Association). *Journal of the Anthropological Institute* 33: 41–43.

Layard, N.F. 1904a. Notes on some English paxes, including an example recently found in Ipswich. *Archaeological Journal* 61 (2nd Series XI): 120–130.

Layard, N.F. 1904b. Further excavations on a Palaeolithic site in Ipswich (text of paper to British Association). *Journal of the Anthropological Institute* 34: 306–310.

Layard, N.F. 1906a. A winter's work on the Ipswich Palaeolithic site (text of paper to British Association). *Journal of the Anthropological Institute* 36: 233–236.

Layard, N.F. 1906b. Account of a Palaeolithic site in Ipswich. *Proceedings and Communications of the Cambridge Antiquarian Society* 11 (New Series V): 493–502.

Layard, N.F. 1907a. An Anglo-Saxon cemetery in Ipswich. *Archaeologia* 60: 325–352.

Layard, N.F. 1907b. Anglo-Saxon cemetery, Hadleigh Road, Ipswich. *Proceedings of the Suffolk Institute of Archaeology and Natural History* 13 (1): 1–19.

Layard, N.F. 1908a. An ancient land surface in a river terrace at Ipswich. *East Anglian Daily Times* 26 Sept. 1908.

Layard, N.F. 1908b. Palaeolithic implements &c. in the valley of the Lark (text of paper to British Association). *East Anglian Daily Times* 3 Oct. 1908.

Layard, N.F. 1909a. The Older Series of Irish flint implements. *Man* 9 (6): 81–85.

Layard, N.F. 1909b. Alabaster figures from Fornham All Saints Church, Suffolk. *Proceedings of the Society of Antiquaries of London,* 2nd Series, 22: 502–503.

Layard, N.F. 1910a. Notes on some early crucifixes, with examples from Raydon, Colchester, Ipswich and Marlborough. *Archaeological Journal* 67 (2nd Series XVII): 91–97.

Layard, N.F. 1910b. Antiquity of Man – Latest lessons from flint discoveries. *Standard* 17 Nov. 1910.

Layard, N.F. 1910c. Animal remains from the railway cutting at Ipswich. *Proceedings of the Suffolk Institute of Archaeology and Natural History* 14 (1): 59–68.

Layard, N.F. 1911a. The Treasure Trove inquest. *East Anglian Daily Times* 17 Apr 1911.

Layard, N.F. 1911b. "Treasure Trove" – "Inquest" on coins found on Suffolk coast. *Standard* 19 Apr. 1911.

Layard, N.F. 1912. Opening of the "New Excelsior Club". *East Anglian Daily Times* (letter dated Oct. 1912).

Layard, N.F. 1913. The Nayland figure-stone. *Proceedings of the Suffolk Institute of Archaeology and Natural History* 15: (1): 3–8.

Layard, N.F. 1915. "Coast Finds" by Major Moore at Felixstowe Ferry. *Proceedings of the Prehistoric Society of East Anglia* 2 (2): 132–134.

Layard, N.F. 1917a. Wooden scratching-tools made by an African parrot. *Knowledge* 40 (New Series XIV Part 2) no. 583: 32–35.

Layard, N.F. 1917b. Finger grips – An interpretation of worked hollows found on many surface flints. *Man* 17 (6): 89–90.

Layard, N.F. 1919a. The Mundford pebble industry. *Proceedings of the Prehistoric Society of East Anglia* 3 (1): 150–157.

Layard, N.F. 1919b. Flint tools showing well-defined finger-grips. *Proceedings of the Suffolk Institute of Archaeology and Natural History* 17 (1): 1–12.

Layard, N.F. 1920. The Stoke Bone Bed, Ipswich. *Proceedings of the Prehistoric Society of East Anglia* 3 (2): 210–219.

Layard, N.F. 1921. Religion and Science – I. *East Anglian Daily Times* 26 Aug. 1921.

Layard, N.F. 1922. Prehistoric cooking-places in Norfolk. *Proceedings of the Prehistoric Society of East Anglia* 3 (4): 483–498.

Layard, N.F. 1924a. *Selections From Poems*. Ipswich: Ancient House.

Layard, N.F. 1924b. Solutrean blades from south-eastern England. *Proceedings of the Prehistoric Society of East Anglia* 4 (1): 55.

Layard, N.F. 1924c. 7. Bronze Ceremonial Crowns. (Early Roman), (Exhibited by Miss Layard). *Catalogue of the Conversazione of the Royal Society, 18 June 1924.*

Layard, N.F. 1925a. Recent excavations on the Neolithic site of Sainte-Gertrude, Holland. *Proceedings of the Prehistoric Society of East Anglia* 5 (1): 35–55.

Layard, N.F. 1925b. Bronze crowns and a bronze head-dress, from a Roman site at Cavenham Heath, Suffolk. *Antiquaries' Journal* 5: 258–265.

Layard, N.F. 1927. A Late Palaeolithic Settlement in the Colne Valley, Essex. *Antiquaries' Journal* 7: 500–514.

Layard, N.F. 1934. Evidence of Human Sacrifice in Seacliff Cave, Scotland. *Proceedings of the Prehistoric Society of East Anglia* 7 (2): 399–401.

Layard-Whytehead MSS. Albums and Photographs of the Layard family. Private Collection.

McCabe, J. 1932. *Edward Clodd – A Memoir*. London: Bodley Head.

Moir, J.R. MSS Letters to James Percy Tufnell Burchell 1916–1944. (Ipswich Museum R.1945.143).

Moir, J.R. 1912. The occurrence of a human skeleton in a glacial deposit at Ipswich. *Proceedings of the Prehistoric Society of East Anglia* 1: 194–202.

Moir, J.R. 1916. Pre-Boulder Clay Man. *Nature* 98: 109.

Moir, J.R. 1921. Excavation of two tumuli on Brightwell Heath. *Journal of the Ipswich and District Field Club* 6: 1–14.

Moir, J.R. 1927. *The Antiquity of Man in East Anglia*. Cambridge: Cambridge University Press.

Moir, J.R. 1935. *Prehistoric Archaeology and Sir Ray Lankester*. Ipswich: Norman Adlard & Co.

Moir, J.R. 1936. Obituary: Nina Frances Layard, F.L.S., F.S.A., 1853–1935. *Proceedings of the Prehistoric Society* 1: 160–161.

Pfeiffer, L. 1912. *Die Steinzeitliche Technik und ihre Beziehungen zur Gegenwart.* Festschrift zur XLIII. Allgemeinen Versammlung der Deutschen Anthropologischen Gesellschaft, Weimar 4–8 Aug. 1912. Jena: Gustav Fischer.

Plunkett, S.J. 1994a. Nina Layard, Hadleigh Road and Ipswich Museum, 1905–1908. *Proceedings of the Suffolk Institute of Archaeology and History* 38: 164–192.

Plunkett, S.J. 1994b. *Guardians of the Gipping. Anglo-Saxon Treasures From Hadleigh Road, Ipswich.* Ipswich: Borough Council.

Plunkett, S.J. 1995. Nina Layard and the Sub-Crag Committee of 1910. In A. Longcroft and R. Joby (Eds.), *East Anglian Studies – Essays presented to J.C. Barringer on his Retirement,* pp. 211–222. Norwich: Marwood Publishing.

Plunkett, S.J. 1997. Hamlet Watling 1818–1908: Artist and Antiquary. *Proceedings of the Suffolk Institute of Archaeology and History* 39 (1): 48–75.

Prestwich, Sir J. 1892. On the primitive characters of the flint implements of the chalk plateau of Kent, with reference to the question of their glacial or pre-glacial age. With notes by Messrs. B. Harrison and De Barri Crawshay. *Journal of the Anthropological Institute of Great Britain and Ireland* 21: 246–276.

Proceedings 1899. Royal Archaeological Institute Annual Meeting at Ipswich, July 25th-August 1st 1899. *Archaeological Journal* 56 (2nd Series 6): 388–405.

P.S.E.A. MSS. Prehistoric Society of East Anglia Correspondence Files 1922–1935. (Ipswich Museum).

Roth, J., and S. Hooper (Eds.) 1990. *The Fiji Journals of Baron Anatole Von Hügel 1875–1877.* Suva: Fiji Museum *with* Cambridge: University Museum of Archaeology and Anthropology.

Salter, E. 1972. *Daisy Bates; The 'Great White Queen of the Never Never'.* Sydney: Angus and Robertson.

Slater, G. 1911. Excursion to Ipswich, Saturday, July 16th, 1910. *Proceedings of the Geologists' Association* 22: 11–16.

Smith, R.A. 1921. Implements from plateau brickearths at Ipswich. *Proceedings of the Geologists' Association* 32: 1–16.

Schwartz, A. (*A.S. Barnes*) and H.R. Beavor 1909. The dawn of human intention. An experimental and comparative study of eoliths. *Memoirs and Proceedings of the Manchester Literary and Philosophical Society, Session 1908–9, 53 Pt. 2.*

Sturge, W.A. 1911a. Early Man. *Victoria County Histories – Suffolk* I, 235–277. London: HMSO.

Sturge, W.A. 1911b. Report of the Special Committee. *Proceedings of the Prehistoric Society of East Anglia* 1: 24ff.

Summers, R.F.H. 1975. *A History of the South African Museum 1825–1975.* Cape Town: South African Museum.

Woodhouse, A.E. [n.d.] The Biography of a South Canterbury Sheep Station, 1856–1970.

18

Nova et vetera: Reworking the Early Upper Palaeolithic in Europe

William Davies

"I think it is true to say that [Breuil] was the first prehistorian to develop a genuine world-outlook, and his investigation and correlation of a mass of evidence from widely-separated areas has led directly to that change of axis which to-day we are beginning to take for granted."   (Garrod 1938: 2)

Dorothy Garrod (1928), in her Presidential Address to the Prehistoric Society of East Anglia, announced that Palaeolithic studies were entering a new era of research objectives. The great battles to establish stratigraphic successions were largely won, and in future archaeology would concentrate more upon the relationships and detail the attributes of cultures. It was natural for Garrod to say this: as a student of the great Abbé Breuil, she was thoroughly inculcated in global perspectives, and they both were really the first Palaeolithic prehistorians of this type. 'Global perspectives' are here used to denote not just a familiarity with the literature, but also an extensive *practical* experience of sites and artefacts from around the world. All other researchers at this period were more concerned with their own particular fields of interest, concentrating upon limited areas, and frequently at a loss to relate their discoveries to the wider picture. Both Garrod and Breuil were less susceptible to narrow perspectives, owing to their experience of world-wide material, and both were astute enough to realise that our interpretations of the past were ephemeral, and depended not only upon available evidence but also the *patterning* within that evidence. Neither was above revising their opinions and interpretations in the light of fresh evidence, and it is this protean adaptability and intelligence which makes them great prehistorians.

Breuil on troubled waters

It has become customary to pay no more than lip-service to the work of Henri Breuil, relegating it to a lower level in the inexorable development of archaeological thought. This view holds that Breuil was superseded by the work of his elder and better, Denis Peyrony (1933), and that he can now be safely ignored. Travesty as this is, it seems to be justifiable to those who believe that the development of archaeological thought is linear and not cyclical. I shall argue that, certainly in the Palaeolithic, a limited number of [sustainable] theoretical options have waxed and waned in favour, depending upon the available evidence. A prominent example of this is the oscillation between multi-regional and Eden-type hypotheses for the origins of anatomically-modern humans, but there have been other examples of wheel re-invention, as we shall see later.

Breuil seems to have had a consuming interest in prehistory, initially studying the Bronze Age remains around Paris. However, his over-riding concern was the Palaeolithic, and he was strongly encouraged to adopt a career in prehistory after his ordination in 1900. From 1906 to 1912, Breuil began to refine and alter the old schemes of de Mortillet and others, creating a more subtle sub-division of the Mousterian and Upper Palaeolithic industries which was based primarily upon the presence/absence of certain *fossiles directeurs*. Gabriel de Mortillet (1870: 50–1; de Mortillet and de Mortillet 1881) had had a strange notion that, in spite of the stratigraphic evidence, the Aurignac site (with its bone and stone artefacts) must post-date the Solutrean (the apex of stone-working), and form part of the Magdalenian (with its complex bone and antler/ivory artefacts); this had already been destroyed by several researchers in the 1890s, notably Edouard Piette, the excavator of Brassempouy. Piette was one of Breuil's mentors at the seminary of Issy-les-Moulineaux at this time, and it is tempting to speculate that this academic debate must have had a profound formative influence.

Breuil maintained a peripatetic existence throughout his sixty-odd years of research, including trips to central and eastern Europe (Breuil 1923, 1924, 1925), Iberia (Breuil 1920, 1921, 1922, *etc.*), China (Breuil 1931a, 1931b, 1932, 1935b, *etc.*), South Africa (Breuil 1930, 1943, 1944, 1949, *etc.*) and the Near East, with an interest in Asia, Australia and the Americas. He first visited Britain in 1912, having been invited to assess the Red Crag material from East Anglia, and made more trips on many occasions, looking at the Paviland artefacts (Swainston, this volume) amongst other things. He received an honorary doctorate from the University of Cambridge in 1920, and when the Prehistoric Society of East Anglia was re-formed as the Prehistoric Society in 1936, the election of Breuil as its President emphasised its re-creation as an entity with a wider remit. Garrod, who had preceded him as Vice-President some ten years earlier, was a personal friend and pupil, as was Miles Burkitt and many others in the British Palaeolithic establishment. This close involvement with anglophone researchers ensured a productive cross-fertilisation of his ideas and methods. His curiosity and energy meant that he never became too closely wedded to any of his hypotheses, as he was always moving on to new ideas and regions. It is this protean quality, the willingness to try out various ideas, and then to modify or reject them, which sets Breuil above many of his contemporaries.

Palaeolithic art was perhaps Breuil's consuming interest, but his approach to it was not dogmatic: he was not particularly interested in creating typological systems for it, being more concerned with its diversity and techniques. His dedication to the recording of the art and the frequent privations he appeared to suffer in this process are testament to his commitment. Palaeolithic art was only authenticated in 1901 at La Mouthe (in Ripoll Perelló 1994), and Breuil was involved right from the start in its documentation and interpretation. The resulting publications served to establish the integrity of the art, even if some of his reproductions can with hindsight be seen as subjective interpretations (Bahn and Vertut 1988). Palaeolithic art became a global discipline under Breuil's influence, and many of his travels, *e.g.* to South Africa in 1942–45, 1947–49 and 1950–51, were for the specific purpose of recording it.

a. Lower Aurignacian *(Châtelperron Type)*
Characteristics: This consisted of curved, backed knives, generally thick, with abrupt retouch: sometimes short and squat, sometimes thin and tapering. There also appeared to be a persistence of numerous Mousterian tool types, and bone tools were at best rare and poorly-defined.

b. Middle Aurignacian *(Aurignac Type)*
Characteristics: This saw the culmination of "Aurignacian retouch": used to make "Aurignacian blades", which were generally large and sometimes strangulated, frequently carrying an end-scraper on one, if not both, extremities. Another technique, lamellar retouch, was identified on thick flakes or cores (more rarely upon thick blades). This removed thin and narrow parallel bladelets from the lithic blank, creating thick, carinated and nosed end-scrapers, and "rabots" (large, heavy-duty scraping or shaving tools), as well as busked burins. Bone tool industries are both varied and abundant, comprising several different types of bone point; the split-based bone points being known as *pointes d'Aurignac* ("Aurignacian points").

c. Upper Aurignacian *(Gravette Type)*
Characteristics: This witnessed the general disappearance of the above-mentioned tools, and the development of a different type of assemblage, comprising very large quantities of angled burins fashioned on retouched truncations. The type-fossil was defined as well-made flint points of variable size, made on blades and sometimes upon bladelets, which had been created by abrupt retouch on one side of a knife-like blank to form a thick backed edge, the latter more-or-less rectilinear [sometimes gibbous] in section. These Gravettian points are accompanied by Font-Robert points (with distinctive tanged ends), Noaillian burins and *fléchettes* (thin, often laminar, leaf-points, carrying only semi-abrupt marginal retouch); grattoirs on the ends of both retouched and unretouched blades, truncated pieces, marginally-retouched blades and bladelets are also present. Breuil saw no logical evolution from the Middle to the Upper Aurignacian, believing them to have had independent origins.

Figure. 18.1: Breuil's (1912, 1937) sub-divisions of his Aurignacian.

Breuil's (1906, 1907, 1909a, 1909b) gradual refinement of his classification for the early Upper Palaeolithic culminated in his seminal paper of 1912. The 'Aurignacian' of Piette, *et alii*, was subdivided into three [broadly chronological] phases (Figure 18.1). This classification held sway for over twenty years before it was challenged by Peyrony's (1933) work, which was based somewhat optimistically upon just a few sites in the Périgord. This new scheme just renamed Breuil's original sub-divisions, with the outer phases (Fig. 18.2: a & c) being called the Lower and Upper Perigordian, respectively; only the middle phase retained the name 'Aurignacian'. Within these groups, further sub-divisions were made with reference to the stratigraphies from the Grand Abri de La Ferrassie and Laugerie-Haute, although they were still made on the presence/absence of 'type fossils' or, failing that, their relative quantities. This essentially parochial classification was enthusiastically promoted across Europe by its disciples, even though it was flawed from the outset. Breuil (1935a) and Garrod (1937) were unimpressed, but this is unsurprising as they were prepared to allow different regions their own characteristics, and not impose a preconceived template derived from one or two sites. Breuil (1935a) responded to Peyrony initially by questioning his ideas on population movement in the Périgord: what happened to the 'Lower Perigordians' when they were displaced by the 'Aurignacians'? They must have survived somewhere if, as Peyrony claimed, they developed into the 'Upper Perigordians'. The lack of such evidence supported Breuil's contention that there was no evolution between these industries [in France], and that Peyrony's (1938) later [desperate] interpretation of the hearths from level B at Laugerie-Haute as 'Middle Perigordian' (*i.e.* intermediate) was a gross chronostratigraphic error.

Breuil's (1937) sub-division of his Middle Aurignacian into three sub-phases appears to be a concession to Peyrony's 1933 scheme, especially when he uses the term 'Aurignacian I', but this is in fact a slight revision of the text in the original 1912 version. It is significant that Garrod uses her mentor's Aurignacian sub-divisions, rather than those of Peyrony.

Breuil was prepared to see a morphological evolution between type fossils, *e.g.* from Abri Audi points into Châtelperron knives (Breuil 1909b), but was less inclined to believe that industries evolved into other ones. This arose from his belief that stone tool industries reflected ethnicity, and that the remains of these ethnic groups should not necessarily be expected to evolve into new ones. The tenet that ethnicity could be detected in material artefacts was not of course restricted to Breuil; it was a widespread assumption, and held by his contemporaries.

Breuil and Garrod

Garrod first met Breuil in 1921, and arrived in Paris in 1922 to study with him. They formed a close and productive working relationship which began with Breuil initiating Garrod's international excavation career by suggesting one of his old sites (Devil's Tower in Gibraltar), and which lasted until his death in 1961. Garrod recalled that he tested her assiduity by asking her to read all Commont's publications on the gravels of the Somme at their first meeting, and this rigour in his dealings with others was typical:

> "...if no questions or ideas had been forthcoming from me, I do not think he would have suggested any. It was the pupil who must take the initiative and think for himself."   (Garrod, speaking on BBC Radio, 1962)

Breuil's views exerted a great influence on Garrod, and they both built upon each other's ideas, especially in the mid–1930s, when the debate over Peyrony's renaming of Breuil's Aurignacian phases was at its peak. Garrod accepted Breuil's Aurignacian sub-divisions, and shared his catholicity of interests. The acceptance of migration of cultural groups was widespread at the time, and Garrod's application of this to explain the spread of archaeological cultures is not especially noteworthy: it is the geographical range of her practical expertise which makes her work significant.

There are many references to Breuil's work in Garrod's seminal paper of 1938, especially in the footnotes: she obviously had unrestricted access to her mentor's voluminous experience, suggesting a concerted attempt by both of them to unseat Peyrony's (1933) re-evaluation of the Aurignacian *sensu lato*. She first coined her terms 'Châtelperronian' and 'Gravettian' in 1936 (Garrod 1936) to replace the terms 'Lower Aurignacian' and 'Upper Aurignacian' of Breuil, respectively, and to emphasise their discreteness. Although by instinct a lumper, not a splitter, she agrees with Breuil (1912, 1935a, 1937) that there is no cultural or technological linkage between Lower Aurignacian/Châtelperronian and Upper Aurignacian/Gravettian industries in western Europe. She is ambiguous about the possibility of such a transition between these two industries in central or eastern Europe, but she does consider the possibility of convergence in the development of backed knives in both industries:

> "...I would suggest that both [the Capsian and the Gravette-Font-Robert industries] are derived from the Chatelperronian, but that their common features are due in part to convergent development, certain forms, such as the Gravette point, being evolved almost necessarily from their Chatelperronian prototypes."
> (Garrod 1938: 22)

It must be noted here that, although Garrod invented the terms 'Châtelperronian' and 'Gravettian', these terms were applied on a wider geographic scale than they are today: 'Châtelperronian' industries were identified by Garrod in the Near East, and she gave them an extra-European origin in the Capsian. The Aurignacian (*sensu stricto*) was recognised as comprising a "large number of diverse strains" (1938: 4), permitting Garrod to trace it over an enormous area: the distribution did not just include material from Europe, western parts of the U.S.S.R. and the Near East, but it also extended into Kenya (if one believed Louis Leakey). Rather than support the established belief that the Aurignacian represented an indigenous European industry (unlike the two backed blade industries), she believed that it originated in the Near East, perhaps in the Iranian plateau or even further east, setting the stage for all subsequent *ex oriente lux* explanations of the Aurignacian spread across western Eurasia.

Garrod appears to have had a greater bias towards lithic analysis than did Breuil, although it is difficult to gauge this on the basis of her publications alone. She was strongly critical of attempts to define differences between Middle and Upper Palaeolithic industries on typological and technological grounds:

> "The time has come when the labels Lower, Middle and Upper Palaeolithic should be used exclusively in a chronological sense, without any typological connotation whatsoever, to cover approximately the periods from the beginning of the Pleistocene to the end of the Riss Glacial, from the end of the Riss to the middle of the Würm, and from the middle of the Würm to the close of the Pleistocene respectively."
> (Garrod 1938: 2)

Her perceptive assessments of the variable presence of 'Upper Palaeolithic' blade industries in Europe exhorted prehistorians to be more flexible, although she did concede that blades are generally most common in the European Upper Palaeolithic. She cautioned against the exclusive application of 'Upper Palaeolithic' monikers to blade industries in general, arguing that the state of knowledge in 1938 was too incomplete and that "industries of Mousterian [flake] tradition lingered on into Upper Palaeolithic times" in certain areas. Although she states that the clues to the development of blade industries are very faint, Garrod (1938) believed that they must have developed *initially* outside Europe during the Middle [or even Lower] Palaeolithic period.

Garrod and Posterity

> "...there is a tendency to-day unnecessarily to create distinct labels for industries which are essentially the same, though found in widely-separated areas which it should be our major interest to trace and interpret."   (Garrod 1938: 2)

Garrod's ideas rarely remained fixed, especially when changing evidence demanded revisions; this is not to say that she was fickle and superficial, but rather that she was mature enough to realise that archaeological thought could only be framed with regard to the available evidence. After she retired from Cambridge in 1952, she reworked her 1938 paper (Garrod 1953), retaining some elements (see Fig. 18.2), while changing other [major] aspects. Her underlying methodology and attitudes, of course, remained: she was still inclined to 'lump' industries, and she still believed in the migration of Palaeolithic peoples to explain the distribution of cultures. However, the geographical ranges of industries *had* changed, generally covering smaller areas, as Garrod disassociated the Near Eastern Emiran from the Châtelperronian, and the Aurignacian shrank likewise, being now confined to Europe and parts of Palestine. There are fewer quoted comments and information from the Abbé Breuil in the 1953 paper, perhaps reflecting a more Near Eastern bias to the paper, which permitted greater confidence.

When the 1938 and 1953 papers are compared, the strongest impression gained is one of *refinement* and of a more empirical use of theory; her retirement from Cambridge at the age of 60 permitted her to return to her work, fitting her discoveries in Palestine within a geological framework (^{14}C determinations were nearly non-existent in 1952/3). Using the sedimentary sequences in the Near East to date her finds in that region, she came to the conclusion that the origins of the Aurignacian could not be located with any confidence in Iran, but were likelier to have been in Europe, perhaps in the Balkans, with a later movement into the former region. This idea has been recently revived (Kozłowski 1992; see also Belfer-Cohen and Bar-Yosef, this volume), using ^{14}C and other absolute technique dates in support, but remains controversial, as some Near Eastern early Upper Palaeolithic industries are contemporary with, or even slightly earlier than, their European counterparts (Hedges *et al.* 1994). As Garrod herself realised, the lacuna in any Europe-Near East scheme is Anatolia, where few sites from this period have been identified.

> "From Anatolia there is a puzzlingly small harvest. As far as I know the only certain find is a handful of flints of Aurignacian type collected on the surface outside an eroded rockshelter at Adiyaman, 60 miles north of the Syrian frontier."   (Garrod 1953: 18)

Garrod's trip to Anatolia in 1938 was abortive; she was compelled to stop her survey after only a few weeks, and moved over to Bulgaria, where she excavated Bacho Kiro for the remaining weeks of the season (Garrod *et al.* 1939).

The association of modern humans with early Upper Palaeolithic (Aurignacian) industries in Europe, which was expounded in 1938, is not developed further in 1953. The proposed change in location for Aurignacian origins in the latter paper leaves an intriguing conundrum: if modern humans spread the early Aurignacian through Europe, only later taking it to the Near East (and co-existing/integrating with the

	1938	1953
a	Aurignacian diverse and widely-distributed	Aurignacian still diverse, although more geographically-restricted
b	Aurignacian originated in Near East: Iran?	Aurignacian as a European phenomenon; subsequent expansion into Near East
c	Aurignacian tools as "carpenter's tools", *i.e.* for wood-working	*Ditto*, although could see little evidence of environmental influences
d	Châtelperronian all over Europe and into the Near East: originated in Asia?	Châtelperronian limited to western Europe, with localised origins
e	Breuil's (1912, 1937) Lower and Upper Aurignacian phases renamed *Châtelperronian* and *Gravettian*	
f	Based sub-divisions on Breuil's 1912 "Aurignacian" [*sensu lato*]	Has adopted Breuil's (1937) tri-partite Aurignacian [*sensu stricto*] phases
g	Population movement used to explain the spread and distribution of lithic industries	
h	Arrival of modern humans in Europe during the earliest Upper Palaeolithic	
i		Although aware of chrono-stratigraphic problems, made much use of Near Eastern environmental sequences to re-date industries
j		Aurignacian as long-lived and innately conservative
k	Concerned about taxonomic rigidity of Lower / Middle / Upper Palaeolithic attributions: should use only as *temporal* indicators	
l		More empirical use of theory than in 1938
m	Many personal communications from Breuil	Fewer Breuil personal communications: more confidence?

Figure 18.2: Tabulation of changes between 1938 and 1953 in Garrod's thought.

resident groups there), then where did they originate? It might imply that the modern human colonists left the Near East with a Mousterian-type industry, which changed as they moved into new environments: did modern humans, moving into Europe (perhaps from the Near East), develop the Aurignacian only when they reached the Balkans? There is also the unsupported possibility that modern humans actually reached and spread through Europe 'invisibly', using Mousterian technology; the Aurignacian only developing and spreading [through acculturation – see below] at a later time from one or more sources, *e.g.* Cantabria and/or the Balkans. In any case, there is no evidence to suggest that Garrod no longer associated the early Upper Palaeolithic in Europe with modern humans in the later paper, although it would be difficult, on any evidence, to postulate that Neanderthals were associated with the early Aurignacian, later moving into the Near East. We have no Near Eastern Neanderthal remains contemporary with the Levantine Aurignacian, so if we must believe that the Near Eastern Aurignacian actually represents a return colonisation from Europe, it would seem most likely to have been carried by, or transmitted through, modern human groups. The Turkish lacuna is a problem, whether one believes in a European or a Near Eastern origin for the Aurignacian, as it effectively isolates the two areas, creating two *de facto* populations. Garrod herself saw a comparatively late Aurignacian in Palestine, which eventually developed into a local variant, the Atlitian (Garrod 1953; see Belfer-Cohen and Bar-Yosef, this volume). She argued that it was unlikely that the Aurignacian would have arisen independently in both Europe and the Near East, and that therefore we must invoke migration to explain its spread.

> "Where a characteristic assemblage can be traced, holding together over great distances – the Aurignacian… is an example of this – there must surely have been a movement of people, perhaps very gradual, and extending over more than one generation."   (Garrod 1953: 16)

Garrod also considered acculturation as a mechanism for cultural transmission in 1953, but she effectively limited it to the small-scale, and used it to explain the movement of one or two tool forms, *e.g.* split-based points in the atypical Aurignacian assemblages from the Balkans. She did not believe that complex industries, with whole suites of characteristics, could be transferred wholesale by acculturation: a conviction which would not be seriously contested by many researchers, even today.

> "The Aurignacian fulfils very completely the conditions proposed earlier… as providing good evidence for cultural diffusion when found at about the same time in separated areas – an assemblage of very distinctive artefacts identical or closely similar in both regions, and produced by the same methods. Of all the Upper Palaeolithic cultures the Aurignacian is one of two [the other being the Magdalenian] which possess the greatest number of rather elaborately fashioned implements peculiar to themselves [end-scraper and burin forms]…" (*ibid.*: 24)

Garrod [and Breuil] was very aware that differential preservation of artefacts, *e.g.* wooden *vs.* osseous and lithic, would lead to the preferential recovery of pieces in more durable materials, and would compound the problems in making industrial attributions on the grounds of just one or two of these more durable *fossiles directeurs*.

The 1953 paper gives serious consideration to the possibility of convergence in tool form. Her favoured example is backed knives: she argues that morphological convergence and similarity in functional demands can combine to produce very similar pieces in the Châtelperronian, the Emiran and the Gravettian, without there being any connection between them. This, to some extent, marks a break with her earlier work, and also with the 1912/1937 papers of Breuil, where evolution within tool types was countenanced. She seems to be implying that although tool types may have changed over time, the presence of convergence make these changes very difficult to determine.

> "The blunted blade is not much more distinctive [than end-scrapers]; in using a stone knife for cutting, as distinct from stabbing, it is useful to blunt one edge in order to protect the finger... and there is only one, very simple way of chipping to produce this result. This widely distributed artefact, then, has little better claim than the end-scraper to be considered a 'type fossil'..."
>
> (Garrod 1953: 23)

All connections between the Châtelperronian and Gravettian have been severed in geographical, as well as typological, terms in the 1953 paper. Whilst in 1938 she was prepared to believe in continuity between both industries *outside* western Europe, her dramatic reduction of the Châtelperronian [and its origins] to *within* western Europe in the later paper makes it difficult to see how one could have evolved into the other, especially when she believed that the Gravettian had a Ukrainian origin. She also speculated (1953) that the Zarzian (Wahida, this volume) perhaps represented a late development of backed industries from this Ukrainian source, which had moved south rather than west.

What, then, is Garrod's contribution to the study of the early Upper Palaeolithic for today's researchers? In both of the papers compared above, she identifies and discusses the main aspects of the Middle to Upper Palaeolithic transition debate: colonisation, diffusion, environmental conditions, dating, and industrial/cultural inter-relationships. She found the fact that the Aurignacian was the earliest Upper Palaeolithic industry in most of Europe 'suggestive', re-inforcing her idea of a colonisation from a particular region. She also treats the Near Eastern material on its own terms, rather than trying to force it into the established [western] European pattern. Most noteworthy of all, however, is her willingness to admit publicly that some of her previously-held opinions might be wrong in the light of new evidence, in contrast to many other workers who clung tenaciously to erroneous perceptions for the whole of their working lives. However, she still retained her underlying theoretical beliefs in population migrations and their associated processes; her revisions were made with regard to these when she incorporated new information. At the risk of seeming facetious, it is perhaps convenient for us that she espoused more than one model of human dispersal during the early Upper Palaeolithic, as we have more choice when we compare her ideas to our current data. Many researchers today would favour her earlier (1938) perspectives on the origins of the Aurignacian: *ex oriente lux* is once more in the ascendant. Just as Garrod set out to work in Palestine in the 1920s in order to test her ideas on the origins of the early Upper Palaeolithic, researchers today need more information from the Balkans and Anatolia to test this hypothesis. Garrod herself was not encouraging about the prospects for early Upper Palaeolithic discoveries in these areas, but that should not discourage us.

Garrod saw the Aurignacian as innately conservative ("obstinate traditionalism") and long-lived, changing little over large areas, and showing disappointingly little evidence [to her] of environmental influences on its [typological] constitution. She defined it as containing "carpenters' tools", *e.g.* carinated scrapers and burins, which she believed to be ideal for working wood and/or antler/ivory/bone, but she saw little difference between assemblages in areas with few trees and in ones with denser woodland. In the end (1953), she was forced to conclude that only in the assemblages with little available wood would people have been obliged to make greater use of bone, antler and ivory in tool manufacture (especially in northern Europe), and that pieces such as split-based points may not have had wooden proto-types after all.

My own work (Davies n.d.) has tended to agree with this idea of a conservative Aurignacian, although it does show a localised, expedient approach to the environment, apparently contemporary with isolated examples of extraordinary forward planning (tool curation and importation of exotic lithic raw materials, marking a break with the preceding Mousterian assemblages). This expediency might be expected of groups moving into unknown territory, while the limited importation of exotic materials might represent some degree of 'insurance' against possible poor raw material quality and/or availability. 'Curation' is problematic, as we cannot now know whether they were left accidentally, or deliberately with the intention of returning at some point; if the latter is true, then we can perhaps assume that occupation of the area was more 'residential' than ephemeral ('pioneer'). The earliest Aurignacian assemblages [in stratified sequences] from a given region tend to be relatively small and typologically-impoverished; the subsequent assemblages are generally more complex and diverse, sometimes including art objects, *etc.*. This could be held to reflect a two-phase colonisation of Europe, with a small-scale pioneer phase, followed by a more substantial and widespread residential phase in many regions. The consistency (with a few exceptions) in end-scraper morphology and retouch patterning across *facies* and reduction strategies throughout the Aurignacian, especially in contrast to late Mousterian and Châtelperronian assemblages, seems to argue against *in situ* evolution to the Aurignacian from local Mousterian industries. This is not directly contrary to either of Garrod's models for the dispersal of the Aurignacian, although it must be said that we are not exactly overwhelmed by evidence from this period in either eastern Europe or Anatolia.

Garrod was very aware of the limitations of typology, believing it to be often a poor indicator of time; she notes that convergence and the cyclical appearance of blank forms such as blades should encourage us to define Palaeolithic sub-divisions less on the grounds of technology, and more with regard to chronostratigraphy and dating. She believed (Garrod 1953) that typology should be used in conjunction with absolute dating techniques, especially where material was 'atypical', *e.g.* the Aurignacian from Potočka cave in Slovenia.

It is interesting to speculate just what Garrod would have made of the methods and theories currently employed in Palaeolithic and Mesolithic archaeology. I suspect that she would have felt reasonably at home: many of her ideas would have been facilitated by new techniques, and the widespread use of absolute dating would have enabled her to give less importance to typology. In any case, being of a generation from before the Bordesian statistical analysis of 'types', her use of typology was different, relying instead more upon the impressionistic comparison of morphology within *types fossiles*. This especially links her categorically to her period; her other ideas and interests are still in currency in this age of more 'scientific' Palaeolithic archaeology. We should not disregard the workers in the pre-Processualist phase of Palaeolithic research out of hand; Breuil and Garrod in particular were trying to test the boundaries of their knowledge and techniques, and frequently touched upon issues of timeless interest. They used the data at their disposal to test their ideas in more subtle ways than the 19th-century prehistorians, as they were more pre-occupied with the relationships between cultural entities than with crude stratigraphical successions (Garrod 1927).

Their methods, as well as their ideas, frequently fell upon stony ground. Breuil's (1938) brave attempt to analyse taphonomic and biological (gnawing, *etc.*) effects on the deposition and working of animal bones in archaeological sites went generally unnoticed, either through lack of interest or through insufficiently developed techniques, and was re-worked and re-invented in the New Archaeology over thirty years later (*e.g.* Binford 1981). The practical breadth of experience which Breuil and Garrod possessed over a wide range of material across much of the world informed their perspectives, and ensured that they would never stagnate. In the face of ever-increasing and diversifying information, we would do well to emulate their catholicity as much as we can, in interests if not in practice.

N.B. The use of the words 'culture' and 'cultural' are used in Garrod's sense, *i.e.* synonymous with 'industry' and 'industrial'. Garrod's original terms 'Châtelperronian' and 'Gravettian' are preferred over Delporte's (1954, 1957) puzzling 'Castelperronian' (the site is called 'Châtelperron', not 'Castelperron'), and his 'Perigordian', respectively.

Acknowledgements

I must thank Prof. Tjeerd van Andel, Dr. Mark White and John Stewart for their valuable comments and suggestions on various drafts of this paper. Any residual idiosyncrasies and errors are, of course, my responsibility. Thanks are also owed to Pamela Jane Smith, for bringing some unpublished material to my attention.

Bibliography

Bahn, P., and J. Vertut 1988. *Images of the Ice Age*. London: Windward.

Binford, L.R. 1981. *Bones: Ancient men and modern myths*. New York: Academic Press.

Breuil, H. 1906. Les gisements Présolutréens du type d'Aurignac: coup d'oeil sur le plus ancien âge du Renne. Paper presented to the *Congrès International d'Anthropologie et d'Archéologie Préhistoriques [XIIIe session]*, Monaco, 1906: 323–350.

Breuil, H. 1907. La question aurignacienne: Étude critique de stratigraphie comparée. *Révue Préhistorique* 2: 173–219.

Breuil, H. 1909a. Études de Morphologie Paléolithique I: La Transition du Moustérien vers l'Aurignacien à l'Abri Audi (Dordogne) et au Moustier. *Révue de l'École d'Anthropologie* 19: 320–340.

Breuil, H. 1909b. L'Aurignacien Présolutréen: Epilogue d'une controverse. *Révue Préhistorique* 4: 5–46.

Breuil, H. 1912. Les Subdivisions du Paléolithique Supérieur et leur Signification. Paper presented to the *Congrès International d'Anthropologie et d'Archéologie Préhistoriques [XIVe session]*, Geneva, 1912: 165–238.

Breuil, H. 1920. Les peintures rupestres de la péninsule Ibérique, XI: Les roches peintes de Minateda (Albacete). *L'Anthropologie* 30: 1–50.

Breuil, H. 1921. Les gravures rupestres préhistoriques et modernes de la péninsule Ibérique. *L'Anthropologie* 31: 519–520.

Breuil, H. 1922. Palaeolithic man at Gibraltar: new and old facts. *Journal of the Royal Anthropological Institute* 52: 46–54.

Breuil, H. 1923. Notes de voyage paléolithique en Europe Centrale, I: Les industries paléolithiques en Hongrie. *L'Anthropologie* 33: 323–346.

Breuil, H. 1924. Notes de voyage paléolithique en Europe Centrale, II: Les industries paléolithiques du loess de Moravie et Bohême. *L'Anthropologie* 34: 515–552.

Breuil, H. 1925. Notes de voyage paléolithique en Europe Centrale, III: Les cavernes de Moravie. *L'Anthropologie* 35: 271–291.

Breuil, H. 1930. The Palaeolithic art of North-Eastern Spain and the art of the Bushmen: a comparison. *Man* 30: 149–151.

Breuil, H. 1931a. The Human remains and artefacts found at Chu-Ku-Tien. *Bull. of the Catholic University of Pekin* 12: 135–137.

Breuil, H. 1931b. Le feu et l'industrie lithique et osseuse à Chu-Ku-Tien. *Bull. of the Geological Society of China* 2: 147–154.

Breuil, H. 1932. Le feu et l'industrie de pierre et d'os dans le gisement du *Sinanthropus* à Chu-Kou-Tien. *L'Anthropologie* 42: 1–17.

Breuil, H. 1935a. Response to: Les industries "aurignaciennes" dans le bassin de la Vézère [Peyrony 1933]. *L'Anthropologie* 45: 114–116.

Breuil, H. 1935b. L'état de nos connaissances sur les industries paléolithiques de Choukoutien. *L'Anthropologie* 45: 740–746.

Breuil, H. 1937. *Les Subdivisions du Paléolithique Supérieur et leur Signification*. Revised version of 1912 Geneva paper. Lagny: Grévin et fils.

Breuil, H. 1938. The use of bone implements in the old Palaeolithic period. *Antiquity* 12: 56–67.

Breuil, H. 1943. Archaic chipped pebble and flake industries from the older gravels of various sections of the Vaal Valley. *South African Journal of Science* 40: 282–284.

Breuil, H. 1944. The old Palaeolthic age in relation to Quaternary sea levels along the southern coast of Africa. *South African Journal of Science* 41: 397–399.

Breuil, H. 1949. Remains of large animal paintings in South West Africa, older than all the other frescoes. *South African Archaeological Bulletin* 4: 14–18.

Davies, S.W.G. [n.d.]. *The Aurignacian as a Reflection of Modern Human Population Dispersal in Europe*. Unpublished Ph.D. dissertation, University of Cambridge.

Delporte, H. 1954. Le Périgordien. *Bulletin de la Société Préhistorique Française [Livre jubilaire]* 51: 44–48.

Delporte, H. 1957. Corrézian ou Brivien? *Bulletin de la Société Préhistorique Française* 54: 43–44.

Garrod, D.A.E. 1928. Nova et Vetera: A Plea for a New Method in Palaeolithic Archaeology. Presidential Address. *Proceedings of the Prehistoric Society of East Anglia* 5: 260–272.

Garrod, D.A.E. 1936. The Upper Palaeolithic in the Light of Recent Discovery. Presidential Address, Section H (Anthropology), Blackpool. *Report of the British Association for the Advancement of Science, 1936*: 155–172.

Garrod, D.A.E. 1937. The Near East as a Gateway of Prehistoric Migration. *Bulletin of the American Society for Prehistoric Research* 13: 17–21.

Garrod, D.A.E. 1938. The Upper Palaeolithic in the Light of Recent Discovery. *Proceedings of the Prehistoric Society* 4: 1–26.

Garrod, D.A.E. 1953. The Relations between South-West Asia and Europe in the Later Palaeolithic Age, with special reference to the Origin of the Upper Palaeolithic Blade Cultures. *Journal of World History* 1: 13–37.

Garrod, D.A.E., Howe, B., and J.H. Gaul 1939. Excavations in the Cave of Bacho Kiro, North-East Bulgaria. Part I: Description, Excavations and Archaeology. *Bulletin of the American Society for Prehistoric Research* 15: 46–87.

Hedges, R.E.M., Housley, R.A., Bronk Ramsey, C., and G.J. Van Klinken 1994. Radiocarbon dates from the Oxford AMS system: *Archaeometry* datelist 18. *Archaeometry* 36: 337–374.

Kozłowski, J.K. 1992. The Balkans in the Middle and Upper Palaeolithic: The Gate to Europe, or a Cul-de-Sac? *Proceedings of the Prehistoric Society* 58: 1–20.

de Mortillet, G. 1870. Notes. In *Matériaux pour l'Histoire Primitive et Naturelle de l'Homme, et l'étude du sol, de la faune et de la flore qui s'y rattachent*. Paris: Reinwald, pp.49–52.

de Mortillet, G., and A. de Mortillet 1881. *Musée Préhistorique*. Paris: Reinwald.

Peyrony, D. 1933. Les Industries "aurignaciennes" dans le bassin de la Vézère. *Bulletin de la Société Préhistorique Française* 30: 543–559.

Peyrony, D. 1938. Laugerie-Haute. *Archives de l'Institut de Paléontologie humaine: Mémoire 19*.

Ripoll Perelló, E. 1994. *El Abate Henri Breuil (1877–1961)*. Madrid: Universidad Nacional de Educación a Distancia.

19
Dorothy A. E. Garrod
A Provisional Bibliography

It should be noted that the following references have been compiled by Brian Boyd and William Davies (with very valuable assistance from the other contributors to this volume) from the sources known to them; omissions are inevitable, and the editors would be very grateful to hear of any works by Garrod currently unknown to them. The personal bibliography compiled by Garrod herself (reaching 1963), kept in the Musée des Antiquités Nationales, St. Germain-en-Laye, could not be accessed for the compilation of this list, and must therefore await subsequent publication.

1924a   Maglemose Harpoons. *Man* 24: 64.

1924b   Excavations at Tor Bryan, 1924. Unpublished report to Torquay Natural History Society dated 12/4/24.

1924c   The Cave of Isturitz. *Proceedings of the Prehistoric Society of East Anglia* 4: 243–244.

1925a   Le niveau inférieur de Kent's Hole: une brèche à *Ursus spelaeus* avec outillage chelléen. *Bulletin de la Société Préhistorique Française* 23: 115–120.

1925b   Solutrean Implements in England. *Man* 25: 84–85, & 151–152 [correspondence].

1925c   The Upper Palaeolithic Age in Britain. Abstract and title in *Report of the British Association for the Advancement of Science, Section H*, p.346.

1926a   The Upper Palaeolithic Age in Britain (talk given 5th Nov., 1925). *Proceedings of the Bristol University Spelaeological Society* 2 (3): 299–301.

1926b   *The Upper Palaeolithic Age in Britain.* Oxford: Clarendon Press.

1926c   Excavation of a Mousterian Site and Discovery of a Human Skull at Devil's Tower, Gibraltar. Abstract and title in *Report of the British Association for the Advancement of Science, Section H*, pp. 385–386.

1926d   and Pittard, E. Pièces inédites de l'aurignacien supérieur de la station Durand-Ruel (Dordogne). *Revue Préhistorique* 36 (7–9): 4pp.

1927   Excavations at Langwith Cave, Derbyshire, April 11–27, 1927. *Report of the British Association for the Advancement of Science (Leeds, 1927)*: 303.

1928a   Nova et vetera: a plea for a new method in Palaeolithic archaeology. Presidential Address for 1928. *Proceedings of the Prehistoric Society of East Anglia* 5 (for 1927): 260–267.

1928b   Notes on some Mousterian finds in Spain and Irak. *Proceedings of the Prehistoric Society of East Anglia* 5 (for 1927): 268–272.

1928c   and Buxton, L.H.D., Elliot Smith, G., and Bate, D.M.A. Excavation of a
            Mousterian Rock-Shelter at Devil's Tower, Gibraltar. *Journal of the Royal
            Anthropological Institute* 58: 33–113.

1928d   Excavation of a Palaeolithic cave in Western Judaea. *Quarterly Statement
            of the Palestine Exploration Fund* 60: 182–185. [Probably the same as a talk
            given under the same title and in the same year to the British Association,
            and whose title and abstract were published in the *Report of the British
            Association for the Advancement of Science, Section H*, p.594.]

1929   Excavations in the Mugharet el-Wad, near Athlit, April-June 1929.
            Quarterly Statement of the Palestine Exploration Fund 61: 220–222.

1930a   Cave exploration in the Near East. (Weekly evening meeting, Friday,
            December 13, 1929.) *Proceedings of the Royal Institution of Great Britain* 26 (2):
            139–150.

1930b   The Palaeolithic of Southern Kurdistan: excavations in the caves of Zarzi
            and Hazar Merd. *Bulletin of the American School of Prehistoric Research* 6:
            8–43.

1930c   Fouilles paléolithiques en Palestine, 1928–1929. *Bulletin de la Société
            Préhistorique Française* 27: 151–160.

1930d   Note on Three Objects of Mesolithic Age from a Cave in Palestine. *Man*
            30: 77–78.

1930e   Excavations in the Caves of the Wady al-Mughara. Title only published
            in *Report of the British Association for the Advancement of Science, Section H*,
            p.366.

1931a   Fouilles préhistoriques au Mont Carmel, 1930–1931. *Congrès Préhistoriques
            de France.* X^e session. 60ff.

1931b   Mesolithic Burials from Caves in Palestine. *Man* 31: 145–146.

1931c   Excavations in the caves of the Wady-el-Mughara, 1929–1930. *Bulletin of
            the American School of Prehistoric Research* 7: 5–11.

1931d   Wadi el-Maghara. *The Quarterly of the Department of Antiquities in Palestine*
            1: 160–161.

1931e   Excavations at the Mugharet el-Wad, 1930. *Quarterly Statement of the
            Palestine Exploration Fund* 63: 99–103.

1931f   Excavations at the Wady al-Mughara in 1931. Abstract and title in *Report
            of the British Association for the Advancement of Science, Section H*, pp.
            444–445. [Possibly the same paper as 1932a.]

1932a   Excavations in the Wady al-Mughara (Palestine), 1931. *Bulletin of the
            American School of Prehistoric Research* 8: 6–11.

1932b   Nuevos descubrimientos prehistóricos en Palestina. *Investigacion y Progreso*
            6: 62ff.

1932c   A New Mesolithic Industry: The Natufian of Palestine. *Journal of the Royal
            Anthropological Institute* 62: 257–269. [Summary in *Man* 32: 19–20 (1932)].

1932d   el-Wad. *Quarterly of the Department of Antiquities in Palestine* 1: 160–161.

1932e   Excavations in the Wady el-Mughara, 1931. *Quarterly Statement of the
            Palestine Exploration Fund* 64: 46–51.

1932f   A New Species of Fossil Man: Great discoveries at Mt. Carmel: "Stone Age deposits so far unparalleled in the Near East" – The finding of *Palaeoanthropus palestinus*. *Illustrated London News* (1932), p.36. [See also pp.33–35: Sir A. Keith]

1933a   el-Wad. *The Quarterly of the Department of Antiquities in Palestine* 2: 184.
1933b   Magharet es Sukhul. *The Quarterly of the Department of Antiquities in Palestine* 2: 189.
1933c   Excavation of the Mugharet et-Tabun, Mount Carmel. Title only in *Report of the British Association for the Advancement of Science, Section H*, p.527.

1934a   The Stone Age of Palestine. *Antiquity* 8: 133–150.
1934b   Excavations at the Wady al-Mughara (Palestine), 1932–33. *Bulletin of the American School of Prehistoric Research* 10: 7–11.
1934c   Wadi el-Maghara. *The Quarterly of the Department of Antiquities in Palestine* 3: 183–184.
1934d   Excavations at the Wady al-Mughara, 1932–3. *Quarterly Statement of the Palestine Exploration Fund* 66: 85–89.

1935a   Excavations in the Mugharet et-Tabun (Palestine), 1934. *Bulletin of the American School of Prehistoric Research* 11: 54–58.
1935b   and Gardner, E.W. Pleistocene Coastal Deposits in Palestine [Letter: 1/6/35]. *Nature* 135: 908–909.
1935c   Wadi Maghara. *The Quarterly of the Department of Antiquities in Palestine* 4: 209–210.
1935d   Cave Deposits on Mt. Carmel (Wady Mughara Expedition). Abstract and title in *Report of the British Association for the Advancement of Science, Section H*, pp. 335–338.
1935e   The Mousterian People of Palestine: their culture. Abstract and title in *Report of the British Association for the Advancement of Science, Section H*, p.421.

1936a   The Upper Palaeolithic in the Light of Recent Discovery. *Report of the British Association for the Adancement of Science, Presidential Address, Section H (Blackpool)*, pp. 155–172. [This is the original version of the 1938a paper below.]
1936b   A summary of seven seasons work at the Wady el-Mughara. *Bulletin of the American School of Prehistoric Research* 12: 125–129.

1937a   The Near East as a gateway of prehistoric migration. *Bulletin of the American School of Prehistoric Research* 13: 17–21.
1937   and Bate, D.M.A. *The Stone Age of Mount Carmel. Vol. 1.* Oxford: Clarendon Press.

1938a   The Upper Palaeolithic in the Light of Recent Discovery. *Proceedings of the Prehistoric Society* 4: 1–26.
1938b   A note on the lithic industries of Ehringsdorf and Wallertheim. Title only, in *Report of the British Association for the Advancement of Science, Section H*, p.473.

[1938c Response to "The Swanscombe Fossil" (E. Le Gros Clark & G.M. Morant). In *Report of the British Association for the Advancement of Science, Section H*, p.469.]

1939a and Gaul, J.H., Howe, B. Report on the A.S.P.R. expedition to Anatolia, 1938. *Bulletin of the American School of Prehistoric Research* 15: 13–27.

1939b and Howe, B. and Gaul, J.H. Excavations in the cave of Bacho Kiro, north-east Bulgaria. Part 1: description, excavations and archaeology. *Bulletin of the American School of Prehistoric Research* 15: 46–76.

1939c and Howe, B. A report on caves in the neighbourhood of Karlukovo in northern Bulgaria. *Bulletin of the American School of Prehistoric Research* 15: 81–84.

1939d Review of *Transjordanien: Vorgeschichtliche Forschungen* (H. Rhotert). *Man* 39: 61–63.

1940 Notes on some decorated skeletons from the Mesolithic of Palestine. *Annual of the British School at Athens* 47: 123–127.

1942 with Bate, D.M.A. Excavations at the cave of Shukbah, Palestine, 1928. *Proceedings of the Prehistoric Society* 8: 1–20.

1943 The cave of Lascaux near Montignac, Dordogne (summary of communication to Society of Antiquaries of London). *Man* 43: 42.

1946 *Environment, tools and man: an inaugural lecture*. Cambridge: Cambridge University Press.

1949a New light on man's remote ancestry: the oldest skull yet found in France; a discovery which revises theories of human evolution. *London Illustrated News*. 4 June 1949.

1949b Finding the Earliest Prehistoric Portrait in the History of Man. *Illustrated London News*. 16 July 1949.

1949c La technique levalloisienne au post-paléolithique. *Bulletin de la Société Préhistorique Française* 46: 391–392.

1949d Review of *The Gate of Horn* (G.R. Levy). *The Antiquaries' Journal* 29: 213.

1949e and Saint-Mathurin, S. de. Fouilles dans un Abri Magdalénien de la Vallée de l'Anglin. *L'Anthropologie* 53: 333–334.

1950 and de Saint-Mathurin, S. Nouvelles découvertes dans l'abri du Roc-aux-Sorciers (anciennement abri Louis Taillebourg) à Angles-sur-l'Anglin (Vienne). *Bulletin de la Société Préhistorique Française* 47: 315–316.

1951a A Transitional Industry from the base of the Upper Palaeolithic in Palestine and Syria. *Journal of the Royal Anthropological Institute* 81: 121–132.

1951b and de Saint-Mathurin, S. La frise sculptée de l'Abri du Roc aux Sorciers à Angles-sur-l'Anglin (Vienne). *L'Anthropologie* 55: 413–424.

1951c The Horses of 12,000 Years Ago. *Illustrated London News*. 7 July 1951.

1951d and de Saint-Mathurin, S. Nouvelles découvertes dans l'abri du Roc-aux-Sorciers à Angles-sur-l'Anglin (Vienne): les Vénus paléolithiques. *Comptes*

rendus de l'Académie des Inscriptions et Belles Lettres, séance du 9 février 1951,
pp. 51–57. Paris: Académie des Inscriptions et Belles Lettres.

1952a　Review of *Les Hommes de la Pierre Ancienne* (H. Breuil & R. Lantier). *The Antiquaries' Journal* 32: 211–212.

1952b　and S. de St.-Mathurin. The Master Sculptors of 12,000 years ago revealed: Exciting "find" in a rock shelter in Vienne, France. *Illustrated London News* (March 15, 1952). In E. Bacon (Ed.) *The Great Archaeologists*, pp. 303–304. London: Secker & Warburg.

1953a　Correspondence re: l'Abbé Breuil, '400 centuries of cave art'. *Antiquity* 27: 108–109.

1953b　The Relations between South-West Asia and Europe in the Later Palaeolithic Age with Special Reference to the Origins of the Upper Palaeolithic Blade Cultures. *Journal of World History* 1: 13–37.

1954a　Excavations at the Mughâret Kebara, Mount Carmel 1931: the Aurignacian industries. *Proceedings of the Prehistoric Society* 20: 155–192.

1954b　and E.M. Clifford, Gracie, H.S. Flint Implements from Gloucestershire. *The Antiquaries' Journal* 34: 178–187.

1955a　The Mughâret el-Emireh in Lower Galilee: Type-Station of the Emiran Industry. *Journal of the Royal Anthropological Institute* 85: 141–162.

1955b　Palaeolithic spear-throwers. *Proceedings of the Prehistoric Society* 21: 21–35.

1955c　Obituary: Pierre Teilhard de Chardin, S.J. (1881–1955). *Man* 55: 70.

1956a　Acheuléo-Jabroudien et "Pré-Aurignacien" de la grotte du Taboun (Mont Carmel): étude stratigraphique et chronologique. *Quaternaria* 3: 39–59.

1956b　and de Saint-Mathurin, S.　L'Abri du Roc-aux-Sorciers (Angles-sur-l'Anglin, Vienne). *Congrès préhistorique de France 15e session, Poitiers*, pp. 89–94. Angoulême: Société Préhistorique Française.

1957a　Notes sur le paléolithique supérieur du Moyen Orient. *Bulletin de la Société Prehistorique Française* 54: 439–446.

1957b　The Natufian culture: the life and economy of a Mesolithic people in the Near East. *Proceedings of the British Academy* 43: 211–227.

1957c　and Henri-Martin, G., Saint-Mathurin, S. de, *et al. Hommage à l'Abbé Breuil pour son quatre-vingtième anniversaire.* Paris: Maçon, Protat.

1958a　Review article on "Rouffignac" publication. *Antiquity* 32: 231–234.

1958b　The ancient shore-line of the Lebanon and the dating of Mount Carmel man. In G.H.R. von Königswald (Ed.) *Hundert Jahre Neanderthaler*, pp. 182–184. Köln: Kemink.

1958c　Review of *Stone Artefacts at and near the Finley Site, near Eden, Wyoming* (Linton Satterthwaite). *Bulletin de la Société Préhistorique Française* 55: 595.

1959a　and Henri-Martin, G. Fouilles à Ras el-Kelb, Liban, 1959. *Actes du 16ᵉ Congrès Préhistorique de France*, Monaco, 1959.

1959b　and Saint-Mathurin, S. de. Datation par le C 14 du Magdalénien III de l'abri sculpté du Roc-aux-Sorciers, à Angles-sur-l'Anglin (Vienne). Paper given to Société Préhistorique Française in June 1959. *Bulletin de la Société Préhistorique Française* 56: 262.

1960a   Prehistoric data Palestine - Lebanon. *Early man and pleistocene stratigraphy in the circum-Mediterranean region.* Burg Warterstein Symposium, 1960.

1960b   and Field, H. *The North Arabian Desert.* Peabody Museum of Anthropology and Ethnology 95, 2. Cambridge, Massachussetts: Peabody Museum of Anthropology and Ethnology 95,2.

1961a   Comments on M. Bordes' article "Sur la chronologie au Paléolithique en Moyen Orient". *Quaternaria* 5 (1958–1961): 71–73.

1961b   Obituary: The Abbé Breuil (1877–1961). *Man* 61: 205–207.

1961c   and Kirkbride, D. Excavation of a Palaeolithic rock shelter at Adlun, Lebanon, 1958. *Actes du Congres International des Sciences Préhistoriques et Protohistoriques (Hamburg, 1958)*, pp. 313–320. Hamburg.

1961d   and Kirkbride, D. Excavation of the Abri Zumoffen, a Palaeolithic rock shelter near Adlun, south Lebanon, 1958. *Bulletin du Musée de Béyrouth* 16: 7–46.

1961e   and Henri-Martin, G. Rapport préliminaire sur la fouille d'une grotte au Ras el-Kelb. *Bulletin du Musée de Béyrouth* 16: 61–67.

1962a   Review of *L'Age de Pierre* (D. de Sonneville-Bordes). *Antiquity* 36: 150–151.

1962b   The Middle Palaeolithic of the Near East and the problem of Mount Carmel man (Huxley Memorial Lecture, 1962). *Journal of the Royal Anthropological Institute* 92: 232–259.

1962c   An Outline of Pleistocene prehistory in Palestine-Lebanon-Syria. *Quaternaria* 6: 541–546.

1963   Recollections of the Abbé Breuil. *Antiquity* 37: 12–18.

1965a   Review of *The Abbé Breuil, prehistorian* (Brodick). *Antiquity* 39: 67–68.

1965b   and Clark, J.D.G. *Primitive man in Egypt, western Asia and Europe.* Cambridge Ancient History, fascicule 30, volume 1. Cambridge: Cambridge University Press.

1966a   and Kirkbride, D. Mugharet el-Bezez, Adlun: interim report, July 1965. *Bulletin du Musée de Béyrouth* 19: 5–10.

1966b   A pebble industry of early Würm, from the Abri Zumoffen, south Lebanon. In D. Sen and A.K. Ghosh (Eds.) *Studies in prehistory*, pp. 41–48. Calcutta: Robert Bruce Foote Memorial Volume.

1968   Recollections of Glozel. *Antiquity* 42: 172–177.

n.d.   *World Prehistory.* Unpublished book type-script [1940s?], in Musée des Antiquités Nationales, St. Germain-en-Laye, Paris.